ENDGAME IN AFGHANISTAN

ENDGAME IN AFGHANISTAN

FOR WHOM THE DICE ROLLS

HIRANMAY KARLEKAR

⑤SAGE www.sagepublications.com
Los Angeles • London • New Delhi • Singapore • Washington DC

First published in 2012 by

 SAGE Publications India Pvt Ltd
B1/I-1 Mohan Cooperative Industrial Area
Mathura Road, New Delhi 110 044, India
www.sagepub.in

SAGE Publications Inc
2455 Teller Road
Thousand Oaks, California 91320, USA

SAGE Publications Ltd
1 Oliver's Yard, 55 City Road
London EC1Y 1SP, United Kingdom

SAGE Publications Asia-Pacific Pte Ltd
33 Pekin Street
#02-01 Far East Square
Singapore 048763

Published by Vivek Mehra for SAGE Publications India Pvt Ltd, typeset in 13/15 pt Perpetua by Diligent Typesetter, Delhi and printed at Saurabh Printers Pvt Ltd.

Library of Congress Cataloging-in-Publication Data

Karlekar, Hiranmay, 1938–
    Endgame in Afghanistan: for whom the dice rolls/Hiranmay Karlekar.
        p. cm.
    Includes bibliographical references and index.
1. Afghan War, 2001—Political aspects. I. Title.
DS371.4.K38   958.104'71—dc23   2012   2012035134

ISBN: 978-81-321-0974-7 (PB)

The SAGE Team: Rudra Narayan, Aniruddha De, Rajib Chatterjee and Dally Verghese

To the memory of my maternal grandmother,
Punyalata Chakraborty, and my maternal grandfather,
Arun Nath Chakraborty.

Thank you for choosing a SAGE product! If you have any comment, observation or feedback, I would like to personally hear from you. Please write to me at <u>contactceo@sagepub.in</u>

—Vivek Mehra, Managing Director and CEO,
SAGE Publications India Pvt Ltd, New Delhi

Bulk Sales

SAGE India offers special discounts for purchase of books in bulk. We also make available special imprints and excerpts from our books on demand.

For orders and enquiries, write to us at

Marketing Department
SAGE Publications India Pvt Ltd
B1/I-1, Mohan Cooperative Industrial Area
Mathura Road, Post Bag 7
New Delhi 110044, India
E-mail us at <u>marketing@sagepub.in</u>

Get to know more about SAGE, be invited to SAGE events, get on our mailing list. Write today to <u>marketing@sagepub.in</u>

This book is also available as an e-book.

CONTENTS

Contents

ABBREVIATIONS

AHAB	AHLE HADITH ANDOLAN BANGLADESH
ALP	AFGHAN LOCAL POLICE
ALTBMD	ACTIVE LAYERED THEATRE BALLISTIC MISSILE DEFENCE
AMISOM	AFRICAN UNION MISSION IN SOMALIA
ANA	AFGHAN NATIONAL ARMY
ANASF	ANA SPECIAL FORCES
ANASOC	ANA SPECIAL OPERATIONS COMMAND
ANP	AFGHAN NATIONAL POLICE
ANSF	AFGHAN NATIONAL SECURITY FORCES
AQAP	AL QAEDA IN THE ARABIAN PENINSULA
AQIM	AL QAEDA IN THE ISLAMIC MAGHREB
BNP	BANGLADESH NATIONALIST PARTY
CACI	CENTRAL ASIA COUNTERNARCOTICS INITIATIVE
CIA	CENTRAL INTELLIGENCE AGENCY
DRS	DESPERATE RESPONSE SYNDROME
EPAA	EUROPEAN PHASED ADAPTIVE APPROACH
FAA	FOREIGN ASSISTANCE ACT
FATA	FEDERALLY ADMINISTERED TRIBAL AREAS

FBI	Federal Bureau of Investigation
FTO	Foreign Terrorist Organization
GCHQ	Government Communications Headquarters
GDP	gross domestic product
GIA	Groupe Islamique Armé (Armed Islamic Group)
GSPC	Groupe Salafiste pour la Prédication et le Combat (Salafist Group for Preaching and Combat)
HUJI	Harkat-ul-Jihad-al-Islami
HUJIB	Harkat-ul-Jihad-al-Islami Bangladesh
HuM	Harkat-ul Mujahideen
HuT	Hizbut Tahrir
IED	Improvised Explosive Devices
IPFM	International Panel on Fissile Materials
ISAF	International Security Assistance Force
ISC	Intelligence and Security Committee
ISI	Inter-Services Intelligence Directorate
ISPR	Inter Services Public Relations
JeI	Jamat-e-Islami
JeIB	Jama'at-e-Islami Bangladesh
JeM	Jaish-e-Mohammad
JMB	Jama'at-ul Mujahideen Bangladesh
JMJB	Jagrata Muslim Janata Bangladesh
JSOC	Joint Special Operations Command
LeT	Lashkar-e-Toiba
MNC	multinational corporation

NATO	NORTH ATLANTIC TREATY ORGANIZATION
NCO	NON-COMMISSIONED OFFICER
NCTC	NATIONAL COUNTERTERRORISM CENTER
NDN	NORTHERN DISTRIBUTION NETWORK
NGO	NON-GOVERNMENTAL ORGANIZATION
NSR	NEW SILK ROAD
NWFP	NORTH-WEST FRONTIER PROVINCE
PAF	PAKISTAN AIR FORCE
PCCF	PAKISTAN COUNTERINSURGENCY CAPABILITY FUND
PCF	PAKISTAN COUNTERINSURGENCY FUND
PHR	PHYSICIANS FOR HUMAN RIGHTS
PPP	PAKISTAN PEOPLE'S PARTY
RPG-7	ROCKET PROPELLED GRENADES-7
RUSI	ROYAL UNITED SERVICES INSTITUTE
SEALs	SEA, AIR, AND LAND TEAMS (OR US NAVY)
SES	SPECTACULAR EPISODES SYNDROME
SIS	SECRET INTELLIGENCE SERVICE
START	STRATEGIC ARMS REDUCTION TREATY
TTP	TEHRIK-E-TALIBAN PAKISTAN
UPS	UNITED PARCEL SERVICE
USAID	UNITED STATES AGENCY FOR INTERNATIONAL DEVELOPMENT
USCYBERCOM	U.S. CYBER COMMAND
USFOR	UNITED STATES FORCES
USSOF	UNITED STATES SPECIAL OPERATIONS FORCES
USSTRATCOM	U.S. STRATEGIC COMMAND
VSO	VILLAGE STABILITY OPERATIONS

PREFACE

THE ENDGAME

I have tried to cover in this book a wide range of issues related to the war in Afghanistan beginning with the stakes the whole world—and not just the United States—has in it. It shows that it is not merely a war for the future of Afghanistan, but a conflict between the regressive world view of the Taliban and al Qaeda and modernity. It dwells in this context on the nature of modernity as it has evolved in post-Renaissance and post-Enlightenment Europe and its fundamental incompatibility with the doctrine and practices of al Qaeda and the Taliban. In this process, it also underlines how what the two organizations stand for is a grossly reductionist distortion of the historic spirit and principles of mainstream Islam.

The book examines the consequences of an American exit from Afghanistan under circumstances suggesting a defeat; the ability of the Karzai government or its successor to hold its own thereafter; and the regional and global geo-strategic consequences, including those on Pakistan, of a Taliban–al Qaeda takeover of Afghanistan. It also explores the possibility of the United States arriving at a peace settlement with the Taliban, particularly weaning away the 'good' Taliban from the 'bad'. Equally, it analyses the chances of Washington DC winning in Afghanistan in terms of realizing the goals President Obama has announced in his major policy declarations.

Given the fact that Pakistan's role will be critical to the outcome of the Afghan war, the book looks at the manner in which Islamabad has been 'cooperating' in Washington DC's war on terror and its objectives in the region. To assess Pakistan's dependability as a US ally, it examines the nature of US–Pakistan relations since the latter's emergence as a separate nation in 1947 and the seriousness with which it has been conducting its counter-insurgency operations against Islamist terror groups. In this context, it studies the rise of intense anti-American sentiments in Pakistan and the spread of Islamist fanaticism in the country and its armed forces, which have a decisive say in its politics.

The book examines whether the United States can win the Afghan war even if Pakistan continues in its present duplicitous course. In the process, it looks at the circumstances that explain America's uneven performance in Afghanistan so far and whether some of these can be rectified. Equally, the book examines whether the United States' defeat in Vietnam and the Soviet Union's in Afghanistan necessarily indicate a similar outcome to America's present war in Afghanistan. It examines the role played by drones and whether the United States' new counter-insurgency strategy can make a major difference.

The question is particularly important because a perceived al Qaeda–Taliban victory in Afghanistan will give a huge fillip to the efforts of al Qaeda and its affiliates to entrench themselves strongly in the Arabian peninsula and North Africa which began with two objectives in mind—to fall back on both if al Qaeda and the Taliban are overwhelmed in their strongholds in Pakistan and establish a stronghold from where it can launch terror strikes on the West, as overwhelming the latter, destroying Israel and imposing their version of Islam and sharia law worldwide is their ultimate objective. Even if a Taliban–al Qaeda victory in Afghanistan and the consequent developments in Central and South Asia remove the need for a fallback area, the other objectives will remain. And al Qaeda and its affiliates, with their morale soaring following victory in Afghanistan, may become an unstoppable force in parts of Africa.

The book analyses the developments in the Arabian peninsula and North Africa, including the violence sweeping the two regions, to assess the seriousness of the threat al Qaeda and its affiliates pose to both. Significant success in their venture will expose Europe and the West to enhanced terrorist threat—there is a brief analysis of that—and further strengthen Islamist forces in Pakistan and Afghanistan by boosting their morale.

The prospect has understandably been causing serious concern because any strengthening of fundamentalist forces allied with the Taliban and al Qaeda will threaten the safety of Pakistan's large and growing nuclear arsenal and the fissile material stocked in its various nuclear establishments. This in turn underlines the enhanced potential for lethality that terrorism has acquired in an age when it can access nuclear and biological weapons of mass destruction and perhaps launch cyber attacks that can cripple countries.

Hence, the book contends, the critical importance of containing al Qaeda, its affiliates and the Taliban and the threats they pose.

SIGNIFICANT ELEVEN

Eleven events with a significant bearing on the book occurred as it was in the final stages of writing. These will largely determine the unfolding of the endgame which has begun in Afghanistan just as the forces and tendencies they represent have shaped the developments in the country since December 1979, when the Soviets invaded it. The latest among these was the Afghan parliament's vote demanding the removal of the country's Defence and Interior Ministers—Abdul Rahim Wardak and Bismullah Khan Mohammadi respectively.[1] The other 10 include US Secretary of State Hillary Clinton's expression of regret to Islamabad for the American air attacks that killed 24 Pakistani soldiers early in the morning of 26 November 2011; Pakistan allowing thereafter the resumption of supplies to North Atlantic Treaty Organization (NATO) troops in Afghanistan through its territory which it had halted after the incident; and its signing on 31 July 2012 of a Memorandum of

Understanding with the United States permitting, until 31 December 2015 in the first instance, such passage by NATO supply convoys.[2]

The 11 also include the grant of the status of a major non-NATO American ally to Afghanistan;[3] the pledge by Western nations at a meeting in Tokyo to provide $16 billion as aid to the Kabul regime over the next four years;[4] the suicide bomb attack that killed an important Afghan Member of Parliament, Ahmad Khan Samangani, and at least 19 others and wounded over 50 in Aybak in northern Afghanistan on 14 July 2012 at the wedding reception of Khan's daughter;[5] the attack on a convey that incinerated 22 tankers carrying fuel for NATO troops in Afghanistan;[6] the removal of Agha Jan Motasim's[7] name from the list of Taliban leaders who are covered by UN sanctions which ban them from travelling or holding bank accounts;[8] and the unanimous vote in the US House of Representatives recommending a cut of $650 million in the US military aid to Pakistan.[9]

Two other events requiring brief mention relate to the developments in Africa. These are the rapidly escalating exodus from harsh Islamist regime in parts of Mali[10] and the ad hoc formation of militias in that country by young men and women determined to oust the Islamists from their country.[11]

Before discussing the two, one must briefly dwell on the 11 developments mentioned. These broadly reflect the three elements— relations between the United States and Pakistan, the United States and Afghanistan, and the United States and the Taliban and al Qaeda— that will largely determine the turn of events in Afghanistan. Each of the three is complex, marked by deep mutual suspicions and vicissitudes caused by conflicting agendas, hiatus between stated and hidden intents and surprising about-turns. Consider the one between the United States and Pakistan.

On 3 July 2012, US Secretary of State Hillary Clinton told the Pakistani Foreign Minister, Hina Rabbani Khar, with reference to the killing of 24 Pakistani army personnel, 'We are sorry for the losses suffered by the Pakistani military.' The US State Department's statement which said this further quoted her as saying, 'We are committed to working closely with Pakistan and Afghanistan to prevent this from ever happening again.'[12] She never used the word 'apology' but Pakistani officials interpreted what she said to mean precisely that and agreed to let the supply convoys roll through its territory from 4 July. And they did.

The two developments underlined two critical aspects of the Afghan narrative. The first is the United States' willingness to go as far as possible to accommodate Pakistan on any issue without compromising what it considers its core interests or strategic options. The second is Pakistan's inability to sustain prolonged opposition to the United States on any issue, to say nothing of affording a break with it. The country's state and edifice of power, including their military component, will be in serious danger of collapsing should American funds stop arriving. Its civilian and military leaders recognize this. During confrontationist phases, they assume seemingly the most intransigent postures, threaten to sever all ties with the United States, talk of an imminent takeover of their country by Islamist fundamentalists and, having done their utmost, accept such straws as may be offered to them.

That even such posturing will not push Americans into compromising on their critical military options was demonstrated on 6 July—three days after the 'apology' episode—when a US drone fired four missiles at a compound in a village in North Waziristan owned by a Taliban commander, Rahimullah. Fifteen suspected Taliban militants were killed. Rahimullah, believed to be a close aid of the warlord Hafiz Gul Bahadur, who controls a large stretch of North Waziristan, was reportedly away at the time.[13]

Despite the incident which reflected continued American disregard for Pakistan's fierce opposition to drone strikes, the question remains whether it will go further and take really tough measures like cutting off aid or imposing sanctions to compel Islamabad to abandon its duplicitous course. Such a development seems unlikely on the face of things and particularly in the light of the fact that following the signing of the Memorandum of Understanding on the resumption of NATO supplies through Pakistan, the latter has already received $1.1 billion from Coalition Support Fund[14] which had been held up. According to an AFP report, the instalment was particularly beneficial to

Pakistan as it tried to head off 'a new financial crisis created by poor tax revenues, mismanagement and overgenerous subsidies'.[15]

DESPITE DUPLICITY?

If the release of the latest instalment from the coalition funds is any indication, the $650 million cut in the military aid to Pakistan, which in any case is subject to the US Senate's approval, is a non-starter. The question is whether all this will end Pakistan's duplicitous approach toward cooperating with the US war on terror. Or will it further confirm Islamabad's belief that it can always manipulate Washington DC to get what it wants without yielding on what it considers to be its interests—even if it is at the cost of basic American goals in the region? It has been doing so and getting away until now and the release of the latest instalment from the Coalition Support Fund is not calculated to make it change its approach. Hence, the question: Can the United States win in Afghanistan with Pakistan continuing to play both sides to achieve, as will be seen later, its goal of installing a pliant government in Afghanistan, even if that means the latter again becoming a staging ground for terrorist strikes against the United States?

Much will depend on the Kabul regime's ability to defeat Pakistan-backed efforts by the al Qaeda–Taliban combine to take over Afghanistan after the United States leaves at the end of 2014. This, in turn, will depend on its internal cohesion, military capability and its ability to deliver reasonably good governance. The Afghan parliament's vote demanding Wardak's and Mohammadi's removal once again underlined the ethnic and other faultiness that bedevil President Hamid Karzai's government, as they had bedevilled most other governments in Afghan history. This is something to worry about, along with the corruption and inefficiency that have been causing concern for quite some time. Significantly, those demanding Wardak's and Mohammadi's resignation have blamed both for the massive corruption flourishing in their respective domains as well as failure to contain the attacks that the Taliban continue to launch from Pakistan.

Afghanistan's ability to hold its own against the Taliban and al Qaeda backed by Pakistan will depend critically on its continuing to receive adequate economic and military aid from the United States and NATO countries. The US Secretary of State Hillary Clinton's declaration of Afghanistan as a major non-NATO American ally, made in Kabul on 7 July 2012 in the presence of Afghan President Hamid Karzai, put Afghanistan in the same league as Israel, Japan, Pakistan and a few other countries close to the United States. It gave Kabul access to American military training and excess supplies as well as loans of equipment and finance for the leasing of the latter. It, however, did not 'entail any security commitment', according to a US State Department statement.[16]

Such a statement could cause a feeling of insecurity in Kabul where people had been talking about the United States' almost total abandonment of Afghanistan shortly after the completion of the withdrawal of Soviet troops from the country on 15 February 1989. Clinton clearly sought to reassure Karzai. She told him, 'We are not even imagining abandoning Afghanistan. Quite the opposite. We are building a partnership with Afghanistan that will endure far into the future.'[17] Her statement reaffirmed the message inherent in President Barrack Obama's signing, along with President Karzai, of a strategic partnership agreement between the United States and Afghanistan setting the terms for relations after the departure of American troops in 2014.[18]

An earlier decision to provide $4.1 billion annually for maintaining Afghanistan's army and police forces, as well as the development assistance $16 billion promised over the next four years, suggest more than ephemeral commitment, as does the United States' plans for long-term engagement with Central Asia, which will be discussed later in the book. Also, its plan to keep contingents of Special Operations forces in Afghanistan even after 2014, for training Afghan forces and executing a new counter-insurgency strategy of relying principally on drone strikes and clinical intelligence-driven strikes against terrorists and their establishments, indicate a resolve not to let the Taliban and al Qaeda take over Afghanistan.

All this will help provided the money comes and the new counter-insurgency strategy delivers. The critically decisive factor, however, will be the ability of the Afghanistan's civilian government and military to fend off the Taliban and al Qaeda. Here, the ability to curb corruption will be a key factor. For one thing, the agreement regarding aid, reached at the International Donors' Conference in Tokyo and called the Tokyo Framework of Mutual Accountability, linked the disbursement of up to 20 per cent of the amount on meeting governance standards, particularly in respect of stronger anti-corruption measures and the establishment of the rule of law.[19] For another, delayed utilization of aid, the siphoning of significant amounts of these to private pockets, the procurement of substandard military equipment for a consideration and corruption in the recruitment of police and military personnel, will undermine national defence.

This will mean trouble, as will any peace settlement which puts the Taliban in a position from where it can subvert the new Afghan government and set up its own dispensation in the country along with al Qaeda. The need to make this point cannot be understated given Washington DC's efforts to woo even leaders like Agha Jan Motasim who are fundamentalist hardliners. Any argument that they have turned a new leaf will remain suspect given the number of released Guantanamo prison detainees who have rejoined al Qaeda and played havoc. Further, the attack on the NATO convoy that incinerated 22 tankers and the killing of the Afghan Member of Parliament and 19 others, which bears the unmistakeable imprimatur of the Haqqani militia, indicates that the latter, a thorn in the flesh of the Karzai regime and US and NATO forces, have not beaten their AK-47s into ploughshares.

It is a tough road that lies ahead in Afghanistan and it will be disastrous if the United States and NATO countries lose patience and heart. The harsh fact, however, is that their economic troubles and weariness with the war in Afghanistan at home is putting them under strong pressure to strike a face-saving deal with Pakistan and the Taliban (which means al Qaeda as well) and dismantle tent. In this context, they would do well to remember that al Qaeda and the Taliban threaten all countries that do not subscribe to their distorted brand of Islam. It is a global phenomenon which requires to be met by a wider global coalition that includes countries like Russia, India and China. The latter has not been affected the way India and Russia have been but Xinjiang remains its soft underbelly and it cannot be comfortable with the goal of worldwide imposition of sharia law which al Qaeda, its affiliates and the Taliban have set before themselves. And even if they fail to achieve their objective, victory in Afghanistan will so increase their strength and prestige that they will inflict large-scale, worldwide death and devastation through terrorism and unconventional warfare before they finally go down. If countries as different as Stalinist Russia on the one hand and the United States and Britain on the other could unite against Nazi Germany and Fascist Italy, there is no reason why the United States, Britain, France, Germany, Russia, China and India, along with the moderate Muslim countries, cannot act together to face a threat which, this book shows later, is in many ways similar to what Hitler and the intellectual garbage that passed for his ideology did.

Finally, having said what the book is all about, it is time to thank those who have played an important role in ensuring that it saw the light of the day and in a remarkably short period. Sunanda and Sugata Ghosh, no kin to each other but pillars of SAGE in sales and commissioning, are old friends; so is Aarti David in charge of marketing. All of them have gone that extra mile that a book of this kind needed. Rekha Natarajan and Rudra Narayan Sharma, two other SAGE stalwarts, have also stretched themselves beyond the call of duty, as have Payal Kumar, head of editorial, and Aniruddha De and Archita Mandal who edited the manuscript with hawk-eyed meticulousness. And, of course, Vivek Mehra, Chief Executive Officer and Managing Director, SAGE India, pulled out all the plugs to ensure that nothing was left undone. Finally, my thanks to Chandan Mitra, Editor, the *Pioneer*, and Ajai Sahani, Executive Director, Institute of Conflict Management, New Delhi, for the support they have unfailingly extended to me.

Now, a word of explanation. The section on Islam in chapter 2 has a great deal in common with the section on the great religion in my book *Bangladesh: The Next Afghanistan?*[20] The reason is that the texts quoted, which account for a large part of the narrative in both, are the same. Also, my understanding of these and what Islam stands for remains the same as when I wrote the book on Bangladesh.

And, of course, I am, as always, deeply indebted to members of my family—my wife Malavika, my son and daughter, Indraneel and Kamini, and their respective spouses, Emily and Duncan, my nephews, Adit and Ranjan, and their respective spouses, Aditi and Saroj, for the affection and help they have unstintingly and unfailingly showered on me. Finally, I am deeply grateful to my family in Kolkata—Jojo, Poli, Munia and Chhanda—for always being there for me.

TAILPIECE

Just as I was about to read the first set of proofs came the report that militants armed with rocket-propelled grenades and automatic weapons had attacked Pakistan Air Force's Minhas Airbase at Kamra, 75 kilometres from Islamabad, before dawn on the morning of Thursday, 16 August 2012. Eight militants were killed in the four-hour gun battle that followed and one perished in a suicide blast just outside the base.[21] Two security officials were also killed.[22] The attack, launched by the Pakistani Taliban, was a shocking development—but of a kind that is in danger of becoming a regular feature of life in Pakistan.

What could mark a departure was a report published in the 15 August 2012 issue of the *Express Tribune* of Pakistan. According to it, United States Defence Secretary Leon Panetta had said that Pakistan was prepared to launch combat operations against Taliban militants in North Waziristan agency, which also served as a safe haven for the al Qaeda–affiliated Haqqani network. He, however, told the Associated Press that he did not know when the operations would start, except that he hoped it to be in the 'near future'. He also felt that the main target would be the Pakistani Taliban[23] rather than the Haqqani network.[24]

Such an offensive, if it comes about, would be a new development only to the extent to which Pakistan had been resisting American pressures to launch operations in North Waziristan. On the other hand, it has been fighting the Pakistani Taliban, which has waged for years a bloody insurgency in the country that has killed over 30,000 people.[25] In contrast, it has been viewing the Haqqani network as a strategic asset for furthering its objectives in Afghanistan after the Americans leave.

The question, however, is whether Pakistan can conduct operations in North Waziristan against the Pakistani Taliban without dragging the Haqqani network into these. The Associated Press quotes Moed Yusuf, South Asia adviser at the United States Institute of Peace, as saying that there was some geographical overlap (in their locations). Besides, both groups had common allies and were closely aligned with al Qaeda and other foreign fighters. Yusuf said he did not think that 'the operations will be feasible beyond a point because they [Pakistani Taliban and the Haqqani network] did coexist geographically' and the army did not want 'to force Haqqani's hand into saving the Pakistani Taliban'. According to him, the Pakistani army 'will do enough against the Arabs, Uzbeks and other foreign fighters and some Pakistani Taliban just to show they have done something there'.[26]

Things, however, can take a radically new course if Pakistan attacks the Haqqani network. That, however, does not seem anywhere near happening. And even if an offensive does begin, it will be advisable not to interpret it as marking a change in Islamabad's approach which will change the course of the Afghan narrative. Jumping to such a conclusion would be yet another example of the Spectacular Episodes Syndrome (SES) involving exaggerated and irrational response to certain kinds of events which has been dealt with in some detail in chapter 1.

It will be salutary to recall the experience of the Pakistani army's offensive entitled Rah-e-Raast (the Right Path or the Straight Path) against the Pakistani Taliban. It started in Lower Dir district of Pakistan's North-West Frontier Province (NWFP) on Sunday, 26 April 2009, and then spread to the neighbouring Buner district of the same province, and from there to Swat, Upper Dir, Shangla and several others of the 24 districts comprising Pakistan's NWFP and large tracts of the country's Federally Administered Tribal Areas (FATA) which includes seven agencies—Khyber, Kurrum, Bajaur, Mohamand, Orakzai and North and South Waziristan.

Launched in the midst of much drumbeating and sabre-rattling, the offensive, discussed in detail in chapter 5, turned out to be a damp squib.

NOTES

1. Alyssa J. Rubin, 'Two Top Afghan Security Ministers Face Dismissal', *New York Times*, 4 August 2012, online edition, http://www.nytimes.com/2012/08/05/world/asia/2-top-ministers-face-dismissal-in-afghanistan.html?pagewanted=2&nl=todays headlines&emc=edit_th_20120805.

2. Richard Leiby, 'U.S., Pakistan Sign Deal to Allow Supply Routes Through 2015', *Washington Post*, 31 July 2012, http://www.washingtonpost.com/world/asia_pacific/us-pakistan-sign-deal-to-allow-supply-routes-through-2015/2012/07/31/gJQA4xeSMX_story.html.

3. Mathew Rosenberg and Graham Bowley, 'U.S. Grants Special Ally Status to Afghans, Easing Fears of Abandonment', 7 July 2012, http://www.nytimes.com/2012/07/08/world/asia/us-grants-special-ally-status-to-afghanistan.html?_r=1&nl=todaysheadlines&emc=edit_th_20120708.

4. Jane Perlez, 'S 16 Billion in Civilian Aid Pledged to Afghanistan, with Conditions', *New York Times*, 8 July 2012, online edition, http://www.nytimes.com/2012/07/09/world/asia/afghanistan-is-pledged-16-billion-for-civilian-needs.html?_r=1&nl=todaysheadlines&emc=edit_th_20120709.

5. Enayat Najafizada and Mathew Rosenberg, 'Prominent Afghan Lawmaker among Bombing Victims at Wedding', *New York Times*, 14 July 2012, online edition, http://www.nytimes.com/2012/07/15/world/asia/afghan-lawmaker-among-victims-at-wedding-bombing.html?1&nl=todaysheadlines&emc=edit_th_20120715.

6. BBC, 'Afghanistan: Taliban Bomb Destroys 22 NATO Fuel Tankers', 18 July 2012, http:www.bbc.co.uk/news/world-asia-18882247.

7. Motasim, a son-in-law of Mullah Omar, was Finance Minister and Chief Administrator in the Taliban government in Afghanistan.

8. Praveen Swami, 'Key Taliban Leader Removed from U.N. Sanctions List', *Hindu*, 21 July 2012, online edition, www.thehindu.com/news/international/articlde366306.ece.

9. Press Trust of India, '$ 650 Million Cut in U.S. Military Aid to Pakistan', *Hindu*, n.d., online edition, www.thehindu.com/news/international/article3661854.ece.

10. Adam Nossiter, 'Jihadists' Fierce Justice Drives Thousands to Flee Mali', *New York Times*, 17 July 2012, online edition, http://www.nytimes.com/2012/07/18/world/africa/jidhadists-fierce-justice-drives-thousands-to-flee-mali.html?pagewanted=2&nl=todaysheadlines&emc=edit_th_20120718.

11.   Marco Gualazzini, 'Saying Mali "Is Our Country," Militias Train to Oust Islamists', *New York Times*, 5 August 2012, online edition, http://www.nytimes.com/2012/08/06/world/africa/mali-militias-poorly-armed-but-zealous-to-oust-islamists.html?nl=todaysheadlines&emc=edit_th_20120806.

12.   Adam Entous and Tom Wright, 'U.S. Apologizes to Pakistan, Says Supply Routes to Reopen', *Wall Street Journal*, 3 July 2012, online edition, http://online.wsj.com/article/SB10001424052702304299704577503914049142208.html.

13.   Salman Masood and Ihsanhullah Tipu Mehsud, '15 Killed in U.S. Drone Strike in Pakistan', *New York Times*, 6 July 2012, online edition, http://www.nytimes.com/2012/07/07/world/asia/15-killed-in-us-drone-strike-in-pakistan-aimed-at-taliban.html?nl=todaysheadlines&emc=edit_th_20120707.

14.   Under the Coalition Support Fund Pakistan is reimbursed the cost of counter-insurgency operation it incurs. It had received $8.8 billion under this head between 2010. Reimbursement had stopped after December 2010.

15.   AFP, 'Pakistan Gets $ 1.1b CSF from US', *Express Tribune*, 2 August 2012, online edition, http://tribune.com.pk/story/416525/pakistan-gets-1-1b-csf-from-us.

16.   Matthew Rosenberg and Graham Bowley, 'U.S. Grants Special Ally Status to Afghans, Easing Fears of Abandonment'.

17.   Ibid.

18.   Mark Landler, 'Obama Signs Pact in Kabul, Turning Page in Afghan War', *New York Times*, 2 May 2012, online edition, http://www.nytimes.com/2012/05/02/world/asia/obama-lands-in-kabul-on-unannounced-visit.html?pagewanted=2&nl=todaysheadlines&emc=edit_th_20120502.

19.   Perlez, '$16 Billion in Civilian Aid Pledged to Afghanistan, with Conditions'.

20.   Hiranmay Karlekar, *Bangladesh: The Next Afghanistan?* (New Delhi: SAGE, 2006).

21.   *Dawn*, 'Terrorists Attack Kamra Air Base: Nine Attackers Dead. Plane Damaged', 16 August 2012, online edition, http://dawn.com/2012/08/17/terrorists-attack-kamra-air-base-%E2%80%A2-nine-attackers-dead-%E2%80%A2-plane-damaged/.

22.   Associated Press, 'Kamra Attack Shows Need for North Waziristan Offensive', *Dawn*, 18 August 2012, online edition, http://dawn.com/2012/08/17/attack-shows-need-for-pakistani-taliban-offensive/.

23.   The name by which Tehrik-i-Taliban Pakistan is generally referred to.

24.   Agencies, 'Pakistani Military Plans to Open New Front: Panetta', *Express Tribune*, 15 August 2012, online edition, http://tribune.com.pk/story/422240/pakistan-military-plans-to-open-new-front-panetta/.

25.   Associated Press, 'Kamra Attack Shows Need for North Waziristan Offensive'.

26.   Ibid.

CHAPTER 1

THE SPECTACULAR EPISODES SYNDROME

A common human failing can be described as 'Spectacular Episodes Syndrome' or SES. A response to spectacular events, it represents a state of mind in which elation has the better of rational judgement. It can be triggered by a wide variety of causes, from winning the World Cup in cricket or soccer, which might prompt one to think that one's country will remain champion for ever, to a battlefield victory. It can be the assassination of a much hated national enemy, which can make one believe, contrary to evidence, that victory in a war against his country or organization is imminent. It can be the start of elusive talks which makes people conclude that peace is round the corner.

Spells of SES can last for a few hours or even a few years before unpleasant reality shatters them, and are followed by what can be called the Desperate Response Syndrome (DRS) representing desperation to escape from harsh reality as intense as the elation obscuring it. Both individuals and countries can lapse into it. The United States and Americans are no exceptions. The vulnerability of both has greatly affected the former's conduct of the Afghan war. Continuing swings from one to the other obscure the basic questions that the United States and the world need to examine in relation to the Afghan war. What is at stake? Is peace with the Taliban possible? Can Pakistan be depended upon to broker a peace with the Taliban which will ensure a peaceful, modern and democratic Afghanistan, or to help the United States and the North Atlantic Treaty Organization (NATO) forces to win the war? Can the Americans win, or could have won the war in Afghanistan? What will be the consequences of an American retreat which seems like a defeat? The book tries to answer these questions which are important to not only the United States but the whole world.

To begin with, three instances need examination—euphoria over the perceived success of the post-9/11 US-led invasion of Afghanistan, the hype generated by Osama bin Laden's killing, and the excitement caused by the Taliban opening an office in Doha in Qatar.

The first followed a campaign lasting a little over a mere two months. The Taliban had mobilized massively, deploying an estimated 60,000 troops from the north-eastern province of Takhar to Kabul, Herat province in the west, and to the south.[1] There were, besides, foreigners—3,000 Arabs from 13 Arab counties on the Kabul front, 9,000 from Pakistan's tribal areas, and about 2,500 combatants from Central Asia sent by the Islamic movement of Uzbekistan. In addition, there were hundreds of Chechens and Uighurs.[2]

Yet troops of the Northern Alliance,[3] aided by massive bombing by the United States and NATO forces and support on the ground by a very small number of American Special Operations Forces personnel, had routed the Taliban in a short and swift campaign. Between 8,000 and 12,000 Taliban were killed, twice that number wounded and 7,000 had been taken prisoners. By the middle of December 2001 the leaders and the rank-and-file militants of both al Qaeda and the Taliban were seeking sanctuary in Pakistan. Against this only one American and several Northern Alliance soldiers were killed.[4] Besides, Americans had won this massive victory incredibly cheaply—the amount coming to just $3.8 billion by January 2002—relative to how much such conflicts cost.[5]

Al Qaeda's plight, already severe, seemed to continue worsening. Its support network in Pakistan—its main strategic backyard in the Afghan war—seemed to collapse. Several of its top functionaries were arrested—including Abu Zubaydah in March and Ramzi bin al-Shib in September—in the course of 2002.[6] Besides, the 300,000 militants, who, the Taliban Central Command in south-west Afghanistan had loudly proclaimed, were to rise at a signal from Mullah Omar, were reabsorbed in the urban and rural tribal population of Hamid Karzai–governed post-Taliban Afghanistan.[7]

The stalwarts of the Bush administration thought they had won a resounding victory, the backs of al Qaeda and the Taliban had been broken and they could sally forth to a new range war—read Iraq—with their loaded six-guns in their tied-down holsters and Winchesters slung across their backs. Unfortunately for them, things turned out differently. By 2003, both militant Islamist organizations were back in business much to the chagrin of the United States and its NATO allies.

ELATION AND ITS CAUSES

Osama bin Laden's killing perhaps led to a bigger outburst of elation. Weary after nearly 10 years of war, Americans were increasingly feeling that they were not going anywhere in Afghanistan and Osama bin Laden would never be found, to say nothing of being killed. At home, the economy was not picking up and the drain of the war was seen as a major obstacle to mobilizing the resources needed for staging a quick recovery. Yet, no honourable end to the conflict appeared in sight. Suddenly, President Obama broke the news of Osama bin Laden's killing in a commando raid whose daring, and the underlying planning, belonged to the realm of movies.

A report in the *New York Times* summed up succinctly what the event meant for the US establishment:

> For an intelligence community that had endured searing criticism for a string of intelligence failures over the past decade, Bin Laden's killing brought a measure of redemption. For a military that has slogged through two, and now three vexing wars in Muslim countries, it provided an unalloyed success. And for a president whose national security leadership has come under question, it proved an affirming moment that will enter the history books.[8]

To Americans, it meant just retribution for a man who was more responsible than anyone else for the ghastly terrorist strike on 11 September 2001, which brought down the twin towers of the World Trade Center in New York and destroyed a part of the Pentagon in

Washington DC, killing nearly 3,000 innocent men and women, a man who, to them, had come to symbolize distilled evil. As the news of bin Laden's death spread, men and women were out in the streets of New York City and Washington DC celebrating.

Nevertheless, given the experience of the Taliban and al Qaeda's second coming, the Obama administration's elation was somewhat tempered by caution. There were warnings about the importance of not being carried away, about the need for continued vigilance against terrorism which would not end overnight and of al Qaeda shifting its operations to the Arabian Peninsula and North Africa and posing a threat to the West from there.

The back and forth between caution and elation was very much in evidence in President Obama's statement in the White House's East Room late on 1 May 2011, when he announced bin Laden's death in Abbottabad in Pakistan where it was then the morning of 2 May. He said that for 'over two decades bin Laden has been al Qaeda's leader and symbol', and that his death marked the 'most significant achievement to date' in the United States' effort to defeat al Qaeda. But his death, he added, did not mark the end of the effort. Al Qaeda would continue with its attacks against the United States which had to 're-main vigilant at home and abroad.'[9]

Optimism, however, seemed increasingly on the ascendant. Announcing a schedule for the withdrawal of American troops from Afghanistan, President Obama declared in a 15-minute address from the East Room of the White House on 22 June 2011 that the United States had largely achieved its goals in Afghanistan, which no longer represented a terrorist threat to it. The 'tide of war' was receding and it was time for Americans to focus on nation building at home. The United States, he further added, was starting its troops drawdown from a position of strength and that al Qaeda was under more pressure than at any time since 9/11. An intense campaign of drone strikes and other covert operations in Pakistan had crippled the organization's original network in the region and its leaders were either dead or pinned down in the rugged border between Pakistan and Afghanistan. Twenty of the 30 top al Qaeda leaders identified by

American intelligence had been killed during the previous year and a half, administration officials said.[10]

Other pronouncements and dispatches also tended to reflect optimism. On board his plane on his first visit to Kabul—where he arrived on 6 July—as United States Defence Secretary, Leon Panetta, told journalists that the United States was 'within reach of strategically defeating al Qaeda' and that America's focus had narrowed to capturing or killing 10 to 20 crucial leaders of the terrorist group in Pakistan, Somalia and Yemen.[11] A report in the *Washington Post* of 27 July 2011 stated that US counterterrorism officials were increasingly convinced that Osama bin Laden's killing and seven years of drone strikes by the Central Intelligence Agency (CIA) had pushed al Qaeda to the brink of a collapse.[12] According to the report, this assessment reflected a widespread view at the CIA and other agencies which felt that a small number of additional blows would effectively extinguish the Pakistan-based organization.

Miller's report also mentioned voices of concern. It quoted American officials as saying that al Qaeda might yet rally and that even its demise would not end the terrorist threat, which was being increasingly driven by radicalized individuals as well as aggressive affiliates. It also stated that officials now saw al Qaeda's offshoot in Yemen as a greater counterterrorism challenge than the organization's traditional base.

Nevertheless, the general mood appeared optimistic. According to the *Washington Post* report, a senior US counterterrorism official had cautioned that even if al Qaeda's base was dismantled, its militant ideology, which had spread, would remain a long-term threat. The official, however, felt that Panetta was 'exactly right' and 'strategic defeat'—an expression he was not sure he would have chosen to use—meant that al Qaeda had been rendered largely incapable of mounting catastrophic attacks against the United States. The official had added, 'We are within reach of rendering them to that point.'[13] Like many others, he believed that Osama bin Laden's death had been a turning point as the al Qaeda leader had remained active in managing the organization's network and keeping it focused on attacking the United States.

Also, his charisma was critical to the strength of al Qaeda's brand and the proliferation of its franchises overseas.

WITHDRAWAL AND APPREHENSIONS

The question of al Qaeda's defeat doubtless owes much of its present salience to President Obama's plan for a phased withdrawal of American troops from Afghanistan. According to the schedule announced by him on 22 June 2011, a total of 10,000 troops were to leave by the end of 2011. The remaining 20,000 from the 2009 'surge', which saw the infusion of 30,000 additional soldiers in Afghanistan, were to leave by the summer of 2012. The drawdown would continue at 'a steady pace' until the United States handed over security management to the Afghan authorities in 2014.[14]

There was anxiety over what would follow. Afghan security forces, to be in charge of their country's defence after 2014, did not yet seem capable of coping with the Taliban and al Qaeda. Besides, the departure of American and NATO troops would hit the Afghan economy hard. According to a report in the *New York Times* of 22 June 2011, thousands of Afghans who worked at or around American bases and under grants and contracts financed by the United States' State Department and the United States Agency for International Development (USAID) would lose their jobs as American military and civilian presence—and spending—decreased over the next three years.[15] The report stated that Afghan and American civilian and military planners feared that the country would fall into an economic abyss which would deepen poverty and drive some Afghans back into insurgency. The hope that the private sector would create some jobs hinged on a possibility that still seemed to be years away.

Emphasizing Afghanistan's dependence on aid, another report in the *New York Times* of 31 January 2012 cited a World Bank estimate stating that international assistance amounted to roughly 97 per cent of the country's gross domestic product (GDP). The report further stated that real estate prices, salaries, store sales and factory orders were shrinking, leaving Afghans almost everywhere to wonder what was happening. Growth, the World Bank forecasted, could fall to 5 or 6 per cent for the next few years as aid was withdrawn. The slowdown could be more severe if the security situation worsened or if Afghans could not maintain their new infrastructure.[16]

The discovery of $1 trillion worth of untapped mineral deposits in Afghanistan by a Pentagon task force transferred from Iraq to Afghanistan in 2009 promises much for the Afghan economy. According to a report in the *New York Times* in June 2010, the biggest mineral deposits discovered were of iron ore and copper, the quantities being such as to make Afghanistan a major producer of both. Other finds include large deposits of niobium, a soft metal used in producing superconducting steel, rare earth elements and large gold deposits in Pashtun areas of southern Afghanistan.[17]

The report further stated that, according to an internal Pentagon memo, Afghanistan could become the 'Saudi Arabia of lithium', a key raw material in the manufacture of batteries for laptops and BlackBerrys. Also, US officials believed that the previously unknown deposits— including huge veins of iron, copper, cobalt, gold and critical industrial metals like lithium—were so big, and included so many minerals that were essential to modern industry, that Afghanistan could eventually emerge as one of the most important mining centres in the world. The report quoted Jalil Jumriany, an adviser to Afghanistan's Minister of Mines, as saying that deposits 'will become the backbone of the Afghan economy'.

The issue of control over the deposits and their exploitation is bound to be a critical factor in any calculation of the stakes involved in the war. American, European, Russian, Chinese and Indian corporations will be interested in exploiting them. Even before the full magnitude of Afghanistan's mineral deposits were known, China forged ahead of the others by winning the rights to operate the Aynak copper mines for a staggering $4 billion in an international bid in 2008.[18] In 2009, five Indian companies—Vedanta group's Sesa Goa, Essar Minerals, Ispat Industries, JSW Steel and Rashtriya Ispat Nigam—joined the Chinese to bid for the 1.8 billion tonne Hajigak iron ore mines in the Hindu Kush mountain ranges. These mines account for a part of

Afghanistan's total iron ore deposits estimated at between five to six billion tonnes.[19]

Successful conduct of negotiations with multinational corporations (MNCs) and conglomerates for the exploitation of mineral resources, and the ensuring of a security environment in which investments follow agreements and mining units come up and begin functioning, will require a high level of governance and military and policing effort. One has to see whether the post-2014 Afghan government can ensure this. The matter is critically important to avoiding a destructive cycle, with lack of security undermining economic progress, and lack of economic progress undermining security.

People who have lost their jobs and livelihoods, and, with that, their hopes for the future, are the new poor who are easy recruits, or returnees, to the Taliban or organizations like al Qaeda leading mass movements resorting to terrorism and insurgency. In his seminal work *The True Believer: Thoughts on the Nature of Mass Movements*, Eric Hoffer writes, 'It is usually those whose poverty is relatively recent, the "new poor," who throb with the ferment of frustration…. They are the disinherited and the dispossessed who respond to every rising mass movement.'[20] He shows that it was the new poor who ensured the success of the Puritan revolution in 17th-century England and it was members of the ruined middle class who flocked to Nazis in Germany and Fascists in Italy.[21]

While the Obama administration can rightly claim considerable success in cornering the Taliban and al Qaeda, the latter remain active at the global level and, with the pressure of the American forces gone, can powerfully attract the discontented. Besides, as the revival of both after their ouster from Afghanistan by the post-9/11 US-led invasion shows, the success so far achieved against them provides no guarantee against their staging a comeback once the American and NATO troops have left.

Of course, the phased withdrawal of American troops from Afghanistan may not mean the end of the United States' war on terror. Instead, it would, according to American officials, mean a switchover to an intensified and focused counterterrorism strategy with a political dimension.[22] Operationally, it would put greater emphasis on drone strikes based on enhanced and effective intelligence-gathering, and clandestine missions by special forces teams, including of the kind that led to Osama bin Laden's killing. Politically, it would involve talks to wean the Taliban away from al Qaeda and make them a part of an Afghan peace settlement.

The picture is not terribly clear as the United States' position on the deployment of its troops in Afghanistan has undergone several major changes. Barring any totally unexpected development, however, a broad scenario can be seen as emerging. The *New York Times* of 20 December 2011 cited members of the Obama administration and other American officials as saying that 2014 was not a hard deadline for an American military withdrawal. It also quoted the American ambassador in Kabul, Ryan C. Crocker, as saying that the United States was open to keeping its forces in Afghanistan if the Afghan government asked for them. According to General John R. Allen, head of the American and NATO forces in Afghanistan, more American trainers and mentors would arrive in Afghanistan from 2012, and, even more in 2013.[23] Besides, the United States' plan to wind down its combat role in Afghanistan from 2013 relied on the Special Operations Forces playing a greater role in ensuring security. The *New York Times* reported on 4 February 2012 that under the emerging plan, the conventional forces, focused on policing large parts of Afghanistan, would be the first to leave while thousands of Special Operations Forces personnel would remain even after the NATO's mission ended in 2014. In fact, their number might increase. They would train a variety of Afghan security forces while elite commando units would continue with raids to hunt down, capture or kill insurgent commanders and terrorist leaders and keep terrorist/insurgents under pressure to prevent them from attacking.[24]

Questions, some of them uncomfortable, arise. Can the strategy lead to victory? Have bin Laden's death and drone strikes actually crippled al Qaeda or can it again rise from the ashes? Does it have the strategic vision, resources and capacity to do that? Will circumstances permit? Of crucial significance will be its relations with the

Taliban, which gave it space in Afghanistan after 1996 to grow, did not deliver Osama bin Laden to the Americans despite intense pressure, and which, and its kindred militant organizations in Pakistan, gave refuge to its cadre and leaders after their flight from Afghanistan in 2001 and helped them to regroup and strike back. Hence, from the American point of view, it is very important to draw the Taliban, or significant sections of it, away from al Qaeda. Can such an effort succeed?

Success in any dialogue with the Taliban would require Pakistan's active cooperation, which will also be critical to the constant inflow of accurate intelligence critical to the success of drone strikes and targeted clandestine operations, which constitute the central element in the American strategy. Equally, any regime taking over in Afghanistan following an American withdrawal might find survival difficult if the Taliban, nursed, protected, armed and guided by Pakistan, launches a renewed offensive.

Here is a problem. Washington DC's relations with Islamabad, its 'non-NATO ally', never quite smooth, became particularly nettlesome after al Qaeda's attacks on American embassies in Nairobi and Dar es Salaam on 7 August 1998 and Washington DC's retaliatory missile strikes of 20 August of the same year. Many Americans felt that Pakistan had alerted Osama, who was supposed to be at the al Qaeda camp targeted, to escape, and that it was not doing enough to compel the Taliban to hand him over to the United States. The improvement and euphoria, and of course, massive aid, which followed Pakistan's participation in the post-9/11 war on terror, began waning as al Qaeda and the Taliban recovered and struck back and Pakistan did little to contain them. Pakistan, Americans complained, was not only not pulling its weight but playing both sides and helping the Taliban and al Qaeda. Things became particularly acrimonious after the helicopter-borne commando raid that led to Osama bin Laden's killing, and which left Pakistan's top brass red-faced as the country's armed forces remained blissfully unaware of it until the United States' Navy SEALs had left with bin Laden's body and a treasure trove of intelligence-yielding material! They further worsened after the killing of 24 Pakistani soldiers in American airstrikes early in the morning of 26 November 2011.

It is not just a question of al Qaeda and the Taliban. Will Pakistan genuinely act against organizations like Lashkar-e-Toiba (LeT), Jaish-e-Mohammad (JeM) and Harkat-ul Mujahideen (HuM) which, spawned by its premier intelligence organization, the Inter-Services Intelligence (ISI) Directorate, function unhindered despite being banned? These, as well as the Haqqani network, had provided critical help to al Qaeda and Taliban leaders and combatants fleeing to Pakistan following the US-led post-9/11 invasion, and maintain close links with them. Failure to act against these outfits and stanch their assistance to al Qaeda and Taliban may not only hobble the fight against both but also lead to a steady accretion of strength to these and other fundamentalist organizations, creating a situation where they threaten the already-fragile Pakistani state. One can hardly rule out the danger of the latter being then overwhelmed, particularly if American forces withdraw in circumstances which appear to indicate their defeat.

THE JIHADI SHADOW

The steep boost the development will give to the prestige of the Taliban and al Qaeda will also enhance the appeal of fundamentalist Islam and the prestige of the LeT, JeM, HuM and other fundamentalist militant organizations and allied political parties and leaders. It will also encourage the jihadi segment of the Pakistani army, now lying low, to flex its muscles. On the other hand, it will profoundly demoralize the secular segment of Pakistan's military as well as the country's secular political parties and leaders. Even now—as the murders of Salman Taseer, the Governor of Pakistan's Punjab province, and Shahbaz Bhatti, the country's Minister for Religious Minorities, on 4 January and 2 March respectively in 2011, showed—they live under the shadow of death. Consequently, they are often afraid to speak out on contentious issues in public. Following what appears as an American defeat, they will hardly be in a position to prevent a takeover by jihadi groups. Having once withdrawn from Afghanistan, the United States will be unwilling to return to foil such a development. Even if so inclined, it may not be able to act if its economy sinks deeper into a crisis or there is stiff opposition at home. After all, the United States did not intervene in Afghanistan despite gross human rights violations by the Taliban regime and the attacks on its embassies in Nairobi and Dar es Salaam in August 1998. It took 9/11 for it to launch 'Operation Enduring Freedom'.

Of course, the post-exit situation will not be without serious threats to America. Jihadi groups that take over Pakistan will control its very considerable nuclear assets. Given their close and subservient ties with the Taliban and al Qaeda, the development would also enable the latter to access these, clandestinely if not openly. Bruce Riedel, a former CIA official, chaired, at President Obama's request, the US government's inter-agency review of policy towards Afghanistan and Pakistan for the White House, completed in March 2009. In his insightful work, *The Search for Al Qaeda: Its Leadership, Ideology and Future*, he said that al Qaeda seemed to think that it had to outdo 9/11 in its next attack on the United States and that it had obviously to be a raid using weapons of mass destruction.[25]

Riedel then referred to former CIA Director George Tenet's detailed account in his memoirs of al Qaeda's prolonged efforts to acquire a nuclear device and his conclusion that this was among al Qaeda's highest priorities. Riedel observed that the most likely place for al Qaeda to acquire a nuclear weapon was Pakistan, which had been the focus of the organization's attention. Stating that Pakistan possessed up to 200 nuclear bombs according to most accounts, he added, 'Although the security surrounding them has improved significantly in the past decade, at least on paper, the growing presence of al Qaeda and its allies in Pakistan should serve as a cause for deep concern.'[26]

The Pakistani state may, of course, continue to limp along and not collapse. Al Qaeda's efforts to acquire weapons of mass destruction may continue to draw a blank. That, however, would not mean an end of the threat the organization poses to the United States and the world as it will persist in its efforts to realize its objectives. The question arises: What are these? According to Syed Saleem Shahzad, al Qaeda's first objective is to defeat the West in Afghanistan, and the next is to extend the fighting all the way from Central Asia to Bangladesh to exhaust the US resources, before taking it to the Middle East for the final battles to revive the Muslim political order under a Caliphate, which would lead to the liberation of all Muslim territories.[27]

Shahzad further states that though al Qaeda was primarily an Arab organization, it chose to launch its struggle from South Asia because, according to a saying attributed to Prophet Muhammad, 'End of Time' battles would start after victory in the East, which then meant Khurasan. Geographically defined, Khurasan included parts of modern Iran, Central Asia, Afghanistan and parts of Pakistan. After victory in Khurasan, the triumphant army of Islam would launch *Ghazwa-e-Hind* (a term used in Prophet Muhammad's sayings), or the battle for India (which then included what is now Pakistan and Bangladesh). Muslims believe that having won the battles of Khurasan and India, their armies will march to the Middle East to join forces with the promised Mahdi (the ultimate reformer) and fight for the liberation of Palestine.[28]

Meanwhile, as Shahzad writes, al Qaeda is fighting for complete ideological control over all Muslim resistance movements worldwide. It wants these to fight their wars within the broader al Qaeda parameter, perceiving the United States to be the root cause of all problems affecting the world, and believing that it must fail on every front for peace to prevail.[29]

What al Qaeda Wants

As will be seen later in this book, al Qaeda wants not territory but an end to the United States' global hegemony, the subjugation of the West, and the establishment of a global Muslim Caliphate implementing its version of reductionist Islam. It knew from the beginning that the task would be difficult given the awesome powers that Americans command, and hence, sought to entrap it in a prolonged war in Afghanistan which would enfeeble it and bring it to the verge of a collapse as it happened with the Soviet Union. This would combine the beginning of the Khurasan battles with the process of undermining the United States.

An integral part of al Qaeda's strategy for defeating the United States in Afghanistan was interdicting its supply lines through Pakistan. According to Shahzad, an attempt to disrupt America's and the West's international trade and supply routes has been a corollary. This, as well as an effort to open up another front against the United States and prepare an alternative base of operations in case its strongholds in the tribal areas of Pakistan crumble, explains its expanding operations in Yemen and Saudi Arabia. The two countries, he points out, straddle the strategic Bab-el-Mandeb Strait which connects the Red Sea to the Gulf of Aden and commands a key oil supply route to the West.[30] Besides, control over Yemen, 'the strategic backyard of the whole Arab world', is key to controlling the struggles in Iraq and Palestine.[31]

Also, North Africa and West Asia, particularly the Arabian peninsula, which are often together referred to as the Middle East when they are not separately mentioned by their respective names, are key producers of oil. According to figures cited by the *Oil and Gas Journal*, reproduced on the official website of the International Energy Agency, the world's total proven oil reserves came to 1,342,207 billion barrels, of which the Middle East alone accounted for 745,998 billion. Of the African countries hit by the upheaval, Libya, the most severely affected, has 43,660 billion barrels, and Egypt and Algeria 3,700 and 12,200 billion barrels respectively.[32]

Any power which controls the Middle East will also control the economic regimes of both West Asia and North Africa. This would mean control over the imports of consumer and capital goods, trained labour power and contracts for infrastructural development, from which the United States, countries of Europe and countries like India, Japan and China benefit considerably. Besides, such a power will dominate some of the principal routes through which international trade moves from Europe to South, South-East and East Asia as well as countries of the Asia-Pacific rim. It is easy to imagine the kind of economic, political and military clout any power controlling the two regions will command.

One can also easily imagine the kind of economic blow the West will suffer if the Taliban, al Qaeda or their affiliates control the region.

A critical goal of these organizations is the disruption of the West's economy and supplies, which in turn has led them to encourage Somali piracy. Shahzad has cited an Internet posting (http://www.alqimmah. net) to show al Qaeda exhorting Somalis to engage in it, pointing out that the 'spoils of war from the sea' were legitimate and were to be divided in 'the same way as bounty from the land'. In fact, they were to be preferred because 'what might be captured from one infidel ship can be much more than the spoils obtained by dozens of land raids'. The mujahideen, who 'weep' for lack of money, need them.[33]

The importance al Qaeda attaches to its operations in Somalia and Yemen, indeed, the whole of Middle East, becomes clear on looking at the way it has mended its ties with Iran, which had been severely damaged by Abu Musab al-Zarqawi's[34] anti-Shi'ite violence in Iraq. Profoundly angered by it, Iran had changed its policy of not acting against al Qaeda operatives passing through it and had arrested several of them and handed them over to Saudi and Egyptian authorities.[35] The abduction of an Iranian diplomat, Heshmatollah Attarzadeh, from Peshawar in 2008, however, led to investigations by Tehran which eventually led to the Taliban commander, Sirajuddin Haqqani, and a deal under his aegis. Under the latter, Attarzadeh was exchanged in lieu of several al Qaeda leaders held in Iran, including Osama bin Laden's daughter, Iman, and an important commander, Saif al-Adel.[36]

The popular upsurge in the countries of North Africa and the Arabian Peninsula has assumed a special relevance in this context. Success in establishing its sway over Somalia and Yemen will greatly enhance al Qaeda's prestige in the entire region. An al Qaeda/Islamist takeover of the Middle East will radically alter the global balance of political and economic power. Even if there is no takeover but al Qaeda, its affiliates and allies come to control parts of some countries, they may use the latter, like areas of Afghanistan under Taliban control prior to their ouster post-9/11, to launch terrorist strikes worldwide. The implications of this require no elaboration given not only 9/11 but also a number of vicious terrorist strikes, and attempted strikes, in the United States, Europe, India (repeatedly for three decades), Russia, Indonesia and several African and West Asian countries.

Al Qaeda's regional affiliates like Al Qaeda in the Islamic Maghreb (AQIM) and Al Qaeda in the Arabian Peninsula (AQAP), the political parties and front organizations supporting them, as well as their sympathizers in the general population, have been active in the Middle East for some time. Their presence, earlier not much in evidence in countries like Libya, Syria, Egypt and Tunisia, swept by movements for change beginning in the winter of 2010, is beginning to be felt. Their morale, standing and public support will rise sharply if al Qaeda and the Taliban win in Afghanistan or are perceived to have won. This, in turn, may tilt the balance in their favour and against the moderate Muslim and the secular, democratic and modernist forces which are also active in the region, and which would be demoralized by a perceived American defeat in Afghanistan. Nor may the United States, defeated in Afghanistan, be inclined or be able to help them to prevail.

Al Qaeda's triumph in the Middle East will also hasten Pakistan's takeover by al Qaeda surrogates—whose prestige will shoot up while the moderate Muslim and secular elements will be demoralized—if it had not happened by then. The danger of their then accessing Pakistan's nuclear arsenal has been mentioned. A sharp increase in the chances of a nuclear terror strike in the United States will be one consequence; another will be a devastating war in South Asia which may involve the use of nuclear weapons.

If al Qaeda accesses Pakistan's nuclear arsenal with its delivery systems, it may be able to stage a nuclear attack on the United States from outside it. Even if it fails to do so, it will continue trying to stage a clandestine nuclear strike. The question arises whether the United States, or for that matter, any other country, can render itself immune to terrorist strikes by passing laws and erecting security structures that convert it into a virtual fortress, and severely restricting inward and outward international travel. The fact that there has been no large-scale terrorist strike in America post-9/11 suggests that it can. Equally, however, the Pakistani terrorist Faisal Shahzad's attempt to set off a car bomb at Times Square, New York, on 1 May 2010, failed because the bomb began smoking prematurely, thus attracting attention of a

T-shirt vendor who, in turn, alerted the police. It did not fail because security arrangements in place in New York City prevented him from placing his Nissan Pathfinder with its deadly cargo at the heart of Manhattan.[37]

Besides, despite leaving clues virtually at every step, Shahzad almost succeeded in flying out of the United States and was taken off a plane he had already boarded at Kennedy Airport, New York.[38]

GHAZWA-E-HIND

As for South Asia, the beginnings of Ghazwa-e-Hind or 'battle for India' can be traced to the early 1980s. The ISI, which had been training Kashmiri terrorists at al-Badr's camp in Afghanistan's Paktia province where they were training Afghan mujahideen, shifted its preference later to the HuM, Hizb-ul Mujahideen and Harkat-ul-Jihad-al-Islami (HUJI). The unconventional war through cross-border terrorism these organizations have waged against India has taken a heavy toll of life for over 20 years now.[39]

According to a report, officials of India's External Affairs Ministry said on 7 December 1999 that while a total of 25,267 persons had been killed in terrorist attacks in the States of Punjab and Jammu & Kashmir in 10 preceding years, 12,316 Indians had lost their lives in the wars the country had fought since 1947.[40] The number of casualties from terrorist attacks in two states has gone up since then, as has the figure for whole of India as terrorism now stalks large parts of the country. Another report published on 25 September 2008 pointed out, citing the US State Department's National Counterterrorism Center (NCTC), that, on an average, terrorist violence killed seven persons daily in India in 2007. Pointing out that terrorists killed a total of 2,300 persons in India during that year, it stated that India was third on the international terror list in terms of those killed after Iraq (13,611) and Afghanistan (4,673).[41]

The situation continues to be grim despite a fall in the number of terrorist strikes. The United States' State Department's country report for 2010 states:

In 2010, India continued to see a reduction in the number of deaths attributable to terrorist violence, as it ramped up its counterterrorism capacity building efforts and increased cooperation with the international community, especially the United States. However, the loss of nearly 1,900 lives (civilian, security forces, and terrorists) still made India one of the world's most terrorism-afflicted countries. Sustained violence in Kashmir over a six-month period and attempted infiltrations from Pakistan across the Line of Control remained serious concerns for the Indian government.[42]

Over the years, the LeT and JeM have emerged as the principal striking arms of the ISI and al Qaeda against India. Besides, LeT has also been carrying out international strikes on behalf of al Qaeda. Judging by the evolving pattern of developments, the unconventional war that these two and other Islamist surrogates of al Qaeda have been waging against India will be transformed into a full-fledged war between India and Pakistan once al Qaeda and the Taliban win in Afghanistan and take over Pakistan. Those who dismiss the idea need to consider the following scenario. In the course of roughly two years after the withdrawal of American troops, the Taliban, assisted by Pakistan and the remnants of al Qaeda, defeat the forces of the Kabul government and come to rule Afghanistan. Pakistan, even if it has not been taken over by the jihadis, will be under increasing pressure from them to escalate the Ghazwa-e-Hind. Initially, it will follow the pattern it did in 1947, 1965 and, to an extent, in 1999. On the first occasion, it unleashed tribal levies on Kashmir under the leadership of the Pakistani army's officers and men. This led Maharaja Hari Singh to seek India's help, Kashmir's accession to India and the despatch of Indian troops to defend the former mountain kingdom. This in turn led to the open deployment of Pakistan's army and the first India–Pakistan war.

Pakistan again unleashed groups of infiltrators to stir up a revolt in Kashmir in 1965. The locals alerted the government which easily dealt with the situation. As the effort petered out, Pakistani army launched an offensive against India in the latter's Chhamb-Jaurian region to cut off its main supply route to its State of Jammu & Kashmir. India launched a counteroffensive in the Lahore sector to ease the pressure on the Chhamb-Jaurian sector and the second India–Pakistan war got into full flow.

The third India–Pakistan war, which led to the emergence of Bangladesh as an independent country, arose out of circumstances unrelated to Kashmir and not from Pakistani-engineered infiltration. The fourth India–Pakistan war of 1999 was triggered by Pakistan's infiltration of its regular troops, along with jihadi irregulars, into the daunting heights of the Indian territory of Kargil which Indian troops had abandoned, as they did every year, during the freezing months of winter. India regained the heights, from which artillery barrages could disrupt supplies to Kashmir, in the primarily localized war that followed.

TRANS-BORDER TERROR

Meanwhile, the end of the jihad in Afghanistan, following the withdrawal of Soviet troops in 1989, had left thousands of mujahideen, trained only to wage war and without the skills required for income-yielding civilian work, with very little to do. That year saw the beginning of a massive escalation of violence in Kashmir resulting from both local and cross-border terrorism, with the latter being much more devastating in its strikes than the local ones. If things did not proceed beyond terrorist strikes, it was because the Kabul regime did not fall with the departure of the Soviets. Confounding most forecasts, the government of the People's Democratic Party of Afghanistan, headed by Mohammad Najibullah, continued to defy its opponents. It fell in 1992 after the disintegration of the Soviet Union deprived it of the aid that sustained it. Civil war in Afghanistan followed Najibullah's ouster and ended when the Taliban, aided by the Pakistani army and al Qaeda, captured Kabul in September 1996, and then extended its sway over most of the country, except a small sliver of territory in the north controlled by the legendary Ahmed Shah Massoud, 'The Lion of Panjshir'.

Much will depend on whether the Afghan regime, disproving most prophesies, survives, and if it does not, how long it continues to resist. Much will also depend on whether countries like India, Russia and Iran come to its assistance. Assuming that it lasts for two years on its own, Ghazwa-e-Hind will receive a massive impetus in the form of a sharp escalation of Pakistan-based cross-border terrorism after its fall. Beyond a point, India will be forced to retaliate, perhaps by striking at terrorist training and launching sites in Pakistan. A full-scale conventional war between the two countries will then follow as Pakistan strikes back. As India's superior military might begins to tell, Islamabad will be tempted to threaten a nuclear attack and may even use its nuclear weapons if India does not back down. It is well known that it had activated its nuclear arsenal during the Kargil War in 1999. India, whose nuclear doctrine permits only a retaliatory second strike, will then unleash its own nuclear weapons. South Asia will be in ruins.

Even if a nuclear conflagration does not occur, a devastating conventional war raging over most of South Asia is a distinct possibility, particularly if Sheikh Hasina and her party, the Awami League, lose the general elections in Bangladesh scheduled for early 2014. With an overwhelming majority in Bangladesh's Jatiya Sangsad or National Parliament, she has taken firm action against fundamentalist Islamist terrorists groups. These, like the Harkat-ul-Jihad-al-Islami Bangladesh (HUJIB), a branch of the HUJI, Jagrata Muslim Janata Bangladesh (JMJB), Jama'at-ul Mujahideen Bangladesh (JMB), Ahle Hadith Andolan Bangladesh (AHAB) and Hijb-ut Tawhid, ran riot in the country when Begum Khaleda Zia headed a coalition government from 2001 to 2006. Though her Bangladesh Nationalist Party (BNP) had a huge majority in parliament, its coalition partner, the fundamentalist Jama'at-e-Islami Bangladesh (JeIB), which has close ties with Islamist terrorist organizations, had a disproportionately large say in the running of the government.

HUJIB, formed in 1992 to recruit volunteers to fight in Afghanistan and Kashmir, has close links with al Qaeda. Rohan Gunaratna writes in *Inside Al Qaeda: Global Network of Terror* that 'Bangladeshi authorities now believe that Al Qaeda had funded it'. He adds, 'The group also operated in north-eastern India in tandem with several small Islamist groupings. Osama is said to have sent his private secretary to attend a meeting of Harkar-ul-Jihad-al-Islami Bangladesh to draft a strategy to intensify their violent campaign in the region.'[43] Further, Yossef Bodansky, a former Director of the United States' Congressional Task Force on Terrorism and Unconventional Warfare, points out in *Bin Laden: The Man Who Declared War on America* that one of the six signatories to the fatwa issued by the World Islamic Front for Jihad Against Jews and Crusaders on 23 February 1998 was Sheikh Abdul Salam Muhammad, 'Emir of the Jihad Movement in Bangladesh'.[44]

A Taliban/al Qaeda victory in Afghanistan would give a huge boost to the morale of these organizations and send their stock as well as that of the JeIB soaring. This as well as the disadvantage of incumbency may make victory difficult for Sheikh Hasina. Should the BNP win in alliance with the JeIB and the Islamist militants, Bangladesh will become an important base of the Taliban and al Qaeda's operations against the United States and war with India, and of Islamist terrorism as such. The next target will be Nepal. The ISI has spread its tentacles far and wide in the country which continues to be unstable.

Two Zero One Four

Should such a scenario unfold, a war in Central Asia will either begin simultaneously with the war in South Asia or occur during the course of it. Al Qaeda's interest in the region and close links with Chechen, Uighur, Tajik and Uzbek Islamist militants are well known. This will bring Russia, and perhaps China as well, into the war's vortex. Thus, 2014 will be a critical year. With American troops gone except for a small contingent of Special Operations Forces personnel, the Afghan National Security Forces (ANSF) will have to defend their country against the Taliban, al Qaeda and the supporting forces. In fact, it may have to do it as early as mid-2013, when, as the United States Defence

Secretary, Leon Panetta, said in Brussels on 1 February, American forces would step back from a combat role, more than a year before the start of their departure from Afghanistan.[45] Will the ANSF be able to deliver?

As of now, the answer is 'unlikely'. A report in the *New York Times* of 22 June 2011, which covered President Obama's announcement of the phased troops withdrawal, also stated that the effort to transfer responsibility for security to Afghan forces remains elusive because the Afghan troops are proving unprepared for the job.[46] According to another report in the same paper on 27 June 2011, the many problems that still plagued the Afghan army and police included 'the danger of Taliban infiltration, the divided loyalties of many recruits and even officers, and the sometimes explosive tensions between them and the foreign forces who are supposed to train them'.[47]

Talking to reporters on 23 June 2011, President Hamid Karzai described President Obama's announcement about troops withdrawal as 'a moment of happiness for Afghanistan'. He added that in keeping with 5,000 years of their history, 'Afghans would take the responsibility for the preservation of their soil, the security of their people and educating their children by the end of 2014.'[48] Afghans have a great martial tradition. But, as the Taliban had no army, the Afghan National Army (ANA) had to be built from a scratch after the ouster of their government. Major General Dhruv C. Katoch (Retired) writes in his chapter, 'The Afghan National Army', in *Afghanistan: A Role for India*, 'Despite the many problems faced in its [Afghan army's] reconstitution, it remains a story of success in a conflict with few bright spots and will undoubtedly prove pivotal to stabilizing Afghanistan and in the ongoing counter-insurgency campaign in the country.'[49]

The performance of Afghan troops has improved and is set to improve further. But it would be unrealistic to expect it to so improve by 2014, to say nothing of 2013, that they can bear the major brunt of defending their country against powerful enemies fully supported by Pakistan. The report in the *New York Times*, which quoted Karzai, also pointed out that views were 'far less optimistic 300 miles to the south in Kandahar Province, a spiritual heartland of the Taliban, and to a lesser extent in neighbouring Helmand, the country's largest producer of opium poppy and a place where the northern districts continue to have active fighting.' It quotes a tribal leader from Maiwand district, Hajji Kala Khan, as saying, 'The drawdown will embolden the morale of the Taliban, and actually it has already emboldened them.' The Taliban, he added, who had been telling the elders that they would be killed if they supported the Americans, were now telling them, 'The Americans are leaving and your lives will not be spared.'

One needs to give a close look to the ANSF to gauge whether it will be able to defend its country by 2014. ANSF consist of the ANA, the Afghan National Police (ANP), the Afghan Border Police, the Afghan National Civil Order Police and other smaller authorized militia across the country. Its primary component is the ANA of which the Afghan National Army Air Corps (formerly Afghan Air Force) is a part.[50] The first handicap is numbers. According to a report in the *New York Times*, ANSF numbered 305,000 in December 2011, and were expected to expand to 352,000 by the end of 2012.[51] As of March 2011, there were 160,000 troops on the ANA's rolls, 4,000 ahead of the March goal. There is a proposal to increase its strength to between 195,000 and 208,000 by October 2012.

The expansion, however, may not take place. United States Defence Secretary Panetta said in Brussels on 1 February 2012 that a NATO meeting, which would focus on Afghanistan, would also discuss a potential downsizing of the ANSF from the proposed 350,000, largely because of the expenses involved in maintaining such a large body. A downsizing will be disastrous. In his chapter, 'Afghanistan Today', Lieutenant General R. K. Sawhney (Retired) wrote in *Afghanistan: A Role for India* that the US military's counter-insurgency doctrine prescribed the presence of 20 to 25 counter-insurgency personnel for every 1,000 residents. Afghanistan's population of approximately 28.4 million (some put it at 30 million) would require anything between 568,000 and 710,000 troops.[52] These figures, which he cited to underline the numerical inadequacy of the International Security Assistance Force (ISAF), would also apply to the ANA's strength.

The other problem is the ANA's inconsistent performance—ranging from excellent to very poor. This, however, was only to be expected. It takes time and a great deal of money and effort to build an efficient army. Even an abundance of both may not be enough. An army fights for *izzat* (pride) which in turn is closely linked to regimental traditions and tales of indomitable courage against indescribable odds, of which the Indian Army has a surfeit since World War I and earlier. Afghans have a martial tradition that any country should be proud of. These, however, relate to tribal history and traditions. The challenge will be integrating these into a national motivational framework for the ANA.

DIFFICULT, NOT IMPOSSIBLE

The challenge is difficult but not impossible to meet. India has developed an excellent military force that displays a high degree of professional and operational excellence and also reflects the country's tradition of unity in diversity. This, however, has happened over a long period. The ANA, with little time on its hand, has to depend on another factor critical to military performance, leadership at the levels of planning and strategy as well as combat. In the case of the latter, the role of officers like lieutenants, captains and majors will be very important. Unfortunately, performance at this level has sometimes not been good enough.

There is another problem. Major General Dhruv C. Katoch (Retired) points out in his chapter, 'The Afghan National Army', in *Afghanistan: A Role for India*, that while the ethnic composition of the ANA is generally representative of all the ethnic communities of the country at the level of foot soldiers, the commissioned and non-commissioned officers (NCOs) are mostly Pashtuns and Tajiks. This imbalance has to change if the ANA is to be perceived as a genuine national army.[53] Besides, Afghanistan's feudal tradition, and the fact that commissioned officers generally come from the landed and privileged sections, tend to create a barrier between them and the men they lead. This has sometimes created difficulties in counter-insurgency operations in which officers and men have often to live and function closely together.

There are two other problems. Writing in the *Long War Journal*, a website that reports on terrorism and Islamist insurgencies, C. J. Radin pointed to a significant shortage of both commissioned officers and NCOs in the ANA. According to him, there were 18,191 officers where 22,646 were required, and 37,336 NCOs where 49,044 were required, in November 2010. Stating that training capacity was being increased to address the shortage, he mentions the opening of two additional Officer Candidate School establishments in December 2010 and two more in April 2011. The additional capacity, he added, was expected to reduce, but not entirely eliminate, the shortage by October 2012.[54]

Radin also pointed out that about 86 per cent of ANA's enlisted recruits were not literate. An illiterate soldier could not read a map, a training manual or the serial number of his rifle. Furthermore, specialized fields such as medicine, logistics and communications could not be taught to him. The problem, Radin wrote, was being addressed by the establishment of an extensive literacy training programme. Starting in March 2010, mandatory basic literacy and numeracy training was instituted for all ANSF enlisted personnel in both ANA and ANP. The goal was to train every member of the ANSF to at least third-grade level. The curriculum was the equivalent of 312 hours of training. The programme applied to enlisted personnel and NCOs.[55]

There, besides, has been the major problem of raising an army under conditions of insurgency when the writ of the central government does not run in many parts. According to a report in the *New York Times* of 6 September 2011, Afghan and NATO officials have long struggled to entice young men in the heavily Pashtun south—the Taliban heartland—to join the Afghan army. An analysis of recruitment patterns by the newspaper showed that, despite their efforts, the number of people joining remained relatively minuscule, 'reflecting a deep and lingering fear of the insurgents, or sympathy for them, as well as doubts about the stability and integrity of the central government in Kabul, the capital'.

The report further pointed out that the two provinces of Kandahar and Helmand had a total population of nearly two million people but had contributed only 1,200 soldiers since 2009, 'less than 1 percent of the nearly 173,000 enlistees in that period'. On the other hand, Kunduz, a northern province of about 900,000 people, enlisted more than 16,500 recruits.[56]

Recruitment has also been slow given the need to keep out Taliban and al Qaeda infiltrators. Afghans alone, however, cannot be blamed for the state of the country's army. The United States' preoccupation with the Iraq War accounted for ANA's slow and haphazard development in the initial years.[57] Equipment have been late in coming. A backgrounder by Greg Bruno for the United States' Council on Foreign Relations based in New York City, cites the Pentagon as saying that just over half the number of promised up-armoured Humvees, with which coalition forces trainers were trying to augment the Afghan forces' capabilities, had been delivered by March 2010.[58] Nor does the ANA have tanks, heavy artillery and combat aircraft, which a full-fledged army needs to fight determined enemies like the Taliban and al Qaeda.

Nor is the Afghan National Army Air Corps worth much. In 2011, it had a strength of 2,876 men and women and 34 rotary-wing and 12 fixed-wing aircraft. The target is 8,000 personnel and 152 rotary and fixed-wing aircraft by December 2016.[59] An air-arm, which has neither bombers nor fighters, is hardly equipped to fight a serious unconventional war, which combines insurgency with terrorism, that the Taliban and al Qaeda are waging in Afghanistan.

While all this is true, it is also true that the Afghans are trying hard to enhance their overall military capability. C. J. Radin further mentions in the Long War Journal the ANA's setting up of a Special Operations Forces Organization. ANA commandos and ANA Special Forces (ANASF) are both under the ANA Special Operations Command (ANASOC). ANA commandos are the ANASOC's 'direct action' force. The ANASF is meant to operate at the level of Afghan tribes and villages and implement the Village Stability Operations (VSO) programme, which is designed to help individual villages fight insurgency. An ANASF brigade A-team is attached to each village under the VSO programme to train and advise the Afghan Local Police (ALP), the village's own defence unit. It is also meant to support the village leadership in the overall project of village defence and mediate in local disputes. In fact, the team will replace the United States Special Operations Forces (USSOF) in running the VSO programme.[60]

This is a tall order. The ANASF brigade A-team will have the advantage of familiarity with local culture, traditions and customs which the USSOF does not have, and the lack of which often created problems. A great deal will, however, depend on the A-team's combat ability as well as capacity for securing local cooperation. Besides, it will not be able to deliver unless the ANA's overall capability also enhances significantly. Also, the 134,000-strong ANP has a vital role to play in counter-insurgency in the form of intelligence-gathering and apprehension of terrorists lying low and preparing to strike. Unfortunately, it is the weakest link in Afghanistan's security chain. In his backgrounder, Greg Bruno cites the Pentagon as saying that the development of Afghanistan's police force 'has been hindered by a lack of reform, corruption, insufficient U.S. military trainers and advisors, and a lack of unity of effort within the international community'.[61]

Not Just Afghanistan's Future

It is a complex and mixed picture. The stakes go beyond Afghanistan's future. The first to feel the aggressive consequences of a Taliban–al Qaeda takeover of Afghanistan will be India and the Central Asian republics. India is a big and powerful country. A war will severely damage but not overwhelm it. The Central Asian republics may not be able to defeat without American assistance the expanded and intensified fundamentalist Islamist militancy which will follow. There are indications that the United States recognizes this as well as the importance of preventing Afghanistan from being overrun by the Taliban and al Qaeda. Releasing a report titled *Central Asia and the Transition in Afghanistan* by the majority staff of the United States Senate Committee on Foreign

Relations, the Committee's Chairman, Senator John Kerry, said on 19 December 2011:

> Central Asia matters. Its countries are critical to the outcome in Afghanistan and play a vital role in regional stability. As we reassure our partners that our relationships and engagement in Afghanistan will continue after the military transition in 2014, we should underscore that we have long-term strategic interests in the broader region.

The report itself categorically states:

> The U.S. role in Afghanistan is changing, but Washington should repeatedly stress that its engagement is not ending. Afghanistan's neighbours fear the 2014 security transition and withdrawal of coalition forces could mean abandonment. The United States must keep working to change the narrative by making it clear that we will protect our long-term interests in the region. The top priority is regional stability, and that is why 2014 will mark the beginning of a new phase of U.S. engagement in the region. The U.S. military will continue to work with the Afghan National Security Forces to prevent the return of terrorist safe havens. Much as it is doing in Iraq, the United States will remain vigorously engaged on security, governance, and economic and social development.[62]

The report makes three recommendations dealing with America's ties with Tajikistan, Kazakhstan, Uzbekistan and Kyrgyzstan with reference to their as well as Afghanistan's stability and security. The first calls for striking a balance between the security and political priorities in the region. It further states that while increasing security cooperation with the countries of Central Asia to support the efforts in Afghanistan, the United States must also lay the foundation for a long-term strategy that 'sustains these gains and protects U.S. interests in the region'. It calls for the United States promoting political and economic reforms and, 'given the tight fiscal climate', for the use of 'the existing Afghanistan resources on cross-border projects that

promote regional stability'. Significantly, it calls for increased assistance to Tajikistan and Kyrgyzstan 'given their fragility and importance
for broader regional stability'.[63]

The second recommendation is for translating the New Silk Road
(NSR) vision into a working strategy for the broader region beyond
Afghanistan. This, the report says, will require identifying needs, available resources, the United States' comparative advantages, and the
economic reforms regional governments must undertake to support
increased trade and investment. It states that the NSR's vision of con-
necting Central to South Asia through Afghanistan will not be a pana-
cea for the latter's economic woes, but has the potential for promoting
private sector investment if projects are prioritized and steps taken to
create an enabling environment. The United States, it says, can play a
vital role by supporting political and economic reforms and leveraging
its resources.[64]

The third recommendation calls for linking the Central Asia
Counternarcotics Initiative (CACI) with bilateral initiatives that offer
traction in the context of constraints on regional cooperation. CACI
provides an important vision for reform and information sharing to
tackle narcotics trafficking in the region. Mentioning hurdles like corruption and lack of political will, it asks the United States to consider
piloting a task force in countries with the greatest chance for success,
and an enhancement of cross-border cooperation between Afghan and
Central Asian law-enforcement and military officials and the establishment of joint training facilities.[65]

All this as well as the maintenance of the ANSF will require huge
expenditure. A report in the *Guardian* estimates that maintaining the
ANA and the ANP will require $6–8 million a year. This may be a
fraction of the $120 billion the United States was spending on its own
military operations in Afghanistan in 2011, but would mean the country receiving more direct American military aid than Israel and Egypt
together.[66] Leon Panetta said on 1 February 2012 that the United
States and the NATO countries spent around $6 billion in supporting
the ANSF but now European countries were balking at the amount
because of the financial crisis in the continent.[67]

THE PEACE PIPE ... OR A PIPE DREAM?

It is a heavy financial burden to bear at a difficult time. This is clearly one of the main reasons why the United States is trying to arrange a peace settlement in Afghanistan, which brings one to the third instance of SES—the start of the talks for peace talks with the Taliban in Doha, Qatar. It all began with the Taliban announcing on 3 January 2012 that they would open a political office in Qatar to facilitate peace talks to end the Afghan war. The step, the *New York Times* reported the same day, was meant to give Western and Afghan peace negotiators 'an address' where they could openly contact legitimate Taliban intermediaries.[68] This, the report quoted American officials as saying, would open the way for discussing confidence-building measures on which Americans sought progress. The principal among them would be the possibility of transferring a number of 'high risk' detainees to Afghan custody from Guantanamo Bay, which might in turn lead to their subsequent release.

Among the names discussed was that of Muhammad Fazl, former Taliban Deputy Defence Minister, who was accused of killing thousands of Shi'ite Muslims during Taliban rule. The others were two provincial governors, Khairullah Khairkhwa of Herat and Noorullah Nori of Balkh; Abdul Haq Wasiq, a former top Taliban intelligence official; and one of the Taliban's top financiers, Muhammad Nabi. According to American officials, also under consideration was the establishment of ceasefire zones, though the prospect was both uncertain and distant.[69]

Things seemed to have been moving. A report in the *New York Times* of 28 January 2012 quoted several former Taliban officials as saying that several Taliban negotiators had been meeting American officials in Qatar where their organization had set up a political office.[70] The Taliban had not formally stated that they would participate in peace talks but were discussing preliminary confidence-building measures including the transfer of prisoners from Guantanamo Bay. Maulavi Qalamuddin, who was the head of the *Amar Bil Maroof Wa Nahi* (the Department of the Promotion of Virtue and Prevention of Vice) in

Afghanistan's Taliban government, and was a member of the High Peace Council[71] in Kabul, told the paper that what was under way was not peace negotiations but talks for the release of Taliban prisoners from Guantanamo Bay.

Former Taliban officials in Qatar said that the talks on prisoners were in a fairly advanced stage. According to one of them, Syed Muhammad Akbar Agha, who had been a Taliban military commander, five Taliban prisoners were to be transferred in two phases, two or three in one group and then the remainder. The discussions had also touched the issue of removing some Taliban members from NATO's 'kill or capture' lists, the former Taliban officials said.[72]

Pakistan appeared to be on board. The *New York Times* report quoted Maulavi Qalamuddin as saying that it 'definitely supported the holding of talks and was also helping'. It would, he had added, have otherwise arrested the Taliban delegates to Qatar, just as it had arrested Mullah Baradar, a senior Taliban official, in 2010 after he began secret talks with the Afghan government. The report further stated that the Afghan government, which was initially angry at being left out, had accepted the talks in principle but was not directly involved.

All this suggested that the ball had been set rolling. It is, however, too early to say whether it will continue to roll or where it will end up. Consider Pakistan's role. Marc Grossman, the United States Special Envoy to Afghanistan and Pakistan, wanted to visit the latter along with Turkey, Saudi Arabia, United Arab Emirates and India during a trip that culminated in his talks with the Afghan government and a press conference in Kabul on 22 January 2012, which he addressed along with Mr Jawed Ludin, Afghanistan's Deputy Foreign Minister. He was rebuffed, with a Pakistani government spokesman telling the British news agency Reuters, 'Ambassador Grossman asked to visit Pakistan, but we conveyed to him that it was not possible at the moment.' Islamabad said it first had to complete a parliamentary review of the troubled bilateral relationship with Washington DC. Grossman admitted at the Kabul press conference, 'There really can't be a comprehensive peace process unless Pakistan is part of it,' reportedly adding in a conciliatory tone and with a smile, 'I would be happy to meet them at any time or any place.'[73] Clearly, the United States was prepared to go more than that proverbial extra mile to woo Pakistan.

But Afghanistan too has to be on board. And here too an uncertain course lies ahead. The fiercest opposition to a German proposal for a push for a political reconciliation in Afghanistan, made at the international conference for Afghanistan's security and development in Bonn on 5 December 2011, came from Afghanistan's President Hamid Karzai who initially rejected a plan for the Persian Gulf state of Qatar hosting an insurgent negotiating office.[74] He acquiesced under Obama administration's pressure but signs of resentment soon surfaced. One of these was his renewed demand for an immediate end to the night commando raids which Americans considered vital to getting at insurgent field commanders. Another was public condemnation of NATO forces for killing civilians. Then came his denunciation of abuses at the main American prison at Bagram Air Base and demand that Americans cede control of it within a month. The matter was important. The prison played a key role in the war effort, housing almost all the detainees that forces of the American-led coalition deemed 'high value', including Taliban operatives.[75] The recall of the Afghan ambassador from Qatar following the latter's grant of permission to the Taliban to open an office there was another protest gesture.

The Karzai government is doubtless critically dependent on economic and military assistance from the United States for its survival. It may resort to brinkmanship but will try to go with the Americans until it is so endangered that it is ready to gamble on a break. The talks, however, may run aground on several contentious shoals even if President Karzai tags along. One of these is the role of the Taliban office in Qatar. Asked about the significance of its opening, Marc Grossman had stated at the news conference in Kabul that 'nothing has been concluded' and 'more work needs to be done'.[76] The usefulness of the office would depend on whether the Taliban use it to facilitate serious negotiations or as a ploy to buy time until 2014 when American troops are supposed to withdraw from Afghanistan. Many believe the latter to be the case. They may well be right. The Taliban had not committed themselves to peace talks even after the opening of their Qatar office.

Also, while there is general recognition that Qatar and Afghanistan needed to be in direct contact with each other, there is, at the time of writing, no Afghan ambassador in Doha or a Qatari ambassador in Kabul and the two sides appeared to be talking past each other.[77]

Nor will the transfer of high-level Guantanamo Bay detainees be easy. In the United States, there is likely to be a political backlash. Criticizing Obama's plans to close the prison there, Republicans have cited several instances of those released having returned to terrorism or insurgency. Besides, legislators from both Republican and Democratic parties have tied the administration's hands by imposing new restrictions on transfers.[78] Mr Grossman has, doubtless, played down talk of the release of detainees and said that the Obama administration had not decided on the issue as it was a matter of meeting the requirements of the country's law. Besides, it had to consult the Congress.[79]

Two Questions

There is another hurdle. According to Grossman, the United States needed a clear statement by the Afghan Taliban against international terrorism and in support of the peace process to end the armed conflict in Afghanistan.[80] Two questions arise. Would the Taliban do it? Or would they just sit tight expecting the United States to capitulate? The chances of the latter happening can hardly be ruled out. Announcing his new policy for Pakistan and Afghanistan on 27 March 2009, President Barack Obama had said in Washington DC:

> So let me be clear: Al Qaeda and its allies—the terrorists who planned and supported the 9/11 attacks—are in Pakistan and Afghanistan. Multiple intelligence estimates have warned that al Qaeda is actively planning attacks on the United States homeland from its safe haven in Pakistan. And if the Afghan government falls to the Taliban—or allows al Qaeda to go unchallenged— that country will again be a base for terrorists who want to kill as many of our people as they possibly can.[81]

President Obama had further stated:

> So I want the American people to understand that we have a clear
> and focused goal: to disrupt, dismantle and defeat al Qaeda in
> Pakistan and Afghanistan, and to prevent their return to either
> country in the future. That's the goal that must be achieved. That
> is a cause that could not be more just. And to the terrorists who
> oppose us, my message is the same: We will defeat you.[82]

Further, he had stated that a return to Taliban rule would condemn Afghanistan to

> brutal governance, international isolation, a paralyzed economy,
> and the denial of basic human rights to the Afghan people—
> especially women and girls. The return in force of al Qaeda
> terrorists along with the core Taliban leadership would cast
> Afghanistan under the shadow of perpetual violence.[83]

President Obama had stated in his Address to the Nation on the
Way Forward in Afghanistan and Pakistan from West Point, New York,
on 1 December 2009:

> Over the last several years, the Taliban has maintained common
> cause with al Qaeda, as they both seek an overthrow of the
> Afghan government. Gradually, the Taliban has begun to control
> additional swaths of territory in Afghanistan, while engaging in
> increasingly brazen and devastating attacks of terrorism against
> the Pakistani people.
> We will support efforts by the Afghan government to open
> the door to those Taliban who abandon violence and respect the
> human rights of their fellow citizens.[84]

The following averments are clear from President Obama's statements: Afghanistan would again become a base for terrorists if the
'Afghan government falls to the Taliban—or allows al Qaeda to go
unchallenged'. Also, the United States sought to defeat, disrupt and
dismantle al Qaeda and prevent its return to Afghanistan. Further, a

return to Taliban rule would condemn Afghanistan to 'brutal governance' and 'the denial of basic human rights to the Afghan people—
especially, women and girls'. Over the 'last several years', the Taliban
had maintained common cause with al Qaeda as they both sought the
overthrow of the Afghan government. Finally, the United States supported the Afghan government's efforts to 'open the door to those
Taliban who abandoned violence and respected the human rights of
their fellow citizens'.

The United States started talks about confidence-building measures without Taliban officials of the Quetta Shura, headed by Mullah
Mohammad Omar, making any commitment about abandoning violence or respecting the human rights of 'the Afghan people—especially
women and girls'. To all appearances, Taliban II will be a clone of
Taliban I in the area of gender equality and justice and human rights,
and under their rule Afghanistan will revert to being the repressive
nightmare it was. An important indication is the fact that Maulavi Qalamuddin is playing an important role in the talks. In *Taliban: Islam, Oil
and the New Great Game in Central Asia*, Ahmed Rashid observes that the
edicts of the Department of the Promotion of Virtue and Prevention
of Vice he presided over 'had changed the lifestyles of Kabul's once
easy-going population and forced Afghan women to disappear from
public view'. The entire repressive and joyless system rested on terror
and ubiquitous espionage. Maulavi Qalamuddin ran a most elaborate
intelligence set-up. He told Rashid that he had 'thousands of informers
in the army, government ministries, hospitals and Western aid agencies'. His department's writ was enforced by thousands of young men,
many of them with no more than madrasa education from Pakistan,
walking about with whips, long sticks and Kalashnikov rifles.[85]

Nor had the Shura given any indication of shedding its ties with al
Qaeda. Hence, there is every likelihood of the al Qaeda leadership, now
in the border regions of Pakistan, returning to Afghanistan along with
the Taliban, regrouping and recovering its strength and again planning
terrorist strikes against the United States. Besides, it is clear that not
only did the initiative for the talks come from the United States but
also that Grossman and a few other American officials secretly met a

representative of the Taliban for a year in Doha before the organization indicated its willingness to participate in talks for confidence-building measures. One, therefore, needs hardly be surprised if the Taliban's leadership believed that they would be holding talks with a supplicant United States desperate for peace and it was a matter of time before the Americans conceded all their demands.

Many Taliban already believed that victory was theirs. According to a report in the *New York Times* of 1 February 2012, a classified NATO report dated 6 January and entitled *The State of the Taliban*, portrayed an insurgency that was far from vanquished or demoralized even as the United States and its allies entered what they hoped would be the final phase of the war. The report, first carried by the BBC and the *Times*, London, and based on 27,000 interrogations of 4,000 prisoners, provided a sobering counterpoint to the coalition's decidedly more up-beat public assessments of progress in the war and the Afghanistan that NATO claimed it would leave behind. It abounded with accounts of cooperation between the insurgents and local government officials or security forces, as well as accounts from Taliban detainees who claimed that in areas from where coalition soldiers were withdrawing, the Afghan military was cooperating with the insurgents. The report further stated that many Afghans were already bracing themselves for an eventual return of the Taliban. While the Afghan government continued to declare its willingness to fight, many of its personnel had secretly reached out to insurgents, seeking long-term options in the event of a possible Taliban victory, it added.[86]

There is nothing illegible about the writing on the wall. Americans are on the back foot at the start of the talks. The Taliban know this and, barring something totally unexpected happening, will prolong the proceedings until most American troops leave Afghanistan in 2014, and then make a bid for power. Judging by the drift of events, they are more than likely to succeed. Many in the United States and the NATO countries will say that fighting the global war on terrorism should not be their business. But one should remember that the rise of global Islamist terrorism has principally been the result of the Reagan administration's decision to sponsor the mujahideen's jihad against

Soviet occupation of Afghanistan and the appointment of Pakistan as its sole agent for managing the war. A number of books, including Yossef Bodansky's *Bin Laden: The Man Who Declared War on America* and Steve Coll's *Ghost Wars: The Secret History of the CIA, Afghanistan and bin Laden, from the Soviet Invasion to September 10, 2001*, show how the decision and the events that followed led to the rise of Osama bin Laden and Islamist fundamentalism as a formidable force.

Besides, simply because the United States wants to stay away from the war does not mean that the war will stay away from it. Al Qaeda believes that the United States is the root cause of all problems facing the world. Osama bin Laden's 'Letter to America' of November 2002, which sought to explain why he and al Qaeda were fighting the United States, reflected his searing hatred of the country. The 'Letter' first appeared in the Internet in Arabic and was later translated into English by Islamists in London. The full text of the translation, carried by the *Observer* of the United Kingdom on 24 November 2002, was reproduced in the *Guardian* of the United Kingdom on the same day.

THE REASONS WHY

The reasons for opposition to the United States and its people that bin Laden cited included America's creation of Israel and support to the Jews, and their oppression of Palestine. These also included the United States' support to governments acting as its agents in the land of Muslims, preventing the imposition of Islamic sharia and surrendering to the Jews. The other reasons included its starving of Iraqi children through the imposition of sanctions on their country, operations in Somalia, the theft of the oil wealth of Muslim countries at paltry prices, and the establishment of military bases in these. The United States' 'crimes' also included support to Russia's 'atrocities' in Chechnya, India's 'oppression' in Kashmir and Jewish 'aggression' in Lebanon. Then he warned:

> These tragedies and calamities are only a few examples of your
> oppression and aggression against us. It is commanded by our

religion and intellect that the oppressed have a right to return the aggression. Do not await anything from us but Jihad, resistance and revenge. Is it in any way rational to expect that after America has attacked us for more than half a century, that we will then leave her to live in security and peace?!!

Osama bin Laden called the United States 'the worst civilisation witnessed in the history of mankind' which, 'rather than ruling by the *Shariah* of Allah in its Constitution and Laws', had chosen to invent its 'own laws' as it willed and desired and separated religion from its policies, 'contradicting the pure nature which affirms Absolute Authority to the Lord and your Creator'. He then called upon the United States to accept Islam, stop its 'oppression, lies, immorality and debauchery' and 'be a people of manners, principles, honour and purity' to reject 'the immoral acts of fornication, homosexuality, intoxicants, gambling and lending with interest'. Then came the warning:

> If the Americans refuse to listen to our advice and the goodness, guidance and righteousness that we call them to, then be aware that you will lose this Crusade Bush began, just like the other previous Crusades in which you were humiliated by the hands of the Mujahideen, fleeing to your home in great silence and disgrace. If the Americans do not respond, then their fate will be that of the Soviets who fled from Afghanistan to deal with their military defeat, political breakup, ideological downfall, and economic bankruptcy.[87]

Bin Laden's scalding indictment of what has been called the American way of life and what he calls the United States' war on Muslims is not related to any issue of material power and military success. As Bruce Riedel has analysed, al Qaeda's 'ultimate goal' is

> to create (or in its view restore) the Islamic Caliphate from Spain to Indonesia, uniting all the lands of modern Muslim world and some territories lost in Christian reconquests over the

past centuries. Although it has no blueprint for governing this caliphate, it plans to impose *sharia* (Islamic law) on the model of the Taliban's Islamic Emirate of Afghanistan, whose government barely functioned in its brief history.[88]

Riedel points out that al Qaeda's leaders were well aware that they were not close to achieving this objective and hence were not dealing with its practical implications for the moment. They knew they did not have a mass following in the Muslim world and were not on the verge of taking over even a single Muslim country. They regarded themselves as constituting a small vanguard of 'knights' showing the *ummah* the way.[89] They were focussed on more immediate objectives: How to defeat the United States the way they had defeated the Soviet Union, how to defeat its allies in the Muslim world, and how to destroy Israel.

These objectives were to be achieved through a three-pronged strategy, the first prong of which was wearing down the United States and its allies in 'bleeding wars' in Iraq and Afghanistan just as the mujahideen wore down the Soviet invaders. The second was consolidating its safe haven in South Asia while 'creating new al Qaeda "franchises" or allies across the Muslim world' and, the third, building an infrastructure of supporters in the West, particularly in Europe, that could be used to stage 'raids' into the West, perhaps even armed with weapons of mass destruction, to spread fear and terror besides serving to bait the West into more quagmires.[90]

A look at the doctrinal aspect of al Qaeda's ultimate goal makes clear that the United States—indeed, the whole of the modern world—is facing a fundamental challenge that the Taliban and al Qaeda and their obscurantist brand of Islam pose to the culture of modernity as it has evolved in the West and has influenced governance, politics, institutional growth and developmental paradigms, as well as ideas of freedom, democracy, gender justice and allied issues, over large parts of the whole world. In this sense, the conflict between the United States and its allies—in fact the entire modern and democratic world—and al Qaeda and the Taliban raises the question as to which way of life would prevail.

This, in turn, raises four critical questions. Is the Taliban and al Qaeda's version of Islam such a huge and monstrous threat to modernity as their opponents claim? How does their faith relate to what is regarded as mainstream Islam and would, at some future date, affect the whole world? Is it possible to achieve a settlement with them except on their terms? If not, can both be defeated militarily? For an answer to the first two, one would have to give a close look to their doctrine, its application in terms of social, political and economic measures in Afghanistan under Taliban rule, and the true character of Islam as distinct from al Qaeda's version of it. For the third, one will have to look at the history of efforts being made to win the Taliban over and the chances of success.

Defeating the Taliban and al Qaeda militarily will call for action across multiple and widely disparate areas requiring the mobilization of considerable military, technological and financial resources. The critical factors will be intelligence gathering, which will determine the success of drone strikes, clandestine surgical operations, like the one which killed Osama bin Laden, and dialogue with the Taliban to detach at least a section from al Qaeda, which constitute the cornerstones of the Obama administration's new counterterrorism policy. Whether the Americans will succeed will depend on how well they perform in these areas and how al Qaeda counters their moves. Does it have the strategic vision, infrastructure and the strike capacity needed to defeat the new counterterrorism strategy? For an assessment of the United States' capability one must examine in some detail the jewel in its counterterrorism crown—the daring raid that killed Osama bin Laden, its impact and al Qaeda's ability to recover and strike back. There will also have to be an analysis of why the only superpower in the world has not been able to win in Afghanistan after more than 10 years of warfare and whether things can change. To begin at the beginning, one must first consider whether the Taliban and al Qaeda do present a monstrous threat to both modernity and humanity.

NOTES

1. Ahmed Rashid, *Descent into Chaos: How the War against Islamic Extremism Is Being Lost in Pakistan, Afghanistan and Central Asia* (London: Allen Lane, 2008), p. 80.
2. Ibid., pp. 80–81.
3. An anti-Taliban coalition commanded by the legendary Ahmed Shah Massoud forged during the civil war in Afghanistan in the 1990s. Al Qaeda had Massoud assassinated two days before 9/11. During the war it was commanded by Mohammad Fahim, who later became a leading functionary in the Karzai government.
4. Rashid, *Descent into Chaos*, p. 96.
5. Ibid., p. 97.
6. Syed Saleem Shahzad, *Inside Al-Qaeda and the Taliban: Beyond Bin Laden and 9/11* (London: Pluto Press, 2011), p. 3.
7. Ibid., p. 25.
8. Mark Mazetti, Helene Cooper and Peter Baker, 'The Death of Osama bin Laden: Behind the Hunt for Bin Laden', *New York Times*, 2 May 2011, online edition, http://www.nytimes.com/2011/05/03/world/asia/03intel.html?pagewanted=4&nl=todaysheadlines&emc=tha2.
9. Peter Baker, Helene Cooper and Mark Mazzetti, 'Bin Laden Is Dead, Obama Says', *New York Times*, 1 May 2011, online edition, http://www.nytimes.com/2011/05/02/world/asia/osama-bin-laden-is-killed.html?pagewanted=3&nl=todaysheadlines&emc=tha2.
10. Mark Landler and Helene Cooper, 'Obama Will Speed Pullout from War in Afghanistan', *New York Times*, 22 June 2011, online edition, http://www.nytimes.com/2011/06/23/world/asia/23prexy.html?pagewanted=2&nl=todaysheadlines&emc=tha2.
11. Elizabeth Bumiller, 'Panetta Says Defeat of Al Qaeda Is "Within Reach"', *New York Times*, 9 July 2011, online edition, http://www.nytimes.com/2011/07/10/world/asia/10military.html?_r=1&ref=leonepanetta.
12. Greg Miller, 'U.S. Officials Believe al-Qaeda on Brink of Collapse', *Washington Post*, 27 July 2011, online edition, http://www.washingtonpost.com/world/national-security/al-qaeda-could-collapse-us-officials-, it say/2011/07/21/gIQAFu2pbl_story_1.html.
13. Ibid.
14. Landler and Cooper, 'Obama Will Speed Pullout from War in Afghanistan'.
15. Alissa J. Rubin, 'As the US Pulls Back, Fears Abound over Toll on Afghan Economy,' *New York Times*, 22 June 2011, online edition, http://www.nytimes.com/2011/06/23/world/asia/23kabul.html?nl=todaysheadlines&emc=tha22.
16. Graham Bowley, 'Afghans Fear Downturn as Foreigners Withdraw', *New York Times*, 31 January 2012, online edition, http://www.nytimes.com/2012/02/01/world/asia/afghans-fear-economic-downturn-as-foreigners-leave.html?pagewanted=2&_r=1&nl=todaysheadlines&emc=tha22.

17.   James Risen, 'US Identifies Vast Riches of Minerals in Afghanistan', *New York Times*, 13 June 2010, online edition, http://www.nytimes.com/2010/06/14/world/asia/14minerals.html?pagewanted=2&th&emc=th.

18.   Times News Network, '5 Indian Firms to Bid for Afghan Mines', *Times of India*, 15 June 2010, New Delhi.

19.   Ibid.

20.   Eric Hoffer, *The True Believer: Thoughts on the Nature of Mass Movements* (New York: HarperPerennial, 1989 reprint), p. 26.

21.   Ibid., pp. 26–27.

22.   Landler and Cooper, 'Obama Will Speed Pullout from War in Afghanistan'.

23.   Alissa J. Rubin, 'U.S. General in Afghanistan Says Troops May Stay Post-2014', *New York Times*, 20 December 2011, online edition, http://www.nytimes.com/2011/12/21/world/asia/american-commander-in-afghanistan-john-allen-hints-at-post-2014-military-presence.html?pagewanted=2&nl=todaysheadlines&emc=tha22.

24.   Thom Shanker and Eric Schmitt, 'U. S. Plans Shift to Elite Units as It Winds Down in Afghanistan', *New York Times*, 4 February 2012, online edition, http://www.nytimes.com/2012/02/05/world/asia/us-plans-a-shift-to-elite-forces-in-afghanistan.html?pagewanted=all.

25.   Bruce Riedel, *The Search for Al Qaeda: Its Leadership, Ideology and Future* (Washington DC: Supernova Publishers and Distributors (P) Ltd licensed by Brookings Institution Press, 2008), p. 132.

26.   Ibid., p. 133.

27.   Shahzad, *Inside Al-Qaeda and the Taliban: Beyond Bin Laden and 9/11*, p. xi.

28.   Ibid., pp. xvi, 73.

29.   Ibid., p. 53–54.

30.   Ibid., pp. 121–22.

31.   Ibid., p. 121.

32.   International Energy Agency, 'World Proved Reserves of Oil and Natural Gas, Most Recent Estimates', *Oil & Gas Journal*, posted on 3 March 2009, http://www.eia.doe.gov/international/reserves/html.

33.   Ibid., p. 120.

34.   Abu Musab al-Zarqawi was the *nom de guerre* of a Jordanian Arab militant born in 1966 as Ahmed al-Khelayleh. He ran a training camp for the mujahideen in Afghanistan during the anti-Soviet Jihad in the 1980s and formed his own organization, al-Tawhid wal-Jihad (Group Monotheism and Jihad), in 1990. It became known as al Qaeda in Iraq after he pledged his allegiance and joined al Qaeda in 2004. He led the organization until his death in a US air strike in 2006.

35.   Shahzad, *Inside Al-Qaeda and the Taliban: Beyond Bin Laden and 9/11*, p. 57.

36.   Ibid., p. 58.

37.   Al Baker and William K. Rashbaum, 'Police Find Car Bomb in Times Square', *New York Times*, 1 May 2010, online edition, http://www.nytimes.com/2010/05/02/nyregion/02timessquare.html?pagewanted=2&th&emc=th.

38. William K. Rashbaum and James Baker, 'Smoking Car to an Arrest in 53 Hours', *New York Times*, 4 May 2011, online edition, http://www.nytimes.com/2010/05/05/nyregion/05tictoc.html?pagewanted=2&nl=nyregion&emc=ura1. Also see Jim Dwyer, 'A Suspect Leaves Clues at Every Turn', *New York Times*, 4 May 2011, online edition, http://www.nytimes.com/2010/05/05/nyregion/05trictoc.html?pagewanted=2&nl=nyregion&emc=url.

39. Shahzad, *Inside Al-Qaeda and the Taliban: Beyond Bin Laden and 9/11*, pp. 206–07.

40. Apratim Mukharji, 'Terrorism Claimed More Lives Than Wars', *Hindustan Times*, 8 December 1999, Delhi.

41. Haidar Naqvi, 'Frightening Figures', *Hindustan Times*, 25 September 2008, Delhi.

42. The United States' Department of State, *Country Reports on Terrorism 2010*, Chapter 2, 2011, http://www.state.gov/s/ct/rls/crt/2010/170258.htm.

43. Rohan Gunaratna, *Inside Al Qaeda: Global Network of Terror* (New Delhi: Roli Books, 2002), p. 219.

44. Yossef Bodansky, *Bin Laden: The Man Who Declared War on America* (Rocklin, California: Prima Publishing, 1999), pp. 225–26.

45. Elisabeth Bumiller, 'Panetta Says U.S. to End Afghan Combat Role as Soon as 2013', *New York Times*, 1 February 2012, online edition, http://www.nytimes.com/2012/02/02/world/asia/panetta-moves-up-end-to-us-combat-role-in-afghanistan.html?nl=todaysheadlines&emc=tha22.

46. Landler and Cooper, 'Obama Will Speed Pullout From War in Afghanistan'.

47. Ray Rivera, 'Afghans Build Security, and Hope to Avoid Infiltrators', *New York Times*, 27 June 2011, online edition, http://www.nytimes.com/2011/06/28/world/asia/28infiltrate.html?pagewanted=2&_r=1&nl=todaysheadlines&emc=tha22.

48. Alissa J. Rubin and Taimur Shah, 'Karzai Welcomes Withdrawal, but Many Afghans Are Wary,' *New York Times*, 23 June 2011, online edition, http://www.nytimes.com/2011/06/24/world/asia/24afghanistan.html?nl=todaysheadlines&emc=tha22.

49. Dhruv C. Katoch, 'The Afghan National Army' in *Afghanistan: A Role for India*, eds. R. K. Sawhney, Arun Sahgal and Gurmeet Kanwal (New Delhi: Centre for Land Warfare Studies and KW Publishers, 2011), p. 31.

50. Ibid., p. 21.

51. Thom Shanker, 'U.S. Shift May Push Afghans into Lead Role', *New York Times*, 13 December 2011, online edition, http://www.nytimes.com/2011/12/14/world/asia/us-plans-afghan-shift-to-lessen-nato-combat-role.html?_r=1&nl=todaysheadlines&emc=tha22.

52. R. K. Sawhney, 'Afghanistan Today', in *Afghanistan: A Role for India*, eds Sawhney, Sahgal and Kanwal, pp. 13–14.

53. Dhruv C. Katoch, 'The Afghan National Army', in *Afghanistan: A Role for India*, eds Sawhney, Sahgal and Kanwal, p. 34.

54. C. J. Radin, 'Afghan National Army Update, May 2011', *Long War Journal*, 9 May 2011, http://www.longwarjournal.org/archives/2011/05/afghan_national_army_4.php#ixzz1lnihQgZk.

55. Ibid.

56. Ray Rivera, 'Afghan Army Attracts Few Where Fear Reigns', *New York Times*, 6 September 2011, online edition, http://www.nytimes.com/2011/09/07/world/asia/07afghanistan.html?pagewanted=2&nl=todaysheadlines&emc=tha2.

57. Dhruv C. Katoch, 'The Afghan National Army', in *Afghanistan: A Role for India*, eds Sawhney, Sahgal and Kanwal, p. 31.

58. Greg Bruno, *Afghanistan's National Security Forces*, backgrounder, Council for Foreign Relations, New York City, 19 August 2010, http://www.cfr.org/afghanistan/afghanistans-national-security-forces/p19122.

59. Dhruv C. Katoch, 'The Afghan National Army', in *Afghanistan: A Role for India*, ed p. 32.

60. C. J. Radin, 'Afghan National Army update, May 2011.'

61. Bruno, *Afghanistan's National Security Forces*.

62. Majority Staff Report, *Central Asia and the Transition in Afghanistan*, Committee on Foreign Relations, United States Senate, 19 December 2011, pp. 1–2, http://www.fdsys.gpo.gov.

63. Ibid., pp. 2–3.

64. Ibid., p. 3.

65. Ibid.

66. Jon Boon, 'Afghan National Army Prepares for Life after Nato', *Guardian*, the United Kingdom, 20 July 2011, http://www.guardian.co.uk/world/2011/jul/20/afghan-national-army-prepares-nato.

67. Elisabeth Bumiller, 'U.S. to End Combat Role in Afghanistan as Early as Next Year, Panetta Says', *New York Times*, 1 February 2012, online edition, http://www.nytimes.com/2012/02/02/world/asia/panetta-moves-up-end-to-us-combat-role-in-afghanistan.html.

68. Mathew Rosenberg, 'Taliban Opening Qatar Office, and Maybe Door to Talks', *New York Times*, 3 February 2012, online edition, http://www.nytimes.com/2012/01/04/world/asia/taliban-to-open-qatar-office-in-step-toward-peace-talks.html?pagewanted=2&nl=todaysheadlines&emc=tha22.

69. Ibid.

70. Alissa J. Rubin, 'Former Taliban Officisals Say U.S. Talks Had Started', *New York Times*, 28 Janurary 2012, online edition, http://www.nytimes.com/2012/01/29/world/asia/taliban-have-begun-talks-with-us-former-taliban-aides-say.htmlr=1&ref=alissa johannsenrubin.

71. Set up by the Afghan government for peace negotiations with the Taliban.

72. Ibid.

73. John Wendle, 'A U.S. Peace with the Taliban? Don't Hold Your Breath', *Time*, 23 January 2011, online edition, http://www.time.com/time/world/article/0,8599,2105150,00.html#ixzz1kxn04jpv.

74. Myers Steven Lee, Mathew Rosenberg and Erich Schmitt, 'Against Odds, Paths Open Up for U.S.—Taliban Talks', *New York Times*, 11 January 2012, online edition, http://www.nytimes.com/2012/01/12/world/asia/quest-for-taliban-peace-talks-at-key-juncture.html?pagewanted=3&_r=1&nl=todaysheadlines&emc=tha2.

75. Mathew Rosenberg, 'Karzai Ultimatum Complicates U.S. Exit Strategy', *New York Times*, 8 January 2012, online edition, http://www.nytimes.com/2012/01/09/world/asia/karzais-ultimatum-on-afghan-prison-complicates-us-exit-strategy.html?pagewanted=2&_r=1&nl=todaysheadlines&emc=tha22.

76. John Wendle, 'A U.S. Peace with the Taliban? Don't Hold Your Breath.'

77. Ibid.

78. Myers Steven Lee, Mathew Rosenberg and Erich Schmitt, 'Against Odds, Paths Open Up for U.S.—Taliban Talks.'

79. Alissa J. Rubin, 'Former Taliban Officials Say U.S. Talks Had Started.'

80. Ibid.

81. Barack Obama, 'Remarks by the President on a New Strategy for Afghanistan and Pakistan', Office of the Press Secretary, The White House, 27 March 2009, http://www.whitehouse.gov/the_press_office/remarks-by-the-president-on-a-new-strategy-for-afghanistan-and-pakistan/.

82. Ibid.

83. Ibid.

84. Barack Obama, 'Address to the Nation on the Way Forward in Afghanistan and Pakistan', Office of the Press Secretary, The White House, Washington DC, 1 December 2009, http://www.whitehouse.gov/the-press-office/remarks-president-address-nation-way-forward-afghanistan-and-pakistan.

85. Ahmed Rashid, *Taliban: Islam, Oil and the New Great Game in Central Asia* (London: I.B. Tauris & Co., 2000), pp. 105–06.

86. Rod Nordland and Alissa J. Rubin, 'Taliban Captives Dispute U.S. View on Afghanistan War', *New York Times*, 1 February 2012, online edition, http://www.nytimes.com/2012/02/02/world/asia/nato-plays-down-report-of-collaboration-between-taliban-and-pakistan.html?pagewanted=2&_r=1&nl=todaysheadlines&emc=tha2.

87. 'Full Text: bin Laden's Letter to America', *Guardian*, the United Kingdom, 24 November 2002, http://www.guardian.co.uk/world/nov/24/theobserver.

88. Bruce Riedel, *The Search for Al Qaeda: Its leadership, Ideology and Future*, p. 121.

89. Ibid.

90. Ibid., pp. 121–22.

CHAPTER 2

A WAR FOR THE WORLD

S ome may smirk on hearing that the Taliban and al Qaeda seriously threaten modernity and its values. They may argue that Osama bin Laden is dead and al Qaeda is in tatters. The Taliban may call the shots in Afghanistan and parts of Pakistan, but lack the reach to cause trouble elsewhere. Such a view would reflect dangerous complacence. We have seen in the previous chapter the wider conflict that is likely to follow a Taliban takeover of Afghanistan. Besides, it will be dangerous to dismiss as exaggerated the major ideological threat the distorted and reductionist version of Islam both organizations stand for pose to modernity. One is talking here not of what may happen tomorrow or the next year, but in terms of a historical time frame of several decades over which the United States and the West, increasingly hobbled by economic crises, may become progressively unable to resist the resurgent Islam of the Taliban and al Qaeda variety.

Such a dismal scenario is not an inevitability. But nor can it be ruled out given the economic prostration of Europe, the United States' slow and limping recovery from the worst economic crisis visiting it since the Great Depression of the 1930s, and the general erosion of the will to fight in the West. Besides, as seen in the previous chapter, even if reductionist Islam fails to overwhelm the West, the chances of its sweeping most of the Muslim majority countries are more than even. The question is: Can the rest of the world coexist comfortably with such an Islamist bloc—without its life being thrown completely out of gear by the strains of a continuing and bitter confrontation?

Historical events take at least decades to achieve their full potential. For example, the Bolshevik Revolution of 1917 came as a culmination of events spread over decades. An important landmark was the army revolt in St. Petersburg in December 1825. Known as the Decembrist Revolt, its leaders refused to swear loyalty to the new czar, Nicholas, and swore to defend the relatively liberal institutional reforms the previous czar, Alexander I, had effected. Poorly planned and organized, it was suppressed with great severity.[1] Yet a revolutionary movement, rooted in the literary and cultural ferment of mid-19th century Russia, sustained a demand for change spearheaded by an intelligentsia deeply influenced by the West.

A more specifically radical revolutionary movement emerged in the 1860s expressing itself more through journalism than literature.[2] Comprising a multiplicity of elements like romantics with a powerful, albeit not precisely defined, yearning for liberty, constitutional democrats, anarchists, socialists and Marxists, it trudged an uneven course as Russia alternated between liberal phases marked by Czar Alexander II's reform—particularly the emancipation of Serfs in 1861—and repression, such as the crackdown that followed his assassination at the hands of an anarchist in 1881. Political activity had to be clandestine or conducted from exile. It was from his exile in Switzerland that George Plekhanov formed the first Russian Marxist Party in 1883. In 1898 an attempt was made to form a Marxist Social Democratic Revolutionary Party in Russia. The Social Revolutionary Party, which appealed more directly to peasants than to industrial workers, was formed in 1902.

The rise of an industrial working class following urbanization and industrial development, growing political consciousness and discontent over exploitation of the peasantry in the countryside and of workers in factories, and the decline in the prestige of Czardom following defeat in the Russo-Japanese war of 1904–05, led to strikes and demonstrations. Nineteen hundred and five was a year of turmoil. The brutal firing of 9 January that year on demonstrators at St. Petersburg demanding a constituent assembly based on universal adult franchise, transfer of land to the people and an eight-hour working day, triggered massive countrywide protests that slowly gathered momentum through spring and summer.[3] It led to a naval mutiny and a general strike in Odessa in June and climaxed in October with a wave of strikes, the promise by the czar of a liberal constitution and the formation of the first Soviets of Workers' Deputies.[4]

The revolt, in which Bolsheviks, Mensheviks, Social Revolutionaries and constitutional democrats were active, lacked organizational support in the countryside and was crushed by December. The period of Stolypin Reaction, named after Prime Minister Pyotr Stolypin, who almost turned the whole of Russia into a prison, followed. The system he had established continued after his death in 1911 and Czardom appeared as secure as ever on the eve of World War I in 1914. The circumstances created by the war and Russian reverses in it led to the revolution of February 1917 which overthrew the Romanov dynasty! And then, in October, the Bolshevik Revolution paved the way for the formation of the Soviet Union.

Equally, the process that led to the Soviet Union's end took decades. The East Berlin bread riots of June 1953 constituted the first explosion of anger against the Soviet Union's domination of Eastern Europe. It was suppressed, as were the Hungarian uprising and the Poznan riots (in Poland) in 1956, and Czechoslovakia's peaceful upheaval in 1968 for 'communism with a human face'. Finally, the Berlin Wall, the symbol of Soviet domination over Eastern Europe, fell in November 1989 and the Cold War, of which Eastern Europe was perhaps the most important theatre, ended in 1991 with the break-up of the Soviet Union.

MODERNITY AND ITS ENEMIES

Thus it will be unwise to write off the threat the Taliban and al Qaeda, and the distorted version of Islam that they, their allies and affiliates profess, pose to modernity. Before discussing that, however, one must have a clear idea of what one means by 'modernity', of which there are many definitions. Given the context of the present discourse, one should obviously begin by examining Samuel P. Huntington's view expressed in his controversial but thought-provoking work, *The Clash of Civilisations and the Remaking of World Order*. Set in the wider backdrop of the West's relationship with Islam, of which the Afghan war and its implications constitute a crucial element, its relevance is obvious.

According to Huntington, modernization 'does not necessarily mean Westernization. Non-Western societies can modernize and have modernized without abandoning their own cultures and adopting wholesale Western values, institutions and practices.'[5] He also says that Islamic Resurgence, a 'broad, intellectual, cultural, social and political movement prevalent throughout the Islamic world', represented an effort to achieve the goal of accepting modernity along with a 'recommitment to Islam as the guide to life in the modern world'. Also, 'Islamic "fundamentalism", commonly conceived as political Islam, is only one component in the much more extensive revival of Islamic ideas, practices and rhetoric and the rededication to Islam by Muslim populations'. It 'is mainstream, not extremist, pervasive, not isolated'.[6]

Four issues arise here. The first two concern the validity of Huntington's definition of modernization and the compatibility of the fundamentalist brand of Islam, which al Qaeda and the Taliban profess, with modernity. The third and the fourth are respectively whether Political Islam or Islamic fundamentalism is only one component of the Islamic Resurgence and whether the latter is mainstream and pervasive.

According to Huntington, modernization involved 'industrialisation, urbanisation, increasing levels of literacy, education, wealth, and social mobilisation, and more complex and diversified occupational structures'. According to him, it was a product of 'the tremendous expansion of scientific and engineering knowledge beginning in the eighteenth century' that enabled humans to control and shape their environment in totally unprecedented ways. It was 'a revolutionary process comparable only to the shift from primitive to civilized societies, that is, the emergence of civilization in the singular, which began in the valleys of the Tigris and Euphrates, the Nile, and the Indus about 5000 B.C.'[7]

This is a very instrumental and narrow definition of modernity which focuses on its technological, industrial and economic dimensions and ignores its political, cultural and intellectual aspects. It is like saying that humans are bipeds who walk, eat, sleep, use implements, have wives and children and partners, live in cities or villages, drive cars and/or use mass transportation, and remaining silent on their possessing intelligence, will, emotions, intuition, speech—faculties whose complex interplay with the environment has produced the progress in scientific and engineering knowledge Huntington talks about. Such progress, in turn, was a part of a much wider intellectual, social, cultural and political transformation brought about by nine major historical events—the Renaissance, Reformation, the rise of nation states in Europe, the great geographical discoveries, the 18th-century Enlightenment in Europe, the struggle against royal absolutism and for representative government, the industrial and French revolutions and the establishment of colonies by European nation states.

The Renaissance revived the Humanism of the classical Greeks whose essence has been best encapsulated by the aphorism, 'Man is the measure of all things,' attributed to the Greek sophist, Protagoras. Humanism ascribed to humankind the position of being the yardstick for judging the worth and relevance of all other things, because of its possession of reason. This undermined the primacy that medieval Christianity accorded to faith in every area of human life including the arts, social and economic spheres and knowledge. Any progress in any area of human effort and creativity which challenged the Church's position on the subject was regarded as heresy and the person had to recant or face persecution. Galileo Galilei (1564–1642), who is regarded, among other things, as the father of modern science and observational astronomy, was forced by the Roman inquisition in 1632 to recant for supporting Copernicus' heliocentric view, which put the sun and not the earth at the centre of the universe, and had to spend the rest of his life under house arrest.

THE SCRUTINY OF REASON

By subjecting the doctrine and practices of the Roman Catholic Church to the scrutiny of reason in the light of the new status it ascribed to human beings, Humanism facilitated the rise of Reformation. The rise of Protestant churches and monarchs like Henry VIII of England who supported them, and the role of the increasingly prosperous and powerful class of merchants, undermined both feudalism and the autocracy of the Papacy. This unchained the spirit of inquiry that characterized the classical Greeks but had been restrained by the Church, and catalysed unprecedented creativity in every area of human activity, including science and engineering.

The nation states emerging in Europe in the 16th and 17th centuries, and sometimes clashing with the Pope, sought to enhance their strength by harnessing the new learning of the Renaissance and, sometimes, allying with the forces of Reformation. They also encouraged manufacture, foreign trade, geographical discoveries and the establishment of colonies to increase their economic, military and political power and prestige. The rising manufacturing and trading communities demanded freedom from arbitrary taxation and greater say in the affairs of the realm through an increase in the powers of representative institutions like parliaments.

If this planted the seed for a clamour for democracy and republicanism, the 18th-century Enlightenment radicalized discourse through a proliferation of ideologies, a development which led Alvin W. Gouldner to call the 18th and 19th centuries as the Age of Ideology.[8] He adds:

> The rise and development of modern ideologies was shaped by the rise of modern science, by the growing prestige of technology and new modes of production, and by the development of publics whose favourable judgement of modern science was rooted in the decline of the older authority-referencing discourse.[9]

According to Gouldner, there was a profound link between the proliferation of ideologies and the '"communications revolution" grounded in the development of printing, printing technologies, and the growing production of printed products'.[10] The demand for clothes generated by the 19th-century population expansion in the area of western European culture and the technological advances in Britain and the United States, which enabled an unprecedented production of cotton textiles ending Europe's perennial shortage of clothes, caused an immense increase in the supply of worn-out clothes or rags from which paper was made. This ended the shortage of paper that had inhibited the expansion of printing and publishing industries whose further growth was facilitated in the first decade of the 19th century through the perfection of a paper-manufacturing machine by the Fourdnier brothers.[11]

Gouldner quotes Morse Peckham as writing:

> By 1830, publishing had been revolutionised. Printed matter was now cheap—for the first time in human history literacy could be massively extended through all levels of the population. In England the population grew by a ratio of one to four; but the literate population grew by a ratio of one to thirty-two. Not only book manufacture was affected, but every type of communications and record-keeping involving paper—magazines, newspapers, letters; business, government and military correspondence and orders.[12]

A deluge of information followed. The proliferation of ideologies represented, in part, an effort to provide meaning where the overall supply of information was greater than ever.[13] News presented a fragmented image of the world as news items often appeared as a series of independent incidents and 'not in the form of an independent story'.[14] An interesting dialectic developed between news and everyday life and news-generated conversation became the vehicle of public rationality[15] while individual rationality was enhanced by efforts to integrate information contained in news items into one's personal world view to cope with life. Ideologies also represented efforts to mobilize the public for projects. With the undermining of authority, reason became the principle instrument of persuasion.

The Age of Ideology was marked by the emergence of doctrines like Utilitarianism, Liberalism, Laissez-faire capitalism, Socialism and Marxism that have profoundly influenced contemporary political discourse and structures and practices of governance. The intellectual climate the Enlightenment created in Paris salons was the ideological seed bed of the American and French Revolutions. The former, which ended the rule of the British emperor over what is now the United

States of America, and the latter, which executed the Bourbon king of France, delivered severe blows to monarchy as an institution. The ideals of individual freedoms enshrined in the American Constitution and the strident call for liberty, equality and fraternity, arising from the turmoil of the French Revolution, fired the imagination of intelligentsia far and wide. The Napoleonic Wars spread the concept of the rule of law through the introduction of the Code Napoleon by the regimes he established.

If the French Revolution galvanized the spread of republicanism and the cause of democracy despite the excesses of the Reign of Terror, the Bolshevik Revolution put Marxism at the centre of the global political discourse. The great political debate of the 20th century was between Marxism and capitalism, with the various hues of socialism and social democracy straddling the no-man's-land in between. The fierce polemic that characterized the Cold War revolved round the doctrinal contents of these three broad ideological streams.

Progressing in the matrix of history, modernization has played an important role in the evolution of an entire way of life that stands for individual freedom, particularly of thought, speech, inquiry and movement; respect for reason; cultural pluralism; religious tolerance; separation of the powers and functions of spiritual and temporal authorities; and gender, social and economic justice. In its applied form, modernity stands for a value system upholding political democracy, fundamental rights enshrined in constitutions, independent judiciaries, free media, academic autonomy, action to empower the disprivileged and so on. In fact, it has created a culture which may, much sooner than later, transform itself into a civilization. This civilization-on-the-anvil, which does seem to have a large following in India, the United States and several other countries, is under vicious attack from Islamist fundamentalists.

THE TALIBAN CREED

The Taliban and al Qaeda violently reject the values, social and political structures and the way of life associated with modernity. Their religious beliefs and views on almost all issues are identical. Osama bin Laden said in an interview to the Qatari satellite news channel, Al Jazeera, in December 1998, shortly after the United States' continuous 70-hour day-and-night bombing of Iraq, 'So our relationship with the Taliban is very strong and firm, and it is a doctrinal relationship based on us sharing the same belief, not a political or business relationship.'[16] In an audiotaped statement for the delegates to an international conference of Deobandis held near Peshawar from 9 to 11 April 2001, bin Laden described Mullah Mohammad Omar as 'the ruler and the rightful commander' who ruled by 'God's laws in this age', thereby signifying full approval for the Taliban's oppressive policies and orders. He particularly lauded Omar's 'great Islamic decisions' including those pertaining to the destruction of the historic Buddha statues in Bamiyan, the cultivation of opium and 'the proud stance against the campaign of global unbelief.'[17] Clearly, the Taliban's policies and actions in Afghanistan were those of al Qaeda as well.

Both organizations stand for a theocratic order in which political authorities govern according to the principles of Islam as administered and interpreted by the clergy. In the audiotaped message to delegates to the international conference of Deobandis mentioned above, Osama bin Laden identified 'the Islamic Emirate of Afghanistan under the leadership of the Commander of the Faithful Mullah Mohammad Omar' with the 'Islamic state that abides by God's law and raises the banner of his unity'.[18] As pointed in chapter 1, one of the charges he levelled against the people of the United States was that they chose to invent their own laws as they willed and desired instead of being ruled by the sharia of God. He accused them of separating their religion from their policies 'contradicting the pure nature which affirms Absolute Authority to the Lord and your Creator'.[19]

Separation of the spheres of spiritual and temporal authorities, which in the West meant the separation of the powers and functions of the Church and the State, is one of the basic attributes of a modern State. Its rejection is an important count on which the Taliban and al Qaeda fail the modernity test. Besides, Ahmed Rashid, the noted expert on Pakistan, Afghanistan and Central Asia, points out that

'the Taliban are vehemently opposed to modernism and have no desire to understand or adopt modern ideas of progress or economic
development'.[20] They 'recognized no Islam except their own.'[21] They
have emerged from the ranks of the Deobandis but have moved away
significantly in the areas of practice and policy.[22]

Terrorism is a very major area of divergence between genuine
and the Taliban/al Qaeda versions of Islam. The Taliban and all fundamentalist Islamist groups allied with them practise and laud it and kill
indiscriminately. In *The Quranic Concept of War*, Brigadier S. K. Malik
of the Pakistani army writes:

> Based on instructions issued on the subject by the Holy Prophet
> (peace be upon him) and by the Early Caliphs, the muslim ju-
> rists have conducted several studies to identify the acts forbid-
> den to the Muslim armies during the fighting. According to Dr.
> Hamid Ullah, all cruel and torturous ways of killing the enemy
> are prohibited. The killing of women, minors, servants and
> slaves, who might accompany their masters in war but do not
> take part in the actual fighting, is also not allowed. The Muslim
> armies must also spare the blind, the monks, the hermits and
> old, the physically deformed and the insane or the mentally
> deficient. Forbidden also is the decapitation of the prisoners of
> war; the mutilation of men and beasts; treachery and perfidy;
> devastation and destruction of harvests; excesses and wicked-
> ness; and adultery and fornication with captive women. The
> killing of enemy hostages, and resorting to massacre to van-
> quish an enemy is forbidden. The killing of parents except in
> absolute self-defence; and the killing of those peasants, traders,
> merchants, contractors and the like who do not take part in
> actual fighting is also not allowed.[23]

It is then hardly surprising that an antiterrorism conference convened by the Darul Uloom Deoband on 25 February 2008 adopted a
resolution declaring terrorism un-Islamic and against the Islamic principle of peace. Adopted by about 10,000 participants, including scholars, clerics and Islamic leaders from several sects and groups across
the country, the declaration said, 'Islam is a religion of mercy for all

humanity' and 'sternly condemns all kinds of oppression, violence and terrorism. It has regarded oppression, mischief, rioting and murder among severest sins and crimes.' Adding that Islam 'prohibits killing of innocent people', the declaration also expressed deep concern and agony over the present situation the world over in which most nations were adopting an adverse attitude toward Muslims. While the gathering condemned attempts to implicate Muslims, and particularly religious institutions, in terrorist acts, Adil Siddiqui, Public Relations Officer, Darul Uloom, stated, 'The disease (terrorism) has been diagnosed in a wrong way. Whenever there is any incident of terrorism, every possible attempt is made to link it to Muslims and particularly who have studied in madrassas and some religious institutions. This is totally wrong.'[24]

There were other issues of doctrinal emphasis and practice. Rashid writes that while the Deobandis took a restrictive view of the role of women, opposed all forms of hierarchy in the Muslim community and rejected the Shia, 'the Taliban were to take these beliefs to an extreme which the original Deobandis would never have recognized.'[25] Rashid further holds that the Taliban 'have clearly debased the Deobandi tradition of learning and reform, with their rigidity, accepting no concept of doubt except as sin and considering debate as little more than heresy'.[26] Not surprisingly, an inhuman, savage and regressive dispensation prevailed over the parts of Afghanistan they controlled, which, at the height of their power (1997–2001), comprised 90 per cent of the country.

APARTHEID OF GENDER

In a report entitled *The Taliban's War on Women: A Health and Human Rights Crisis in Afghanistan*, published in 1998, Physicians for Human Rights (PHR), a distinguished human rights organization based in the United States, presented a nightmarish picture of the conditions of Afghan women under Taliban rule.[27] One of the original steering committee members of the International Campaign to Ban Landmines, which was a joint recipient of the 1997 Nobel Peace Prize along with its founding coordinator, Jody Williams, the organization conducted as exhaustive field investigations as possible under extremely difficult conditions, and showed in its report how women suffered unbearable oppression in almost every walk of life from health to even day-to-day movement.

After capturing Kabul on 26 September 1996, the Taliban imposed on the city, as on every other place they came to control, a virtual gender apartheid. They also issued a series of orders which robbed life of all joy and entertainment, hemming it with restrictions and reducing it to mechanical performance of rituals in a climate of sheer terror. Three orders, issued by them on 20 February 1997, put together most of the prohibitions and instructions announced earlier. These forbade women from venturing or travelling out of their homes without being escorted by a close male relative (husband, father, brother or son), and without wearing a burqa[28] or a similar outfit. It also prohibited them from sitting on the front seats of carts or jeeps without 'legal relatives'.[29] It forbade shopkeepers from selling to or buying from women who had not covered their faces, the invitation of women to hotels or wedding parties and their travelling in taxis without close (male) relatives, and specified that the person in charge of collecting fares for 'sisters'—as women are described throughout the order—should be less than 10 years old. It warned that 'professional delegates of this department (Department of the Promotion of Virtue and Prevention of Vice) were in charge of punishing the violators 'according to Islamic principles'.[30]

The third order prohibited drivers from picking up women 'using Iranian burqa'.[31] Violation would cause the driver to be imprisoned. If women so attired were observed in the street, their houses would be found out and husbands punished. Drivers 'should not pick up women using stimulating and attractive clothes, and without a close male relative with them'.[32]

Some of the restrictions relating to the treatment of women and their segregation in hospitals, featuring in the order, might have been dismissed as products of lunacy but for their disastrous consequences. The order stated that women patients had to go to women doctors and had to be accompanied by a close relative (husband, father, brother, son) when seeing male doctors. Both female patients and male physicians had to be dressed in Islamic hijab during examinations. Male physicians were not to touch women patients except in the parts of their bodies affected.[33]

Under the order, waiting rooms for women patients had to be adequately covered. Women alone could regulate the turns of women patients waiting to see doctors. Unless called by a patient, male doctors were not to enter at night rooms where women were hospitalized. Male and female doctors were not allowed to sit together and talk. Women doctors had to wear simple clothes and were not allowed to wear 'stylish clothes or use cosmetics and makeup'. Women doctors were not allowed to enter rooms for male patients in hospitals. Every hospital director had to assign a place and appoint a mullah for prayer.[34]

The specific orders were reflective of the general thrust of Taliban policies which made life an agony for Afghan women. The severe restriction of their access to medical attention drastically curtailed the most basic of their rights, the one to live. In January 1997, the Taliban announced that men and women had to go to separate hospitals. The fiat was not strictly enforced until September 1997 when the Ministry of Public Health ordered all hospitals in Kabul to suspend medical services to the city's 500,000 women who could henceforth go only to the temporary Rabia Balkhi facility which had at that time only 35 beds and no clean water, electricity, surgical equipment, X-ray machines, suction equipment and oxygen. The Taliban also banned women from working in Kabul's 22 hospitals. Under intense international pressure, the Taliban partially relaxed its restrictions and agreed to reopen some of the hospitals and made a limited number of beds available to women.[35]

On 25 June 1998, the Taliban reissued and amplified its earlier edict forbidding physicians from treating women unaccompanied by an 'appropriate' male relative.[36] This created severe problems for women in Kabul—a city with 30,000 widows—and elsewhere who did not have such relatives.[37] Indeed, the dress restrictions imposed on women and the savage beatings to which they were subjected by the Taliban's religious police in case of transgressions—however arbitrarily decided upon—made women so scared that they hesitated to venture out of their homes for medical attention or otherwise even when accompanied by male relatives. Women's treatment also suffered because male physicians could not examine them properly thanks to prohibitions on touching or looking at their bodies.[38]

Access to education was also drastically restricted. One of the first edicts of the Taliban regime forbade girls and women from attending school. Humanitarian groups sought to alleviate the order's impact by establishing hundreds of girls' schools in private homes, teaching thousands of women and girls to sew and weave, through philanthropy. On 16 June 1998, the Taliban ordered the closure of more than 100 privately funded schools which were training young women and girls in skills that would have helped them in supporting their families. They issued new rules for non-governmental organizations (NGOs) restricting schooling for girls up to eight years of age and that, too, limited to instructions in the Quran.[39]

REPRESSED AND CONFINED

Before the Taliban came to control Kabul, women accounted for 70 per cent of all teachers, about 50 per cent of civil servants and 40 per cent of medical doctors.[40] PHR's researchers visiting the city in 1998 found that 'women who had once been teachers and nurses [were] now moving in the streets like ghosts under their enveloping *burqas* selling every possession and begging so as to feed their children'.[41] Pointing out that forces opposed to the Taliban had also violated human and gender rights, the PHR's report said in ringing condemnation:

> The Taliban was the first faction laying claim to power in Afghanistan which had targeted women for extreme repression and punished them brutally for infractions. To our knowledge, no other regime in the world has methodically and violently forced half of its population into virtual house arrest, prohibiting

them on the pain of physical punishment from showing their faces, seeking medical care without a male escort or attending school.

It is also difficult to find another government or would-be government in the world that has deliberately created such poverty by arbitrarily depriving half the population under its control of jobs, schooling, mobility, and health care. Such restrictions are literally life-threatening to the women and their children.[42]

Physical health was not the only area affected. Eighty-one per cent of the respondents in PHR's health and human rights survey of 160 Afghan women reported a decline in their mental health compared to the two preceding years. Overall, 98 per cent of the respondents met criteria for post-traumatic stress disorder, major depression or significant symptoms of anxiety, with 52 per cent meeting criteria for two and 59 per cent for all the three.[43]

While women were special victims, men too lived bleak, fearful lives as the Taliban turned Afghanistan into a proscription-ridden, terror-driven nightmare. The third order of 20 February 1997 prohibited music and the presence of music cassettes in shops. Shopkeepers were to be imprisoned and their shops locked if any music cassette was found. A shop could be reopened and the 'criminal' released if five persons guaranteed that such a thing would not recur. Similarly, the driver and owner of a vehicle in which a music cassette was found were to be imprisoned and they and the vehicle would be released if five persons stood guarantee against the offence being repeated.[44] The order further prescribed that after a month of its issue anyone found to have shaved and/or cut his beard would be arrested and imprisoned until his hair got 'bushy'. People had to gather for prayer at mosques exactly at the time announced. The matter was to be monitored and 'young people' seen in shops (at prayer time) would be immediately imprisoned for 10 days unless five persons stood guarantee against a recurrence of the offence.[45] The keeping of pigeons and playing with birds had to stop within 10 days of the ban being announced and 'pigeons and any other playing bird' had to be killed.[46]

The Taliban seemed to make no distinction between such 'offences' and addiction which, albeit not specified, obviously referred to drugs. It had to be eliminated through imprisonment of the addicts and owners of shops selling them, which had to be locked. The order also banned kite-flying, and prescribed the closure of Kabul's kite shops. To prevent idolatry, it prohibited the display of pictures in vehicles, shops, rooms, hotels or any other place.[47] The main centres of gambling were to be found and gamblers imprisoned for a month.

The order further prescribed the arrest of people with 'long hair' and the shaving of their hair with the 'criminal' paying the barber. Interest charges on loans, charges on changing small denomination notes and charges on money orders were banned and violators were to be imprisoned for a long time. Young women were debarred from washing clothes by water streams in the city. Violators were 'to be picked up with respectable Islamic manner, taken to their houses and their husbands severely punished'.[48] Music and dancing were forbidden at wedding parties; heads of families were to be arrested and punished in case of violation. Tailors were to be imprisoned if women or fashion magazines were seen in their shops. All books on sorcery were to be banned and the magician imprisoned until he repented.[49]

ENFORCERS AND SPIES

The impact of these draconian rules was aggravated by the manner of their enforcement. Under the order of 20 February 1997, staff of the Department of the Promotion of Virtue and Prevention of Vice were allowed to go into hospitals 'for control at any time' and 'nobody could prevent them. Those violating the order would be punished according to Islamic regulations' (of course, as interpreted by the Taliban).[50] The staff could intervene at will and beat up women nurses and other health workers for not being covered completely according to their specifications. Cases of wrong punishment were numerous. Ahmed Rashid tellingly writes that edicts issued by the department had 'dramatically changed the lifestyles of Kabul's once easy-going population and forced Afghan women to disappear from public view'.[51]

The PHR report rightly rejected mitigation of the Taliban's tyranny on the ground that they had at least restored order and did not
indulge in crimes like rape. It stated:

> The peace imposed on that portion of the country under Taliban
> rule is the peace of the *burqa*, the quiet of women and girls
> cowering in their homes, and the silence of a citizenry terrorized
> by the Taliban's violent and arbitrary application of their version
> of *Shari'a* law.[52]

Kamal Matinuddin, who retired as a Lieutenant General of the
Pakistani army, gives some idea of what it was like. He writes:

> Doctors have been compelled to cut off the hands and feet of
> thieves in accordance with the *shariah*; killers have been tried by
> the local *qazis* and the punishment has been handed down in a
> matter of hours ... Cinemas have been closed and their buildings
> turned into mosques. Taking photographs and displaying por-
> traits, posters and pictures is banned to prevent idolatry.[53]

Steve Coll tells us that the Taliban rechristened Kabul Radio as the
Voice of Sharia or Islamic law and announced over it a list of things
prohibited. These included toothpaste, which had to be abandoned in
favour of the natural root the Prophet favoured, playing with marbles
and television-watching.[54] Referring to the persecution of women,
Coll points out that 8,000 girls who were undergraduates in Kabul
University lost their places. A similar number of schoolteachers lost
their jobs.[55] Collateral damage followed. 'Education for boys,' Rashid
writes, 'is also at a standstill in Kabul because most of the teachers are
women, who now cannot work. An entire generation of Afghan children are growing up without any education.'[56]

NOT REAL ISLAM

A great deal has been written about the Taliban's savage and regressive
order to require more than a brief illustrative recall like the one above.
Huntington's book does not discuss Osama bin Laden and al Qaeda. It

does not indicate whether the term 'political Islam' or Islamic 'funda-mentalism' covers their version of the religion. It is, however, clear that the latter is not compatible with modernity in the proper and compre-hensive sense of the term. As for Huntington's assertion that 'political Islam' or Islamist fundamentalism is only one element of a far wider and comprehensive phenomenon of Islamic Resurgence which is main-stream in character, one can only say that Islamic Resurgence is a diverse and complex phenomenon characterized by many local editions shaped by history and tradition. Whether Huntington has described it correctly and political Islam of the Taliban and al Qaeda variety can be considered an element of that is an issue that can generate a furious debate and falls outside the scope of the present discourse.

The fact is that Islam itself is very different from the reactionary, intolerant and violent version that the Taliban and al Qaeda preach and practice. While the Taliban severely curtailed the rights and entitlements of Muslim women, Islam played a revolutionary role in advancing these at the time of the Prophet, according to them a position higher than what most other religions did contemporaneously. Muhammad pro-claimed the equality of men and women and their equal rights to the fruits of their labour at a time when they had few rights in the feudal societies of the West. *Ayats* 193 and 194 in the third sura of the Quran, entitled 'The House of Imran', states, 'And their Lord answers them: "I waste not / the labour of any that labours among you / be you male or female—the one of you / is as the other."'[57] The Quran says in the fourth sura, entitled 'Women', ayats 36 and 37, 'To the men a share of what they have earned, / and to the women a share of what they / have earned. And ask God of his bounty. / God knows everything.'[58]

Islam also provided women a share of parental inheritance. The Quran states in the fourth sura, ayats 7 and 8:

> To the men a share of what parents and kinsmen
> leave, and to the women a share of what
> parents and kinsmen leave, whether it be
> little or much, a share apportioned;
> and when the division is attended by
> kinsmen, orphans and the poor,

      make provision for them out of it
      and speak to them honourable words.[59]

In the same sura, the Quran specified the exact share of the inheritance to which each relative was entitled. While the men enjoyed a higher share the very fact that women were given a precisely defined share marked a major step forward in the context of the time. Muhammad did much more. According to the principles of Islam he narrated, a woman had the same capacity for freedom as a man. She could propose marriage to a man, freely choose her husband, reject a suitor and get a divorce from an estranged husband against his will. She could not be forcibly married. According to Islamic jurisprudence, women were competent to own and dispose of property in any manner. If all this was very different in fact and spirit from the hell to which the Taliban confined them, so is the Quran's stand on their role in public. Women were present on the battlefield, providing water to the wounded, carrying them to places of safety and treating their wounds—thus anticipating the remarkable work that Florence Nightingale did during the Crimean War (1854–60) more than 12 centuries later. Several important ladies, including the Prophet's wife, Syeda Ayesha, rendered such services at the battle of Uhud (March AD 625).

Muhammad, of course, prescribed a severe dress code for women and prohibited the display of any part of their bodies except hands and faces, in public. Islam allows only close relatives of women to see them wearing ornaments. Muhammad prohibited women wearing perfume from passing close to men. Intermingling was strictly limited. Women could meet other men only in the presence of their husbands. They were—and are—unequal to men as witnesses; rape laws are severely tilted against them. Adultery by them, however, is also very difficult to prove.

One must, however, consider the times and the fact that the position of women was worse not only in West and Central Asia but also in Europe. Islam had to take the existing realities into account and perhaps avoid radical departures which would have been rejected or ignored in practice. Given, however, the direction of his pronouncements,

Islam should have been the trailblazer in the struggle for gender justice and equality. Unfortunately, the reverse is the case today. Even in
Islamic countries that have not adopted the extreme policies of the
Taliban, women labour under restrictions from which their counterparts in modern democracies are free. Compulsion on women to wear
the burqa or the hijab is an anachronism in the modern world, where
gender justice and equality are critical elements in the social, political,
cultural and economic discourse.

THE INTELLECTUAL CONTRIBUTION OF ISLAM

Equally unacceptable in the 21st century is the violently proselytiz-
ing, intolerant, obscurantist and socially reactionary version of Islam
that the Taliban and al Qaeda seek to impose on the world. In sharp
contrast to the bigoted anti-intellectualism of the Taliban led by people whose education has been mostly limited to madrasas or religious
seminaries, rulers in the early period of Islam encouraged scholarship
and intellectual inquiry.

The Abbasid Khalif, Al Mansur, who built Baghdad in AD 762,

> invited religious scholars and intellectuals to come from far and
> near, and encouraged the rendering of books in various languages
> into Arabic. The work started under the patronage of the State.
> In 830 Al Mamun established in Baghdad his famous Bayt al
> Hikmah, a combination [of] library, academy and translation
> bureau, and an astronomical observatory. The work of transla-
> tion continued with such speed and on such a vast scale that,
> within eighty years after the establishment of Baghdad, most of
> the books in Greek had already been rendered into Arabic.[60]

As Maulana Wahiduddin Khan shows, by destroying the Holy Roman
Empire and the Persian Empire, both of which suppressed freedom
of thought, Islam enabled people to pursue scientific and metaphysi-
cal explorations, their own religions and ways of life without fear
of persecution. Islam's severe monotheism was an important factor. Pre-Islamic polytheistic cultures in the Arabian Peninsula and

the adjoining areas, with their veneration of a multiplicity of deities and the fear of offending them, had created a diffident mindset and hindered the unfettered and enthusiastic investigation of natural and human phenomena, in the search for knowledge. Wahiduddin Khan writes:

> Through the Arabs, monotheism, and a civilisation born under its influence, spread everywhere. Its impact was felt in the major parts of the inhabited world of the time. Thus an atmosphere and an environment was produced in which scientific research, leading to the conquest of nature's phenomena, could be freely and independently undertaken.[61]

Scholarship and scientific experimentation thrived. The large-scale manufacture of paper in the Abbasid era greatly facilitated the publication of books.

> There were more than 400,000 books in the library at Cordova (Spain) in the tenth century, whereas in Europe at that time, according to the Catholic Encyclopaedia, the library at Canterbury was at the top of the list of European libraries with 1800 books in the 13th century.[62]

Arabs gave a significant boost to the progress of astronomy and physics, and made tremendous progress in medicine, not only learning from the Greeks but making their own contribution. Khalif Harun al-Rashid took the initiative to establish the first hospital in Baghdad in AD 800. Muslims from Spain put agriculture on a scientific basis. The numeral system in use now, including the critically important figure of zero, was invented in India. Introduced in Baghdad at the time of Khalif Al Mansur, by an Indian traveller whose works were translated into Arabic, it was adopted for general use after the great Arab mathematician Al-Khawarizmi had certified its usefulness. It revolutionized mathematics in Europe, liberating it from the confining straitjacket of Roman numerals, after it was introduced there by Leonardo of Pisa.[63]

The Arab intellectual efflorescence during the rule of the khalifs, which was certainly more impressive than the 12th-century renaissance in Europe, was largely made possible by the fact that policies governing the State were not formulated by bigoted ruling clerics who saw heresy and blasphemy in whatever they disliked. These were 'determined and directed'[64] by Arab traders and encouraged industry, agriculture and trade. The result was a marked quickening of economic activity. The ruling classes in the 'Roman world' as well as other 'lands of antique civilisation' detested productive labour. The noble professions were those of war and worship. It was different with the Arabs. M. N. Roy writes:

> Nomadic life in the desert had taught them to appreciate labour as a source of freedom. With them trade was an honourable as well as lucrative occupation of the free man. Thus the Islamic State was based upon social relations entirely different from those of the old. Religion extolled industry, and encouraged a normal indulgence of nature. Trade was free, and as noble a profession as statecraft, war, letters and science.[65]

COMPASSION AND TOLERANCE IN WAR AND PEACE

The natural pragmatism of traders, who wanted peace to pursue profit, tended to turn them away from extremism and violence; so did their mindsets which were oriented toward give and take in the world of commerce, and their wide experience of dealing with people from different parts of the world. Their essentially peaceful approach to life was in harmony with the message of the Quran. While some passages in the latter and the words of Prophet Muhammad suggest sanction for violence and intolerance, and appear socially regressive, the broad thrust of the religion is toward tolerance, mercy and peace. The 10th sura, ayat 100 of the Quran clearly states:

> And if thy Lord had willed, whoever
> in the earth would have believed
> all of them, all together. Wouldst thou

> then constrain the people, until
> they are believers?
> It is not for any soul to believe
> save by the leave of God.[66]

Further, the Quran rules out hate and calls for piety and mutual help. Thus the fifth sura, ayat 2 says:

> Let not detestation for a people who
> barred you from the Holy Mosque move you
> to commit aggression. Help one another to
> piety and godfearing; do not help each other
> to sin and enmity. And fear God; surely God is
> terrible in retribution.[67]

In the early days of Islam, conquered people were treated generously and left free to practice their religion. M. N. Roy points out that the inhabitants of Jerusalem were left in possession of their worldly goods and allowed freedom of worship after the city had capitulated to Khalif Umar. For a nominal tax of two pieces of gold, the entire Christian community, along with their patriarch and his clergy, was granted a special quarter of the city to live in. Muslim conquerors stimulated pilgrimage to the city of Jerusalem primarily for the commercial returns it brought.[68] It is hardly surprising that everywhere Saracen invaders were welcomed 'as deliverers by people oppressed and tyrannised by Byzantine corruption, Persian despotism and Christian superstition'.[69]

Makhan Lal Roy Choudhury, who left his mark as an outstanding scholar of Islam in India, affirms that the early history of the khalifs provides examples of tolerance of which any religion should be proud. Umar ordered payment of compensation for damage done to people of the country through which he marched during his Syrian expedition.[70] When Muhammad bin Qasim informed Khalif Walid that he had destroyed temples, converted Hindus to Islam and had successfully waged war against them, the Khalif reprimanded him because his actions were contrary to the sanctions and usages of the Holy

Law, and asked him to provide compensation for the damages he had done.[71]

Roy Choudhury's testimony is particularly valuable because he never shies away from citing acts of savagery and intolerance by Muslim rulers like Mahmud of Ghazna and Mohammad of Ghor. He mentions how Sikandar Lodhi killed 15,000 Hindus in one day to prove his love of Islam and how Timur is credited to have killed 600,000 human beings in a day to change the 'the land of infidels to that of believers'.[72] These instances, however, do not relate to the early days of Islam. The latter, which Roy Choudhury talks about, were marked by tolerance, economic prosperity and a quest for intellectual excellence. The period also involved conflict. Islam united in a single state under a khalif[73] the tribes that inhabited the Arabian Desert and were perpetually engaged in feuds and warfare.[74] This and the expansion that followed involved military conquests, which in turn involved inspiring the 'Army of God' with religious fervour and zeal for conversion. Yet, as M. N. Roy says:

> There is no end of testimonies to prove that even in the predominantly martial period of their history, the Saracens were far from being barbaric bands of fanatical marauders, spreading pillage and rapine, death and destruction, in the name of religion.[75]

The legendary first commander of the faithful, Abu Bakr, said in his famous injunction to his troops:

> Be just; the unjust never prosper. Be valiant; die rather than yield. Be merciful; slay neither old men, nor women, nor children. Destroy neither fruit trees; nor grains nor cattle. Keep your word even to your enemy. Molest not those men who have retired from the world.[76]

Terrorism, Karen Armstrong points out, is repugnant to the Quranic view of warfare which, according to her, is very similar to the West's view of a 'just' war.[77] She points out that Islam regards war as always an 'awesome evil', which Muslims sometimes have to undertake to prevent persecution. She adds:

> They [Muslims] may never initiate hostilities, however, and aggressive warfare is always forbidden. The only permissible war, therefore, is a war of self-defence, but the moment the enemy sues for peace, hostilities must cease. Retaliation is permitted to avenge an attack, but it must be proportionate, and patience is the best option; it is better to refrain from any retaliation at all.[78]

AL QAEDA, TALIBAN AND THE WEAPON OF MASS KILLING

Very different is the conduct of the Taliban, al Qaeda and terrorists groups like the Lashkar-e-Toiba (LeT), Jaish-e-Mohammad (JeM), Tehrik-e-Taliban Pakistan (TTP), Afghan Taliban and the Haqqani network. They think nothing of killing old men, women and children. In fact, Osama bin Laden said in an interview to Al Jazeera in December 1998, which has already been cited earlier, that men were fighters whether they carried arms or merely helped by paying taxes. He referred to a news item stating that 'three-quarters of American people' supported President Clinton's attack (actually prolonged aerial bombing, as we have seen) on Iraq and said, 'This is a people whose votes are won when innocents die, whose leader commits adultery and great sins and then he sees his popularity rise—a vile people who have never understood the meaning of values.'[79]

The fatwa issued by Osama bin Laden and others on 23 February 1998 while announcing the formation of the Global Islamic Front against Jews and Crusaders, generally called World Islamic Front, identified three elements in what it described as the United States–led conspiracy against Muslims and Islam—American occupation and economic exploitation of the Arabian peninsula, the continued 'slaughter of Muslims in Iraq' and the furthering of the interests of the 'Jews' petty state' in conspiring to destroy Iraq, 'the strongest neighbouring Arab state, and their endeavour to fragment all the states of the region such as Iraq, Saudi Arabia, Egypt and Sudan into paper statelets' and through their disunion and weakness, guarantee the survival of Israel.[80]

Stating that all these 'crimes and sins committed by the Americans are a clear declaration of war on Allah, his messenger and Muslims', Osama bin Laden and other signatories declared in the fatwa:

> The ruling to kill the Americans and their allies—civilians and military—is an individual duty for every Muslim who can do it in any country in which it is possible to do it, in order to liberate the al-Aqsa mosque [in Jerusalem] and the Holy Mosque [in Mecca] from their grip, and in order for their armies to move out of all the lands of Islam, defeated and unable to threaten any Muslim ... We—with God's help—call on every Muslim who believes in God and wishes to be rewarded to comply with God's order to kill the Americans and plunder their money wherever and whenever they find it.[81]

Practice has followed fatwas, speeches and sermons. Indiscriminate, mass killing on a large scale was the aim of both 9/11 and the terrorist attack on Mumbai on 26 November 2008, the first perpetrated by al Qaeda and the second by the LeT and the ISI. Innocent men and women were brutally killed in both outrages.

What is now happening to Islam is in some ways a repeat of what happened to it in the 13th and 14th centuries as a culmination of the process of conversion of Turks and Central Asian tribes to the religion. Makhan Lal Roy Choudhury points out that to these violent people 'Islam offered two worlds—power in this world and pleasure in the next. Consequently, in their hands, the true precepts of Islam underwent distortion, as was the case with Christianity in the hands of the barbarian conquerors of Europe.'[82] The violent, intolerant and socially reactionary stream of Islam that they came to represent gained ascendency after the Mongol conquest of the domains of the Omayyad (AD 660–750) and Abbasid (AD 750–1258) khalifs. It was in many respects a response to the humiliating defeat and the atrocities inflicted by Mongols, which were attributed to the Arabs abandoning the pristine and austere ways they followed during the Prophet's lifetime and for a century thereafter. An important proponent of this view was the Hanbali jurist, Taqi Al-Din Ahmed Ibn Taimiyya, who was born in AD

1263, five years after the Mongol ruler Hulagu captured Baghdad and killed the last Abbasid khalif. He advocated a return to Sunni orthodoxy as Ibn Hanbali had left it.[83]

Ibn Taimiyya condemned Sufism—which he blamed for Islam's decline—and Shi'ism as un-Islamic.[84] He severely condemned dancing and the playing of music at *khanqas*[85] as un-Islamic and worship at the *mazar*s (tombs) of Sufi saints and holy men as idolatrous.[86] He was severely critical of the dilution of the rigorous punishments provided for crimes under the sharia law through the grant of remissions and imposition of fines. He was the first to oppose the uncritical acceptance of the tenets of Islam as interpreted by the *ulema* who always bent to the will of rulers.[87] The ulema, however, proved too powerful for him and threw him into prison, where he died.

In contemporary terminology, what Ibn Taimiyya stood for was fundamentalist Islamist extremism. After his death, it was kept alive by many Muslims who venerated him, and received a massive boost when the Ottoman Turks established their sway over the Arabian Peninsula, Persia, Asia Minor and large parts of Europe including Greece and Eastern Europe. In the 18th century it found a powerful advocate in the Saudi Arabia–born cleric, Muhammad Ibn Abd al-Wahhab (AD 1703–92). A follower of Hanbali, he conducted an aggressive campaign against Sufis and worship at mazars, and declared that all knowledge not based on the Quran and the Sunnah was outside the pale of Islamic belief.[88] He stood for the compulsory performance of obligatory prayers, a puritanical life and legal penalties for smoking and drinking.

The large body of al-Wahhab's followers included Abdul Rahman Al Saud and his son, Abdul Aziz, known as Ibn Saud, who was engaged in prolonged warfare with the Sheikh of Riyadh. In the first decade of the 19th century, Abdul Aziz won a series of victories and set up a kingdom in what is now Saudi Arabia. From the very beginning Saudi Arabia has been an exporter of the militant and extremist Wahhabi school of Islam. Not surprisingly, the House of Saud played, at the behest of, and in close coordination with, the United States, a critical role in sustaining and funding the mujahideen forces fighting Soviet troops in Afghanistan from 1980 to 1989, when the defeated Soviet forces finally left the country. Osama bin Laden played a critical role in that war.

SISTERS UNDER THE SKIN?

Clearly, the version of Islam that the Taliban and al Qaeda enforce reflects the views and background of the two protagonists rather than the tenets of the religion whose message is contained in the Quran. Rather, their blinkered vision, smouldering hatred, violent orientation, savagery and dictatorial ways remind one of the Nazis and Fascists. Those who oppose putting them in the same category would argue that unlike the latter, the Taliban and al Qaeda did not have a racist ideology. Nor have they conducted anything like Hitler's mass extermination of Jews, nor run concentration camps like Auschwitz or Buchenwald. They are religious people whom power and responsibility, and the task of rebuilding a war-devastated Afghanistan, will sober down. One only needs to engage with them in a prolonged dialogue.

Nothing could be further from reality. One does not compare the Taliban and the followers of al Qaeda with the Nazis because they propagate the same doctrine. The comparison lies in the exclusivist, totalitarian and savage mindsets, and the obsessive tendency toward persecuting and incarcerating large sections of humanity, that their creeds reflect. The Nazi ideology was based on racism and stood for Aryan superiority over all other races and denunciation and persecution of Jews. The Nazis excluded Jews from their moral universe, tried to exterminate them and herded them into concentration camps where most perished under murderously cruel conditions. The Taliban excluded women from public spaces and most kinds of employment, and virtually put them under house arrest with highly restricted access to the outside world.

Hitler viewed Jews as universal corruptors and the source of all evil. In his outstanding work, *Hitler: A study in Tyranny*, which remains a benchmark despite the decades, Alan Bullock writes:

> In whatever direction one follows Hitler's train of thought, sooner or later one encounters the satanic figure of the Jew. The Jew

is made the universal scapegoat. Democracy is Jewish—the secret domination of the Jew. Bolshevism and social democracy; capitalism and 'interest slavery' of the money lender; parliamentarianism and the freedom of the Press; liberalism and internationalism; anti-militarism and the class war; Christianity; modernism in art (kultur-bolschewismus), prostitution and miscegenation—all are instruments devised by the Jew to subdue the Aryan people to his rule. One of Hitler's favourite phrases, which he claimed—very unfairly—to have taken from Mommsen was: 'The Jew is the ferment of decomposition in peoples.' This points to the fundamental fact about the Jew in Hitler's eyes; unlike the Aryan, the Jew is incapable of founding a state and so incapable of anything creative.[89]

The mere presence of Jews seemed to make Hitler feel ill. Thus he wrote in *Mein Kampf*:

Cleanliness, whether moral or of another kind, had its own peculiar meaning for these [Jews] people. That they were water-shy was obvious on looking at them and, unfortunately, very often also when not looking at them at all. The odour of these people in caftans often used to make me ill. Beyond that, there were the unkempt clothes and the ignoble exterior.[90]

Hitler's hatred for Jews was visceral and absolute. This is clear from his observance:

Was there any shady undertaking, any form of foulness, especially in cultural life, in which at least one Jew did not participate? On putting the probing knife carefully on that kind of abscess, one immediately discovered, like a maggot in a putrescent body, a little Jew who was blinded by sudden light.[91]

Again:

The greater the intelligence of the individual Jew, the better he will succeed in deceiving others. His success in this line may even go so far that the people who grant him hospitality may be led to believe that the Jew among them is a genuine Frenchman, for instance, or Englishman or German or Italian, who just happens to belong to a different denomination which is different from that prevailing in these countries.[92]

Jews were projected as utterly unscrupulous persons who would stop at nothing in pursuit of their designs. Thus,

> he [the Jew] will stop at nothing. His utterly low-down conduct is so appalling that one really cannot be surprised if in the imagination of our people [Germans] the Jew is pictured as the incarnation of the Satan, and the symbol of evil.[93]

Hitler also saw Jews as sexually depraved people ever on the lookout for German girls to seduce. He wrote in *Mein Kampf*:

> The black-haired Jewish youth lies in wait for hours on end, satanically glancing at and spying on the unconscious girl whom he plans to seduce, adulterating her blood and removing her from the bosom of her own people.... In his systematic efforts to ruin girls and women he strives to break down the last barriers of discrimination between him and other peoples.[94]

FUEHRER PRINZIP

Hitler made no secret of his hatred for democracy. In the first chapter, entitled 'Weltanschauung and Party', in Volume II of *Mein Kampf*, he refers to parliamentarians as 'parliamentary worms' and parliament as 'House of Puppets', and to elections as 'repeatedly occurring frauds'. William L. Shirer says in his exhaustive chronicle, *The Rise and Fall of the Third Reich*, that Hilter's ideas on the nature of the future Nazi state was less clearly stated than his assertion that Germany would occupy vast areas in eastern Europe and the Soviet Union in search of *lebensraum* or living space. He, however, made it clear that there would be 'no democratic nonsense' and that the Third Reich would be ruled by the *Fuehrer Prinzip* or the Leadership Principle.[95]

Osama bin Laden held democracy to be incompatible with Islam. In a 53-minute-long audiotape, circulated on 14 February 2003, he stated that the Hadith of the Prophet contained a warning that the war against the enemy will be decided by fighting and killing and not by a paralysis of the powers of the Islamic *umma* 'for decades through other means, like the deceptive idea of democracy'.[96] In his second message to the people of Iraq, conveyed to Al Jazeera through a videotape in October 2003, he described the 'legislative council of representatives' as 'council of polytheism' and called democracy 'the religion of ignorance'. He added, 'Islam is the religion of God, and the legislative councils of representatives are the religion of ignorance.'[97]

The Taliban and al Qaeda believe that Islam is the only true religion and draw a clear line between 'believers' and 'unbelievers'. In an interview with Taysir Alluni, head of Al Jazeera's network in Kabul, Osama bin Laden had, on 20 October 2001—less than two weeks after the beginning of the United States–led offensive in Afghanistan following 9/11—called upon Muslims to 'trust in the victory of God, and to answer the call of God, and the order of his Prophet, with *jihad* against world unbelief'.[98] In his message of 16 December 2004, which was a blistering attack on the regimes of the Arabian peninsula, including Saudi Arabia and its religious establishment, Osama bin Laden said that it was partly an internal regional struggle against Arab rulers but 'in other respects it is a struggle between global unbelief, with the apostates today under the leadership of America on one side, and the Islamic *umma* and its brigades of *mujahidin*, on the other'.[99] He provided a stark idea of the hostility with which he viewed the relationship between the believers and infidels (a more pejorative term than 'unbeliever') when he said in a letter sent to Al Jazeera on 3 November 2001, 'We cannot ignore the enmity between us and the infidels, since it is a doctrinal one.' He spoke of the need to show loyalty to believers and those who professed that there was 'no God but God', and called for renouncing 'idolators, infidels and heretics' and sought God's help against them.[100]

One sees here traces of the same exclusivist mindset that characterized Hitler's view of the distinction between Germans, who were Aryans, and non-Germans, particularly Jews, who had to be exterminated, and Slavs, who had to be kept in a state of slavery. Summing up the Fuehrer's attitudes toward them, Shirer wrote, 'The Jews and the Slavic people were the *untermenschen*—subhumans. To Hitler they had no right to live except as, some of them, among the Slavs, might be needed to toil in the fields and mines as slaves of their German masters.'[101]

Osama bin Laden's references to Jews reflected an intense hatred that sometimes reminded one of Hitler. He said in his audiotape of 14 February 2003 that 'these Jews' were 'masters of usury and leaders in treachery'.[102] He had earlier said in his interview with Al Jazeera in December 1998 that every Muslim, from the moment he realizes the distinction in his heart, 'hates Jews, and hates Christians. This is a part of our belief and our religion'.[103] Even earlier, he had in a statement issued on 29 December 1994 described them as 'an attacking enemy and a corruptor of religion and the world' to whom applied Ibn Taymiyya's assertion that there was 'no greater duty after faith than unconditionally fighting the attacking enemy who corrupts religion and the world'.[104]

Much of Osama bin Laden's hostility toward the United States stems from its support to the Jews. In his absorbing work, *The Bin Ladens: Oil, Money, Terrorism and the Secret Saudi World*, Steve Coll quotes the al Qaeda leader as saying, with reference to the United States' support to Israel 'with weapons, aid and men', which affected the outcome of the 1973 Arab-Israeli war, 'It appears to us from the writings of the Prophet, that we will have to fight the Jews under his name and on this land [Palestine].... And the United States has involved itself again and again ....'[105] Coll also quotes him as describing Jews as 'idiots of the age' who, when confronted by righteous Palestinian youth, 'have become like agitated wild asses fleeing from a lion'.[106]

Osama's animosity toward Jews was largely the result of the creation of Israel, the latter's conflict with the Arabs and, of course, the issue of Palestine. As already discussed in chapter 1, this becomes clear from, among other documents, his 'Letter to America', which first appeared in the Internet in Arabic and was later translated into English by

Islamists in London. The full text of the translation, carried by the *Observer* of the United Kingdom on 24 November 2002, was reproduced in the *Guardian* of the United Kingdom on the same day. Referring to Palestine, Osama wrote:

> The British handed over Palestine, with your [America's] help and your support, to the Jews, who have occupied it for more than 50 years; years overflowing with oppression, tyranny, crimes, killing, expulsion, destruction and devastation. The creation and continuation of Israel is one of the greatest crimes, and you are the leaders of its criminals. And, of course, there is no need to explain and prove the degree of American support for Israel. The creation of Israel is a crime which must be erased. Each and every person whose hands have become polluted in the contribution towards this crime must pay its price, and pay for it heavily.[107]

In an audio tape which the Arabic-language channel, Al Jazeera, received on 24 January 2010, Osama bin Laden praised the Nigerian youth, Umar Farouk Abdulmutallab, who tried in vain to blow up a Northwest Airlines flight from Amsterdam to Detroit on Christmas Day 2009. The channel quoted him as saying, 'The message I want to convey to you through the plane of the hero Umar Farouk [Abdulmutallab], reaffirms a previous message that the heroes of 9/11 conveyed to you.'[108] Bin Laden added:

> America will never dream of living in peace unless we live it in Palestine. It is unfair that you enjoy a safe life while our brothers in Gaza suffer greatly.
>
> Therefore, with God's will, our attacks on you will continue as long as you continue to support Israel.
>
> If it was possible to carry our messages to you by words we wouldn't have carried them to you by planes.[109]

The tape indicated not only that the al Qaeda chief's attitude toward Israel remained unchanged but also that America could 'never dream of living in peace' unless Arabs did so in Palestine, which clearly meant as long as Israel occupied Palestine, or perhaps even existed. This was hardly surprising. He had said in his 2002 'Letter to America' that the creation of Israel was a crime that had to be erased and every person whose hands had become polluted through contribution toward the crime must 'pay its price, and pay for it heavily'.[110]

The language Osama bin Laden generally used in respect of Jews and women was doubtless far less abusive than Hitler's in respect of Jews. But his hostility toward Jews was perhaps only a shade less intense than Hitler's. No doubt, he neither sent women to concentration camps nor contemplated a 'final solution' for them in the form of a genocide which the Fuehrer sought to implement in respect of the Jews. But he, al Qaeda and the Taliban condemned them virtually to house arrest and to a status comparable to what the Nazis accorded to Jews and the Slavic people—whom Hitler regarded as *untermenschen* or subhuman.

RULE BY TERROR

Hitler and the Nazis, as well as the Taliban ruled by terror and repression spearheaded by ubiquitous and barbarous secret police forces. In Germany, it was the feared Gestapo. In Afghanistan, it was Maulavi Qalamuddin's Department of the Promotion of Virtue and Prevention of Vice with its thousands of spies in the army, government ministries, hospitals and Western aid agencies. In Germany under Hitler, governmental repression was reinforced and facilitated by the thousands of lumpens who flocked to the SA and the SS.[111] In Afghanistan, the writ of Maulavi Qalamuddin's department was enforced by thousands young men, many of them with no more than madrasa education, from Pakistan, walking about with whips, long sticks and Kalashnikov rifles.

Significantly, neither Hitler nor Osama bin Laden had come out with a clear idea of the social and economic order they wanted established. Shirer points out that there is almost no mention of economics in *Mein Kampf*. The subject bored Hitler and he never bothered to try to learn something about it beyond toying with the 'crackpot ideas of Gottfried Feders, the crack, who was against interest slavery'.[112] Bullock writes, 'Hitler neither understood nor was interested in economics, but he was alive to the social and economic consequences of events which, like the inflation of 1923, affected the life of every family in Germany.'[113] Nor was he particularly interested in governance. According to Bullock, he refused to outline any programme for his government throughout the campaign for the 1933 election. He said at Munich:

> If, today, we are asked for the programme of this movement, then we can summarise this in a few quite general sentences— programmes are of no avail, it is the human purpose which is decisive.... Therefore, the first point in our programme is: Away with all illusions.[114]

In his perceptive introduction to *Messages to the World: Statements of Osama bin Laden*, Bruce Lawrence states that one of the most striking features of Osama's statements carried in the collection was the absence of any social dimension. 'Bin Laden,' he says, 'was barred from the kind of analysis that would have allowed him to distinguish the different structural features of the various Muslim societies in which *Jihad* had to be awakened.' While some—like unemployment, inflation and corruption—of the host of evils he morally denounced were social, he never offered an 'alternative conception of the ideal society'. There was 'almost a complete lack of any social programme'. Lawrence adds, 'In place of the social there is a hypertrophy of the sacrificial. Bin Laden's messages rarely hold out radiant visions of final triumph.' He lays far more emphasis on the 'glories of martyrdom than the spoils of victory. Rewards belong essentially to the hereafter.'[115]

The Taliban, al Qaeda and the Nazis belong to the same category of totalitarian forces hostile to democracy and human freedom, given to persecution of large sections of people by consigning them to domestic slavery or subjecting them to extermination drives, and perpetuating their hold on power through savage repression. Bin Laden is doubtless dead but his ideology is alive and well at all levels of the Taliban and al Qaeda. This, in turn leads us to the question: Is it possible

to come to a peace settlement with them which does not violate the
fundamental principles of democracy and freedom and does not make
women the subject of a vicious apartheid of gender?

Notes

1. David Thomson, *Europe Since Napoleon* (Harmondsworth: Penguin Books, 1975), pp.
   157–58.
2. Ibid., p. 336.
3. E. H. Carr, *The Bolshevik Revolution 1917–23*, vol. I (Harmondsworth: Pelican Books,
   1966), p. 58.
4. Ibid., p. 58.
5. Samuel P. Huntington, *The Clash of Civilisations and the Remaking of World Order* (New
   Delhi: Viking, 1996), p. 78.
6. Ibid., p. 110.
7. Ibid., p. 68.
8. Alvin W. Gouldner, *The Dialectic of Ideology and Technology: The Origins, Grammar and
   Future of Ideology* (New York: Oxford University Press paperback, 1982), p. 91.
9. Ibid., p. 7.
10. Ibid., p. 91.
11. Ibid., pp. 91–92.
12. Ibid., p. 92. Gouldner quoted this passage from Morse Peckham, *Beyond the Tragic
    Vision* (New York: George Braziller, 1962).
13. Gouldner, *The Dialectic of Ideology and Technology*, p. 93.
14. Ibid., p. 94.
15. Ibid., p. 107.
16. Osama Bin Laden, ed. and introduction by Bruce Lawrence, trans. James Howarth,
    'A Muslim Bomb', in *Messages to the World: Statements of Osama bin Laden* (London and
    New York: Verso, 2005), p. 85.
17. Ibid., p. 98. 'Unbelief' is the opposite of 'true belief' or Islam. Osama bin Laden
    has talked both of 'unbelief' and 'global unbelief' synonymously as anti-Islam forces
    spearheaded by the United States and Israel and supported by pliant regimes in West
    Asia.
18. Osama bin Laden, *Messages to the World: Statements of Osama bin Laden*, p. 98.
19. 'Full Text: bin Laden's Letter to America', *Guardian*, the United Kingdom, 24 November
    2002, http://www.guardian.co.uk/world/nov/24/theobserver.
20. Ahmed Rashid, *Taliban: Islam, Oil and the New Great Game in Central Asia* (New York and
    London: I.B. Taurus, Publishers, 2002), p. 93.
21. Ibid., p. 88.
22. Deobandis are followers of the Deoband movement which has grown up around the
    Darul Uloom madrasa continent, including what is now Pakistan, and Afghanistan.
    Deobandis are conservative Sunnis who primarily follow the Hanafi school of law
    though they also accept the validity of the Maliki, Asha'ri and Maturidi schools.

23. S. K. Malik, *The Quranic Concept of War* (New Delhi: Adam Publishers & Distributors, 2008), pp. 47–48.

24. Press Trust of India, 'Muslim Clerics Declare Terror "Un-Islamic"', *Times of India*, 25 February 2008, online edition, http://timesofindia.indiatimes.com/india/Muslim-clerics-declare-terror-un-Islamic/articleshow/2813375.cms#ixzz1BYIlGHu2.

25. Rashid, *Taliban: Islam, Oil and the New Great Game in Central Asia*, p. 88.

26. Ibid., p. 93.

27. Physicians for Human Rights (PHR), *The Taliban's War on Women: A Health and Human Rights Crisis in Afghanistan*, Boston and Washington DC, 1998, http://physicians-forhumanrights.org/library/documents/reports/talibans-war-on-women.pdf.

28. Burqa: A head to toe covering for women that has only a mesh cloth to see and breathe through.

29. Physicians for Human Rights (PHR), *The Taliban's War on Women*, p. 113.

30. Ibid., p. 114.

31. Perhaps because it is not as all-covering as the Afghan burqa.

32. Ibid., pp. 117–18.

33. Ibid., p. 115. Hijab means modest clothing for both men and women that varies from Islamic country to country.

34. Ibid., p. 116.

35. Ibid., p. 2.

36. Ibid., p. 65.

37. Ibid., p. 8.

38. Ibid.

39. Ibid., p. 75.

40. Ibid.

41. Ibid., p. 34.

42. Ibid. .

43. Ibid., p. 49.

44. Ibid., p. 118.

45. Ibid.

46. Ibid.

47. Ibid.

48. Ibid., p. 119.

49. Ibid.

50. Ibid., p. 116.

51. Rashid, *Taliban: Islam, Oil and the New Great Game in Central Asia*, p. 105.

52. Ibid., pp. 3–4.

53. Kamal Matinuddin, *The Taliban Phenomenon: Afghanistan 1994–99* (Karachi: Oxford University Press, 1999), p. 35.

54. Steve Coll, *Ghost Wars: The Secret History of the CIA, Afghanistan and Bin Laden, from the Soviet Invasion to September 11, 2001* (United States: Penguin Books, 2004), p. 334.

55. Coll, *Ghost Wars*, p. 334.

56. Rashid, *Taliban: Islam, Oil and the New Great Game in Central Asia*, p. 106.

57. Arthur J. Arberry, *The Koran Interpreted* (Oxford: Oxford University Press, 1979), p. 70.

58. Ibid., p. 77.

59. Ibid., p. 73.

60. Maulana Wahiduddin Khan, trans. Farida Khanum, *Islam: Creator of the Modern Age* (New Delhi: The Islamic Centre, 1995), pp. 35–36.

61. Ibid., p. 32.

62. Ibid., p. 36.

63. Ibid., pp. 88–89.

64. M. N. Roy, *The Historical Role of Islam* (Delhi: Ajanta Publications, 1981), p. 16.

65. Ibid., p. 17.

66. Arberry, *The Koran Interpreted*, p. 208.

67. Ibid., p. 99.

68. Roy, *The Historical Role of Islam*, pp. 35–36.

69. Ibid., pp. 11–12.

70. Makhan Lal Roy Choudhury, *The Din-I-Ilahi or the Religion of Akbar*, second ed., (Kolkata: Das Gupta & Co. Ltd., 1952), p. 2.

71. Ibid.

72. Ibid., p. 1.

73. A khalif is a civil and military head of a Muslim state who is regarded as a representative of Allah.

74. Roy, *The Historical Role of Islam*, p. 22.

75. Ibid., p. 14.

76. Ibid., p. 11.

77. Karen Armstrong, 'Was This Inevitable? Islam Through History', in *How Did This Happen? Terrorism and the New War*, eds. James P. Hoge Jr and Gideon Rose (New York: The Perseus Press, 2001), p. 60.

78. Ibid., pp. 60–61.

79. Osama bin Laden, *Messages to the World*, p. 70.

80. Yossef Bodansky, *Bin Laden: The Man Who Declared War on America* (Atherton, California, United States: Forum, an imprint of Prima Publishing, 1999), p. 226.

81. Ibid., pp. 226–27.

82. Roy Choudhury, *The Din-i-Ilahi or the Religion of Akbar*, p. 3.

83. M. A. Karandikar, *Islam in India's Transition to Modernity* (New Delhi: Orient Longmans, 1968), p. 100.

84. Ibid., p. 99.

85. A khanqa is an abode of Sufi saints and holy men.

86. Karandikar, *Islam in India's Transition to Modernity*, p. 99.

87. Ibid.

88. Ibid., p. 101.

89. Alan Bullock, *Hitler: A Study in Tyranny*, Penguin Books (The United Kingdom: Harmondsworth, 1964), p. 407.

90. Adolph Hiter, *Mein Kampf*, unexpurgated edition, trans. James Murphy (New Delhi: ABC Publishing House, 1968), pp. 59–60. The edition combines the first and second volumes of the book written in 1924 and 1925 respectively.

91. Ibid., p. 60.

92. Ibid., p. 256.
93. Ibid., p. 272.
94. Ibid., p. 273.
95. William L. Shirer, *The Rise and Fall of the Third Reich: A History of Nazi Germany* (London: Secker and Warbug, 1962), p. 84.
96. Osama bin Laden, *Messages to the World*, p. 191.
97. Ibid., pp. 208–09.
98. Ibid., p. 129.
99. Ibid., p. 250.
100. Ibid., pp. 134–35.
101. Shirer, *The Rise and Fall of The Third Reich*, p. 937.
102. Osama bin Laden, *Messages to the World*, p. 190.
103. Ibid., p. 87.
104. Ibid., p. 9.
105. Coll Steve, *The Bin Ladens: Oil, Money, Terrorism and the Secret Saudi World* (Penguin, 2009), p. 205.
106. Ibid., p. 571.
107. 'Full Text: bin Laden's Letter to America', *Guardian*, The United Kingdom, 24 November 2002, http://www.guardian.co.uk/world/nov/24/theobserver.
108. Al Jazeera, 'Bin Laden Warns US of More Attacks', online edition, 25 January 2010, http://english.aljazeera.net/news/middleeast/2010/01/201012415287209336.html.
109. Ibid.
110. 'Full Text: bin Laden's Letter to America', *Guardian*.
111. SS stands for Schutzstaffel, which means Protection Squadron or Defence Corps in English. Formed as a small permanent guard unit to provide security for Nazi Party and its meetings in the early 1920s, it grew to become the largest and most powerful organization of the Third Reich and was responsible for many of the crimes against humanity perpetrated by it. Led by the notorious Heinrich Himmler from 1929 onwards, it was banned after Germany's defeat in 1945.

    SA is the abbreviation of Sturmabteilung, whose English equivalent is Assault Division, and its members were generally referred to as storm troopers or Brown Shirts after the colour of their uniform. SA, which played a key role in Hitler's rise to power until 1934 by protecting Nazi assemblies, disrupting those of its opponents and launching violent attacks on Jews and Hitler's opponents, was crippled by Hitler's 'blood purge' of it in 1934, in which most of its important leaders were killed. Thereafter, it lost its salience and the SS became the Nazis' principal instrument of terror and atrocities. It was banned after 1945.
112. Shirer, *The Rise and Fall of the Third Reich*, p. 84.
113. Bullock, *Hitler: A Study In Tyranny*, p. 152.
114. Ibid., p. 259.
115. Osama bin Laden, *Messages to the World*, p. xxii.

CHAPTER 3

WOOING THE 'GOOD TALIBAN'

The killing of Osama bin Laden gave a new thrust to a persistent American dream—winning over the 'good' or 'moderate' Taliban. It, however, will be a miracle if the dream is realized. Ahmed Rashid writes, 'The most elusive chimera that the CIA pursued, with the encouragement of the ISI, was that "moderate" Taliban Pashtuns would rise to denounce Mullah Omar, hand over bin Laden to the Americans, and join a new coalition government in Kabul.' The Inter-Services Intelligence (ISI) Directorate, however, never produced any of them. It had no intention of splitting the Taliban. 'There were moderates among the Taliban earlier on,' Rashid adds, 'but the ISI had betrayed them to Mullah Omar long ago.'[1]

The Americans, nevertheless, marched bravely onward. Speaking on the CNN programme, 'State of the Union', on 19 June 2011, Robert Gates, the US Defence Secretary at the time, publicly acknowledged the ongoing talks with the Taliban for the first time but said that these had begun only a few weeks ago. Officials, he added, were still uncertain whether the Taliban participants were genuine representatives of Mullah Omar. He also said that other countries—whose names he did not specify—were also participating in the effort.[2]

Afghan President Hamid Karzai had publicly referred to talks with the Taliban in a speech on 18 June 2011, in which he had stated that 'negotiations have started with these people and God willing these talks will continue.' He, however, made clear that 'foreign military forces and especially America are continuing this process'.[3] The *New York Times* dispatch stating this added that American officials had reportedly met a senior aide to the Taliban chief, Mullah Muhammad

Omar, at least three times in recent months in the first direct explora-
tory peace talks.[4] According to a Press Trust of India report, a former
Afghan Taliban spokesman, Abdul Haqiq, who used the alias Mohammad Hanif, played a crucial role in enabling Washington DC reach
Mullah Omar. Arrested by Afghan and American intelligence agents
in Afghanistan in June 2007, he was a high-profile Taliban spokesman
along with Yousaf Ahmadi, appointed after chief spokesman Abdul Latif
Hakimi was arrested in October 2005 in Pakistan.[5]

It is not terribly difficult to understand the causes of the spurt in
the reports. A report in the *New York Times* of 7 May 2011 had said that
'many leaders in Europe saw in bin Laden's death another reason to
pull out of a war' they had promised to quit anyway in the next three
years. They believed that bin Laden's death offered them a unique opportunity to unnerve the Taliban leadership and engage them in political negotiations which they had so far resisted doing. 'If you are Mullah
Omar,' the report quoted one of President Obama's top advisers as
saying, 'you've got to wonder whether the next set of helicopters is
coming for you.' Though the Taliban and al Qaeda were 'entwined',
their goals were perceived to be different. The Taliban's primary goal
was to control Afghanistan while al Qaeda wanted to establish a global
terrorist network.[6]

The implication of the difference was that the Taliban could be
detached from al Qaeda and engaged in negotiations. To set the perspective right, this assumption and efforts to wean at least a section of
the Taliban away from al Qaeda have been integral to President Barack
Obama's policy on Afghanistan and Pakistan—or Af-Pak policy as
it has come to be generally known. Announcing it a little over two
months after assuming office as US President, he said at room 450 of
the Dwight D. Eisenhower Executive Office Building in Washington
DC on 27 March 2009:

> We will support efforts by the Afghan government to open the
> door to those Taliban who abandon violence and respect the human
> rights of their fellow citizens. And we will seek a partnership
> with Afghanistan grounded in mutual respect—to isolate those

who destroy; to strengthen those who build; to hasten the day when our troops will leave; and to forge a lasting friendship in which America is your partner, and never your patron.[7]

President Obama has not been alone in wanting to reach out to the 'good Taliban'. United States Secretary of State Hillary Clinton indicated the same intention to the press at the end of the London Conference of 28 January 2010, which marked the first coordinated attempt to bring the Taliban on board for talks through international cooperation. She said:

Now, we have a very clear understanding of what we expect from this process. We expect that a lot of the foot soldiers on the battlefield will be leaving the Taliban because many of them have wanted to leave, many of them are tired of fighting. We believe the tide is beginning to turn against them, and we need incentives in order to both protect them and provide alternatives to them to replace the payment they received as Taliban fighters. This is similar to what the American military did in Iraq. As it became clear that a number of Iraqis were tired of the brutality and barbarism of al-Qaida, as they began to see the potential alternatives available to them in the political system, they began to talk with our military personnel about changing allegiance and becoming part of the forces fighting against the terrorists.[8]

She added:

So we have some experience in this.... Some of the same people, including a British general who is active in this area in Iraq, are advising General McChrystal. We've already seen some examples. In fact, we saw—there's an article in one of the American papers today talking about a whole tribe, a whole tribe of Pashtuns, about 400,000 members, who want to fight the Taliban. But you've got to realize the circumstances. There was a tribe in a village in Pakistan who decided to fight the Taliban and they were targeted with these brutal suicide bombings, killing more than a hundred people at a volleyball match.[9]

The purpose of the London conference, according to the communiqué issued at its conclusion, was to enable Afghanistan to emerge as a secure, prosperous and democratic nation.[10] It was convened by the then British Prime Minister, Gordon Brown, and co-hosted by the Afghan President Hamid Karzai and the UN Secretary General Ban-Ki-moon. It outlined a formidable agenda. The latter included expanded and improved Afghan forces gradually taking over security responsibilities and military operations against the Taliban and al Qaeda from American and North Atlantic Treaty Organization (NATO) troops over increasingly wider areas in Afghanistan; provision of an institutionalized format and earmarked funds for winning over 'the vast majority' of the Taliban; and enhancement of the ability of the Afghan government to deliver the fruits of development by improving efficiency and eradicating corruption. Conditions enabling the Afghan government to do all this were to be created by a surge in the deployment of American and NATO troops, taking their total number to about 150,000 in August 2010. Besides, there would be an increase in the presence of civilian officials from the United States and NATO countries to step up training and economic and social welfare activities that would bring home to Afghans the fruits flowing from peace and accelerated development.

Secretary of State Hillary Clinton further said at the London Conference:

> Among the decisions made today was to establish a Peace and Reintegration Trust Fund to support the Government of Afghanistan's efforts to draw disaffected Taliban back into society so long as they renounce violence, renounce al-Qaida, agree to abide by the laws and constitution of Afghanistan.[11]

The London Conference, in its communiqué, welcomed the 'Government of Afghanistan's commitment to reinvigorate Afghan-led reintegration efforts by developing and implementing an effective, inclusive, transparent and sustainable national peace and reintegration programme'. It also affirmed the international community's 'commitment to establish a Peace and Integration Trust Fund to finance the programme' and encouraged all those who wished to support 'peace-building and stabilisation efforts in Afghanistan to contribute to this important initiative'.[12] As a follow-up measure, the communiqué emanating from the conference declared:

> The London Conference will be followed by a conference in Kabul later this year, hosted by the Afghan Government, where it intends to take forward its programme with concrete plans for delivery for the Afghan people. These should be based on democratic accountability, equality, human rights, gender equality, good governance and more effective provision of government services, economic growth, as well as a common desire to live in peace under the Afghan Constitution. We remain convinced that together we will succeed.[13]

THE ROAD FROM LONDON

In keeping with the announcement, President Karzai held a three-day Peace Jirga in Kabul from 3 June 2010. According to a report in the *Hindu* of 3 June 2010, its purpose was to prepare a road map for reconciliation with the vast sections of the people who had been associated with the Taliban. The report attributed to diplomatic sources the Afghan assessment that only around 1 per cent of the people within the movement could be designated as 'hard-core Taliban' and had terror links with al Qaeda. The rest, outside this hardened inner circle, had been with the Taliban in anticipation of political patronage and protection. It is mainly this majority of lower rung Taliban foot soldiers that the Karzai government wished to engage.[14]

Following the conference, Karzai set up a 70-member High Peace Council to facilitate reconciliation and find a political solution.[15] As will be seen at some length later, he had been trying to reach out to the Taliban as early as after his victory in Afghanistan's presidential elections in 2004. Others have also been at work for some time. The British have been for reconciliation before not only the conference but also President Obama's assumption of office. Following the London conference, David Miliband, then British Foreign Secretary, gave a major boost to the move for a reconciliation with the Taliban when in a speech in Boston, United States, in March 2010, he called upon President Karzai to make as concerted an effort to reach out to disaffected Taliban leaders as British and American troops were making to integrate lower-level Taliban soldiers.[16]

Shortly after Miliband said his piece, Kai Eide, the UN Secretary General's former Special Representative in Afghanistan, told the BBC in an interview on 19 March 2010 that his organization had been involved in quiet negotiations with the Taliban in Dubai for the past year. The United Nations had not only been reaching out but also talking to them. These talks, he told the BBC, had been upended by Pakistan's arrest of Taliban leaders, including Mullah Baradar, the second-ranking person in the organization. The *New York Times* of 19 March 2010, which mentioned the interview, confirmed with him that he had said that Pakistan did not play the role it should have and that the arrests undermined efforts to start talks and build trust that were necessary for substantive peace talks to get under way.[17]

Nor had the Americans been watching from the sidelines. A report in the *New York Times* of 20 May 2009 stated that talks had been under way for months,[18] which indicated that these might have begun soon after Obama's becoming President or even earlier. According to the report, Daoud Abedi, an Afghan-American businessman from California and a member of Hekmatyar's Islamic Party, said he conducted negotiations in March.[19] Another interlocutor has reportedly been the former Taliban ambassador to Pakistan, Mullah Abdul Salam Zaeef.

Given all this and the course formally set by the London conference, President Karzai, whose relations with the Americans had become increasingly acrimonious during the Obama presidency, did not want to be outflanked and left high and dry. He stepped up his own efforts after the Kabul Peace Jirga, having announced at the end of it the formation of a commission to review the case of every Taliban fighter held in custody and release those not considered very dangerous.[20] Face-to-face talks to end the war in Afghanistan were, according to a report in the *New York Times* of 19 October 2010, under way in Afghanistan between members of his inner circle and Taliban commanders at the highest level.[21] At least four Taliban leaders, one of them a member of the family of Jalaluddin Haqqani, who heads one of the most ruthless and fanatical Islamist militia from North Waziristan, attended the talks. An Associated Press report filed on 31 October 2010 stated that the three Taliban leaders who met President Karzai during the peace talks in Afghanistan were Mullah Abdul Kabir, the Governor of Nangarhar province during Taliban rule and the head of the Taliban's Peshawar Shura at the time when the report was being written, Mullah Sadre Azam, his Deputy Governor in the Taliban regime, and Anwar-ul-Haq Mujahed, a militant leader from eastern Afghanistan who is said to have helped Osama bin Laden escape from the Americans attacking Tora Bora to capture him.[22]

OMAR AND HEKMATYAR TOO

The *New York Times* of 20 May 2009 had also stated that discussions had been held not only with Sirajuddin Haqqani, Jalaluddin's son, but also the Taliban leadership group associated with the 'Quetta Shura' or the Quetta Council.[23] Headed by Mullah Muhammad Omar, it included representatives of Gulbuddin Hekmatyar, a long-time warlord with a record of extreme brutality[24] who is the leader of the fundamentalist Islamist party, Hizb-e-Islami (Islamic Party), and the militia, Lashkar-e-Israr (Army of Sacrifice), both instruments of the ISI.

In fact, a delegation representing Hekmatyar had reportedly arrived in Kabul on 23 March and handed over a 15-point peace plan entitled National Rescue Agreement. Among other things, the latter called for the withdrawal of all foreign forces from the country by July 2010, a deadline that is long past, and the holding of new elections. Until foreign forces left and elections were held, it was agreeable to the Karzai government remaining in power with the Afghan police, army and intelligence services assuming responsibility for security, while a seven-member national council was formed as the ultimate decision-making body. The document also demanded that an elected government would have the right to review the Afghan Constitution, and the Afghan courts would prosecute those accused of corruption, drug smuggling, theft of the national wealth, and war crimes.[25]

One has not heard much about Hekmatyar's plan since then, which perhaps suggests that it did not find favour with the Americans. It is difficult to say for sure because the dialogue process has been not only secretive but, by all indications, extremely tortuous and duplicitous with many subplots. This, in turn, has been in character with the tangled nature of the Afghan narrative as it has unfolded from the time of the Great Game of the 19th century when Britain and Russia fought for domination over Afghanistan and Central Asia through various proxies. An interesting example of a subplot in the context of the secret talks is a remarkable revelation by Kathy Gannon of Associated Press. She quotes a former official of the Afghan government as saying that the talks with Mullah Abdul Kabir, Mullah Sadre Azam and Anwar-ul-Haq Mujahed were not directly linked to the Afghan government's efforts to broker a peace with the Taliban and find a political resolution to the insurgency. Rather, they were part of an effort to weaken the Haqqani network.[26]

Gannon sounds plausible because the Haqqani network has been a thorn in the flesh of both Karzai and the Americans and both would like to put it out of action. The question is whether the venture would have succeeded and, if it did, what impact that would have had on the war with the Taliban and al Qaeda. Mullah Kabir and Jalaluddin and his son Sirajuddin Haqqani belong to the powerful Zadran tribe of eastern Afghanistan which is estimated to number about 500,000 and from which the Haqqani network derives much of its strength. The Americans and Karzai hoped that Mullah Kabir's crossing over would divide tribal loyalties and sap the Haqqani network's strength.[27]

A weakening of the Haqqani network would have helped tilt the balance of political and military advantage in favour of the United States, its NATO allies and the Karzai government. Otherwise, it might not have had much impact on the course of the war. Gannon quotes a former Afghan official as saying that the three leaders who met President Karzai were only 'mid-level' contacts as they belonged to the Peshawar Shura and had little, if any, influence over the Quetta and the Waziristan shuras, which provided leadership to most of the Taliban fighters in Afghanistan and were overseen by Mullah Omar himself. According to the official, Kabir was powerful during Taliban rule as the Governor of Nangarhar and Deputy Prime Minister but now had no influence over the shuras in the south which took the military decisions. Mullah Sadre Azam was not viewed as a major player within the Taliban movement. Mujahed was the son of Maulvi Younis Khalis, founder of Hizb-e-Islami Khalis, an offshoot of the larger Hizb-e-Islami organization led by Gulbuddin Hekmatyar who, an ally of the United States during the war with the Soviets, was now a wanted terrorist.[28]

Manoeuvres aimed at weakening the Haqqanis fell in the realm of strategy. The success of the strategy in terms of the final objective hinged to a very great extent on whether the leaders, with whom talks were being held, could deliver besides being the kind of people who could be expected, in the words of President Obama, to 'abandon violence and respect the human rights of their fellow citizens'. Could they and the others being wooed be relied upon to work toward creating a secure, prosperous and democratic Afghanistan and prevent it from becoming a base for launching future terrorist strikes in the West and against countries like India and Russia?

The Haqqani militia is headed by Jalaluddin Haqqani, who has been ill since 2007 and whose son Sirajuddin has been running it since then. It has close links with al Qaeda and is believed to be sheltering its leader, Ayman al-Zawahiri. A minister in the Taliban government in Afghanistan and a fearless commander during the resistance movement against the Soviet Union, Jalaluddin operated out of Miranshah in North Waziristan in Pakistan's Federally Administered Tribal Areas (FATA). It was with him that Osama bin Laden found refuge after escaping from Afghanistan following the Taliban rout of 2001.[29]

Pakistan allowed thousands of Taliban and al Qaeda escapees to settle in FATA, create bases and restart military operations. Jalaluddin became the key organizer by hiring FATA tribesmen to provide sanctuary in, or safe passage out of, the region. Young Waziri and Mehsud tribes-men became rich by providing logistical services for a price.[30]

Hekmatyar has been very close both to the ISI and al Qaeda. He is a dyed-in-the-wool Islamist fundamentalist who and the ISI had jointly launched a relentless attempt to physically eliminate and politically rout all secular, democratic and pro-American elements among the Afghan mujahideen in the period after Soviet withdrawal from Afghanistan. According to Steve Coll, shortly after arriving in Pakistan, Edmund McWilliams, United States' Special Envoy to Afghan Resist-ance during 1988–89, went on a tour of Afghanistan to converse with as many Afghan commanders, intellectuals and refugees as possible. The purpose was to identify the problems facing the mujahideen, American interests in post-Soviet Afghanistan and what was happen-ing on the ground. What he heard from them and the circumstantial evidence he gathered were chilling. They said that as the Soviet soldiers had pulled out, Hekmatyar and the ISI had embarked upon 'a con-certed, clandestine plan to eliminate his rivals and establish his Muslim Brotherhood-dominated Islamic Party as the most powerful national force in Afghanistan'.[31] Also, Hekmatyar is pathologically anti-American. Despite receiving hundreds of millions of dollars in aid from the United States, he once refused to travel to New York and shake hands with the 'infidel' Ronald Reagan.[32]

Given their backgrounds, Hekmatyar and the Haqqanis are hardly the kind of leaders who can be counted upon to 'abandon violence and respect the human rights of their fellow citizens'. Nor can they be relied upon to work toward creating a secure, prosper-ous and democratic Afghanistan and prevent it from becoming a base for launching future terrorist strikes against the West. In fact they will almost certainly do the opposite. Even at the level of strategy, efforts to wean the Haqqanis and Hekmatyar away from al Qaeda and persuade them to shed their hard-line Islamist fundamentalism were unlikely to succeed.

The message that stood out from the confusing flurry of reports about the talks was that the United States and NATO countries were desperate to quit Afghanistan and were beginning to clutch at straws.

Despite this, hope soared in the bosoms of Afghan and NATO officials because one of the most senior Taliban commanders, Mullah Akhtar Muhammad Mansour, was thought to be participating in the talks. Senior American and Afghan officials, including General Petraeus, said that the talks indicated that Taliban leaders, whose rank-and-file fighters were under immense pressure from the American-led offensive, were at least willing to discuss an end to the war.[33] Then the unthinkable happened. It was found that it was not Mullah Mansour but an imposter who sat at three rounds of talks with Afghan and NATO officials and even met President Karzai![34] And, of course, the huge amount of money he had collected, had vanished with him. It is not difficult to imagine faces in Washington DC turning red and loud guffaws exploding at the ISI's headquarters and the Quetta Shura.

PERHAPS A PURELY STRATEGIC MOVE

As remarkable as the failure of American, NATO and Afghan officials to spot the imposter before loading him with money was their overlooking the possibility that Sirajuddin Haqqani or any of his authorized representatives were participating in the talks purely as a strategic move. They were, as the Americans had been themselves saying, increasingly feeling the pressure of frequent and successful drone strikes which had taken a heavy toll of al Qaeda and Talban leaders, operations by the United States Special Operations Forces (USSOF) and the surge in the deployment of American troops which had started producing results. They not only wanted the pressure to be off but knew that the United States and the NATO were under increasing domestic pressure to withdraw from the war.

This means that the Taliban, al Qaeda and formations like the Haqqani network, needed to do just two things to accelerate the pace of American troops withdrawal. The first was to step up the tempo of terrorist strikes inside Afghanistan which would indicate that they were not only not cornered but resurgent and would fight their way back to power once the foreign troops had left. This would ensure that those who were considering leaving them did not do so and those supporters of the Karzai regime and the American and NATO forces, who were worried about their future in case the Taliban and al Qaeda emerged triumphant, would switch to their side. Also, the resultant increase in American casualties would intensify the pressure on President Obama to withdraw American troops. The second move would be to ease the pressure of the American and NATO operations through participation in peace talks. They believed that time was on their side and they had only to conserve their strength. With American and NATO troops gone, the way would be open for them to begin a new round of hostilities and take over Afghanistan with active help from Pakistan. The United States, having retreated under tremendous domestic pressure, will be in no position to intervene again and undo the mischief, even if it knows that, very soon, Afghanistan would again become a staging ground for terrorist attacks against itself and its allies.

Things, of course, may be different if one can detach the Taliban from al Qaeda, and the 'hard core' of the Taliban from the rank and file, many of whom, Hillary Clinton said at the end of the London Conference, were tired of war. Here one needs to examine how effective the conference's decisions can be as well as some of the other measures taken by the United States and the Karzai government to win them over permanently. This lends a critical significance to American efforts to reintegrate elements of the Taliban, who had declared that they had abjured violence and shed their links with the extremist organization, into Afghan society. The first question here was: What was the number of people who could and needed to be reintegrated and how much money was required for that. A report in the *New York Times* of 23 May 2010 cited Major General Richard Barrons, a British Army commander in Kabul who had helped oversee the reconciliation effort, as saying that the Afghan government now estimated that there were 40,000 fighters to be brought back into the fold, with the 1,000 at the top, including Mullah Mohammad Omar, as the most important.[35]

The report quoted United States military officials as saying that they did not have a clear idea of how many Taliban had been reintegrated so far, including those who had crossed over during the early years of the war, but that the number was small. Against this, the report cited the Kabul government, which was implementing a programme of giving jobs to defecting Taliban, as claiming that 9,000 insurgents had turned in their weapons during the previous year.[36] A report in the *New York Times* published three days before 22 June 2011, when President Obama announced his troops withdrawal schedule, quoted Major General Phil Jones, the director of the NATO unit monitoring the programme for bringing over Taliban combatants to the Afghan government's side, as putting the number of Taliban enrolled in the programme at 1,700. Two-thirds of them were from the north, where insurgency was much weaker than in the south, and only a handful of them were mid-level commanders.[37] The report stated that the total was only a fraction of the ranks of Taliban insurgents numbering from 20,000 to 40,000, and that many of those who had taken advantage of the programme might not even have been Taliban but just men with weapons. Taliban leaders, most of whom were in Pakistan, were yet to accept reconciliation.[38]

The poor progress of the reintegration programme was unlikely to have been for lack of money. During the publicity fanfare that preceded the London Conference, it became widely known that a $500 million fund would be set up to woo the Taliban. The United States Special Envoy to Afghanistan and Pakistan, Richard Holbrooke, who died on 13 December 2010, said during an interview with MSNBC television on Monday, 25 January 2010, 'We are going to go to London to affirm our international support for it.' He added, 'Money will be forthcoming for it. I can't say how much. The Japanese are going to take the lead.' He further stated that the initiative would fill a gap in dealing with the Taliban because 'there's no good programme to invite them back into the fold'.[39]

According to a report in the *Dawn* of 27 January 2010, which quoted Holbrooke, the United States was offering $100 million to set up the fund. The report further quoted the German Chancellor, Angela Merkel, as telling journalists in Berlin that her government would contribute $14 million a year for five years to the proposed fund. 'This is an international accord to set up a fund to allow reintegration in cooperation with the Afghan government,' she said.

The *Dawn* report further stated that the plan was to be presented at the London Conference to muster money and support for an Afghan war strategy. Aimed at integrating into the main stream those Taliban who were not a part of the al Qaeda network, it was a response to Afghan President Hamid Karzai's call for help to get the insurgents to stop fighting his government. At the conference itself, attended by 70 countries, President Karzai, said, 'We must reach out to all of our countrymen, especially our disenchanted brothers.' He added that in the coming weeks he would invite Taliban leaders to a tribal assembly and try to persuade them to lay down arms.[40]

Much would, of course, depend on how much money actually comes in. The West's record in honouring development aid commitments to Afghanistan has not been impressive. There, however, will be problems even if the funds arrive. Insurgency conditions hinder the implementation of development projects. Besides, there have been logistical problems impeding the rehabilitation of Taliban fighters laying down arms. Each Afghan province had to have a peace and reconciliation committee to serve as intermediary between active Taliban commanders and the government. Special bank accounts had to be opened to keep track of the money sent to provincial governors to run the programme. There were problems of confirming the identities of those announcing a desire to switch.[41] All this caused delay. Understandably, American military officers have described the progress of reintegration as 'sporadic, at best an interim effort ahead of a more formal process that they hoped the Afghan government would adopt at a political summit meeting in Kabul in the coming weeks'.[42]

The Kabul Conference came and went. Efforts to make peace with the Taliban and reintegrate Taliban fighters continue. Two questions arise here. What are the chances of weaning away a sufficiently large number of foot soldiers that would significantly weaken the Taliban? Many, of course, joined the Taliban because the latter ruled almost the whole of Afghanistan from 1997 to 2001 and some parts of the country after 1994 when they were formed. An example is the case of 23-year-old Juma Khan who was arrested following the discovery of opium, a bomb triggering device and ammunition from his yard. Released after senior members of his family, including his father, and local elders vouched in writing that he will never again support the Taliban or fight for it, he reportedly said through a military interpreter, that he joined the Taliban because 'everybody was like with the Taliban, so it's like the force of the Taliban, I was under pressure'. Captain Scott A. Cuomo, the 32-year-old United States Marines commander who arrested and later released him, understood what drove him into the ranks of the Taliban. He said after Juma Khan's release, 'I can understand why they're Taliban.' He added, 'Well of course they are [Taliban], what do you want them to do? I want to do anything, I had to be part of the Taliban, man.'[43]

The question arises: What would prevent the returnees from re-joining the Taliban? In the case of Juma Khan, the Marines believed that the elders who vouched for him would keep him in check. Also, they would meet him regularly and pump him for information about his friends and expect that he will be employed in a canal clean-up project. According to Captain Cuomo an overture had to be made at the point when they came to believe that the cause they had been fighting for was not a worthy one and the Americans were there to bring stability.[44]

NOT MUCH CHANCE

Frankly, the chances of success through persuasion were bleak from the beginning. The most important reason for this was the fact that the Taliban constituted a mass movement. It is very difficult to engineer defections from mass movements because even those of their members and followers, who may be less motivated, are likely to be deterred from leaving by the fear of reprisals by leaders and hard-core follow-ers. This holds true particularly in the midst of a conflict in which defeat may mean a fatal blow to the organization. Since most mass movements are headed by leaders who maintain tight control and sur-veillance over their flock—particularly if they are violent and involve clandestine organizations—attempts to defect or organize defections are generally found out and foiled. Significantly, Brigadier Mohammad Yousaf, who, as the head of the ISI's Afghan Bureau, played a critical role in the Soviet defeat, once chuckled morbidly and told Steve Coll with reference to Gulbuddin Hekmatyar, 'Once you join his party, it was difficult to leave.'[45]

This does not mean that people who belong to a mass movement do not defect. But they generally defect from one mass movement to another. Eric Hoffer points out:

> Where mass movements are in violent competition with each other, there are not infrequent instances of converts—even the most zealous—shifting their allegiance from one to the other. A Paul turning into a Saul is neither a rarity nor a miracle. In our day, each proselytising mass movement seems to regard the zealous adherents of its antagonist as its own potential converts. Hitler looked at German communists as potential National-al Socialists ... On the other hand, Karl Radek[46] looked on Nazi Brown Shirts (SA) as a reserve for future Communist recruits.[47]

To understand why people switch from one mass movement to another, one must recognize that the most important element in a mass movement's appeal and ability to hold on to its following is the refuge and feeling of security it offers to people to whom life is barren and meaningless. As Hoffer points out, it does this 'by enfolding and absorbing them into a closely knit and exultant corporate whole'.[48] Hoffer further points out that 'of all the cults and philosophies which competed in the Graeco-Roman world, Christianity alone developed from its inception a compact organisation'. None of its rivals possessed a compact and coherent structure like the church's and gave to its adherents quite the same feeling of joining a close-knit community. The Bolshevik movement 'outdistanced all other Marxist movements in the race for power because of its tight collective organisation'.[49] The National Socialist movement also won out over all other folkish movements which were active in the Germany of the 1920s because Hitler recognized early that a rising mass movement could 'never go too far in advocating and promoting collective cohesion' and that the chief passion of the frustrated was 'to belong' and there could not be 'too much of cementing and binding to satisfy this passion'.[50]

Hoffer points out that the 'problem of stopping a mass movement' is often that of finding a substitute. A social movement can be halted by promoting a religious or nationalist movement.[51] The strategy of promoting one mass movement to destroy another or bring down a regime, however, can have the most damaging and unintended consequences. Thus the building up of Nazis to contain the spread of Communism led to the holocaust, World War II and the establishment of communist States over most of Eastern Europe. In Afghanistan itself, the consequences of the Americans and Saudi Arabians promoting fundamentalist mujahideen formations to fight the Soviet Union in the 1980s, are now visiting the promoters. The United States is also paying for its indulgence of Pakistan's promotion of the Taliban in 1994 to establish its hegemony over Afghanistan.

The issue, however, is largely of academic interest at the time of writing. There is now no mass movement in Afghanistan that is opposed to the Taliban and al Qaeda, has an organization that is tighter and is armed with a doctrine that claims to embody the absolute truth encompassing all aspects of existence in the universe and providing answers to all dilemmas and contingencies that may confront an individual. This makes surrender by a significant section of the Taliban foot soldiers virtually impossible. The $500 million fund to woo the Taliban will not help. Imtiaz Gul, the author of *The Al Qaeda Connection: The Taliban and Terror in Tribal Areas* and *The Most Dangerous Place—Pakistan's Lawless Frontier*, writes in an article, 'Hoping to Separate Afghan Taliban and Qaida':

> ... as far as the Mulla Omar-led Afghan Taliban are concerned, one has to bear in mind that even two earlier 'disarmament and reintegration' campaigns made no dent in the insurgency. The reason: unlike the British minister's estimate,[52] the majority of Taliban fighters, a rag-tag army of a few thousand, take up arms out of commitment and not for economic considerations. The 'reintegration trust' therefore may not work the way its advocates would wish it to.[53]

Nor will the prospect of defeat make many of them change sides. To most of those who constitute the rank and file of the Taliban and al Qaeda, and particularly those who choose to become suicide bombers, suicide or death in a jihad means a direct passage to heaven where rewards, much richer than any the US or the NATO forces or any temporal government can offer, await them. Why should they grab peanuts in this world when riches await them in the next? Besides, they have seen many ups and downs during the course of the jihad against the Soviet Union, the war against Najibullah that followed Soviet withdrawal in 1989 and the civil war among mujahideen that ensued after the fall of Kabul and Najibullah's execution on 27 September 1996. They have seen the Taliban, who ruled over almost the whole of Afghanistan, being ousted by the post-9/11 US-led offensive, and then stage a comeback. One needs hardly be surprised if all this makes them believe that setbacks are temporary and they will eventually emerge victorious.

Significantly, an US Delta Force troop commander and senior ranking military officer in the battle of Tora Bora, whose orders were to kill or capture Osama bin Laden, wrote under the pen name of Dalton Fury in *Kill Bin Laden: A Delta Force Commander's Account of the Hunt for the World's Most Wanted Man*, 'The CIA bought loyalty out of duffel bags filled with American cash only to learn later that money does not buy everything in Afghanistan. Some of this might have been funny had it not been so serious.'[54] People who have fought the Taliban and al Qaeda on the ground ought to know a bit more about them than theorists in Washington DC or London.

PAKISTAN'S AXE

Besides, there remains the question of Pakistan's role. As it will be seen in detail later, the Pakistani military establishment considers the Taliban, particularly the Afghan segment of it led by Mullah Omar, and the Haqqani network, as its principal assets for establishing its hegemony over Afghanistan after an American withdrawal under the cover of a face-saving peace agreement. Similarly, it considers terrorist organizations like the Lashkar-e-Toiba (LeT), Jaish-e-Mohammad (JeM) and Hizb-ul Mujahideen as its strike formations in its unconventional war through cross-border terrorism to weaken and dismember India. It will not be willing to see any of these dispersed or destroyed until both objectives are met.

Pakistani officials had been resentful about the negotiations conducted by the Karzai regime and the Americans with sections of the Taliban because they felt these had been held behind their back. They were reportedly trying desperately to wedge themselves in. Most significant in this context was the arrest in January 2010 of Mullah Abdul Ghani Baradar, who held the second position in the Taliban hierarchy, next only to Mullah Mohammad Omar. He was also a close associate of Osama bin Laden before 9/11 occurred.[55] His capture was followed by the arrests of two Taliban 'shadow governors' elsewhere in Pakistan.[56]

The New York Times reported on 16 February 2010 that a senior Pakistani intelligence officer, interviewed three weeks before Mullah Baradar's arrest, as saying, 'We are after Mullah Baradar.' Then, stating that the American action of excluding Pakistan from talks with the Afghan Taliban was making things 'difficult,' he had added, 'You cannot say that we are important allies and then you are negotiating with people whom we are hunting and you don't include us.'[57]

According to the report, Mullah Baradar was one of the main conciliators within the Talban who were fiercely divided on the issue of peace and the only Taliban leader for peace negotiations. Pakistanis suspected that the Americans were talking to him, keeping them out of the loop. An American official in Washington DC, who had been briefed on the arrest, denied both that the Americans had been negotiating with Baradar and that Pakistani intelligence had engineered the arrest to ensure a role in the negotiations. An American intelligence officer in Europe, speaking on the condition of anonymity, however, admitted that 'our people had been in touch with people around him [Baradar] and were negotiating with him'.[58]

The New York Times report quoted officials in Pakistan and Afghanistan as saying that the arrest was potentially a strategic coup for Pakistan.

It added that by arresting him, Pakistan had 'removed a key Taliban commander, enhanced cooperation with the United States and ensured a place for itself when political parties explored a negotiated settlement of the Afghan war'.[59] The report further pointed out that the arrest followed 'weeks of signals by Pakistan's military chief, General Kayani—to NATO officials, Western journalists and military analysts—that Pakistan wanted to be included in any attempts to mediate with the Taliban'.

Understandably, the arrest led to much speculation, allegations, airing of grievances and acrimony. As seen earlier, Kai Eide, former special representative in Afghanistan for the United Nations Secretary General, Kofi Annan, told the BBC in an interview, broadcast on 19 March 2010, that, for the past year, the United Nations had been quietly involved in discussions with the Taliban in Dubai. He said those talks were upended by the arrests of senior Taliban leaders, including Mullah Baradar. The former Taliban ambassador to Pakistan, Mullah Abdul Salam Zaeef, who has led efforts on behalf of President Karzai to persuade the Taliban to negotiate an end to the war, has also attacked Pakistan's action as destroying all chances of reconciliation with the rest of the Taliban leadership.

Speculation is all the more intense because even the circumstances of Mullah Baradar's arrest are wrapped in controversy. According to one report, it was purely accidental. American intelligence agencies, which had intercepted communications saying that militants with possible links with the second-ranking Taliban leader were meeting in a house outside Karachi, had tipped off Pakistani counterterrorist officers. The latter conducted a raid and arrested several men without resistance. It was only after a careful process of identification that Pakistani and American officials realized that they had captured Mullah Baradar himself. According to the report, the arrest was not necessarily a result of Pakistan's new determination to go aggressively after the Taliban or a bid to improve its strategic position in the region. It quoted an American official as saying that it was a lucky accident.[60]

Certain aspects of the arrest, however, are significant. It came at a delicate time, when the Taliban were in a fierce internal debate about whether to negotiate for peace or continue fighting as the United States prepared to send 30,000 more troops to Afghanistan in 2010. Mullah Baradar was among the main Taliban leaders in favour of conciliation.[61] Besides, the arrest of Mullah Abdul Kabir in Nowshera in Pakistan's North-West Frontier Province (NWFP) in February 2010 was the result of a strictly Pakistani operation, and was kept secret from the Americans. His arrest, that of Mullah Mohammed Yunis, Taliban's shadow governor for Zabul Province in Afghanistan, and of several others including two shadow governors, seemed to mark a shift in Pakistan's behaviour. The *New York Times* report, which indicated this, quoted Bruce Riedel as stating with reference to the arrests, 'This indicates Baradar was not a one off or an accident but a turning point in Pakistan's policy toward the Taliban.' He then added, 'We still need to see how far it goes, but for Obama and NATO this is the best possible news. If the safe haven is closing then the Taliban are in trouble.'[62]

The shape of things to come is still unclear, particularly since one does not quite know how the ties between the Karzai regime and the Pakistanis will end up. The former's talks with the representatives of the Taliban and a member of the Haqqani family, which were reportedly held in Afghanistan in October 2010, could certainly not have been possible without Pakistan's cooperation. According to a report in the *New York Times* of 24 June 2010, Washington DC had watched with some nervousness as General Kayani and Lieutenant General Ahmad Shuja Pasha, shuttled between Islamabad and Kabul, telling President Karzai that they agreed with his assessment that the United States could not win in Afghanistan, and that a post-war Afghanistan should incorporate the Haqqani network, a long-time Pakistani asset. The report added that the ISI chief, Lieutenant General Shuja Pasha's dash to Kabul on the eve of Karzai's visit to Washington DC in May 2010 was seen as a revealing and significant indication of the growing proximity between the two countries.[63]

The reportedly increasing closeness between Kabul and Islamabad was principally due to President Karzai's belief that the Americans could not win the war in Afghanistan. A senior analyst of the ISI told the *New York Times* in June 2010 that the Taliban were gaining in strength and, despite the impending arrival of new troops, the situation would become more dangerous for the Americans resulting in an erosion of Washington DC's will to fight. 'That is the reason why Karzai is trying to negotiate now,' he added.[64] The increasing sourness characterizing Karzai's relations with the Americans was also a major factor.

The *New York Times* report cited above further quoted Pakistani and American officials as saying that Pakistan was exploiting the United States' troubled military campaign in Afghanistan to drive home a political settlement that would give it important influence in Afghanistan at Washington DC's cost. According to it, the thaw between Kabul and Islamabad, though encouraged by Washington DC, heightened the risk that the United States would find itself cut out of what amounted to a separate peace between the Afghans and Pakistanis that did 'not necessarily guarantee Washington's prime objective in the war: denying Al Qaeda a haven'.[65] It also said that the thaw provided another indication of how Pakistan, ostensibly an American ally, had worked 'many opposing sides in the war to safeguard its ultimate interest in having an Afghanistan that was pliable and free of the influence of its main strategic obsession, its more powerful neighbour, India'.

The report quotes Rifaat Hussain, a professor of international relations at Islamabad University, and a confidante of top generals, as saying that the making of the Haqqanis a part of the solution in Afghanistan was now Pakistan's basic policy. 'The establishment,' Hussain stated, 'thinks that without getting the Haqqanis on board, efforts to stabilize the situation in Afghanistan will be doomed.... Haqqani has a large fighting force, and by co-opting him into a power-sharing arrangement a lot of bloodshed can be avoided.' General Kayani's recent trips to Kabul, according to him, were aimed at making this happen.

General Kayani, the report further says, had offered to broker a deal with the Afghan Taliban leader, Mullah Mohammad Omar, and had sent envoys to Kabul from Hekmatyar in March with a 15-point peace plan—a development discussed earlier in this chapter. Now the question arises: What are the chances of the Karzai regime agreeing to make the Haqqanis and the Afghan Taliban led by Mullah Omar a part of a future Afghan dispensation? Pakistan, the report pointed out, has already won what it saw as an important concession from Kabul, the resignations in June 2010 of the Afghan intelligence chief, Amrullah Saleh, and the Interior Minister, Hanif Atmar. The two officials, favoured by Washington DC, were viewed by Pakistan as major obstacles to its vision of hard-core Taliban fighters being part of an Afghanistan settlement, though the circumstances of their resignations did not suggest any connection with Pakistan.

KARZAI AND THE TALIBAN: SUPPORT AND ALIENATION

The question naturally arises whether this indicated the Karzai regime's willingness to include Mullah Omar and the Haqqanis in a postpeace accord dispensation. Karzai was one of the early promoters of the Taliban. Steve Coll gives an engrossing account of this phase as well as of his subsequent falling out with the Taliban in *Ghost Wars: The Secret History of the CIA, Afghanistan and Bin Laden from the Soviet Invasion to September 10, 2001*. In 1994, Karzai had been held captive and beaten up by men of Fahim Khan, then Ahmed Shah Massoud's security chief, who had received a report that he had been working for Pakistani intelligence. Escaping in the confusion created by a rocket explosion near where he was being interrogated, he joined his father in Quetta in 1994 Spring and decided to support the Taliban as that would be one way of challenging the Kabul regime, which had beaten him and forced him into exile.[66] Described by Coll as 'not especially wealthy by Western standards' he gave the Taliban $50,000 of his own funds and a huge cache of weapons he had hidden away besides introducing them to prominent Pashtun tribal leaders as they began to organize themselves around Kandahar.[67]

Gradually, however, he became profoundly alienated from the Taliban. An important factor was clearly the murder of the wife and children of Abdul Haq, a colourful and brave fighter against Soviet forces during the days of the jihad who had become a bitter opponent of the ISI and the Taliban, on 12 January 1999.[68] It presaged a new opposition to Mullah Omar by the Pashtuns, the tribe to which Karzai's family belongs. According to Coll, Haq's aides, who investigated the crime, concluded that it had been organized with help from Pakistani intelligence. Peter Tomsen, United States State Department's Special Envoy to the mujahideen between 1989 and 1992, later reported that the killers had been trained at the Taliban's intelligence school supported by bin Laden.[69]

As the situation in Afghanistan changed, the Karzais began to consider opposition to the Taliban. At Hamid Karzai's wedding in Quetta in April 1999, his father, Abdul Ahad Karzai, the family patriarch and a former Afghan Senator, called his sons and spoke of resistance to the Taliban and overtures to Ahmed Shah Massoud.[70] Hamid Karzai worked with his father from his family compound in Quetta, organizing meetings among royalist Pashtuns and tribal elders and promoting a loya jirga to discuss Afghan politics. His father pushed for the return of former King Zahir Shah from his exile in Rome. Hamid Karzai invited Mullah Omar to these meetings but warned that the Taliban had to change their ways and get rid of the foreigners—clearly referring to bin Laden and al Qaeda—who had been ruining Afghanistan through violence and murder. The answer was his father's assassination in the streets of Quetta on 15 July 1999. Hamid Karzai, who inherited his father's political mantle, sought to avenge his death.[71]

Given the background of his father's killing, it is highly unlikely that President Karzai would reach out to Mullah Omar and his associates and followers unless his arm is severely twisted or his survival requires it. This would become clear on looking at his first attempt to reach out to the Taliban, which began after his victory in the first presidential election in 2004. His first tangible step in this direction was the setting up in May 2005 of the Takhim-e-Solh (Strengthening Peace), a mechanism for providing followers of the Taliban not guilty of criminal activity a way to return to society. It failed because reintegration did not happen in many cases, the promised security remained elusive, and the promised payments were not made. Most of the prodigals soon returned to the Taliban, which was the more lucrative thing to do.[72]

Significantly, Karzai's initiative came after the invasion of Iraq by the United States and its allies in March 2003, and the diversion to

Iraq of resources that should have gone to fighting the Taliban, had enabled the latter to make their presence felt in many parts of Afghanistan. One needs also to recall here Ahmed Rashid's observation that the invasion of Iraq 'was critical to convincing Musharraf that the United States was not serious about stabilising the region' and that it was 'safer for Pakistan to preserve its own national interest by clandestinely giving the Taliban refuge.'[73] One, therefore, needs hardly be surprised by the *New York Times* report of 24 June 2010 referred to earlier. It quoted a senior analyst of the ISI as saying that Karzai was trying to negotiate because the situation in Afghanistan would become increasingly dangerous for Americans and that this would undermine their will to fight. It is hardly surprising that he would like to keep all options open in such a situation.

It is, however, too early to say that a reconciliation is on the cards. The October 2010 talks between President Karzai and representatives of the Taliban were very preliminary.[74] NATO and Obama administration officials could not tell how serious the Taliban were about reaching an accord. They could not even spot an imposter in time. Meanwhile, the question remains whether the Americans will accept a government of Afghanistan that includes the Haqqanis, Mullah Mohammad Omar and Gulbuddin Hekmatyar.

The report in the *New York Times* of 24 June 2010 stated that, according to Pakistani intelligence officers, the Haqqanis were ready to break with al Qaeda. They could tell the latter to move elsewhere because they had given nine years of protection after 9/11.[75] The chances of their actually doing so, however, are rather slim. The report quotes an official as acknowledging that the Haqqanis and al Qaeda had provided each other with fighters, money and other resources over a long period and were 'too thick' with each other for a separation to happen.

PROBLEMS OF INCORPORATION

This raises some basic questions for Americans. Some officials in the Obama administration, who have not ruled out incorporating the

Haqqani network in an Afghan settlement, also say that President Obama's policy for Afghanistan and Pakistan requires the network's separation from al Qaeda. They are also sceptical about this happening and rightly so. Jalaluddin Haqqani is completely bedridden and incapable of giving directions to his militia. His son Sirajuddin cannot be detached from al Qaeda for two reasons. First, as Syed Saleem Shahzad has pointed out, the Haqqani militia comprises mainly of Punjabi combatants from the ranks of Pakistani jihadi organizations like Harkat-ul Mujahideen (HuM) and Harkat-ul-Jihad-al-Islami (HUJI). They had a tough time in Pakistan after 9/11 and particularly after the attempts on President Musharraf's life in 2003. Hundreds were rounded up and held without trial for months.[76] Shahzad further pointed out that thousands of Punjabi jihadis fled to North Waziristan from 2005 to 2007 and added, 'Although most of them were connected to the Haqqani network, Al Qaeda was the source of their inspiration even before their arrival in North Waziristan.'[77]

Their experience had engendered in these Punjabi jihadis' intense hatred of the Pakistani army, civilian establishment and the United States which was supposed to be manipulating both. Much of this hatred had rubbed off on Sirajuddin through close association. Similarly, interaction with the Arabs had influenced him profoundly, albeit gradually and, perhaps, imperceptibly even to himself. On its part, al Qaeda seized the opportunity of Jalaluddin's incapacitation to develop strategic ties with Sirajuddin. Shahzad points out that the latter's attack on NATO's Bagram base near Kabul in February 2007 was, for instance, recognized as having been guided by the Arab Islamist ideologue, Abu Laith al-Libi, who made all his expertise available for carrying it out. Subsequently, al Qaeda coordinated several other attacks carried out by the Haqqani network in Ghazni, Khost and Kabul.[78]

Pakistani army's operations in North Waziristan and the Central Intelligence Agency's (CIA) drone attacks on the Haqqani home in Dand-e-Darpa Khail (also spelt Danda-e-Darpa Khel) in 2008 and 2009, which killed several of his family members, destroyed the network's ties with the Pakistani army, which were strong when Jalaluddin was in charge. The Pakistani army was considered responsible for providing intelligence for the strikes.[79] The younger Haqqani's growing proximity to al Qaeda had led the NATO command in Kabul to view him as a possible rival to Mullah Omar. There was doubtless tension between the two. The Afghan Taliban, headed by Mullah Omar, considered fighting the foreign forces in Afghanistan as their first priority and did not want to fight the Pakistani army. Al Qaeda considered fighting the Pakistani army as the first priority. The Afghan Taliban were particularly taken aback when the leader of the Islamic Movement of Uzbekistan, Tahir Yaldochiv, issued a fatwa prioritizing the fight against the Pakistani army over the war in Afghanistan. Uzbeks and Chechens were among the foreign fighters gathered in North and South Waziristan who were affiliated to al Qaeda.

Shahzad, who has given a detailed account of these developments,[80] has said that the Pakistani army, which sought to exploit these differences, gave Mullah Nazir, the Taliban commander in Wana in South Waziristan, and the only important Taliban commander who had maintained his distance from al Qaeda, money and arms to eliminate the Uzbeks. This led to clashes in early 2007 in which hundreds of Uzbeks were massacred. The rest fled and sought refuge with Baitullah Mehsud. This had implications in terms of tribal rivalry which worried al Qaeda leaders. Mullah Nazir was a Wazir, a tribe which were traditionally rivals of Mehsuds, and he was a rival of Baitullah Mehsud as a militia commander. Al Qaeda leaders did not want tribal, personal and other rivalries to create divisions among those operating under its ideological banner. Their attempts to forestall such an eventuality led to the formation in early 2008 of the Tehrik-e-Taliban Pakistan (TTP) with Baitullah Mehsud as its chief and Hafiz Gul Bahadur and Moulvi Faqir as his lieutenants. Mullah Omar was proclaimed its patron-in-chief. It was a purely ornamental position and the TTP was used to draw the Afghan Taliban out of the ambit of his influence.[81]

Al Qaeda helped Baitullah to increase his strength and, by the end of 2008, the TTP had established its presence in seven of Pakistan's tribal agencies and the bordering regions of Afghanistan, and its influence ran all the way down to Balochistan province in southern Pakistan. From 2008 onward the TTP paid no heed to Mullah Omar's repeated urgings to shun violence against Pakistan's security establishment.[82] Al Qaeda, on the other hand, now had an instrument for realizing its strategic objectives in Pakistan, which were two. The first was to foil the dialogue process through which the United States, its allies and the Karzai regime sought to detach the 'good Taliban' or the Taliban foot soldiers from al Qaeda. The second was to trigger revolts in Pakistan's cities to tie down the Pakistani army in the country's interior and prevent them from acting against the TTP and al Qaeda in FATA and NWFP. Besides, if the Afghan Taliban and the Pakistani military establishment ever wanted to have a reconciliation with the West, the TTP would oppose them and remind them 'that the jihadi agenda did not end in Afghanistan, but was set to circle the world'. Meanwhile, al Qaeda could use the TTP to remove any obstruction set up by Pakistan's government.[83]

Mullah Omar and the Afghan Taliban did not like the dilution of the focus of jihadi operations through the inclusion of the Pakistani army as a target and giving attacks against it priority over waging the Afghan war. But they were in no position to condemn the TTP as long as it continued to pledge its allegiance to him and send a significant number of combatants to Afghanistan. In 2008, Baitullah alone sent 250 groups to Helmand province.[84] The question arises: If Mullah Omar and the Afghan Taliban are unable to condemn TTP and al Qaeda even when they disapprove of what they are doing, can they be expected to break from both and enter into a peace agreement with the Karzai regime and the United States?

As things stand now, Mullah Omar and the Afghan Taliban can be expected to join peace talks only if al Qaeda, completely routed by the US-led forces, is in no position to oppose, and they too are reduced to a position in which talks offer the only route to survival. Equally, they will participate if the TTP and al Qaeda are agreeable to it. The same goes for their participation in an Afghan peace settlement. The first is out of the question at this juncture. The TTP, the Haqqani network and al Qaeda are nowhere near being completely defeated. Al Qaeda will be agreeable to the Afghan Taliban, Mullah Omar, Hekmatyar or even the Haqqani network, participating in talks or a settlement only as a strategic gambit. That is, if it is convinced that the talks would lead to a settlement which would help it and its allies to take over Afghanistan. It might even agree to the TTP and the Haqqani network formally renouncing their ties with it because nothing prevents them from reneging on their statement.

'WE WILL DEFEAT YOU'

And, what may happen if the United States agrees on an Afghan settlement that includes the Haqqanis and Hekmatyar without the latter jettisoning al Qaeda? Simply put, it would be regarded as a humiliating defeat. This will become clear on recalling an important statement that President Obama made while unfolding his strategy for Afghanistan and Pakistan on 27 March 2009. Spelling out America's role in the region, he had said:

> So I want the American people to understand that we have a clear and focused goal: to disrupt, dismantle and defeat al Qaeda in Pakistan and Afghanistan, and to prevent their return to either country in the future. That's the goal that must be achieved. That is a cause that could not be more just. And to the terrorists who oppose us, my message is the same: We will defeat you.[85]

He categorically stated the reason for setting the goal:

> Al Qaeda and its allies—the terrorists who planned and supported the 9/11 attacks—are in Pakistan and Afghanistan. Multiple intelligence estimates have warned that al Qaeda is actively planning attacks on the United States homeland from its safe haven in Pakistan. And if the Afghan government falls to the Taliban—or allows al Qaeda to go unchallenged—that country will again be a base for terrorists who want to kill as many of our people as they possibly can.[86]

Like any withdrawal from Afghanistan without disrupting, dismantling and defeating al Qaeda, a withdrawal following a settlement which gives the Haqqanis, Hekmatyar's outfits and Mullah Mohammad

Omar's Taliban a role in the government, would also be regarded as a defeat. Their formally renouncing their ties with al Qaeda will not help if they do not do so in reality and al Qaeda's terrorist infrastructure remains intact. People will find out that the pronouncements were made to provide a face-saving exit for the Americans and conclude that it was a matter of time before the Taliban and al Qaeda once again controlled Afghanistan.

Two consequences will follow. First, the development will confirm the Taliban, al Qaeda and their associated and affiliated organizations in their belief in their own invincibility. They will conclude that they had, despite a severe initial setback, defeated the United States and will be able to win the world if they persevere. The likelihood of their drawing such a conclusion would appear very strong on recalling their interpretation of the history of Islam and of the significance of the Russian withdrawal from Afghanistan, completed on 15 February 1989, which had made them feel that they had defeated a super powerer and were invincible. Osama bin Laden wrote in his 'Letter to the American People':

> The Islamic Nation that was able to dismiss and destroy the previous evil Empires like yourself; the nation that rejects your attacks, wishes to remove your evils, and is prepared to fight you. You are well aware that the Islamic Nation, from the very core of its soul, despises your haughtiness and arrogance.
>
> If the Americans refuse to listen to our advice and the goodness, guidance and the righteousness we call them to, then be aware that you will lose this crusade Bush began, just like the other previous crusades in which you were humiliated by the hands of the Mujahideen, fleeing to your home in great silence and disgrace. If the Americans do not respond, their fate will be that of the Soviets who fled from Afghanistan to deal with their military defeat, political breakup, ideological downfall, and economic bankruptcy.[87]

Many more such examples can be cited. Osama bin Laden is dead but al Qaeda persists with its militant ideology and line of relentless opposition to the United States and the West. The next serious threat comes from Ayman al-Zawahiri who has since succeeded Osama bin Laden to al Qaeda's leadership. Zawahiri, who had remained silent for a long time, finally spoke out in a YouTube recording posted on 8 June 2011. In his eulogy for bin Laden entitled 'The Noble Knight Dismounted',[88] he asked Americans not to gloat and vowed to continue 'on his [bin Laden's] path of jihad to expel the invaders from the land of Muslims and to purify it from injustice'.[89] Not surprisingly, Zawahiri issued another threat after the announcement of his succession to bin Laden on 16 June 2011. The statement by al Qaeda, which announced his appointment, also declared that under his leadership, the organization will relentlessly pursue its jihad against the United States and Israel.[90]

One can be told that however strident the rhetoric of leaders like al-Zawahiri, they are rational people and know the limits of their power. This would be a totally unwarranted assumption. The fact is that they are not rational people familiar with the unfolding of world history and the lessons it offers. In *The Bin Ladens: Oil, Money, Terrorism and the Secret Saudi World*, Steve Coll points out that Osama bin Laden's own 'gifts of foresight and political analysis had always been limited....'[91] In this regard, there is a marked difference between the al Qaeda leader and his followers on the one hand and the Vietnamese revolutionaries and their leaders.

In his monumental work, *The Vietnamese War: Revolution and Social Change in the Mekong Delta 1930–1975*, David W. P. Elliott shows how the dislocation and social change caused by the Vietnamese revolution and the efforts of the Viet Minh and the Communists to indoctrinate the peasantry raised the latter's awareness to new heights. At the end of the Vietnamese War in 1975, even the ordinary peasant in Vietnam was better informed about national and international affairs than at its beginning. Citing the developments in Thanh Phu village in My Tho province's Cai Lay district to illustrate the progress made by the Viet Minh's popular education programme implemented between October and December 1945, he mentions the anti-illiteracy drive. Seventy per cent of the inhabitants could read and write at the end of it. This, he said, had a significant impact on the political education of the population. According to Elliott, reading opened up a new world of information that peasants increasingly saw as vital to their survival. 'This', he adds, 'was the beginning of a long process of political education that, in the end, did produce "rational peasants" at every socio-economic level, who were able to acquire and process the information necessary to make decisions about their own interests.'[92]

Elliott further points out that the transformation of the mental world of the peasants brought about by the 1975 revolution constituted far more fundamental a change than its destruction of the old power structure in the rural areas. No longer resigned to their fates or gripped by the feeling that their lot in life had been predetermined, they were now keenly aware of the political world around them, the larger national situation, and even the global forces that shaped their lives. While constant indoctrination was onerous and the framework of Marxist class analysis limited, they did provide rural people with powerful tools for making sense out of the society and the economy they lived in.[93]

Enlightened Peasants, Tall Leaders

Vietnamese revolutionaries also had outstanding leaders, headed by the legendary Ho Chi Minh, who were not only ideologically sound but had a sharp awareness of military tactics and international affairs and a deep understanding of Vietnamese realities. They had an outstanding general in Vo Nguyen Giap. They knew what they could and could not do and when to stop. Besides, Communism had lost much of its shine worldwide by the time the Vietnamese War ended in 1975. The Soviet Union's harsh suppression of the East Berlin bread riots of 1953, Nikita Khrushchev's revelation of Stalin's monstrous crimes at the 20th Congress of the Soviet Communist Party in February 1956, Moscow's gory intervention in Hungary in 1956 and the Poznan riots in Poland in the same year had severely undermined its image; so had its intervention in Czechoslovakia in 1968 and the acrimonious Sino-Soviet rift, marked by harsh polemic and clashes between Soviet and Chinese armies along the Ussuri river border. The Sino-Soviet split precluded a global revolutionary surge by a monolithic communist bloc. The nuclear deterrent froze the Cold War boundaries and both Soviet Union and China became status quoist powers unwilling to go beyond brinkmanship. The chances of Vietnam playing a critical role in a violent global revolutionary surge to spread socialism and communism were, therefore, remote.

The Vietnamese leaders who came to power in 1975 had the intelligence to realize this. Besides, they had problems at home. David Elliott points out that the social base on which the revolution was founded was fundamentally transformed by the end of the war. In fact, he says that the revolution was a victim of its own success. Its land reform began a fundamental transformation of South Vietnam's rural social structure but the prolonged and disruptive war itself became the main engine of social change and took the country in a direction very different from what the Communist Party had originally planned. Subsidized American consumer goods and equipment flooded the market during the war. Dislocation of peasant communities and the depopulation of the countryside led to more sweeping changes in the rural class structure than anything the party could have engineered. An unintended result was the emergence of a rural middle class that included 70 per cent of the rural population in the Mekong Delta that stubbornly resisted collectivization after the war. Elliott points out:

> Eventually, this brought social transformation in South Vietnam to a halt and created a crisis that spread to North Vietnam. It ultimately forced the entire country to abandon collective agriculture and many other features of state socialism and adopt a sweeping programme of market reforms.[94]

It is important here to note that the Vietnamese leaders had the wisdom to recognize the strength of the demand for a course correction and implement it though it meant going against the fundamentals of their ideology. The Taliban and al Qaeda, on the other hand, have displayed nothing even remotely approximating these qualities. They stuck to their barbaric medieval ways despite severe international pressure and sanctions and refused to expel Osama bin Laden from Afghanistan even after al Qaeda's bomb attacks on United States' embassies in Nairobi and Dar es Salaam on 7 August 1998, which led to the retaliatory American missile strikes on al Qaeda's camps in Afghanistan on 20 August. They continued to refuse to hand the al Qaeda chief over to the Americans even after 9/11. Even after their ouster from Afghanistan in the wake of the US-led invasion that followed, they persist with terrorist strikes against Americans and their allies the world over.

Nothing has happened to indicate a change in their mindset or any intention on their part to give up terrorist attacks and their jihad against countries like the United States, Israel, Russia and India. Nor is there any likelihood of their followers recognizing the futility of their efforts and the irrationality and medieval character of the order they seek to establish. This is hardly surprising. Eric Hoffer writes that 'the chief preoccupation of a mass movement is to instil in its followers a facility for united action and self-sacrifice'.[95] He further states:

> The readiness for self-sacrifice is contingent on an imperviousness to the realities of life. He who is free to draw conclusions from his individual experience and observation is not usually hospitable to the idea of martyrdom. For self-sacrifice is an unreasonable act. It cannot be the end product of a process of probing and deliberating. All active mass movements strive, therefore, to interpose a fact-proof screen between the faithful and the realities of the world. They do this by claiming that the ultimate and absolute truth is already embodied in their doctrine and that there is no truth nor certitude outside it. The facts on which the true believer bases his conclusions must not be derived from his experience and observation but from holy writ.[96]

Hoffer adds that the effectiveness of a doctrine does not come from the profundity, sublimity and truth it embodies, but from how thoroughly it insulates the individual from his self and the world.'[97] He continues:

> To be in possession of an absolute truth is to have a net of familiarity spread over the whole of eternity. There are no

surprises and no unknowns. All questions have already been answered, all decisions made, all eventualities foreseen. The true believer is without wonder or hesitation.... The true doctrine is the master key to all the world's problems. With it the world can be taken apart and put together.[98]

THE TROUBLE WITH TRUE BELIEVERS

Leaders of the Taliban, al Qaeda and organizations like the Haqqani network and the Hizb-e-Islami, to say nothing of their followers, are true believers. Apart from the limited and essentially instrumental nature of their mental world, their failure to distinguish the possible from the impossible and the limits of their own capacity is a result of their judgement being clouded by not only their fanaticism but also their intense hatred for the United States and Israel, indeed the whole of the West. The virulence of his hatred is clear from Osama bin Laden's 'Letter to the American People' in which he tells Americans, 'It is saddening to tell you that you are the worst civilisation witnessed by the history of mankind.'

As seen before, he levels in the same document a series of charges against the United States including that of choosing to invent its own laws as it chooses and desires instead of being ruled 'by the Shariah of Allah in its Constitution and laws'. He also presented Americans with a list of demands such as stopping their support to Israel, 'Indians in Kashmir, Russia against the Chechens and also to cease supporting the Manila Government against the Muslims in Southern Philippines.' He asked them to get out of Arab lands, stop supporting corrupt leaders of these and discontinue their support to Israel. He wrote, 'The Nation of Monotheism, that puts complete trust on Allah and fears none other than him,' is

> addressed by its Quran by the words, 'Do you fear them? Allah has more right that you should fear Him if you are believers. Fight against them so that Allah will punish them by your hands and disgrace them and give you victory over them and heal the

breasts of believing people. And remove the anger of their [be-
lievers'] hearts.'

'The nation of Monotheism'[99] is, therefore, divinely instructed
to fight the United States and the West. This has, as in the case of all
religion-inspired terrorism, also an impact at the individual level.
Ekaterina Stepanova writes that 'in contrast to many secular militant
organisations or groups whose ideology is not dominated by [a] religious imperative, religious terrorists perceive their attacks as "acts of
faith". Accordingly, self-sacrifice attacks are carried out as acts of religious martyrdom.'[100] Stepanova adds that the 'upgradation of a terrorist
event to a "sacred act" effectively removes some of the basic constraints
on incurring mass civilian casualties and facilitates the perpetration of
deadlier, larger attacks addressed to a much broader audience'.[101]

It also makes them court death, and not just immune from the
fear of it. For a religious terrorist, life finds its fulfilment in martyrdom. He or she lives for it. Organizations like al Qaeda, Taliban,
LeT and Lashkar-e-Israr derive the rationale for their existence from
jihad. Besides, without the latter, there will be the serious problem of
finding occupation for thousands of militant members of their cadre
programmed to kill or suicide. So the jihad will continue even after
al Qaeda and Taliban have established their sway over Afghanistan. As
noted earlier, the targets will be Israel, the United States and the West,
India, Russia and even China—in fact, all countries that do not subscribe to the Taliban and al Qaeda's distorted view of Islam and do not
impose sharia law.

One will doubtless be told that Pakistan, which will play a major
role in a settlement that gives the Haqqanis, Mullah Mohammad Omar
and the followers of Hekmatyar places in an Afghan government, will
prevent such a thing from happening. Apart from the question of its
alliance with the United States, it would be guided by the compulsions
of its own survival which is threatened not only by the TTP but other
internal fundamentalist groups. The assertion merits a laugh and no
more. Pakistan's record both in combating terrorist groups and keeping promises is dismal.

History shows it would be unwise of the United States to expect Pakistan to deliver on its promises. It was uneasy about Pakistan's support to Hekmatyar and the consequences of the Taliban's dispensation established in Afghanistan. Yet, as Coll points out in *Ghost Wars*, the CIA was content to let the ISI take the lead in respect of Afghan politics even if it installed Hekmatyar in Kabul. Officers of its Near East Division felt that Pakistan's hegemony over Afghanistan, whether or not achieved through the ideology of political Islam, did not pose any significant threat to American interests. Coll adds, 'even if they had qualms about Hekmatyer—and most of them did—they did not see what they could do to block the ISI's plans. So they moved to help ISI succeed.'[102]

In the event, Pakistan did not—rather, could not—install Hekmatyar in power in Afghanistan. It installed the Taliban. What did the United States do? Coll states that on 28 September 1996, the day after Kabul fell to the Taliban, the State Department sent out a cable to embassies abroad saying that it wanted to engage the 'new Taliban interim' government at an early stage. In official meetings with the Taliban, American diplomats should strive to demonstrate their country's 'willingness to deal with them as the new authorities in Kabul and seek information about their plans, programmes, and policies and express the United States' government's key concerns—stability, human rights, narcotics and terrorism'. Bin Laden, according to Coll, 'ranked last on the cable's more detailed list of issues for discussion'.[103]

One knows the results of that. The question is: Can the United States win the Afghan war if peace with the Taliban is not possible. The question has become particularly relevant following the Taliban's announcement on 15 March 2012 that they were breaking off the negotiations with the Americans and accused the latter's representative of changing the preconditions for the talks.[104]

NOTES

1. Ahmed Rashid, *Descent into Chaos: How the War against Islamic Extremism Is Being Lost in Pakistan, Afghanistan and Central Asia* (London, 2008), pp. 72–73.

2. Ray Rivera and Ginger Thompson, 'U.S. Ambassador Responds to Karzai's Criticism', *New York Times*, 19 June 2011, online edition, http://www.nytimes.com/2011/06/20/world/asia/20afghanistan.html?nl=todaysheadlines&emc=tha22.

3. Rod Nordland, 'Lashing Out, Karzai Says U.S. Is Talking to the Taliban', *New York Times*, 18 June 2011, online edition, http://www.nytimes.com/2011/06/19/world/asia/19afghanistan.html?pagewanted=2&nl=todaysheadlines&emc=ha22.

4. Ibid.

5. Press Trust of India, 'US Establishes Contact with Mullah Omar', *Times of India*, Delhi, 15 June 2011.

6. Alissa J. Rubin and David E. Sanger, 'Bin Laden's Death and the New Unknown in Afghanistan', *New York Times*, 7 May 2011, online edition, http://www.nytimes.com/2011/05/08/world/asia/08taliban.html?pagewanted=2&_r=1&nl=todaysheadlines&emc=tha22.

7. Barack Obama, *Remarks by the President on a New Strategy for Afghanistan and Pakistan*, Office of the Press Secretary, Washington DC, http://www.whitehouse.gov/thepressoffice/remarks-by-the-president-on-a-new-strategy-for-Afghanistan-and-Pakistan.

8. Hillary Rodham Clinton, 'Remarks at the International Conference on Afghanistan', U.S. Department of State, London, 28 January 2010, http://www.state.gov/secretary/rm/2010/01/136159.htm.

9. Ibid.

10. Communiqué, 'Afghan Leadership, Regional Cooperation, International Partnership', HM Government, London, 28 January 2010, http://afghanistan.hmg.gov.uk/en/conference/communique/.

11. Clinton, 'Remarks at the International Conference on Afghanistan'.

12. Communiqué, 'Afghan Leadership, Regional Cooperation, International Partnership'.

13. Ibid.

14. Atul Aneja, 'Karzai Escapes Attempt on life', *Hindu*, 3 June 2010, online edition, http://www.hindu.com/2010/06/03/stories/2010060364901700.htm.

15. Kathy Gannon, 'Taliban Hold Secret Talks with Afghan president', The Associated Press, MSNBC website, 31 October 2010, http://www.msnbc.msn.com/id/39936327/ns/world_news-south_and_central_asia.

16. Helene Cooper and Mark Landler, 'White House Weighs Talks with Taliban after Afghan Successes', *New York Times*, 12 March 2010, online edition, http://www.nytimes.com/2010/03/13/world/asia/13prexy.html?th&emc=th.

17. Alissa J. Rubin, 'Taliban Arrests Have Halted Early Talks, Former Envoy Says', *New York Times*, 19 March 2010, online edition, http://www.nytimes.com/2010/03/20/world/asia/20afghan.html.

18. Dexter Filkins, 'U.S. Pullout a Condition in Afghan Peace Talks', *New York Times*, 20 May 2009, online edition, http://www.nytimes.com/2009/05/21/world/asia/21kabul.html.

19. Ibid.

20. Dexter Filkins, 'Karzai Is Said to Doubt West Can Defeat Taliban', *New York Times*, 11 June 2010, online edition, http://www.nytimes.com/2010/06/12/world/asia/12karzai.html?th&emc=th.

21. Dexter Filkins, 'Taliban Elite, Aided by NATO, Join Talks for Afghan Peace', *New York Times*, 19 October 2010, online edition, http://www.nytimes.com/2010/10/20/world/asia/20afghan.html?_r=1&th&emc=th.

22. Kathy Gannon, 'Taliban Hold Secret Talks with Afghan President', *Guardian*, 31 October 2010, online edition, http://www.guardian.co.uk/world/feedarticle/9337587.

23. A militant organization comprising the top leadership of Afghan Taliban, the Quetta Shura has been based in Quetta Balochistan since 2001, when the Taliban were ousted from Afghanistan by an American-supported Northern Alliance of Ahmed Shah Massoud. The Shura is directing the insurgency in Afghanistan.

24. Filkins, 'U.S. Pullout a Condition in Afghan Peace Talks'.

25. Carlotta Gall, 'Insurgent Faction Presents Afghan Peace Plan', *New York Times*, 23 March 2010, online edition, http://www.nytimes.com/2010/03/24/world/asia/24afghan.html?pagewanted=2&th&emc=th.

26. Gannon, 'Taliban Hold Secret Talks with Afghan President'.

27. Ibid.

28. Ibid.

29. Rashid, *Descent Into Chaos*, p. 99.

30. Ibid., p. 268.

31. Steve Coll, *Ghost Wars: The Secret History of the CIA, Afghanistan and Bin Laden, from the Soviet Invasion to September 11, 2001* (United States: Penguin Books, 2004), p. 181.

32. Ibid., p. 165.

33. Dexter Filkins and Carlotta Gall, 'Taliban Leader in Secret Talks Was an Imposter', *New York Times*, 22 November 2010, online edition, http://www.nytimes.com/2010/11/23/world/asia/23kabul.html?pagewanted=all.

34. Ibid.

35. Elisabeth Bumiller, 'U.S. Tries to Reintegrate Taliban Soldiers', *New York Times*, 23 May 2010, online edition, http://www.nytimes.com/2010/05/24/world/asia/24reconcile.html?pagewanted=2&th&emc=th.

36. Ibid.

37. Alissa J. Rubin, 'Few Taliban Leaders Take Afghan Offer to Switch Sides', *New York Times*, 19 June 2011, online edition, http://www.nytimes.com/2011/06/20/world/asia/20afghanistan-taliban.html?pagewanted=2&nl=todaysheadlines&emc=tha2.

38. Ibid.

39. Anwar Iqbal, 'US, Allies Plan $500m Fund to Woo Taliban, *Dawn*, 27 January 2010, online edition, http://archives.dawn.com/archives/44634.

40. Mark Landler and Alissa J. Rubin, 'War Plan for Karzai: Reach Out to Taliban', *New York Times*, 29 January 2010, online edition, http://www.nytimes.com/2010/01/29/world/asia/29diplo.html?th&emc=th.

41. Rubin, 'Few Taliban Leaders Take Afghan Offer to Switch Sides'.

42. Bumiller, 'U.S. Tries to Reintegrate Taliban Soldiers.'

43. Ibid.

44. Ibid.

45. Coll, *Ghost Wars*, p. 119.

46. Active in Germany and Poland as a Socialist leader before World War I, Karl Radek emerged as an international Communist leader after the Russian Revolution.

47. Ibid., p. 17.

48. Ibid., p. 41.

49. Ibid.

50. Ibid., pp. 41–42.

51. Ibid., p. 19.

52. The reference actually is to the then British Prime Minister Gordon Brown.

53. Imtiaz Gul, 'Hoping to Separate the Taliban and the Al Qaeda', *Times of India*, 6 February 2010, online edition, http://timesofindia.indiatimes.com/world/south-asia/Hoping-to-separate-Afghan-Taliban-and-Qaida-/articleshow/5542195.cms.

54. Dalton Fury, *Kill Bin Laden: A Delta Force Commander's Account of the Hunt for the World's Most Wanted Man* (New York: St. Martin's Press, 2008), p. xxvi.

55. Mark Mazzetti and Dexter Filkins, 'Secret Joint Raid Captures Taliban's Top Commander', *New York Times*, 15 February 2010, online edition, http://www.nytimes.com/2010/02/16/world/asia/16intel.html?pagewanted=2&th&emc=th.

56. Scott Shane and Eric Schmitt, 'In Pakistan Raid, Taliban Chief Was an Extra Prize', *New York Times*, 18 February 2010, online edition, http://www.nytimes.com/2010/02/19/world/asia/19intel.html?th&emc=th.

57. Carlotta Gall and Souad Mekhennet, 'Taliban Arrest May be Crucial for Pakistanis', *New York Times*, 16 February 2010, online edition, http://www.nytimes.com/2010/02/17/world/asia/17intel.html?th&emc=th.

58. Ibid.

59. Ibid.

60. Shane and Schmitt, 'In Pakistan Raid, Taliban Chief Was an Extra Prize'.

61. Gall and Mekhennet, 'Taliban Arrest May be Crucial for Pakistanis'.

62. Pir Zubair Shah and Dexter Filkins, 'Pakistani Reports Capture of a Taliban Leader', *New York Times*, 22 February 2010, online edition, http://www.nytimes.com/2010/02/23/world/asia/23islamabad.html.

63. Jane Perlez, Eric Schmitt and Carlotta Gall, 'Pakistan Is Said to Pursue a Foothold in Afghanistan', *New York Times*, 24 June 2010, online edition, http://www.nytimes.com/2010/06/25/world/asia/25islamabad.html?pagewanted=2&th&emc=th.

64. Ibid.

65. Ibid.

66. Coll, *Ghost Wars*, pp. 286–87.

67. Ibid., p. 289.

68. Ibid., p. 445.

69. Ibid.
70. Ibid., pp. 461–62.
71. Ibid., p. 462.
72. Indrani Bagchi, 'Is India's Neighbourhood Set to Get Even More Dangerous?' *Times of India*, Crest, 6 February 2010.
73. Rashid, *Descent into Chaos*, p. xli.
74. Filkins, 'Taliban Elite, Aided by NATO, Join Talks for Afghan Peace'. Also see Perlez, Schmitt and Gall, 'Pakistan Is Said to Pursue a Foothold in Afghanistan'.
75. Perlez, Schmitt and Gall, 'Pakistan Is Said to Pursue a Foothold in Afghanistan'.
76. Syed Saleem Shahzad, *Inside Al Qaeda and the Taliban: Beyond Bin Laden and 9/11* (London: Pluto Press, 2011), p. 105.
77. Ibid., p. 106.
78. Ibid.
79. Ibid., pp. 106–07.
80. Ibid., pp. 54–55.
81. Ibid., p. 55.
82. Ibid., p. 56.
83. Ibid., pp. 62–63.
84. Ibid., pp. 56, 63.
85. The White House, 'Remarks by the President on a New Strategy for Afghanistan and Pakistan', Office of the Press Secretary, Washington DC, 27 March 2009.
86. Ibid.
87. 'Full Text: bin Laden's Letter to America', *Guardian*, the United Kingdom, 24 November 2002, www.guardian.co.uk/world/2002/nov/24/theobserver.
88. Press Trust of India, 'Zawahiri Threatens US, Vows Jihad in bin Laden Eulogy', *Times of India*, New Delhi, 9 June 2011.
89. Reuters, 'In Osama Eulogy, Zawahiri Vows Jihad', *Indian Express*, New Delhi, 9 June 2011.
90. Press Trust of India, 'Zawahiri Takes Over Qaeda, Vows Jihad', *Pioneer*, Delhi, 17 June 2011.
91. Steve Coll, *The Bin Ladens: Oil, Money, Terrorism and the Secret Saudi World* (Penguin, 2009), p. 409.
92. David W. P. Elliott, *The Vietnamese War: Revolution and Social Change in the Mekong Delta 1930–1975* (New York: M.E. Sharpe Inc. Armonk, 2007), p. 51.
93. Ibid., p. 83.
94. Ibid., p. 4.
95. Eric Hoffer, *The True Believer: Thoughts on the Nature of Mass Movements* (New York: Haper Perennial, 1951), pp. 83–84.
96. Ibid., p. 79.
97. Ibid., p. 80.
98. Ibid., p. 82.
99. The 'nation of Monotheism' means Islam in this context.

100. Ekaterina Stepanova, 'Al-Qaeda Inspired Transnational Terrorism: Ideology and Organisational Forms', in *Terrorism: Patterns of Internationalisation*, eds. Jaideep Saikia and Ekaterina Stepanova (New Delhi: SAGE Publications, 2009), p. 192.
101. Ibid.
102. Coll, *Ghost Wars*, p. 174.
103. Ibid., p. 334.
104. Rod Nordland, Elisabeth Bumiller and Matthew Rosenberg, 'Karzai Calls on U.S. to Pull Back as Taliban Cancel Talks', *New York Times*, 15 March 2012, online edition, http://www.nytimes.com/2012/03/16/world/asia/taliban-call-off-talks-as-karzai-urges-faster-us-transition.html?nl=todaysheadlines&emc=edit_th_20120316.

CHAPTER 4

POOR PROGRESS AND ITS CAUSES

T
hose arguing that the United States cannot win the Afghan war cite the examples of the Soviet retreat from Afghanistan and the United States' own defeat in Vietnam. The circumstances of the Soviet Union's defeat in Afghanistan were different in critical aspects from those that confront the US and North Atlantic Treaty Organization (NATO) forces in that country. In *The Bear Trap*, Brigadier Mohammad Yousaf, who co-authored the book with a former British Army officer, Major Mark Adkin, gives a detailed account of how the Afghan Mujahideen defeated what was still then a superpower with the help of the United States, Saudi Arabia and Pakistan. Pakistan's Inter-Services Intelligence (ISI) Directorate was the nodal agency for training the mujahideen formations, providing them with money and arms, drawing up and implementing an integrated strategic and tactical approach, and, often, extending operational leadership.

As head of ISI's Afghan Bureau from 1983 to 1987, Brigadier Yousaf played a key role in the entire process along with the organization's head, Lieutenant General Akhtar Abdul Rahman Khan, who was later made a General following his elevation to the office of Chairman of Pakistan's Joint Chiefs of Staff Committee in 1987. *The Bear Trap* is markedly tilted in favour of the ISI and its favourite mujahideen groups and leaders but provides a whole range of useful analyses and information. Of particular relevance here is its account of the causes of the Soviet defeat, the first one being the essentially defensive nature of its strategy. Soon after joining the ISI, Brigadier Yousaf concluded from a study of the deployment pattern of Soviet troops and Afghan forces allied to them that the Russians were, by and large, 'content to hold a series of military bases or strategic towns, and the routes between them, which indicated a mainly static, defensive posture. They did not seem to want to occupy large tracts of the countryside.'[1]

Yousaf further pointed out that even after being in Afghanistan for four years, the Soviets provided no 'evidence that they wished to escalate the war in terms of numbers'.[2] Their emphasis was on improving their own tactics, rationalizing their own forces, developing the use of air power, bolstering their Afghan allies and introducing more suitable weapons. In short, they sought to increase the quality, and not the number, of their forces.

The strategy, and the tactics employed to implement it, did not work. The reasons will become clear if we look at an operation Yousaf describes in some detail. On 26 November 1983 Soviet forces comprising armoured personnel carriers, tanks and guns drove up the Salang Highway, a critical supply route. Splitting into three columns, they moved into three valleys, Shakadara, Farzia and Istalef, north of Kabul. By nightfall, the columns had positioned themselves astride the highway exits of each valley. On 27 November fighter-bombers from the nearby Bagram airbase screamed up the valleys, targeting the houses and people below, dropping 500 lb bombs, killing indiscriminately, spreading terror, destroying houses and entrapping such mujahideen as might have been there. There were further air attacks, supplemented by firing from helicopter gunships, on mountains and valley floors, on 28 November as the ground forces moved toward Shakadara, Farzia and Istalef villages which had been reduced to rubble. When the Soviet forces arrived, they found in each of these dead and wounded civilians lying around, and a few old men and women and children who had survived by cowering behind rocks.

The mujahideen, who had been watching the open, ponderous movement of Soviet troops, were obviously not there to receive them. Yousaf writes, 'The pretence of attacking and securing ground continued for another week before the entire force pulled back to Kabul.'[3] The whole operation, he added, reminded him of a 'boxer with his punchbag. Just so long as the boxer keeps his fist on the bag after making his punch, an impression is maintained. When he removes his fist to strike again elsewhere the bag resumes its original shape'.[4] This enabled the mujahideen to move across much of Afghanistan which remained without effective Russian presence and, as they became better organized and armed, to increasingly strike at will. If raids of the kind described above served any purpose, it was only to further infuriate the local population and alienate it from the Soviet forces.

CONSTRAINTS, NOT CHOICE

The Soviet strategy, however, perhaps owed more to constraints than choice. The Soviet economy was doing poorly. The burden of the war was crushing at $12 million a day.[5] Afghanistan's economy having been ruined, the Soviets had to finance the Afghan government and army besides the deployment of their own military. They had also to feed Afghan refugees who had flocked to Kabul and other cities because of the Soviets' scorched earth policy aimed at denying the mujahideen any sustenance.

If the state of the Soviet economy tended to preclude a steep increase in the level of troops, the long and difficult supply line did the same. The main lifeline, the Salang Highway, stretched all the way from Termez in South Uzbekistan to Kabul and, then, for another 500 kilometres, to Kandahar. It was not only very long but had to cross the Hindu Kush and was vulnerable to mujahideen attacks almost throughout. More important, as Yousaf points out, it was 'parallel to the Pakistan border. The mujahideen's main base, with all its jumping off points, was within striking distance' of the highway for over 1,000 kilometres.[6]

Another problem was the poor training of the conscripts who accounted for the bulk of the Soviet troops. Yousaf writes that as a professional solider he was puzzled by 'the almost total lack of even basic training given to men who were posted to operational areas in the early days of the war'.[7] Some efforts were made to improve training standards when it became clear to the Soviets that the Afghan Army was 'totally unreliable' and Soviet units had to spearhead major operations. Even this did not obviate the need for continued training. Nor did it greatly improve the quality of troops thanks to the system of conscription for two years with 25 per cent of the force replaced every six months. This meant that every six months the troop formations, which were anyway under-strength, had 25 per cent of its most experienced soldiers replaced by a roughly equal proportion of greenhorns requiring further training. This, Yousaf says, was one of the reasons why 'Soviet units had so small a portion of their men available for active operations away from their bases' and adds that he doubted whether 'more than 10–12,000 Soviet troops of their 85,000 inside Afghanistan could have been committed to active operations at any one time'.[8]

Low morale worsened matters. Unlike as in World War II, the Soviet forces were not defending their country from savage invaders but were invaders themselves, 'detested by most Afghans, allies or enemy'.[9] Conscripts were subjected to the most degrading bullying even by those who were only six months their senior. Their salaries and living conditions were terrible. They had little money. A conscript private without qualification or experience received the equivalent of $5 per month, which was spent mostly on food.[10] On top of all this, life was incredibly boring, with long hours of sentry duty on hill tops, baking in the sun and freezing in the cold. The result was often a search for refuge in drugs and alcohol.[11]

It is hardly surprising that such soldiers would not want to fight. Most Soviet conscripts, compelled to enlist at 18, just wanted to survive and go home. They were loathe to leave the security of their bases or to get down from their armoured vehicles during operations. Besides, they would sell anything, even arms and ammunition, for money—notwithstanding the draconian punishments meted out to those caught. Yousaf writes:

> Their preferred tactics seemed to be to leave the fighting to the Afghan Army, make maximum use of firepower, both ground and air, and stick to the roads as much as possible, only venturing out on foot when the area had been thoroughly strafed and pounded by shells, bombs and rockets.[12]

The Afghan Army was in an even worse shape. Yousaf points out that right up to 1987, when he left the ISI, the Afghan Army was

believed to have been losing 20,000 soldiers annually through deser-
tion, demobilization and death. Press gangs had to be used for recruitment. Theoretically, men aged 18–25 were to be conscripted for three
years, but in practice those from the 18–55 age group were often
taken. The problem was that Kabul, which had lost all control over the
rural areas, could only conscript from the large cities. By the end of
1980s, severe penalties had to be prescribed to 'keep men in'.[13]

Tension between Soviet and Afghan Army personnel at all levels
compounded matters. The Soviets took all strategic and most tactical decisions. Soviet military advisors conveyed these to their Afghan
opposite numbers, who could disregard such advice at their own
peril. Not surprisingly, there was a widening rift between Soviet and
Afghan commanders, the former regarding the latter as second-rate
and the latter complaining that they were being ordered to undertake risky and dangerous missions while the Soviets remained secure
in the bases.[14]

SOME FOUGHT WELL

Not all Soviet military formations, however, fought poorly and/or un-
willingly. The paratroops (assault) units and their officers were better
trained and fought aggressively. The Soviet Special Forces (Spetsnaz)
were highly trained and motivated. Career officers did not share the
conscripted private's unwillingness to fight. It provided them with an
opportunity to further their careers. Yousaf says that something 'like
60,000 Soviet officers went through the Afghan war, thus qualifying
for membership of the "Afghan Brotherhood", which was so often rewarded with promotions and medals'.[15]

Their efforts, however, could not tilt the balance in favour of
Soviet troops because not only of their own weaknesses but also the
advantages the mujahideen enjoyed. To win, a guerrilla force first requires a loyal local population supporting its efforts at 'great risk to
themselves' and a majority of which 'would supply shelter, food, recruits and information'. Thousands of Afghans in the villages met this
requirement. Also, guerrillas need to believe implicitly in their cause

for them to sacrifice themselves completely to achieve victory. The Afghans had Islam. They fought to protect their homes and families. They further had the advantage of terrain, two-thirds of which was covered by inhospitable mountains, which were known only to the local people. Fourth, they had a safe haven in Pakistan, 'a secure base area to which the guerrilla could withdraw to refit and rest without the fear of attack'.[16]

The mujahideen could not gain the upper hand early in the war because they could not combine quickly enough to strike decisively and lacked weapons to take on tanks, armoured personnel carriers and aircraft. This, in turn, enabled the Soviets and the Kabul regime to overcome their deficiencies, which they partially did. By 1983, Yousaf states, the Russian army was 'functioning again as a viable force.'[17] Yet, it was defeated. Why?

According to Yousaf, the reason was the presence of 'possibly [the] most important' requirement for the success of guerrilla warfare—outside backers who not only represent the guerrillas' cause in international fora, but are also a bountiful source of funds.[18] In the case of the mujahideen and Pakistan, the United States and Saudi Arabia played this role.[19] There could, of course, be no comparison of the roles of the two. The United States provided not only funds but sophisticated arms that tilted the military balance in favour of the mujahideen. Besides, the United States' status as a superpower and the diplomatic support it could marshal for the mujahideen's cause played a critical role, as did its military power which perhaps deterred the Soviet Union from taking the kind of drastic steps—attacking Pakistan, for example—it might otherwise have taken. Nor would Pakistan have extended the kind of support it did to the mujahideen without the United State's protective umbrella over its head.

The United States' goal in Afghanistan, which, during the Carter presidency, was primarily harassing the Soviets, changed to one of forcing it to withdraw from the country following Ronald Reagan's assumption of office as President. His administration and the people calling the shots in it and the US Congress included a number of dyed-in-the wool anti-Communist and anti-Soviet elements who wanted to get even with the Soviet Union for its role in defeating the Americans in the Vietnam War. Their efforts led to a sharp stepping up of the United States' efforts to help the mujahideen around the same time when the Soviets had managed to get their military better organized in Afghanistan.

The Central Intelligence Agency's (CIA's) authorized annual budget for its Afghan programme rose from $30 million in fiscal year 1981 to $200 million in fiscal year 1984. By an agreement reached between US President Ronald Reagan and the Saudi royal family, the latter effectively doubled the amount by agreeing to match the CIA's contribution dollar for dollar.[20] Initially, the weapons supplied were .303 Lee Enfield rifles, the standard British Army infantry weapon until the 1950s and Rocket Propelled Grenades-7 (RPG-7) and their launchers.[21] Later, the weaponry expanded to include 60-millimetre Chinese mortars and 12.7-millimetre heavy machine guns.[22]

Pressed constantly by Texas Congressman, Charles ('Charlie') Wilson, and supported eagerly by CIA Director, William Casey, the CIA's 1985 budget for the Afghan programme rose to $250 million. This, as Steve Coll has pointed out, 'was about as much as all the previous years combined'. According to Coll, this would have given the intelligence agency about $500 million on weapon and supplies if the Saudis kept their promise of contributing an equal amount.[23] Money came pouring. The US Congress secretly allocated $470 million in fiscal year 1986 for funding covert operations in Afghanistan, and increased the amount to $630 million—which did not include matching Saudi contribution—for fiscal year 1987.[24]

At William Casey's insistence, the CIA, despite some of its career officers' qualms, shipped to the ISI 'many tons' of C-4 plastic explosives for sabotage operations. Britain's MI6 supplied magnetic depth charges for destroying bridge pylons, particularly those of the bridge spanning the Amu Darya near Termez. Steve Coll further writes in *Ghost Wars* that after 1985, the CIA also supplied electronic timing and detonating devices that made the remote detonation of explosions possible. Developed by the CIA's Office of Technical Services, the 'Time pencil', a chemical device that wore down gradually and set off a bomb or a rocket after a predictable period, was 'the most basic delayed detonator'.[25]

WEAPON OF CHANGE

The weapon that tilted the military balance in the mujahideen's favour was the Stinger missile which the CIA began sending to the Afghan battlefield from 1986. A portable, shoulder-fired weapon with an automated heat-seeking guidance system, it worked with deadly effect bringing down scores of Soviet helicopters and transport planes between 1986 and 1989.[26] Fear of the Stinger made Russian and Afghan pilots to ascend, as often as possible, above the missile's effective ceiling of about 12,500 feet, which severely undermined their ability to mount low-flying sorties. It also ended helicopter evacuation of the wounded, thereby demoralizing front-line Soviet officers. According to Coll, within months, Milton Bearden, CIA's station chief at Islamabad, cabled the agency's headquarters at Langley, Virginia, that the Stingers had become the 'most significant battlefield development'.[27] Yousaf adds that every transport aircraft at Kabul airport and elsewhere had to land or take off protected by helicopters dispersing to divert Stingers. 'Even civilian aircraft, which were not generally attacked, adopted a tight, corkscrew descent to runways causing much nervousness and vomiting among passengers.'[28]

According to Yousaf, the CIA's richest military contribution to the Afghan war, however, 'was in the field of satellite intelligence'.[29] With pictures taken from great heights showing tanks, vehicles, bridges, culverts as well as the results of bombing or rocket attacks with amazing clarity, operational planning and the briefing of mujahideen commanders became 'a comparatively simple business'.[30] It is hardly surprising that he said, 'Without the backing of the US and Saudi Arabia, the Soviets would still be entrenched in that country [Afghanistan].'[31]

The question is: How many of the circumstances that led to the Soviet Union's defeat are present to bedevil the United States in Afghanistan? Despite growing resentment against the Americans for drone strikes and incidents like the burning of copies of the Quran at the Bagram base on 20 February 2012, which led to widespread violence for three days and the killing of several American and NATO troops, the Taliban and al Qaeda do not have the kind of loyal popular support the mujahideen enjoyed. A vast section of Afghans remember the harshness of their regime and dread their return. The support they command is because of the fear their brutal executions have instilled in people and the belief that they will come to power when the American and NATO troops withdraw. Referring to the Taliban's reign of terror in Kandahar, the *New York Times* reported on 26 March 2010, 'Taliban suicide bombings and assassinations have left this city virtually paralyzed by fear. The insurgents boldly walk the streets, visit shops and even press people into keeping guns and other supplies in their houses for them in preparation for urban warfare, residents say.'[32] This was when a full-scale American offensive was expected in the next few weeks.

The Taliban and al Qaeda forces are inspired by their fanatical commitment to their brand of Islam. But their creed is a gross distortion of Islam; its regressive social and cultural content and the savagery of the Taliban and al Qaeda is repulsive to the large majority of Muslims. Besides, many fighters of these two organizations, who are from Pakistan's Punjab and Federally Administered Tribal Areas (FATA), or from Arab countries, Chechnya and the Central Asian republics, are not defending their homes from alien invaders but taking over another country as part of a global jihad. An important motivation that fired the mujahideen against Soviet troops is, therefore, absent in their case. Third, their advantage of the inaccessibility of the terrain where they operate has been severely undermined by the surveillance and striking capacity of American drones.

The drones have also diminished, in the case of the Taliban and al Qaeda, the advantage of a safe haven in an adjacent country and support from the latter's government. A report in the *New York Times* of 4 April 2010 stated that according to a mid-ranking militant in Pakistan's North Waziristan as well as supporters of the government there, 'a stepped-up campaign of American drone strikes over the past three months has battered al Qaeda and its Pakistani and

Afghan brethren'[33] in the tribal agency. The report further stated, 'The strikes have cast a pall of fear over an area that was once a free zone for Al Qaeda and the Taliban, forcing militants to abandon satellite phones and large gatherings in favour of communicating by courier and moving stealthily in small groups, they said.'[34]

The factor of external aid mentioned by Brigadier Yousaf will not be terribly effective in the case of the Taliban and al Qaeda. Pakistan's capacity to provide it is insignificant compared to what the United States could give the mujahideen. The same goes for intelligence. Pakistan just does not have the technological capability to provide its protégés the kind of precise intelligence the Americans could provide to the mujahideen.

Nor has the United States suffered from the same kind of inadequacies that led the Soviet Union to defeat. Unlike the latter, their military strategy has not been purely defensive and status quoist. While there have been no massive offensive for some time, intelligence-driven commando raids and drone strikes continue. Besides, the morale of the American and NATO troops has not been as low as that of their Soviet counterparts in the 1980s. American soldiers are far better paid and looked after than their Russian counterparts were. Nor have the Americans had to contend with game changers like the Stinger missiles which virtually neutralized the advantage of total air-dominance the Soviet forces enjoyed. In fact, the United States' unchallenged air dominance has enabled the unimpeded flight of the drones and commando raids, which have played havoc with the Taliban and al Qaeda.

A weakness Americans have shared with the Soviets is a long and precarious supply line which will be discussed in detail later; another is grossly inadequate deployment of troops which has enabled the Taliban and al Qaeda, routed in December 2001, to stage a comeback. The latter, however, has nothing to do with the inherent nature and dynamics of the Afghan war of 1980s and the one now, and has been the result of poor decision-making in Washington DC. An even bigger instance of poor decision-making has been its announcement that it will withdraw its troops, save for a small presence for training and intelligence-driven counterterrorism operations, by 2014. Given political will, the consequences of both can be remedied.

By No Means Inevitable

Turning to the Vietnam War, one finds nothing in it that points to an inevitable American defeat in Afghanistan. Some circumstances are certainly common. The Viet Cong were determined and skilful fighters; so are the Taliban and al Qaeda militants. The last two are inspired by fanatical, death-defying commitment to their brand of Islam. Viet Cong were inspired in an equal measure by Marxism as interpreted by the Vietnamese Communist Party and a burning desire to unite their country. They hated the Americans as foreign invaders as much as the Taliban and al Qaeda do now.

The Americans, however, faced much greater odds in Vietnam than in Afghanistan. Besides North Vietnam, the Viet Cong were backed by the Soviet Union and China, any day much more powerful than Pakistan which is supporting the Afghan Taliban and, indirectly, the latter's ally, al Qaeda. Also, North Vietnam supported the Viet Cong even at the cost of losing almost its entire agricultural and industrial infrastructure to American bombing, the destruction of many of its cities and villages and suffering thousands of casualties. One can by no stretch visualize Pakistan extending itself that much for its Afghan protégés. Otherwise, it would never have become an ally—however duplicitous and self-serving—of the United States in the current Afghan war. Perhaps because of the kind of support they received, North Vietnamese and Viet Cong air defence was much more effective than that of the Taliban and al Qaeda. American air superiority was bought at a very high price. Besides anti-aircraft guns and missiles, American fighter and bomber aircraft had to deal with MiG-15 interceptor-fighters. The United States Air Force lost over 2,251 aircraft—1,737 to hostile action and 514 to operational causes—in South East Asia (Cambodia and Laos besides North and South Vietnam) during 1961–75.[35]

One can argue that the United States lost so many aircraft and more than a thousand air force personnel because air power played a key role in its waging of the Vietnam War. The use of aircraft in strafing and bombing has no doubt been on a much smaller scale in Afghanistan than in Vietnam but then perhaps the most critical component of the United States' military strategy in its war against the Taliban and al Qaeda has been surveillance and precision killing of targets by drones, and not only in Afghanistan. A prime example of the latter has been the killing of Anwar al-Awlaki, a US-born Islamist preacher and senior al Qaeda leader with a dual American-Yemeni citizenship, and an associate, Samir Khan, also an American citizen and a co-editor of the al Qaeda magazine *Inspire*, in a drone strike in Yemen on 30 September 2011.[36]

The success of the drone strikes, whose flipside is the unpopularity they cause the Americans through civilian casualties they inflict, underlines a major difference between the United States' war in Afghanistan and the Soviet war there and its own war in Vietnam. The present war belongs to the electronic/information technology era. The earlier ones mentioned above were essentially industrial-age wars. Electronic surveillance and interception equipment and computer-linked weapons with precision-guidance systems have given an entirely new dimension to the present Afghan war. According to a report in the *New York Times* of 16 March 2009, the United States Air Force's fleet of drones, considered 'a novelty a few years ago', had grown to 195 Predators and 28 Reapers, a 'new and more heavily armed cousin' of the former. Besides, there have been drones the US Army has been using to counter roadside bombs as well as tiny hand-launched models that can help soldiers to peer past the next hill or building. The total number of military drones had soared to 5,500, from 167 in 2001.[37] According to the *New York Times*, as accessed on 15 April 2012, the Pentagon now had some 7,000 aerial drones compared with fewer than 50 a decade ago, and had asked Congress for nearly $5 billion for drones in the 2012 budget.[38]

This is hardly surprising. The *New York Times* cited the website longwarjournal.com, which closely tracks the strikes as part of its focus on the war on terror, as saying that American drones had killed more than 1,900 insurgents in Pakistan's tribal areas since 2006.[39] Besides, drones render signal service to ground troops. According to another report in the *New York Times* of 19 February 2010, American troops pushing into Marja in southern Afghanistan earlier that month knew where dozens of roadside bombs had been planted, thanks to the drones. Some troops, when they came under fire, called for help by drones. As the flights increased, the military was also finding that the drones could offer continuous protection and a broad view of their surroundings that the army and marines had long asked for.[40]

Like Stingers in the Afghan Mujahideen's war against the Soviet Union, drones can well make a critical difference in the present Afghan war. The examples of the Vietnam War and Soviet Union's defeat in Afghanistan have some relevance but do not indicate the inevitability of an American defeat. The question arises: Why then is one talking about a defeat? The short answer is: Because of the United States' poor performance in the war and the deteriorating situation in Afghanistan from its point of view. The situation is doubtless grim. Announcing a new American policy for Afghanistan a little over two months after assuming office as US President, Barack Obama said in room 450 of the Dwight D. Eisenhower Executive Office Building in Washington DC on 27 March 2009:

> The situation is increasingly perilous. It's been more than seven years since the Taliban was removed from power, yet war rages on, and insurgents control parts of Afghanistan and Pakistan. Attacks against our troops, our NATO allies, and the Afghan government have risen steadily. And most painfully, 2008 was the deadliest year of the war for American forces.[41]

The American President was making a frank statement about the situation in Afghanistan. Shortly after becoming US President, he had ordered a comprehensive review of the situation there under Bruce Riedel, a former US CIA officer. The review was over. The team led by Riedel had submitted its report. And the United States' Supreme Commander was saying how he intended to turn the tide.

The situation has remained critical since then. Despite a large increase in the number of American troops and the implementation of a new, comprehensive counter-insurgency strategy, the Taliban, allied with al Qaeda, have hit back with fluid and effective guerrilla warfare which blends the use of traditional communication techniques and modern weaponry, with terror and intimidation in urban and rural areas, and explosions in the national capital.

TENACIOUS ENEMY

Three weeks after a 4,000-strong force of US Marines launched an offensive in Afghanistan's Helmand province on 1 July 2009, it found it had never met an enemy so tenacious. A report in the *New York Times* quotes Sergeant Tambunga, a squad leader in Company C, First Battalion, Fifth Marines, as saying, 'In Iraq, they'd hit you and run,' and adding, 'But these guys stick around and manoeuvre on you.'

Taliban fighters had made a calculated decision to retreat and regroup to fight where and when they chose. They displayed a keen awareness of when to fight and when the odds against them were too great. American Marines discovered that the Taliban were surprisingly proficient at tactics they themselves had learned at infantry school. According to them, what the Taliban lacked in munitions they made up for in tactics, even practising 'information operations' and disinformation. Knowing the Marines listened to their two-way communications, the Taliban described phony locations of ambushes and bombs.

These tactics, always under a process of improvement, were on further display as the Americans stepped up their offensive from the end of January 2010 with the arrival of reinforcements. Describing the advance of a Marine infantry company, accompanied by a squad of Afghan soldiers, through several villages, a report in the *New York Times* states:

> Mixing modern weapons with ancient signaling techniques, the Taliban have developed the habits and tactics to evade capture and to disrupt American and Afghan operations, all while containing risks to their ranks.[42]

The report adds that seven months after the marines began flowing forces into Helmand province, clearing territory and trying to establish Afghan local government, such tactics had 'helped the Taliban transform themselves from the primary provincial power to a canny but mostly unseen force'. Besides, they had carefully studied American movements and placed pressure plates of Improvised Explosive Devices (IED) where the troops are most likely to be. The result? In areas where they had built bases, 'the Marines have undermined the Taliban's position. But the insurgents have consolidated and adapted, and remain a persistent and cunning presence.'[43]

Taliban use their presence to launch campaigns of intimidation to offset the gains made by American and allied forces. We have seen the example of Kandahar; another is Marja, an important town in Helmand province which had been for months under Taliban control until 13 February 2010, when over 6,000 American and allied forces fought their way into it. The town's capture was a result of a sweep, beginning in the summer of 2009, by American and NATO forces, clearing the Helmand Valley. It was particularly important for the American and NATO forces to hold on to Marja because it was to be a test case of the efficacy of the new American counter-insurgency strategy of capturing territory, holding it and delivering governance. An essential element of the strategy, drawn up under General Stanley A. McChrystal, who had replaced General David McKiernan as the commander of United States and International Security Assistance Force (ISAF) in May 2010, was minimizing civilian casualties and convincing the local population of the ability of the American and NATO forces to protect them.[44] To minimize civilian casualties, leaflets had been dropped into the town from helicopters as early as four months prior to the start of the offensive warning people to stay off the streets from 9 p.m. and to keep away from the windows once it began.[45]

INVISIBLE INTIMIDATION

The warnings, a part of deliberate strategy, also helped the Taliban to leave Marja and regroup to launch their campaign of silent, invisible domination after the US and NATO troops moved in. The methods included beheading, the cutting off of people's hands and feet, the issue of 'night letters', posted at mosques or on utility poles warning people against cooperating with Americans and allied troops, the holding of meetings in selected homes, bringing residents together and asking them to reveal the names of those cooperating with the government and forcing them to provide food and shelter to Taliban fighters. According to a tribal leader in Marja who spoke on the condition of anonymity out of fear of reprisal, 'After dark the city is like the kingdom of the Taliban.'[46] The 'government and international forces cannot defend anyone even one kilometer from their bases'. Walid Jan Sabir, the Afghan member of Parliament for Marja and the surrounding Nad Ali District, was critical of American and Afghan forces for surrendering the night. 'At night the local people are the hostages of the Taliban,' he said.[47]

Things seemed to have picked up in April. People were coming forward to receive government aid, and farmers were taking money for destroying poppy crops, which yielded opium, the main source of Taliban financing. The example of benefits accruing to people encouraged their neighbours to follow their example. But, as a report in the *New York Times* states, though combat operations were over by the end of April and the US military declared victory, much of the local Taliban, including at least four mid-level commanders, never left. They stashed their rifles and resumed their quiet farm lives.[48] People know who they are but are too terrified to identify them. The insurgents' extensive intelligence network remained intact and they maintained their hold on the local population through what local residents described as threats and assassinations.[49]

Clearly, even three months after the Americans proclaimed victory in Marja, the Taliban exercised considerable influence in the district and the government's authority remained quite tenuous. As another report in the *New York Times* indicated, the position in the northern province of Kuduz also remained precarious.[50] The situation in Kandahar, the cradle of the Taliban, was much worse. As American and NATO forces prepared for an offensive to capture the city and secure the province, suicide bombers killed 35 people on 13 March 2010. In the week before, the Taliban had killed one or two policemen every night for several days. The *New York Times* quoted a woman human rights worker, who asked not to be named for fear of reprisal by the Taliban, as saying, 'We do not feel safe in town, and even for the men it is dangerous to go out.' The report also quoted Hajji Agfa Lanai, a provincial councillor and former head of the Peace and Reconciliation Commission in Kandahar, as saying, 'The Taliban can walk around, and government officials cannot.'[51] The fact is that success in counterinsurgency operations needs time; General McChrystal, then Commander of the US and ISAF forces in Afghanistan, said so after his visit to Kandahar with President Karzai on 13 June 2010 and added that some of the affected areas had been under Taliban control for years.[52]

RETHINKING TACTICS

The realization that the capture of Kandahar would pose a formidable military challenge prompted the Americans to do some serious tactical rethinking. In what has been described as 'an unusual public conversation', President Karzai and the United States Secretary of State, Hillary Clinton, 'went to some length to depict a looming coalition offensive around Kandahar as not a full-fledged military assault, but, in Karzai's words, "a process"'.[53] Karzai added, 'We're not calling it an operation.' An operation 'would indicate a military operation, tanks and troops moving. That is not the situation in Kandahar.' Striking almost an identical note, Clinton said that it would be wrong to expect a 'massive military action' in Kandahar. 'That is not the kind of operation that our military leaders believe is warranted,' she said. 'They want to have a successful counterinsurgency operation that, you know, doesn't destroy Kandahar in the effort to save Kandahar.'[54]

The caution that McChrystal and other American civilian and military personnel have often displayed about the war's progress is understandable. Counter-insurgency is one of the most difficult forms of warfare and it has been made particularly difficult in Afghanistan by years of gross neglect caused by America's involvement in the Iraq war and the diversion of attention and resources to it even before it actually began. More about this later. Suffice here to say that, as a result, the United States and its allies had not only to win back large tracts of the countryside which had been lost to the Taliban but also cope with terrorist attacks in the capital city of Kabul.

URBAN ATTACKS

The attacks began during President George Bush Jr's administration. The most serious of these was the one on the Indian embassy in Kabul on 7 July 2008 in which Defence Attaché Brigadier R. D. Mehta and Counsellor V. Venkateswara Rao, were killed along with two guards, Ajai Pathania and Roop Singh, of the Indo-Tibetan Border Police, a crack Indian paramilitary formation. One hundred and thirty-nine persons were injured. Queuing visa-seekers, shoppers across the street and security staff bore the brunt of what was the first direct terror strike on an Indian mission which blew the embassy gates and outer walls off and badly damaged the buildings inside.[55] Accusing a foreign intelligence agency of involvement, the Afghan interior ministry said in a statement, 'The interior ministry believes this attack was carried out in coordination and consultation with an active intelligence service in the region.' Afghanistan had previously accused Pakistani agents of being behind a number of attacks on its soil.[56]

Another attack followed within three weeks of President Obama being sworn in on 20 January 2009. On 11 February 2009, Taliban terrorists launched a coordinated attack on three government buildings housing the Justice Ministry, its Prisons Directorate and the Education Ministry. At least 20 persons and 8 of the attackers, armed with Kalashnikov rifles, explosives and wearing suicide vests (none of which were detonated), were killed and 57 wounded.[57]

The attacks, which underscored the deteriorating security situation in Afghanistan and the growing sense of siege in the capital, were launched on the eve of President Obama's Special Representative to Afghanistan and Pakistan Richard C. Holbrooke's visit to Kabul as a part of the review of American policy on Afghanistan and Pakistan ordered by the American president. The attacks plunged Kabul in panic and unnerved officials. Noting that the 'enemy still has the capability to bring this amount of weapons and explosives' inside Kabul and 'find their way to government institutions', Hanif Atmar, then Interior Minister, promised new and strict security measures that would be uncomfortable for residents but were necessary.[58]

The attacks continued. On 17 September, a powerful car bomb exploded in central Kabul, close to the hub of the American and NATO military command, killing six Italian soldiers and 10 Afghan civilians. Fifty-two were wounded. The explosion, which occurred around noon, was so powerful that the armoured vehicle carrying the Italian soldiers was blown across two lanes of traffic. It prompted the Italian Prime Minister Silvio Berlusconi, a close ally of the Americans who was in political trouble and under considerable pressure to bring the Italian troops back from Afghanistan, to declare that his government had begun planning to 'bring our young men home as soon as possible'.[59]

The Indian embassy again became a target on 8 October when a suicide bomber blew up his car outside its compound killing at least 12 people and injuring 83, including 3 guards of the Indo-Tibetan Border Police. The Taliban claimed responsibility for the attack and said that their target was the Indian embassy.[60] A deadly suicide attack on a UN guest house killed eight people, five of them foreigners working for the United Nations, in the last week of October. A report in the New York Times of 31 October quoted Afghan intelligence chief, Amrullah Saleh, as saying that the three attackers were from Pakistan's Swat Valley and that the operation was jointly directed by two groups. Two of them belonged to the Haqqani network. The other was an al Qaeda operative known as Ajmal, who fled to the Waziristan area. The intelligence chief further stated that al Qaeda and Haqqani networks were thought to have cooperated in many attacks.[61]

On 15 December, a suicide car bomber struck the Heetal Hotel, mainly frequented by foreigners, killing 8 people, including 4 women, and wounding about 40. The blast, which occurred in the Wazir Akbar Khan district, where homes of government officials and diplomats and offices of international organizations are located, was heard across the city at the foreign ministry, where 200 people were attending a three-day conference on corruption in Afghan government. President Hamid Karzai, who was speaking at the time, said that the explosion had occurred near the residence of Ahmed Zia Massoud, a former Vice President of Afghanistan, two of whose guards were killed. Massoud, a brother of the legendary leader of the resistance to the Taliban, Ahmed Shah Massoud, who was assassinated by al Qaeda two days before 9/11, may have been the intended victim.[62] The hotel was only slightly damaged. Three homes, including Massoud's, were severely damaged and windows in buildings were shattered.[63]

On Monday, 18 January 2010, two attackers blew themselves to death and five others fought to death in Kabul. The Pashtunistan Circle where President Karzai's palace, the Justice Ministry and the Central Bank, the target of the attack, are located, was the main scene of action.[64] As the gun battle raged there, another suicide bomber, driving an ambulance, struck a traffic circle a half-mile away, sending a second mass of bystanders fleeing in terror. Afghan officials said that 3 soldiers and 2 civilians—including a child—were killed, and at least 71 people were wounded. The Taliban claimed responsibility for the attack. Their spokesman, Zabiullah Mujahid, reached by telephone, said that the attack was a reply to the American and Afghan proposal for reconciling and reintegrating Taliban fighters into mainstream society.[65]

The next attack, on Friday, 26 February, targeted two guest houses popular with foreigners and located at the centre of the city. According to the Taliban spokesman, Zabiullah Mujahid, the targets were foreigners. Indians, who accounted for at least 9 of the 18 reported killed, seemed, however, to have been the special targets. The rest of the dead were French, Italian and Afghan nationals. More than 30 were reportedly wounded. A car bomb exploded outside a guest house popular with Indians, blowing up the gate. Suicide bombers were among those who attacked the other guest house popular with westerners. The gunfight with security forces that followed lasted 90 minutes.[66]

Yet another suicide attack occurred in Kabul on Tuesday, 18 May 2010, when a bomber in a minibus drove into a convoy of armoured sports utility vehicles carrying four senior military officers and others. Of the four, Colonels Geoff Parker and John M. McHugh were from the Canadian and US armies respectively, and Lieutenant Colonels Paul R. Bartz and Thomas P. Belkofer were from the US Army. On brief visits, they were killed along with two other American military personnel, Staff Sergeant Richard J. Tieman and Specialist Joshua A. Tomlinson, and 12 Afghan civilians in a passing bus. The incident marked the killing of the largest number of ranking officers from the American-led forces in any insurgent attack in Afghanistan since the war that ousted the Taliban from power began more than eight years ago.[67]

The next attack occurred on 2 June 2010 during the first day's session of the three-day Peace Jirga (Council) which President Karzai had convened in Kabul to draw up a road map for reconciliation with elements of the Taliban who were not a part of the organization's hard core. President Karzai was addressing the gathering when a rocket exploded in the compound, within a few hundred yards of the *jirga* tent. 'Some are trying to fire rockets,' he said, shrugging off the attack. 'Everyone is used to it; even my 3-year-old son is used to it.'[68] Minutes after Karzai concluded his speech, a second, larger explosion rocked the jirga tent, and the session was suspended for 90 minutes as the police battled the insurgents.[69] Three persons, wearing burqas, tried to attack the jirga.[70] One was shot to death as the trio approached a checkpoint about a mile from the jirga compound and another detonated his explosives. A third attacker was arrested, said Wahid Omar, President Karzai's spokesman.[71]

The rocket attack was launched from a small house not far from the place where the jirga was being held. Bodies of two dead terrorists were found when the house was recaptured on the afternoon of 2 June. Two Afghan policemen were wounded in the operation, the police said.[72] Two things were significant about the attacks. They occurred despite elaborate security measures.[73] If this was discouraging, the encouraging aspect was that, according to a spokesman of NATO's ISAF, the Taliban attack was handled completely by Afghan authorities. 'It was a quick response by our security forces,' said presidential spokesman Omar, who maintained that all of the actual attackers were killed and that none got close enough to pose a serious threat to the jirga.[74] Nevertheless, the chain of events it unleashed led to President Karzai seeking, and securing, the resignations of Hanif Atmar, Afghanistan's Interior Minister, and the chief of the country's intelligence agency, Amrullah Saleh.

Kabul was not the only city where terrorist attacks were taking place. In Kandahar, Taliban fighters attacked the main prison on the night of 13 June 2008, blowing up the mud walls, killing 15 guards and freeing around 1,200 inmates. Among the escapees were about 350 Taliban members, including commanders, would-be suicide bombers and assassins.[75] Another attack on 1 April 2009 killed 13 persons, 7 civilians and 6 police officers. The blast destroyed the gate of the provincial council office in Kandahar where a meeting of tribal leaders was in progress. While a suicide bomber blew himself and the explosive-laden vehicle he was driving, three tried to storm the building. Policemen shot two of them dead; the third blew himself up, taking the total death toll to 17, counting the terrorist who blew himself up in the car.[76] Qari Yousef Ahmadi, a Taliban spokesman, claimed responsibility for the attack and acknowledged that the target was the compound.[77]

On the night of 25 August, a blast devastated an entire block, gutted shops and homes, reducing them to ash and rubble and shattering lives while people were breaking their day-long Ramzan fast. The death toll finally rose to 41 and the number of the wounded to over 60. The Taliban denied responsibility for the bombing. Few, however, doubted that it was their handiwork and attributed its denial to the popular revulsion generated by the outrage.[78]

The arrival of 2010 provided no respite. According to a report in the *Guardian*, a series of bomb explosions on 13 March 2010 left, according to Afghanistan's interior ministry, at least 35 people, including 13 police officers, dead and 57 wounded. A Taliban spokesman, Qari Yousef Ahmadi, said the bombings showed that the militants were still capable of carrying out major attacks despite the build-up of foreign troops before the push by NATO that summer.[79] Two car bomb explosions in downtown Kandahar left 2 dead and 23 wounded on 15 April.[80]

Nor is Kandahar the only city outside Kabul to come under Taliban attack. The pattern in almost each case has been the same. An example is the coordinated attack by Taliban militants in Khost city, the capital of Khost province in eastern Afghanistan, on 12 May 2009. One of the targets was the palace of the provincial governor, Hamidullah Qalanderzay. A suicide car bomb exploded at the gate of his office, killing two policemen and two other guards. The militants who tried to enter the building were repulsed. The other target was a nearby municipal building which a group of nine suicide attackers stormed. Four blew themselves up in a battle with security guards; five others made their way into the building and took about 20 people hostage. The hostages were later freed. The attackers were eventually killed at the end of a long standoff. American troops from Camp Salerno, who were holding a meeting with Afghan army and police officers a few blocks away at the time of the attack, rushed to the scene on hearing an explosion, and killed two suicide bombers before they could detonate their explosives.[81]

WikiLeaks' Leaks

The broad contours of the difficult military situation facing American and allied troops in Afghanistan was, therefore, clear to analysts who had carefully collated and analysed media reports on the war, even before the WikiLeaks disclosures. These and the WikiLeaks disclosures together provide a comprehensive account of the situation as has been actually unfolding on the ground. As a report in the *New York Times* points out, the secret documents, released on the Internet, are 'a daily diary of an American-led force often starved for resources and attention as it struggled against an insurgency that grew larger, better coordinated and more deadly each year'.[82]

The reports, numbering around 92,000, partially covering the administrations of Presidents Bush and Obama and spanning the period from January 2004 and December 2009, however, convey two pieces of information not publicly disclosed by US military or reported in popular media. The first is that the Taliban had used against American aircraft portable heat-seeking surface-to-air missiles of the kind used so tellingly by the Afghan Mujahideen against Soviet troops in the 1980s. According to an incident report dated 30 May 2007 from Helmand province, an American CH-47 transport helicopter was struck by what witnesses described as such a missile shortly after taking off from the landing zone and crossing the Helmand River. The crash that followed killed seven soldiers—five Americans and a Briton and a Canadian. The *New York Times* report cited above commented:

> Multiple witnesses saw a smoke trail behind the missile as it rushed toward the helicopter. The smoke trail was an important indicator. Rocket-propelled grenades do not leave them. Heat-seeking missiles do. The crew of other helicopters reported the downing as a surface-to-air missile strike. But that was not what a NATO spokesman told Reuters.[83]

The reports, however, make it clear that the Taliban's use of such missiles had been neither common nor terribly effective, with the missiles usually missing their targets.

The second new information provided by WikiLeaks was that the performance of drones had been less impressive than what had been officially portrayed. Some, as the *New York Times* report quoted above mentions, had crashed or collided, forcing American troops to undertake risky retrieval missions before the Taliban could claim their weaponry. An incident report dated 13 September 2009 from Badakshan province details the circumstances of the loss of one of the US Air Force's premier armed drones, a Reaper, which had gone out of control while flying over southern Afghanistan on a combat mission. Carrying advanced radar and sophisticated cameras, as well as Hellfire missiles and 500-pound bombs, it had lost its satellite link with its controller at a base in the United States. Failing to control it after repeated efforts, commanders ordered an Air Force F-15E Strike Eagle fighter jet to shoot down the $13 million aircraft before it soared unguided into neighbouring Tajikistan. This was the first loss of a Reaper with a 66-feet wing span, though reports had mentioned the loss of many of the small 5-pound drones, with names like Raven and Desert Hawk, that American troops tossed out to find out what has happening beyond the next hill.[84]

Another information, conveyed by reports put up by WikiLeaks, concerned the use of Special Operations forces for secret missions to capture or kill about 70 top Taliban commanders. According to the information, not entirely new, while individual commandos had displayed great courage, and some of the missions had notched important successes, the operations, conducted at night, had caused resentment among Afghans for their lack of coordination with local forces, the civilian casualties they often inflicted and the lack of accountability.[85] Media reports tend to confirm some of the criticism. Thus according to a report in the *New York Times* of 15 March 2010, General Stanley A. McChrystal, then commander of US and allied forces in Afghanistan, had brought most American Special Operations forces under his direct control for the first time because of continued civilian casualties and disorganization among units in the field.[86] Rear Admiral Gregory J. Smith, General McChrystal's deputy chief of staff for communications, however, cautioned against putting undue blame on Special Operations forces. Since the raids were dangerous, and conducted at night, most of them were carried out by the more highly trained special groups.[87]

RISING CASUALTIES, GROWING DIFFERENCES

That it is tough going for the United States is also indicated by rising casualty figures and growing differences in the country as to how to wage the war or whether not to wage it at all. There have been differences among generals, between a section of the latter and key personnel of the Obama administration like Vice President Joseph Biden. As accessed on 12 April 2012, http://icasualties.org/oef/, a website tracking US and NATO casualties in Afghanistan, gave 1,932 and 2,956 respectively as the latest figures of American and NATO troops killed since the beginning of the Afghan war in 2001. Having taken

nearly seven years to reach the first 500 dead, the war killed the second 500 in fewer than two.[88] The casualties began rising sharply from
the middle of 2009. July, August, September and October were the
four deadliest months for American troops since the war began.[89] The
total number of American dead reached 1,000 on 18 May 2010.[90]

A cause of the rising casualties and poor progress in the Afghan
war has been sharp differences in the United States' political establishment over strategy and continued involvement. According to a report
in the *New York Times* of 14 June 2010, halting progress in the war had
crystallized long-standing tensions within the government over the
viability of President Obama's plan to turn Afghanistan around and
begin pulling US troops out of it by July 2011. The report states:

> Persistent violence in the southern area around Marja, which was
> supposed to be an early showcase of the new counterinsurgency
> operation, has reinforced doubts in Washington about the cur-
> rent approach—doubts only fuelled by President Hamid Karzai's
> abrupt dismissal of two security officials widely trusted by the
> Americans.[91]

Further, General Stanley A. McChrystal's unceremonious removal on 23 June 2010 as the commander of the United States Forces
(USFOR), as well as the ISAF, in Afghanistan, raised serious questions
about the way the war was being conducted and made people sceptical
about the United States' prospects. General McChrystal was removed
after the contents of an article entitled 'The Runaway General', by a
freelance journalist, Michael Hastings, then to be published in the
Rolling Stone magazine, came to be known. It had quoted him and
some of his close aides as making critical comments about important
members of the Obama administration and even saying that the President himself appeared 'uncomfortable and intimidated' during his
first meeting with the general.

Doubts about the United States' resolve and ability to win have
been all the sharper because General McChrystal was not the first
US commander in Afghanistan to be shown the door. General David

D. McKiernan, his predecessor, had also met the same fate on 11 May 2009. The move was, according to a report in the *New York Times* of that date, intended to bring a more aggressive and innovative approach to a worsening seven-year war. The report quoted the US Defence Secretary Robert M. Gates as saying that 'fresh eyes were needed' and that 'a new approach was probably in our best interest'. When asked if the dismissal ended the general's military career, Mr Gates replied, 'Probably.'[92] The report further quoted US Defence Department officials as saying that General McKiernan, a respected career armoured corps officer, had been removed primarily because he had brought too conventional an approach to the challenge.[93]

Perhaps even more damaging to the United States' image and the credibility of its war effort was the acrimony among those connected with waging it, whether in civilian or military capacity, that the McChrystal episode brought into sharp focus. The *New York Times* reported on 25 January 2010 that the US ambassador to Afghanistan, Karl W. Eikenberry, had, in two secret cables, written on 6 and 9 November 2009, expressed serious doubts about the leadership of the Afghan government, particularly of President Hamid Karzai, and provided a detailed rebuttal of General Stanley A. McChrystal's counter-insurgency plan.[94]

Mr Eikenberry, a retired US Army Lieutenant General, who had served in Afghanistan in a senior capacity, had written on 6 November that the proposed counter-insurgency strategy assumed an Afghan political leadership able to take responsibility and exert sovereignty in furtherance of the goal of 'a secure, peaceful, minimally self-sufficient Afghanistan hardened against transnational terrorist groups'.[95] According to him, Karzai was 'not an adequate strategic partner' and continued 'to shun responsibility for any sovereign burden, whether defence, governance or development. He and much of his circle do not want the U.S. to leave and are only too happy to see us invest further'. He continued, 'Beyond Karzai himself, there is no political ruling class that provides an overarching national identity that transcends local affiliations and provides reliable partnership.'

According to the report, the cables, obtained by the *New York Times*, showed for the first time how Eikenberry had repeatedly cautioned that deploying sizeable American reinforcements would result in 'astronomical costs' and would only deepen the dependence of the Afghan government on the United States. He felt that 'sending additional forces will delay the day when Afghans will take over, and make it difficult, if not impossible, to bring our people home on a reasonable timetable'.

Eikenberry also declared that he had serious doubts about the ability of the Afghan police and military forces to take over security duties in the country by 2013. 'The Army's high attrition and low recruitment rates for Pashtuns in the south are crippling,' he wrote, adding, 'Simply keeping the force at current levels requires tens of thousands of new recruits every year to replace attrition losses and battlefield casualties.' Referring to the dependence of President Obama's Afghan policy on the Pakistani forces eliminating militants' safe havens in the mountainous regions of their country bordering Afghanistan, he stated, 'Pakistan will remain the single greatest source of Afghan instability so long as the border sanctuaries remain.' Pointing out that the gains from sending additional forces might be fleeting as long as the sanctuary problem was not 'fully addressed', he recommended further ratcheting up 'our engagement in Pakistan' without, as the *New York Times* report pointed out, elaborating what he meant.[96]

The debates over United States' Afghan policy became increasingly bitter. On Sunday, 8 November 2009, top military and civilian officials gathered for a regularly scheduled meeting at the American embassy in Kabul, where General McChrystal pointedly addressed many of the issues in the first of the Eikenberry cables. The *New York Times* report, which mentions the meeting, adds, citing an official familiar with what happened there, that General McChrystal did not mention the cable specifically but said, in a reference to the hasty American withdrawal from Saigon in 1975, that no alternative had been offered besides 'the helicopter on the roof of the embassy'.[97] According to the report, Generals McChrystal and Eikenberry had a private conference after the meeting but it was not clear what was said there. It said that American officials stated that the next day General Eikenberry sent another cable softening his stance about the impact of a troop increase in Afghanistan. A spokesman for General Eikenberry declined to comment but since the next day was 9 November, the reference was clearly to the General's second cable dated 9 November.

Eikenberry said in subsequent public hearings that his concerns had been addressed and he supported the White House's decision to send troops. The two cables, which became a subject of serious discussions in the White House, however, stirred a furious controversy at a time when American generals strongly urged dispatch of significant troop reinforcements and the Obama administration was actively debating dispatching a massive reinforcement of American troops. The rancour remained.

According to a report in the *New York Times* of 23 June 2010, 'many of the president's top advisers have continued to criticize one another to reporters and international allies alike, usually in private conversation, and always off the record'. The report quoted a senior European diplomat who worked closely with the United States on Afghanistan strategy as saying, 'Yes, we do hear them disparage each other' and that it was 'never good to hear that'. It also quoted Bruce Riedel as saying, 'This flap shows once again that his [Obama's] team is not pulling together, but is engaging in backbiting.'[98]

Among the fractious relationships was the one between Richard C. Holbrooke, United States' Special Representative for Afghanistan and Pakistan, and Karl W. Eikenberry. The latter had been complaining about Holbrooke, whom many have described as disruptive and whose relationship with President Hamid Karzai of Afghanistan nosedived in 2009 after a 'difficult meeting' following the August elections. Nor were Eikenberry's relations with Karzai smooth.[99] His relations with General Stanley A. McChrystal had been no better. According to a report, they hardly spoke to each other and remained in their separate compartments in the military plane in which they travelled from Kabul to a NATO meeting in Brussels in December 2009.[100]

ALIENATING A PRESIDENT

Nor have the United States' ties with Karzai been smooth. According to a report in the *New York Times* of 9 April 2010,

> The relationship with Mr. Karzai has grown so tense, adminis-
> tration officials said, that the foreign leader who may be most
> important to American interests barely speaks to some of the
> president's senior advisers. His relationship with the two key
> administration emissaries—Richard C. Holbrooke and Karl
> Eikenberry—is deeply strained. He has also clashed with Vice
> President Joseph Biden Jr. Mr. Karzai's ties to Mr. Obama him-
> self are, at best, distant.[101]

The report further stated that the only person with whom Karzai had a solid day-to-day relationship was General McChrystal. Clear-ly, the situation is complex and the roots of the problem run deep. The report points out, 'The tension with Mr. Karzai mirrors internal stresses within the administration's Afghanistan team, including fric-tion between Mr. Eikenberry, who is the American ambassador to Afghanistan, and the military, and between Mr. Holbrooke and the White House.' In fact, Holbrooke was not a part of President Obama's entourage during the latter's visit to Kabul on 28 March 2010, a re-markable omission since he was supposed to be the top official dealing with the region.[102]

Besides, there have been major issues between President Karzai and the US administration. The latter and its NATO allies hold that he has not done enough to curb Afghanistan's rampant corruption, and resents the demand for a major overhaul of the electoral system, made by them as well as the United Nations, following charges of fraud levelled against him after his victory in the presidential elections of August 2009.[103] The Afghan President overhauled the Electoral Com-plaints Commission but his claim to appoint all five of its members, against the prevailing system of three being appointed by the United Nations, infuriated some Western diplomats.[104]

President Obama's aides, who felt that the move was meant to emasculate the independent election panel, sent Karzai a terse message that his invitation to visit the White House had been revoked.[105] Karzai was incensed. He invited the Iranian President, Mahmoud Ahmadinejad, who flew to Kabul and delivered a fiery anti-American speech inside Kabul's presidential palace. An Afghan, who knew what had happened, reportedly said on the condition of anonymity, 'He [Karzai] invited Ahmadinejad to spite the Americans.'[106] Karzai again met the Iranian President in Tehran in the weekend preceding President Obama's visit and the two celebrated the Afghan and Iranian New Year together. He returned to Kabul only hours before Obama landed.[107]

During his visit, President Obama reportedly presented President Karzai with pointed criticism. The language the two Presidents used in private is not known. In public, Obama said standing alongside the Afghan President in the latter's palace in Kabul that while the 'American people were encouraged by the progress made', work remained to be done on governance issues that had frustrated American officials over the preceding one year. Saying that 'we also want to continue to make progress on the civilian process', he mentioned several areas, including fight against corruption and the upholding of the rule of law.[108]

Friction between the Obama administration and Karzai continued. Escalating his criticism of the West, Karzai said at a meeting with 60 Members of Parliament, mostly his supporters, on Saturday 3 April 2010, 'If you and the international community pressure me more, I swear that I am going to join the Taliban.' A Member of Parliament, who was present at the meeting, said this to the New York Times on the condition of anonymity.[109] What seemed to have concerned the United States more was his speech in Kandahar on 4 April, in which he promised local tribal leaders that the coalition forces' planned summer offensive in the area would not proceed without their approval. The New York Times report of 4 April 2010 quoted him as saying, 'I know you are worried about this operation,' and adding, 'There will be no operation until you are happy.'[110] It added, 'Given his tone in the last few days, it was unclear whether he was literally extending the elders veto power over the offensive, or merely trying to quell their fears and bring them on board.'

As the United States pondered its options, many experts felt that public hectoring of President Karzai had undermined the Obama visit and triggered his outburst against the United States and the West that followed shortly afterwards. 'There is a realization that public remonstrances and temper tantrums don't work,' said Bruce O. Riedel. He added, 'It brings out the worst in Karzai, while undermining support for the war effort in Congress, in the media, and in the public. If you disparage Karzai, you're in effect saying the war cannot be won.'[111]

There was a prompt change. On 28 March, on his way from Washington DC to Kabul with President Obama on United States Air Force One, General James Jones, the United States' National Security Adviser, told reporters that Obama would take on his Afghan counterpart for ignoring American demands on corruption and drug trafficking. On 9 April, he told reporters while travelling with President Obama from Washington DC to Prague that Obama had sent a respectful note to Karzai expressing his gratitude to the Afghan leader for the dinner in Kabul.[112] He further said during the flight, 'We believe that we are on an encouraging glide path in Afghanistan' and that the American delegation was 'generally impressed with the quality of the ministers and the seriousness with which they're approaching their job'. President Obama, he said, was reassured by his conversation with President Karzai.[113]

The new emollient approach was taken further forward during President Karzai's visit to the United States in May. At a press conference jointly addressed with him on 12 May at the East Room of the White House, President Obama announced that America would maintain a long-term presence in Afghanistan despite adhering to the timetable of beginning to withdraw its troops from July 2011. His references to corruption were few and the only time he referred to it directly, he praised the progress made in halting it. Karzai did not repeat his threat of joining the Taliban. Both played down the sharp differences that had caused bitterness between the two governments.

Reaffirming 'our shared goal to disrupt, dismantle and defeat Al Qaeda and its extremist allies', the American President added that the differences had been overstated.

Obama expressed support for Karzai's efforts to reach out to a section of Taliban supporters and try for their integration into the Afghan society provided they renounced their ties with al Qaeda and extremism. He also made it clear that whether the Taliban, or at least a part of them, would have the incentive to lay down arms and make peace with the Afghan government would depend on the effectiveness of the efforts to break their momentum militarily. Hence the deployment of additional troops.

KARZAI'S WORRIES

It remains to be seen how the United States–Karzai relations work out. Several things seemed to be understandably worrying Karzai. The first was the apprehension that the United States, which was committed to begin withdrawing its troops from July 2011, might not win the war, and might depart leaving him high and dry. A report in the *New York Times* of 11 June 2010 quoted Amrullah Saleh as saying that Karzai 'had lost his confidence in the capability of either the coalition or his own government to protect this country'. He added that 'President Karzai has never announced that NATO will lose, but the way that he does not proudly own the campaign shows that he doesn't trust it is working'.[114] Saleh was not alone in his readings of Karzai's worries. The report states that according to people close to Karzai, he began losing confidence in the Americans the previous summer after the 'national elections in which independent monitors determined that nearly one million ballots had been stolen on Mr. Karzai's behalf. The rift worsened in December, when President Obama announced that he intended to begin reducing the number of American troops by the summer of 2011'.[115]

The report quoted a Western diplomat in Kabul as stating on condition of anonymity that Karzai believed they 'stole his legitimacy during the elections last year. And then they said publicly that they were going to leave'. It observed that Obama would have a problem if Karzai's resolve to work closely with the United States and use his own army to fight the Taliban was weakening. The American war strategy rested largely on clearing the ground held by the Taliban so that Karzai's army and government could move in, allowing the Americans to scale back their involvement in an increasingly unpopular and costly war.[116]

Particularly disturbing for the Americans was Karzai's attempt to reach out to the Taliban and the Pakistanis and the resultant signs of thaw between Islamabad and Kabul. According to a report in the *New York Times* of 24 June 2010, though the United States had encouraged the process, it now feared that it would 'find itself cut out of what would amount to a separate peace between the Afghans and Pakistanis, and one that did not necessarily guarantee Washington's prime objective in the war: denying al Qaeda a haven'.[117]

Significantly, Saleh resigned along with Interior Minister Hanif Atmar after Karzai told them that the Taliban were not responsible for the attack on the three-day Peace Jirga that opened in Kabul on 2 June 2010.[118] They were showing him evidence of the Taliban's involvement in rocket and suicide attacks on the jirga, whose purpose was to adopt a road map for reconciliation with vast sections of Taliban who did not belong to the organization's hard core which had terror links with al Qaeda.[119]

Karzai's reported remark that it might have been the Americans who had carried out the rocket attack on the Peace Jirga was significant. According to the *New York Times* report cited above, a 'prominent Afghan [not Saleh or Atmar] with knowledge of the meeting' had quoted the remark.[120] If the prominent Afghan was right, Karzai's statement was an indication of the deep distrust of the Americans he had come to harbour, something that did not augur well for America's ability to win the war. Saleh and other officials confirmed that it was Karzai's perception of the inability of the United States and its NATO allies to emerge victorious that made him try to strike a deal with the Taliban and the latter's long-time supporter and Afghanistan's arch rival, Pakistan. His moves involved 'secret negotiations with the Taliban outside the purview of Americans and NATO officials'.[121]

According to the *New York Times* report of 24 June 2010 cited earlier, Pakistan was projecting itself before Karzai, who had 'soured on Americans', as the new viable partner for Afghanistan. Pakistani officials had been telling him that they could set up a power-sharing arrangement with the militia led by Sirajuddin Haqqani, an al Qaeda ally who ran a major part of the insurgency in Afghanistan. Afghan officials said that the Pakistanis were pushing 'various other proxies, with General Kayani personally offering to broker a deal with the Taliban leadership'.[122]

The report added:

> Washington has watched with some nervousness as General Kayani and Pakistan's spy chief, Lieutenant-General Ahmad Shuja Pasha, shuttle between Islamabad and Kabul, telling Mr. Karzai that they agree with his assessment that the United States cannot win in Afghanistan, and that a post-war Afghanistan should incorporate the Haqqani network, a longtime Pakistani asset.[123]

The Americans were particularly worried because the Pakistanis played their cards very close to their chest. The report cited above quoted an American official involved in the administration's Afghanistan and Pakistan deliberations as saying that despite General McChrystal's 11 visits to General Kayani in Islamabad in the past year, the Pakistanis had not been altogether forthcoming on details of their conversations with Karzai. According to the report, this provided another indication of how Pakistan, ostensibly America's ally, had worked 'many opposing sides' in the war to safeguard its ultimate interest in having an Afghanistan that was pliable and free of Indian influence.

The growing proximity between the governments of Afghanistan and Pakistan was further underlined by the way the then ISI chief, Lieutenant General Ahmed Shuja Pasha, dashed to Kabul on the eve of Karzai's visit to Washington in May. The *New York Times* report also stated that Pakistan had already won what it saw as an important concession in Kabul in the form of the resignations of Saleh and Atmar in June 2010. The two officials, favoured by Washington, were viewed by Pakistan as major obstacles to its vision of hard-core Taliban fighters being part of an Afghanistan settlement, though the circumstances of their resignations did not suggest any connection to Pakistan.

Given their strategic interests, the Pakistanis had chosen this juncture to open talks with Karzai because, even before the controversy over General McChrystal, they had, as one of them put it, sensed an uncertainty and 'a lack of fire in the belly', within the Obama administration over the Afghan fight. Also, as Major General Athar Abbas had pointed out, President Obama's commitment to begin withdrawing American combat troops from July 2011 'made it easier for Pakistan to play a more visible role'.[124]

REBUILDING BRIDGES

To rebuild bridges with President Karzai and prevent him from doing a deal with Pakistan, the Obama administration must convince him that it has the fire in their belly to win. For this, it must itself believe that it can win the war if it is determined to do so. This is by no means an impossible task. If the Afghan situation has its grim and discouraging aspects, encouraging developments have also occurred. It must focus on these and shed defeatism.

Second, the Obama administration must stick to its new strategy of treating Karzai with the respect he deserves. An important cause of his alienation has been public berating of him and his government by Western leaders. Admonitions such as the one that President Obama reportedly administered to him on 2 November 2009, urging him to act against rampant corruption and drug trade that, according to American officials, fuelled the Taliban resurgence, did not go down well with him; nor did reportage of pressure on him by Obama administration officials to act against General Abdul Rashid Dostum and Marshal Fahim Khan. In the summer of 2009, President Obama even called for an investigation into General Dostum's activities.[125] Marshal Fahim Khan, one of Afghanistan's Vice Presidents, was accused of drug trafficking, as was Ahmed Wali Karzai, President Karzai's half brother and the Governor of Kandahar, killed on 12 July 2011. Dostum was accused of killing thousands of Taliban prisoners of war early in the Afghan war.[126]

Another instance of public criticism was the then British Prime Minister Gordon Brown's warning on 6 November 2009 that Kabul would forfeit its right to international support against the Taliban if it failed to root out corruption. 'Sadly, the government of Afghanistan had become a byword for corruption,' Brown said in a speech to defence experts, and added, 'And I am not prepared to put the lives of British men and women in harm's way for a government that does not stand up against corruption.'[127]

Harsh public criticism and threats on issues like corruption and electoral malpractices must have been particularly galling to Karzai given the widespread allegation of electoral fraud which is said to have contributed to George W. Bush Jr's victory in the American presidential elections of 2000, which he won by the skin of his teeth. Nor could the Afghan President have been unaware of the widespread incidence of corporate greed and corruption in the United States which caused the subprime loans crisis, brought down giants like Enron and triggered the economic meltdown of 2008 and 2009, which, in turn, produced the worst global crisis since The Great Depression that began in 1929.

OPERATION OUSTER?

Besides public admonitions, reports of bitter differences in Washington DC on the issue of supporting him, as well as repeated allegations of widespread fraud in the 2009 elections that returned him to office for a second term, could not but have given President Karzai the impression that the Americans and their allies wanted him out. The report that Peter Galbraith, then influential in the Democratic foreign policy establishment, was trying to do precisely that when he was the second-ranking UN official in Afghanistan, must have reinforced the impression. According to a report in the *New York Times* in December 2009, Kai Eide, head of the United Nation's Mission in Afghanistan and Galbraith's boss, said that Galbraith proposed to enlist the White House's help in replacing Karzai.[128] The latter, the report stated, became incensed when he learned of the plan and was told that it had been put forth by Galbraith, who had been installed in his position with strong backing from Richard C. Holbrooke, United States' Special Envoy to Afghanistan and Pakistan, who had himself clashed with the Afghan President over the election.

The report created a stir when it was published. It quoted Kai Eide as saying that Galbraith's departure from Afghanistan in early September 2009 came immediately after Eide rejected his proposal to replace Karzai by a more Western-friendly figure. Eide, who left his job in early 2010, said that he had told his deputy that the plan was 'unconstitutional, it represented interference of the worst sort, and if pursued it would provoke not only a strong international reaction' but also civil insurrection. It was during this conversation, Eide said, that Galbraith proposed that he went on leave to the United States, and Eide agreed.[129] In a letter to the International Crisis Group[130] in response to its critical public report on his work, Eide said that Galbraith proposed to undertake a secret mission to Washington and added, 'He [Galbraith] told me he would first meet with Vice President Biden. If the Vice President agreed with Galbraith's proposal they would approach President Obama with the following plan: President Karzai should be forced to resign as president.' Then a new government would be installed led by a former Finance Minister, Ashraf Ghani, or a former Interior Minister, Ali A. Jalali, both favourites of American officials.

Galbraith, who abruptly left Afghanistan in early September and was fired weeks later, said that he believed that he was forced out because he was feuding with Eide, on how to respond to what he termed wholesale fraud in the Afghan presidential election and accused Eide of concealing the degree of the fraud benefiting President Karzai.[131] In response to questions from the New York Times, Galbraith said that he never put forth any full-fledged proposal and that he only considered an effort to persuade Karzai to leave so that an interim government, allowed under the Constitution, could be installed in case a run-off election did not occur until May 2010. He also said that the United Nations had never informed him that these discussions played a role in his firing.[132] Stating that there were 'internal discussions', he said, 'I'm sure I discussed the crisis and I'm sure I discussed a way out. But that is an entirely different matter from acting on it.' He also said that he never promoted the idea with officials outside the United Nations.

The *New York Times* report, however, cited, without naming, a Western diplomat as saying that Galbraith discussed his plan with Frank Ricciardone, the Deputy American Ambassador in Kabul,[133] who was also subsequently alerted by Eide. The report also stated that a spokeswoman for the American embassy in Kabul, Caitlin Hayden, said that Galbraith had brought the plan to the embassy but that it was summarily rejected. She said that 'Galbraith was outspoken within the diplomatic community about his concerns regarding fraud and its consequences, and raised questions about various alternatives to the elections', but the 'U.S. Embassy discouraged consideration of theoretical alternatives to the constitutional elections process whenever they were raised by any party, even while acknowledging flaws in the process'.

While Galbraith also said that he never actually contacted Vice-President Biden or any member of his staff, a spokesman for the Vice-President, James F. Carney, told the *New York Times* that Galbraith had telephoned one of the Vice-President's staff members, Tony Blinken, saying that he had some thoughts about Afghanistan and wanted to talk about them at some point. According to Carney, Blinken received the call when Galbraith was working for the United Nations in Afghanistan but did not say when exactly it was. While Blinken said he would be glad to discuss them, he did not hear from Galbraith thereafter. Nor did he receive from the latter any information about his thoughts or ideas about Afghanistan. The discussion never took place.

The *New York Times* report stated that Galbraith's warnings about fraud were largely confirmed in October 2009, when a UN-backed audit stripped Karzai of almost one-third of his votes, preventing a first-round victory and forcing him into a run-off. He was proclaimed winner in November 2009 after his challenger, Abdullah Abdullah, withdrew, saying the run-off would not be fair. Electoral fraud on a significant scale notwithstanding, Karzai, to all appearances, would have won anyway. He was the best-known Afghan leader at home and abroad and had cobbled together a poll alliance that included people like General Abdul Rashid Dostum and Marshal Fahim Khan who, put simply, called the shots in their respective areas of influence.

KARZAI'S COMPULSIONS

Those who blame Karzai for his alliance with men like Dostum and Fahim Khan ignore that his ties with them were perhaps based more on compulsion than preference. As seen earlier, in *Ghost Wars: The Secret History of the CIA, Afghanistan and Bin Laden from the Soviet Invasion to September 10, 2001*, Steve Coll relates how Karzai was held captive and beaten up by Fahim Khan's men early in 1994 before managing to escape. He, therefore, could not be expected to harbour any great affection for Khan.[134]

The compulsion behind Karzai's alliance with Fahim Khan and Dostum, who was once an ally of the Soviet Union, was not just that of winning the presidential elections in the teeth of bitter hostility from influential sections of the Obama administration; it was also related to securing Afghanistan's future. Pressure from significant sections in the United States and its NATO allies—as well as important sections within the Obama administration—for early withdrawal of American and NATO troops from Afghanistan had created serious doubts about the firmness of Washington's commitment to defeating the Taliban and al Qaeda. This, as well as the suspicion that Washington DC might do a deal with the Taliban and Pakistan at his cost, could only have convinced him of the need not only for reaching out to Pakistan but also having allies in a war for the control of Afghanistan that might follow the withdrawal of American and allied troops.

Karzai could not have forgotten the manner in which the United States virtually forgot all about Afghanistan after the completion of the Soviet withdrawal from the country on 15 February 1989. It did nothing as Gulbuddin Hekmatyar's savage rocket attack killed thousands of civilians in Kabul as the city and its outskirts became a scene of clashing militia, mass murders and rape. Nor could he have forgotten the United States' close links with Pakistan and the way in which it ignored Ahmed Shah Massoud's call for assistance during the Clinton administration, and, willy-nilly, played into Islamabad's hands. Nor could he have failed to note the consequences of the junior George Bush's ill-advised and unwarranted invasion of Iraq instead of consolidating the United States' victory in Afghanistan, diverting to Iraq attention and resources that should have gone to the war in Afghanistan, and enabling the Taliban, with the help of Pakistan and al Qaeda, to stage a comeback. The invasion of Iraq also had a profound impact on President Pervez Musharraf of Pakistan. Ahmed Rashid writes that it was 'critical to convincing Musharraf that the United States was not serious about stabilising the region, and that it was safer for Pakistan to preserve its own national interest by clandestinely giving the Taliban refuge'.[135]

Karzai's distrust of Americans was bound to have been compounded by bitterness and anger over the humiliating manner in which the Americans treated him. It was not just public berating over corruption and electoral malpractices that grated but arrogant behaviour. A shocking example was an incident in February 2008, when Joseph R. Biden, then a Senator and not the United States' Vice-President, and two other American Senators sat down to a formal dinner with him during a visit to Kabul. Questioned by the three about corruption in his government, he told them, as a report in the *New York Times* states, that there was none and, in any case, it was not his fault. The senators gaped in astonishment and, after 45 minutes, Biden threw down his napkin and stood up, saying, 'The dinner is over.' The three senators walked out long before the appointed time.[136]

Whatever the circumstances or the provocation, one does not treat the President of another country in this manner. Besides, Biden's conduct reflected a very poor understanding of Karzai's contributions. The report in the *New York Times* which mentioned the incident, also added that many Afghans and Western officials in Kabul believed that 'it was the Iraq war, more than any other factor, that deprived Karzai of the resources he needed to help the Afghan state stand on its own, and to prevent the resurgence of the Taliban that Mr. Obama is now vowing to contain'. It then stated:

Yet for all the doubts about Mr. Karzai—and for all the strains he labors under—he remains by far the strongest politician in the country. He commands the resources of the Afghan state, including the army and the police, and billions of dollars in American and other aid that flows into the treasury.

In his seven years in office, Mr. Karzai has successfully presided over the transition of the Afghan state from the devastated, pre-modern institution it was under the Taliban to the deeply troubled but largely democratic one it is today. Perhaps most important for his future, Mr. Karzai has assembled a team of senior administrators whose competence and experience would be difficult for any challenger to match.[137]

The tantrum thrown by Biden also suggested a basic lack of understanding of Afghan character, a major component of which is a profound sense of honour and self-pride. An Afghan can be boundlessly generous, helpful and a loyal friend to death if treated with respect, and bitterly unforgiving if slighted. Karzai is an Afghan and much more. He belongs to a Kandahar-based family that is the leader of the Popalzai tribe of none other than Ahmed Shah Durrani, the founder of the Afghan monarchy. Coll writes:

> His royal Pashtun heritage and ease with foreigners allowed him to mediate across Afghan political and ethnic lines after the Soviet withdrawal. He was a born diplomat, rarely confrontational and always willing to gather in a circle and talk.[138]

There are, however, times when even a born diplomat, who is rarely confrontational, feels that enough is enough. President Karzai seems to have been approaching that point for some time. For example, Obama wanted an investigation into General Dostum's activities in the summer of 2009. Karzai not only allowed the General to return from exile but reinstated him to his official position, while the general endorsed his presidential candidature and campaigned for him.[139] President Obama has done well to begin mending fences with Karzai, whose support is more crucial than Pakistan's for retrieving the Afghan situation for Americans.

Stating that things were 'not looking good' and that there was not much sign of the turnaround that people had been hoping for, Riedel told the *New York Times* that 'the [Obama] administration had few attractive alternatives to its current course'. While pouring in more troops was politically unfeasible, an outright withdrawal would make the United States vulnerable to an al Qaeda–type organized terrorist attack originating in a Taliban-dominated Afghanistan. Most significantly, Riedel further stated, 'Staying where you are is not attractive, because sooner or later, it means you'll lose,' and added, 'Obama inherited a disaster in Afghanistan and he faces the same bad options he faced in 2008.'[140]

The situation has been made worse by Pakistan's role. A report in the *New York Times* quotes American and Pakistani officials as saying that Pakistan was 'exploiting the troubled United States military effort in Afghanistan to drive home a political settlement with Afghanistan' that would give Pakistan a decisive influence there but was likely to undermine the United States' interests.[141] The report further stated that General McChrystal's dismissal would almost certainly embolden the Pakistanis in their plan as they detect increasing American uncertainty.

Three questions arise. How important is Pakistan's support? Can Pakistan be made to mend its ways? Can Americans win in spite of Pakistan?

NOTES

1. Mohammad Yousaf and Mark Adkin, *The Bear Trap: Afghanistan's Untold Story* (Lahore: Jang Publishers, 1992), p. 48.
2. Ibid., p. 48.
3. Ibid., p. 53.
4. Ibid.
5. Ibid., p. 49.
6. Ibid., p. 67.
7. Ibid., p. 54.
8. Ibid., p. 55
9. Ibid., p. 54.
10. Ibid., p. 55.
11. Ibid.

12. Ibid., p. 56.

13. Ibid., p. 57.

14. Ibid., p. 58.

15. Ibid., p. 64.

16. Ibid.

17. Ibid.

18. Ibid., pp. 64–65.

19. Ibid., p. 65.

20. Coll Steve, *Ghost Wars: The Secret History of the CIA, Afghanistan and bin Laden from the Soviet Invasion to September 10, 2001* (New York: Penguin Books, 2004), pp. 65–66.

21. Ibid., p. 58.

22. Ibid., p. 66.

23. Ibid., p. 102.

24. Ibid., p. 151.

25. Ibid., p. 135.

26. Ibid., p. 11.

27. Ibid., p. 150.

28. Yousaf and Adkin, *The Bear Trap*, pp. 184–86.

29. Ibid., p. 93.

30. Ibid.

31. Ibid., p. 96.

32. Carlotta Gall, 'Kandahar Becomes Battlefield Before a U.S. Offensive', *New York Times*, 26 March 2010, online edition, http://www.nytimes.com/2010/03/27/world/asia/27kandahar.html?th&emc=th.

33. Jane Perlez and Pir Zubair Shah, 'Drones Batter Qaeda and Allies Within Pakistan', *New York Times*, 4 April 2010, online edition, http://www.nytimes.com/2010/04/05/world/asia/05drones.html?th&emc=th.

34. Ibid.

35. John Schlight, *A War Too Long: The USAF in Southeast Asia 1961–1975*, Air Force History and Museums Programme 1996, ePub Bud, p. 103, 2011, http://www.epubbud.com/read.php?g=KLGLHQ63.

36. Sudarshan Raghavan, 'Awlaqi Hit Misses al-Qaeda Bombmaker, Yemen Says', *Washington Post*, online edition, 30 September 2011 (updated 1 October, 9.15 p.m.), http://www.washingtonpost.com/world/anwar-al-aulaqi-us-born-cleric-linked-to-al-qaeda-killed-yemen-says/2011/09/30/gIQAsoWO9K_story.html.

37. Christopher Drew, 'Drones Are Weapons of Choice in Fighting Qaeda', *New York Times*, online edition, 16 March 2009, http://www.nytimes.com/2009/03/17/business/17uav.html?pagewanted=all.

38. Times Topics, 'Predator Drones and Unmanned Aerial Vehicles (UAVs), *New York Times*, online edition, as accessed on 15 April 2012 and as updated on 20 March 2012, http://topics.nytimes.com/top/reference/timestopics/subjects/u/unmanned_aerial_vehicles/index.html.

39. Ibid.

40. Christopher Drew, 'Drones Are Playing a Growing Role in Afghanistan,' *New York Times*, online edition, 19 February 2010, http://www.nytimes.com/2010/02/20/world/asia/20drones.html.

41. The White House, 'Remarks by the President on a New Strategy for Afghanistan and Pakistan', Office of the Press Secretary, Washington DC, 27 March 2009, http://www.whitehouse.gov/the_press_office/remarks-by-the-president-on-a-new-strategy-for-afghanistan-and-pakistan/.

42. C. J. Chivers, 'Taliban Hit Back in Marya with a Campaign of Intimidation', *New York Times*, online edition, 17 March 2010, http://www.nytimes.com/2010/03/18/world/Asia/18Afghan.html?pagewanted=all.

43. Ibid.

44. Rod Nordland, 'Taliban Hit Back in Marja with a Campaign of Intimidation', *New York Times*, online edition, 17 March 2010, www.nytimes.com/2010/03/18/world/Asia/18afghan.html?pagewanted=all.

45. Rod Nordland, 'Military Officials Say Afghan Fight Is Coming', *New York Times*, online edition, 3 February 2010, http://www.newyorktimes.com/2010/02/04/world/Asia/04Talibanhtml?th&emc=th.

46. Ibid.

47. Ibid.

48. Carlotta Gall, 'Taliban Hold Sway in Area Taken by U.S., Farmers Say', *New York Times*, online edition, 16 May 2010, http://www.nytimes.com/2010/06/09/world/asia/09kandahar.html?pagewanted=2&th&emc=th.

49. Ibid.

50. Carlotta Gall, 'Taliban Open Northern Front in Afghanistan', *New York Times*, online edition, 26 November 2009, http://www.nytimes.com/2009/11/27/world/asia/27kunduz.html?pagewanted=2&_r=1&th&emc=th.

51. Carlotta Gall, 'Kandahar Becomes Battlefield Before a U.S. Offensive', *New York Times*, online edition. 26 March 2010, http://www.nytimes.com/2010/03/27/world/asia/27kandahar.html?th&emc=th.

52. Dexter Filkins, 'In Visit to Kandahar, Karzai Outlines Anti-Taliban Plan', *New York Times*, online edition, 13 June 2010, http://www.nytimes.com/2010/06/14/world/asia/14afghan.html?src=un&feedurl=http%3A%2F%2Fjson8.nytimes.com%2Fpages%2Fworld%2Fasia%2Findex.jsonp.

53. Brian Knowlton and Elsiabeth Bumiller, 'Leaders Put a Different Face on Afghan Drive', *New York Times*, online edition, 13 May 2010, https://mail.google.com/mail/?shva=1#inbox/12895cc2965a0951.

54. Ibid.

55. Our Bureau and Agencies, 'India Target in Kabul's Deadliest Attack', *Telegraph*, Kolkata, online edition, 8 July 2008, http://www.telegraphindia.com/1080708/jsp/frontpage/story_9519558.jsp.

56. Haroon Siddique and Agencies, 'Afghans Accuse Foreign Agents of Involvement in Indian Embassy Attack', *Guardian*, online edition, 7 July 2010, http://www.guardian.co.uk/world/2008/jul/07/afghanistan.india.

57. Richard A. Oppel Jr, Abul Waheed Wafa and Sangar Rahimi, 'At Least 20 Dead in Attacks in Kabul', *New York Times*, online edition, 11 February 2009, http://www.nytimes.com/2009/02/11/world/asia/11iht-   afghan.4.20118990.html?_r=1&pagewanted=2.

58. Ibid.

59. Richard A. Oppel and Rachel Donadio, 'Afghan Blast Raises New Doubts in Europe', *New York Times*, online edition, 17 September 2009, http://www.nytimes.com/2009/09/18/world/asia/18afghan.html?_r=1&th&emc=t.

60. Agencies, 'Blast Near Indian Embassy in Kabul, 12 Dead', *Times of India*, online edition, 8 October 2009, http://timesofindia.indiatimes.com/world/south-asia/Blast-near-Indian-embassy-in-Kabul-12-dead/articleshow/5100417.cms.

61. Dexter Filkins, 'Qaeda Had Role in Attack on U.N. Staff, Official Says', *New York Times*, online edition, 31 October 2009, http://www.nytimes.com/2009/11/01/world/asia/01kabul.html?th&emc=th.

62. Adam Gabbat and Agencies, 'Suicide Car Bomber Strikes Kabul Hotel', *Guardian*, online edition, 15 December 2009, http://www.guardian.co.uk/world/2009/dec/15/afghan-capital-suicide-bomb.

63. Ibid.

64. Dexter Filkins, 'Kabul Attack Shows Resilience of Afghan Militants', *New York Times*, online edition, 18 January 2010, http://www.nytimes.com/2010/01/19/world/asia/19afghan.html?pagewanted=2&th&emc=th.

65. Ibid.

66. Alissa J. Rubin, 'Deadly Attacks in Kabul Strike at Foreigners in Guesthouses', *New York Times*, online edition, 26 February 2010, http://www.nytimes.com/2010/02/27/world/asia/27kabul.html?th&emc=th.

67. Rod Nordland, 'Toll in Kabul Suicide Attack Included U.S. and Canadian Officers', *New York Times*, online edition, 20 May 2010, http://www.nytimes.com/2010/05/21/world/asia/21afghan.html?th&emc=th.

68. Alissa J. Rubin and Rod Nordland, 'Taliban Attacks Shake Afghan Peace Gathering', *New York Times*, online edition, 2 June 2010, http://www.nytimes.com/2010/06/03/world/asia/03afghan.htm.

69. Ibid.

70. The long robes, which cover the entire body from the head to the toes, worn by Muslim women.

71. Alex Rodriguez, 'Taliban Targets Afghanistan Peace *Jirga*', *Los Angeles Times*, 3 June 2010, http://www.latimes.com/news/nationworld/world/la-fg-afghan-jirga-attack-20100603,0,4943931.story.

72. Rubin and Nordland, 'Taliban Attacks Shake Afghan Peace Gathering'.

73. Rodriguez, 'Taliban Targets Afghanistan Peace *Jirga*'.

74. Rubin and Nordland, 'Taliban Attacks Shake Afghan Peace Gathering'.

75. Carlotta Gall, 'Taliban Free 1,200 Inmates in Attack on Afghan Prison,' *New York Times*, online edition, 14 June 2008, http://www.nytimes.com/2008/06/14/world/asia/14kandahar.html?ref=afghanistan.

76. Associated Press, '13 Die in Kandahar Attacks,' *Washington Times*, online edition, 2 April 2009, http://www.washingtontimes.com/news/2009/apr/02/13-die-in-kandahar-attack/.

77. Ibid.

78. Taimoor Shah, 'Bombing Deepens Despair in a Stricken Afghan City', *New York Times*, online edition, 26 August 2009, http://www.nytimes.com/2009/08/27/world/asia/27kandahar.html.

79. Jon Boone, 'Kandahar Bombings a Warning to Nato, Says Taliban', *Guardian*, online edition, 14 March 2010, http://www.guardian.co.uk/world/2010/mar/14/afghanistan-bombings-warning-nato.

80. Taimoor Shah and Richard A. Oppel, 'Taliban Seen behind 2 Car Bomb Attacks in Downtown Kandahar', *New York Times*, online edition, 15 April 2010, http://www.nytimes.com/2010/04/16/world/asia/16afghan.html.

81. Abdul Waheed Wafa and Sharon Otterman, '9 Killed in Coordinated Attacks in Afghanistan', *New York Times*, online edition, 12 May 2009, http://www.nytimes.com/2009/05/13/world/asia/13afghan.html.

82. C. J. Chivers, Carlotta Gall, Andrew W. Lehren, Mark Mazzetti, Jane Perlez and Eric Schmitt, with contributions from Jacob Harris and Alan McLean, 'View Is Bleaker Than Official Portrayal of War in Afghanistan', *New York Times*, 25 July *2010*, http://www.nytimes.com/2010/07/26/world/asia/26warlogs.html?_r=1&th&emc=th.

83. Ibid. The quote from the battlefield report displayed by WikiLeaks is also from the *New York Times* report cited above.

84. Ibid.

85. Ibid.

86. Richard A. Oppel and Rod Nordland, 'U.S. Is Reining In Special Operations Forces in Afghanistan', *New York Times*, 15 March 2010, online edition, http://www.nytimes.com/2010/03/16/world/asia/16afghan.html?pagewanted=2&th&emc=th.

87. Ibid.

88. James Dao and Andrew W. Lehren, 'Grim Milestone: 1,000 Americans Dead', *New York Times*, online edition, 18 May 2010, http://www.nytimes.com/2010/05/19/us/19dead.html?pagewanted=all.

89. Ibid.

90. Dao and Lehren, 'Grim Milestone: 1,000 Americans Dead'.

91. Peter Baker and Mark Landler, 'Setbacks Cloud U.S. Plans to Get Out of Afghanistan', *New York Times*, online edition, 14 June 2010, http://www.nytimes.com/2010/06/15/world/asia/15military.html?th&emc=th.

92. Elisabeth Bumiller and Thom Shanker, 'Commander's Ouster Is Tied to Shift in Afghan War', *New York Times*, online edition, 11 May 2009, http://www.nytimes.com/2009/05/12/world/asia/12military.html.

93. Ibid.

94. Eric Schmitt, 'U.S. Envoy's Cables Show Worries on Afghan Plans', *New York Times*, online edition, 25 January 2010, http://www.nytimes.com/2010/01/26/world/asia/26strategy.html?th&emc=th.

95. Ibid.

96. Ibid.

97. Mark Landler and Jeff Zeleny, 'Among Obama Aides, Debate Intensifies on Troop Levels', *New York Times*, online edition, 12 November 2009, http://www.nytimes.com/2009/11/13/world/asia/13eikenberry.html?th&emc=th.

98. Helene Cooper, Thom Shanker and Dexter Filkins, 'McChrystal's Fate in Limbo as He Arrives at White House', *New York Times*, 23 June 2010, Ihttp://www.nytimes.com/2010/06/24/us/politics/24mcchrystal.html?pagewanted=2&th&emc=th.

99. Ibid.

100. Mark Landler and Helene Cooper, 'Official Try to Unite on Afghan Plan', *New York Times*, 7 December 2009, http://www.nytimes.com/2009/12/08/world/asia/08advisers.html?th&emc=th.

101. Helene Cooper and Mark Landler, 'U.S. Now Trying Softer Approach toward Karzai', *New York Times*, 9 April 2010, http://www.nytimes.com/2010/04/10/world/asia/10prexy.html.

102. Ibid.

103. Alissa J. Rubin and Helene Cooper, 'In Afghan Trip, Obama Presses Karzai on Graft', *New York Times*, 28 March 2010, http://www.nytimes.com/2010/03/29/world/asia/29prexy.html?pagewanted=2&th&emc=th.

104. Ibid.

105. Dexter Filkins and Mark Landler, 'Afghan Leader Is Seen to Flout Influence of U.S', *New York Times*, 29 March 2010, http://www.nytimes.com/2010/03/30/world/asia/30karzai.html?th&emc=th.

106. Ibid.

107. Rubin and Cooper, 'In Afghan Trip, Obama Presses Karzai on Graft'.

108. Ibid.

109. Alissa J. Rubin, 'Karzai Steps Up Attacks on NATO, Boxing In the West', *New York Times*, 4 April 2010, http://www.nytimes.com/2010/04/05/world/asia/05karzai.html?th&emc=th.

110. Ibid.

111. Helene Cooper and Mark Landler, 'U.S. Now Trying Softer Approach Toward Karzai', *New York Times*, 9 April 2010.

112. Ibid.

113. Ibid.

114. Dexter Filkins, 'Karzai Is Said to Doubt West Can Defeat Taliban', New York, *New York Times*, 11 June 2010, http://www.nytimes.com/2010/06/12/world/asia/12karzai.html?th&emc=th. The two officials were Interior Minister Hanif Atmar and chief of intelligence Amrullah Saleh.

115. Ibid.

116. Ibid.

117. Jane Perlez, Eric Schmitt and Carlotta Gall, 'Pakistan Is Said to Pursue a Foothold in Afghanistan', *New York Times*, 24 June 2010, http://www.nytimes.com/2010/06/25/world/asia/25islamabad.html?pagewanted=2&th&emc=th.

118. Ibid.

119. Aneja Atul, 'Karzai Escapes Attempt on Life: Rocket Attacks while President Attacks Peace Conference', *Hindu*, online edition, 3 June 2010, http://www.thehindu.com/2010/06/03/stories/2010060355141700.htm.

120. Dexter Filkins, 'Karzai Is Said to Doubt West Can Defeat Taliban'.

121. Ibid.

122. Perlez, Schmitt and Gall, 'Pakistan Is Said to Pursue a Foothold in Afghanistan'.

123. Ibid.

124. Ibid.

125. Helene Cooper and Jeff Zeleny, 'Obama Warns Karzai to Focus on Tackling Corruption', *New York Times*, onlien edition, 2 November 2009, http://www.nytimes.com/2009/11/03/world/asia/03afghan.html?_r=1&th&emc=th.

126. Ibid.

127. John F. Burns and Alan Cowell, 'Brown Warns Afghan Leader on Corruption', *New York Times*, online edition, 6 March 2009, http://www.nytimes.com/2009/11/07/world/europe/07britain.html?th&emc=th.

128. James Glanz and Richard A. Oppel, 'U.N. Officials Say American Offered Plan to Replace Karzai', *New York Times*, online edition, 16 December 2009, http://www.nytimes.com/2009/12/17/world/asia/17galbraith.html?th&emc=th.

129. Ibid.

130. A non-governmental organization committed to preventing and resolving deadly conflict.

131. Ibid.

132. Ibid.

133. The website of the US embassy in Turkey, however, shows his name as Francis. http://turkey.usembassy.gov/ambassador_francis_j_ricciardone.html.

134. Coll, *Ghost Wars*, pp. 286–87.

135. Ahmed Rashid, *Descent into Chaos: How the War against Islamic Extremism Is Being Lost in Pakistan, Afghanistan and Central Asia* (London: Allen Lane, 2008), p. XLI.

136. Dexter Filkins, 'Afghan Leader Finds Himself Hero No More', *New York Times*, online edition, 7 February 2009, http://www.nytimes.com/2009/02/08/world/asia/08iht-08karzai.20003370.html.

137. Ibid.

138. Coll, *Ghost Wars*, p. 286.

139. Cooper and Zeleny, 'Obama Warns Karzai to Focus on Tackling Corruption'.

140. Ibid.

141. Perlez, Schmitt and Gall, 'Pakistan Is Said to Pursue a Foothold in Afghanistan'.

CHAPTER 5

PATRON OF CHOICE

From the very beginning Pakistan's approach to its relationship with the United States has been simple: extract as much military and economic aid as possible and give as little as possible in return. Husain Haqqani, the scholarly Pakistani diplomat who was forced to resign in November 2011 as Pakistan's ambassador to the United States following the 'memogate'[1] scandal, says that America was Pakistan's 'great-power patron of choice, crucial as a source of weapons and economic aid. Alliance with the United States became as important a part of the plans for consolidating Pakistani nation and state as Islam and opposition to Hindu India.'[2]

The search for a big power as a friend, however, predates the birth of Pakistan. Shuja Nawaz, the country's pre-eminent military historian, refers to a meeting between Muhammad Ali Jinnah and Lord Ismay[3] and quotes the latter as saying that Jinnah told him that Pakistan could not stand alone after the British left, and needed to be 'friends with a superpower'. According to him, Russia had no appeal for Pakistan. France was weak and divided, which left only Britain and the United States. Pakistan preferred the former, 'a natural friend', as the 'known devil'. Nevertheless, Jinnah despatched his trusted friend, M. A. H. Ispahani, to visit the United States, which he did not know well, to survey the landscape and set up contacts.[4]

Shortly after the birth of Pakistan, Jinnah asked the United States to provide some $2 billion in civil and military aid, making it potentially the largest donor for the fledgling economy. The United States rejected the request after the Kashmir war, which began on 22 October 1947 and lasted until formal ceasefire was declared on the night of 1–2

January 1949.[5] Pakistan, however, did not give up. Its leaders continued to emphasize its strategic location and its potential as an American ally against the encroaching Soviet empire as well as the threat it faced internally from communists. The extent to which it went in this quest becomes clear from Ayesha Jalal's revelation that since the 'cease-fire in Kashmir, the joint services intelligence had been fabricating increasingly bizarre reports about the fledgling local communist party and its purported plans to destabilise the state'.[6]

After Jinnah's passing, Liaquat Ali Khan, who became Prime Minister, continued wooing the United States. He made special advance preparations to ensure that his visit to that country in May 1950 opened the floodgates of aid. During his stay there, he made his country's alignment with Washington DC clear. He talked of fighting the communist menace and supported the United States in the Korean War. 'US economic aid began pouring into Pakistan' soon after that.[7] General Ayub Khan, who became the first Pakistani Commander-in-Chief of his country's army in 1951, put in his bit. He stressed the importance of chasing out leftists and communists from Pakistan's political and social system. In addition, he harped on the ability and willingness of the Pakistani army to defend Middle East's oil resources though his eye was really on domestic needs, especially defence against India.[8]

As a part of its strategy, Pakistan meticulously avoided mentioning India during the negotiations which followed President Eisenhower's decision in principle on 5 January 1954 to proceed with military aid.[9] Prior to the arrival of a US military aid review team to Pakistan under the leadership of Brigadier General Harry F. Myers, a highly secret meeting was held under the chairmanship of General Ayub Khan on 24 February 1954 at the army's general headquarters. Defence Secretary Iskander Mirza and the chiefs of Pakistan's air force and navy attended. Major General Mohammad Musa was the secretary of the group. Preparing to war game the exchange with the Americans, Mirza and Ayub Khan had orchestrated a carefully worked out strategy. Mirza, according to Shuja Nawaz, 'spelled out the remit of the group'.

The object of the aid was to be projected as enabling Pakistan to repel communist aggression against itself and provide an expeditionary force for the defence of Middle East 'under certain circumstances, if required'. Any digression from this object was likely to create the impression that 'we were mainly interested in building our forces for some other purpose'. India was never to be mentioned even in internal discourse as that would 'ruin the prospect of getting any assistance from the United States'.[10]

India, however, might be indirectly brought into the picture. When General Ayub Khan reported on his talks with Brigadier General Meyers to Prime Minister Muhammad Ali Bogra and key members of the Pakistani cabinet on 2 April, Finance Minister Chaudhry Muhammad Ali suggested that the US ambassador and the visiting team be told that Pakistan had to shoulder a very heavy defence budget, which had seriously upset its economy and drained its resources. It had antagonized the Soviet Union and India by approaching the United States at a time when most Asian countries were reluctant to take sides in the global conflict for fear of annoying the Soviets. The Americans were also to be told that Pakistan itself had taken the step to approach the Americans to make itself strong to defend itself adequately against communist aggression and effectively contribute to the cause of peace and stability in the Middle East.[11] In keeping with the decision, Chaudhry Muhammad Ali told the visiting team that his country never sought American aid to meet its own deficiencies but had chosen to align itself with the United States and other democratic countries in fighting the communist threat. Pakistan, he added, had suffered from increased hostility from India as a result of its alignment with the United States and was depending on military aid to reduce the burden on its own resources to protect itself and fight communists.[12]

This was a very clever strategy. Pakistan would not mention India but would bring it into the discourse indirectly and would put the United States under moral pressure by suggesting that both India and Russia were annoyed with it because of its seeking to ally with the Americans. Also, by clubbing India and Russia together, it clearly hoped that some of the American Cold War animosity towards the

Soviet Union would also rub off on India. The strategy, however, did not quite work and the United States remained against arming Pakistan against India.

AGREE AND DIFFER

Nevertheless, Pakistan and the United States signed a Mutual Defence Agreement on 19 May 1954. America was now officially on Pakistan's side and vice versa.[13] Differences, however, cropped up on both sides almost immediately thereafter regarding not only the extent of military assistance but also the nature and intent of it.[14] The United States was very clear that it was not for use against India. Even after Eisenhower had decided in principle on 5 January to proceed with arms assistance to Pakistan, American bureaucracy conducted a series of studies on the provision of military aid to that country and the consequences of not providing it. The outcome, however, favoured Pakistan. The sum of the conclusions was that Pakistan was likely to be a dependable ally and despite anything that Washington DC might do to mollify India, Nehru would not accept American actions with understanding. On the other hand, an American pullout from the decision would weaken the pro–United States moderate elements now in control in Pakistan and 'strengthen the reactionary religious elements'. It would also send a wrong signal to America's Middle Eastern allies and encourage elements opposed to the West.[15]

As it turned out, the scale of the assistance was staggering given the purchasing power and price levels of that time. Ahmed Rashid points out that besides agreeing to provide military and economic aid to Pakistan worth $105 million a year, the United States also covertly agreed to 'equip four infantry divisions for the army, six fighter squadrons for the air force, and twelve naval ships. By 1957, the covert US commitment to Pakistan had grown to an astonishing $ 500 million a year.'[16]

Nevertheless, differences between the Americans and Pakistanis continued. Americans made clear that their arms aid was not for use against India but for collective defence against the communist threat.

They were uneasy over Pakistan's neglect of economic development and use of the aid primarily to strengthen its military. They also felt that Pakistan's emphasis on its being able to send troops for the defence of Middle East was a ploy. Towards the end of 1957, the new US ambassador to Pakistan, James Langley, wrote to William Rountree, Assistant Secretary of State for Near Eastern, South Asian and African Affairs, seeking a reappraisal of the situation in Pakistan, where political and economic conditions were deteriorating rapidly. He also sought a reduction in Pakistan's military establishment as the country's military expenditure absorbed 65 per cent of its revenues. Shuja Nawaz, who cites the letter in his book *Crossed Swords: Pakistan, Its Army and the Wars Within*, states that Langley also wrote in the letter that 'it would not be too difficult to make a convincing case that the present [American] military programme [in Pakistan] is based on a hoax, the hoax being that it related to the Soviet threat'.[17]

There were misgivings at the highest level of the Eisenhower administration. The US President himself expressed doubts about the military relationship with Pakistan. Chairing a meeting of the United States National Security Council in January 1957, he said that the decision to have Pakistan as a military ally had proved costly. In fact, the United States was doing nothing for Pakistan except giving military aid, and this represented perhaps the worst form of planning and decision-making by the Americans. This was a terrible error in which they seemed to have become helplessly involved.[18]

Also, the Americans realized that while the government was pro-West the general public opinion was anti-West and, when the political parties were allowed to function again, powerful political forces might emerge and demand a reorientation of Pakistan's foreign policy and a *defenestration* of Americans.[19] Analysts at the American embassy in Pakistan also realized that the defence forces constituted a favoured elite in Pakistan which existed because of its army. Hence, one could not expect very substantial cuts in the country's military expenditure even if it meant risking serious economic deterioration. Having said all this, Americans concluded that their assistance was necessary and would be required for some time to come if Pakistan was to continue making bases and other military facilities available to the United States.[20]

The United States got very little in return. Haqqani reveals that 'Washington's expectation of a centrally positioned landing site for possible operations against the Soviet Union and China was not met'.[21] Shirin Tahir-Kheli informs that General Ayub Khan, then Commander-in-Chief of the Pakistani army, kept on tantalizing Washington DC by saying that it might receive such facilities and manpower as it asked for only if the price was right.[22] Haqqani states that while Pakistan did not provide the military facilities the United States sought, it 'permitted U-2 reconnaissance flights and listening posts that were aimed at the Soviet Union'. In fact, the kind of heads-I-win, tails-you-lose type of bargaining that Ayub Khan did was followed by his successors. General Zia-ul Haq drove a similar hard bargain when the United States sought to expand an anti-communist insurgency in Afghanistan after the 1979 Soviet invasion. General Musharraf too demanded the right price for cooperation in the war against terrorism after 11 September 2001.[23]

DECEIVE AND RECEIVE

The circumstances attending the grant of American arms aid to Pakistan and the developments thereafter underlined a pattern that runs like a thread throughout the relations between Islamabad and Washington DC—Pakistan's deception regarding its real objectives and the United States' falling in line with the former's demands despite reservations. It also shows how Pakistan did precious little in return and deftly manipulated the United States' wider global concerns to coax and browbeat the Americans. The wider concern was the fight against Soviet Union in the 1950s and 1960s and during the Afghan war of the 1980s. Post-9/11 it was the fight against al Qaeda and sections of the Taliban. A new form of duplicity was added later on—doing the opposite of what it had promised and deliberately furthering its own interests at the cost of America's. This was most blatantly manifest both during the mujahideen's jihad against occupying Soviet forces from

1980 to February 1989 and also the war among mujahideen groups that followed after that.

It would be interesting to begin by examining the motives behind the General-turned-President, Muhammad Zia-ul Haq's decision to get Americans to support the mujahideen. The book *The Bear Trap: Afghanistan's Untold Story*, which Brigadier Mohammad Yousaf wrote along with Major Mark Adkin of the British Army, mentions several causes. According to Yousaf, who, as director of the Afghan section of the Inter-Services Intelligence (ISI) virtually ran the mujahideen's war in Afghanistan from 1983 to 1987, Zia called for the Director General of the ISI, Lieutenant General Akhtar Abdul Rahman Khan, generally referred to as General Akhtar, following the Soviet invasion of Afghanistan in December 1979. Zia had wanted from Akhtar what 'soldiers call an "appreciation of the situation" but at a national, grand strategy level'. An appreciation, Yousaf points out, is a 'meticulous, logical, step-by-step examination of a given situation, where all relevant factors are considered, along with likely enemy objectives, to produce a recommended course of action and an outline plan to achieve it'.[24]

In his presentation, General Akhtar forcefully recommended support to the Afghan resistance with arms, ammunition, money, intelligence, training and operational advice, which would become a part of Pakistan's forward defence against the Soviets. He made a strong case for setting out to defeat the Soviet Union in large-scale guerrilla warfare and believed that Afghanistan could be made into another Vietnam with the 'Soviets in the shoes of the Americans'. He also said that this would mean turning the border areas of North-West Frontier Province (NWFP, renamed as Khyber Pakhtunkhwa in 2010) and Baluchistan into sanctuaries for both refugees and guerrillas. Zia agreed.[25] What moved Zia to do it?

Yousaf mentions several factors. In 1979, Zia had provoked worldwide condemnation, and had tarnished his image inside Pakistan, by killing Zulfikar Ali Bhutto. He hoped to regain sympathy in the West by supporting, albeit unofficially, a jihad against a communist superpower and was sure that the United States would rally to his assistance. As a devout Muslim he was eager to help his Islamic neighbours. Indeed, he stood to gain enormous prestige in the Arab world as a champion of Islam, and with the West as a champion against communist aggression. But despite the happy coincidence of political, strategic and religious factors all seeming to point in the same direction, the final, decisive factor for him was Akhtar's argument that it was a sound military proposition, 'provided that the Soviets were not goaded into a direct confrontation, meaning that the water must not get too hot'.[26]

On the part of the United States, the motive was getting even with the Soviet Union for its critical role in America's defeat in the Vietnam War. Shuja Nawaz points out that Zbigniew Brzezinski, National Security Advisor in President Jimmy Carter's administration, had said in an interview with the French newspaper *Le Nouvel Observateur* in 1988 that he had sent a memorandum to President Carter as early as 3 July 1979, the day the latter had signed the first order authorizing secret aid to opponents of the pro-Soviet regime. The memorandum had said that the assistance would lead to Soviet intervention, which would be an excellent thing as the objective was to draw Moscow into the 'Afghan trap', which in turn would give the United States a chance 'to give Russia its own Vietnam'.[27]

Carter was not very forthcoming. There were reservations in the United States about Zia's human rights record and anger over the mob attack on the American embassy in Islamabad which was burned down on 21 November 1979—an incident, which is dealt with in greater detail later in the chapter. Ultimately, however, the urge to get even with the Soviet Union prevailed. The Carter administration initially offered a military and economic package of $400 million. Zia contemptuously spurned it as 'peanuts'.[28]

ENTER REAGAN, AID FLOWS

Things changed after Ronald Reagan became President of the United States, defeating the incumbent, Jimmy Carter, in the 1980 presidential election. Reagan brought with him to the administration a number of conservatives who were committed to challenging the Soviet Union worldwide. William Casey, who took over as director of the Central

Intelligence Agency (CIA) in January 1981, was one of the principal ones. According to Steve Coll, Casey, like his Muslim allies, 'saw the Afghan jihad not merely as statecraft, but as an important front in a worldwide struggle between communist atheism and God's community of believers'. Further, according to Coll, it was Casey, more than anyone else, 'who welded the alliance among the CIA, Saudi intelligence and Zia's army' in support of the mujahideen groups battling Soviet troops.[29]

In a few months, the Reagan administration cobbled together a package of $3.2 billion in economic and military aid to be dispensed over five years. The sanctions imposed on Pakistan were waived and, in 1986, followed another commitment of $4.02 billion to be given during the next six years. Military aid pleased the Pakistani army and solidified its support to Zia's regime, ensuring its continuance.[30] Besides, in July 1980, Prince Turki al-Faisal, then head of the Saudi intelligence service, entered into a formal agreement with the CIA, to match every year the United States' Congressional funding for Afghan rebels.[31] And, of course, the United States rescheduled and wrote off Pakistan's outstanding economic debts.[32]

Pakistan had its own agenda—promoting fundamentalist Islamist groups among the mujahideen to have, at the end of the war, a subservient government in Kabul that would help it to use Afghanistan's territory to gain strategic depth against India, and helping various terrorist organizations that would help it annex Kashmir and achieve its strategic goal of balkanizing, or at least weakening, India. Neither goal was on the American agenda, and their pursuit involved keeping the Americans in the dark about what Pakistan was doing and affecting high dudgeon whenever Washington DC questioned its actions or pressured it to follow a particular course. And, of course, Americans gave in on each occasion because the Soviet Union had to be trapped in the Afghan quagmire, its Vietnam.

One needs to look at the idea of 'strategic depth' before proceeding further. Lieutenant General (Retired), V. R. Raghavan, an expert on multiple aspects of peace and security studies, stated in an article in the *Hindu* of 7 November 2001 that the expression 'strategic depth' first received its official seal of approval when Pakistan's then Chief of Army Staff, General Mirza Aslam Beg, used it during the high-profile manoeuvres, named Zorb-i-Momin, the Pakistani army conducted in 1989–90.[33] The concept, however, had been in circulation for a long time. Aslam Siddiqi, an official in Pakistan's Bureau of National Reconstruction, wrote in a book published as early as 1960 that Iran and Afghanistan could lend depth to Pakistan's defence against India.[34] He had even talked of the safety of the Indo-Pakistani subcontinent against invasions from the north—the reference here was clearly to a threat from the Soviet Union—requiring a fusion of Afghanistan and Pakistan which would take place by force if not peacefully.[35]

Raghavan provided a further elaboration of the concept of 'strategic depth' when he wrote in his article:

> The gaining of strategic depth in Afghanistan has been a major objective of Pakistan's policy. Islamabad's anxieties about its northern neighbour commenced almost immediately after Independence. The combination of ambitions in Pakistan, the uncertain status of the Durand Line, memories of long military campaigns in the North West Frontier Agency and the fierce independence of Afghanistan under King Zahir Shah had made Pakistan anxious. A strong military sense of geo-politics among its largely military rulers also led to the need to gain control over Afghanistan. The notion of strategic depth emerged even stronger after the socialist revolution in Afghanistan and became an obsession after the Soviet intervention in the country.[36]

Raghavan further added:

> Pakistan's beliefs in the value of seeking strategic depth in Afghanistan were influenced by two factors. The support it received from the U.S. in waging an armed response against the Soviet occupation triggered the belief. The success of that, with no apparent costs to itself, gave Islamabad the illusion of being able to play a major role in the geo-politics of Central Asia. This more than anything else led to the belief that Afghanistan provided the strategic leverage Pakistan had long been seeking. The

energy-rich Muslim states of Central Asia beckoned both Pakistan and the energy-seeking multi-nationals. Iran's standing up to western pressures was proving an obstacle to long-term plans for energy extraction from the region. Afghanistan offered both shorter energy routing and political control through Pakistan.[37]

To ensure that the mujahideen's jihad produced in Afghanistan a pliant government, Pakistan began strengthening the fanatical Islamist groups which were patronized by the fundamentalist Jama'at-e-Islami Pakistan and which were rabidly anti-American. Yossef Bodansky, then Director of the US Congressional Task Force on Terrorism and Unconventional Warfare, wrote in *Bin Laden: The Man Who Declared War on America*:

> Islamabad's critical need to conceal the US-financed training infrastructure from the American government resulted from far more than the disagreement between the ISI and Washington over the fact that the prime recipients of military assistance were Islamist groups. The ISI adamantly opposed supporting Afghan resistance organisations associated with the predominantly tribal-traditional Pashtun population, who were essentially pro-Western. Instead, the ISI insisted on diverting some 70 per cent of the foreign aid to the Islamist parties—particularly the Hizb-i-Islami—who were inherently and virulently anti-American. From Washington's perspective, the support for the Afghan jihad was so important as to warrant 'ignoring' the ISI's use, or abuse, of the US-funded training infrastructure for other 'causes'—from Arab Islamists to regional groups serving Pakistan's own interests.[38]

CUTTING INDIA DOWN TO SIZE

Duplicity with the United States was also an offshoot of Pakistan's other objective—taking advantage of the Afghan war to realize its agenda of annexing Kashmir and cutting India down to size. The mindset which produced the objective was in accordance with a study of the 'Hindu' personality traits and Indian history by Lieutenant Colonel Javed Hassan, who later became a Lieutenant General. According to Hassan in his book *India: A Study in Profile*, 'India was hostage to a centrifugal rather than a centripetal tradition.'[39] Stating that India 'had a historical inability to exist as a unified state',[40] he identified Punjab, Jammu & Kashmir, Tamil Nadu and six north-eastern states (it is a small mercy that he leaves one of the seven sisters out) as being completely alienated from mainstream India. Haqqani, who refers to the book, writes that Hassan felt that 'with some encouragement', the alienated regions could become centres of insurgencies that would 'at best, dismember India and, at [the] least, weaken India's ability to seek regional dominance for years to come'.[41]

Hassan's book is particularly significant because it represented a study conducted for the Pakistani army's Faculty of Research and Doctrinal Studies, Command and Staff College, Quetta. It was published and distributed by the Services Book Club, Rawalpindi. None of these could have happened without official sanction from the highest level, which, in turn, indicated that it articulated—at least was in sync with—official policy. Further, Haqqani points out in footnote number 20 in chapter 7 of his book that in several conversations with him, Lieutenant General Hamid Gul, who was Director General of the ISI from 1987 to 1989, referred to an operational plan to encourage the centrifugal forces in India that existed when he was Director General of Military Intelligence from 1984 to 1987.[42]

Haqqani further reveals that after the United States had agreed to support the Afghan jihad (more about which appears later in the chapter) and American economic assistance had begun to flow, Zia-ul Haq wanted a forward policy be drawn up to deal with India.[43] Following a conversation between him and Lieutenant General Akhtar Abdul Rahman, a two-track policy combining clandestine operations to weaken India while simultaneously appearing to seek durable peace was followed, 'throughout the years Zia was in power as well as the subsequent years'.[44] In keeping with the policy, the ISI spread its tentacles deep into India, several files from Prime Minister Indira Gandhi's office were taken to Pakistan, Indian troop movements were constantly watched, conditions in Kashmir were studied and a search was mounted for Kashmiris capable of leading 'the freedom struggle'.[45]

Pakistan used the ISI to arm and train Sikh and Kashmiri terrorists. Referring to the training camps for Afghan Mujahideen which the ISI ran, Yossef Bodansky wrote:

> The main reason the ISI decided to keep the CIA out of the camps was the extent of the training and support non-Afghan 'volunteers' and others were getting in these camps. Most numerous were the thousands of Islamist trainees from Indian Kashmir and to a lesser extent the Sikhs from Punjab. In addition, thousands of Islamists from all over the Arab and Muslim world were routinely trained in these camps originally designed for the training of Afghan Mujahideen.[46]

Pakistan-sponsored terrorism has taken a heavy toll of human lives since it first raised its head in Punjab in 1978 to press the secessionist demand for 'Khalistan' (land of the pure). It triggered widespread violence during the 1980s and petered out after 1992 thanks to the strong measures taken by Punjab Police, then led by its Director General, K. P. S. Gill. By then, however, terrorism had started stalking Kashmir. Soon, it began menacing the whole of India. The first major strike, the serial bomb blasts in Mumbai on 12 March 1993, left 257 persons dead and about 700 injured. According to a report, officials of India's External Affairs Ministry said on 7 December 1999 that while a total of 25,267 persons had been killed in terrorist attacks in Jammu & Kashmir and Punjab in the 10 preceding years, 12,316 Indians had lost their lives in the wars the country had fought since 1947.[47]

THE INCIDENT ON 11/21

Those familiar with the history of Indo-American relations would not expect Washington DC to risk its own perceived interests to force Pakistan to stop terrorist attacks against India. But one would expect it to recognize its own interests and the fact that Pakistan has been blatantly taking it for a ride in Afghanistan. One would also have expected it to act against Pakistan's attempt to hijack the jihad in Afghanistan to achieve its own goals at the cost of American interests. Washington has done nothing of the sort. One, however, would not perhaps be surprised by this if one recalls what happened in Islamabad on 21 November 1979 and the American government's response to it.

Steve Coll gives a graphic account of the incident. As the day rolled on, students, supporters of Jama'at-e-Islami, the most powerful among Pakistan's fundamentalist Islamist political parties, began arriving in buses from Islamabad's Quad-e-Azam University, located three miles from the American embassy. They were demonstrating against the capture on 20 November of Mecca's Grand Mosque, the holiest of all Muslim religious places, by armed followers of a Saudi Arabian, Mohammad Abdullah al-Qahtani, who had accepted him as the Mahdi, or the Saviour who, the Quran had predicted, would appear to deliver Muslims from persecution. They began shooting and killing people who had come to mourn and/or to pray. Men of the Saudi Arabian army and French commandos cleared the shrine of the attackers on Saturday, 24 November. But the failure of the Saudi authorities to immediately reveal the identity and goal of the attackers enabled rumours to fly across the globe. One of these was that Washington DC and Tel Aviv were behind it. Coll writes, 'Absurd on its face, the rumour was nonetheless received as utterly plausible by thousands if not millions of Pakistanis.'[48]

Zia-ul Haq's government should have been particularly careful about the security of the American embassy after 5 November when Islamists had stormed the American embassy in Tehran and held 49 Americans hostage. It did provide an additional two dozen armed policemen following a request from the US ambassador, Arthur Hummel, for enhanced protection.[49] This proved grossly inadequate. The argument that Pakistan's government underestimated the scale and intensity of the attack would not wash. It could not have been unaware of the rumour, which had been reported on radio and television, and the elaborate preparations at the Quaid-i-Azam University since morning to mobilize demonstrators. Nor could it have been unaware of the intense anti-American sentiments being whipped up in the country by political parties like the Jama'at-e-Islami. Even if Pakistan's government had been initially caught napping, which it should not have been, it did absolutely nothing to disperse the attackers as the situation turned ugly.

The rioters had stormed into the embassy compound, burnt down 60 embassy vehicles and set the embassy building ablaze besides wounding a US Marine who died subsequently because the rampaging mobs prevented him from getting timely medical attention and the supply of oxygen being administered to him ran out. They had also attacked residential premises and taken hostages. The latter were saved because a Pakistani police officer, who had not surrendered his weapon to the demonstrators, had taken them to safety from a truck in which they had been loaded for transportation to the university for 'trial'. The Pakistani authorities knew all this but did not act despite dozens of pleas from Arthur Hummel, the ambassador, and John Reagan, the CIA station chief and the enormous black clouds of gasoline-scented smoke rising from the American compound and visible from miles away.[50]

The riot finally petered out in the evening. What was the United States' response to the entire incident? One learns from Coll that State Department spokesman, Hodding Carter, told reporters in Washington DC later in the day, 'All reports indicate all of the people in the compound have been removed and taken to safety thanks to the Pakistani troops.' President Jimmy Carter thanked Zia-ul Haq over the telephone for his assistance and his Pakistani counterpart expressed regret for the loss of life.[51] After this, one could hardly blame Zia for believing that any American slaughtered by a Pakistani mob would die thanking him and the Pakistani army, and perhaps even the mob!

If President Carter's lame-duck administration was weak, Ronald Reagan was a driven crusader against the Soviet Union and, as seen earlier, sanctioned aid on an unprecedented scale to Pakistan. Casey, of course, was the prime mover. Another powerful promoter of Afghan jihad and avid supporter of Pakistan's role in it was the powerful Texas Congressman, Charlie Wilson. From 1984, Wilson, goaded 'by small but passionate anti-communist lobbies' in Washington DC, 'began to force more money and more sophisticated weapons systems into the CIA's classified Afghan budget, even when Langley wasn't interested'.[52] His pressure changed what he described as the agency's lukewarm attitude toward the Afghan jihad and practice of sending just enough weaponry to 'ensure that many brave Afghan rebels died violently in battle but not enough to help them win'.[53]

Wilson's arguments deeply influenced Casey who was perhaps the most influential 'member of the Reagan administration after the president'. Both United States and Saudi Arabia, which were acting in concert to support the jihad in Afghanistan, poured money and increasingly sophisticated weapons for the mujahideen despite the fact that Pakistan relentlessly pursued its own agenda in Afghanistan. Many of the ISI's favoured Afghan leaders—Gulbuddin Hekmatyar, for example—were linked to Islamists like the Muslim Brotherhood. After 1983 particularly, Lieutenant General Akhtar and his colleagues tended to keep out followers of traditional Afghan royalty and tribal leaders, depriving them of weapons. Akhtar told Howard Hart, CIA's chief-of-station in Islamabad, that this was because the royalists did not fight vigorously enough. Mentioning this, Coll observes that as with every other facet of the covert war, 'the CIA accepted the ISI's approach with little dissent'.[54]

Coll further points out that some diplomats in the American embassy in Islamabad became worried that the CIA's dependence on the ISI was causing disunity in Afghan resistance. A secret cable from the embassy to the State Department observed that the Americans were largely content to follow Pakistan's lead since the Soviet invasion and that a change in approach 'would probably require some differentiation' in 'our policy from that of Pakistan'.[55] But few in the US government were concerned. The war bogged the Soviets down in Afghanistan and embarrassed Moscow globally and, according to Hart's calculation, the CIA's covert action programme had become cost effective by 1983.[56]

Protests within the US administration were summarily dismissed. Steve Coll writes:

> The ISI generals saw Casey as a forgiving ally, always focused on the big picture, content to let ISI make the detailed decisions

on the ground, even when working-level CIA case officers disagreed. Casy explained that Akhtar 'is completely involved in this war and certainly knows better than anyone else about his requirements. We simply have to support him'. On one trip Akhtar presented Casey with a $ 7000 carpet.[57]

Casey, Coll points out in endnote 19 to chapter 5 of his book, reported the gift and passed the carpet on to the US government. The incident, however, further underscored the efforts Pakistan made to cultivate Americans. It involved finding out the United States' goals and giving the impression that they were Pakistan's as well. It also meant giving the impression of working all out for these goals while doing everything possible to achieve Pakistan's own goals, even if it involved double-crossing and harming Americans. Simultaneously, it involved creating a situation in which Americans felt that they were totally dependent on the Pakistanis and then turning the screws on them. All the time, from beginning to end, the process involved flattery, wining, dining and giving expensive presents.

The process was on full display during the Afghan war (1979–89). Once the ISI took Casey, who ran the CIA for nearly six years before a stroke disabled him on 15 December 1986, literally for a ride. Coll narrates the hilarious incident. Casey continuously insisted on visiting a training camp for the mujahideen at Pakistan's border with Afghanistan. Pakistan, fearful that the Soviet Special Forces, active across the border, might kidnap him, was resisting. Finally, when the pressure could no longer be withstood, the ISI, with the collaboration of the CIA's Islamabad station, set up a temporary and, in Coll's words, 'essentially fake' training camp in 'the hills that sprawled to the north behind Islamabad, far away from the Afghan border'. They took Casey in a jeep at night and drove him around for the same length of time as taken to reach the border. Finally, they 'unpacked him from his convoy' and showed him a small crew of Afghans training on anti-aircraft guns. Added Coll, 'The Afghans made a lot of noise, and Casey wept tears of joy at the sight of his freedom fighters.'[58]

DECEPTION AND SURRENDER

On the nuclear front too, there was deception on the part of Pakistan and surrender on the part of Americans. General Zia brazenly lied about Pakistan's secret nuclear programme in private meetings with American leaders like President Reagan, Vice President Bush and Secretary of State George P. Shultz, who succeeded General Alexander Haig Jr. on 16 July 1982.[59] Americans were only too willing to swallow the lies. On his part, General Alexander Haig Jr. had told Pakistani officials that American reservations about Pakistan's nuclear programme 'need not become the centrepiece of US Pakistan relationship'.[60]

Despite its best efforts, Pakistan did not have a government of its choice in Afghanistan after the completion of the withdrawal of Soviet troops from there. The Democratic Republic of Afghanistan, installed by the Soviet Union and headed by Mohammad Najibullah who became President on 30 September 1987, remained in power with support from the Soviets. Pakistan, however, never gave up trying. The ISI chief, Lieutenant General Hamid Gul, cobbled together a plan under which the mujahideen were to capture Jalalabad in eastern Afghanistan, install a new government and then move towards Kabul.[61] The plan was scripted for disaster as the attack on well-fortified positions defended by heavy artillery followed the pattern of conventional warfare and not that of mobile guerrilla warfare in which the mujahideen were traditionally well-versed. Predictably, the Afghans were routed amid heavy slaughter.

It is difficult to believe that neither Lieutenant General Hamid Gul nor anyone else in the ISI and the Pakistani army, who was aware of the mujahideen groups' strengths and weaknesses, could foresee the outcome of the attack. Then why did they go for it? Yossef Bodansky observes:

> Islamabad knew that such a frontal attack could only result in a massive carnage of the attackers, who were not tightly controlled by Pakistan. As a result, the Afghan resistance that had endured almost a decade of fighting the Soviet-DRA forces was

so decimated, it could no longer constitute a viable fighting force. The road was open for Islamabad to organize and field its own 'mujahideen' force, now known as Taliban.[62]

One can argue that over four years separated the Jalalabad disaster and the emergence of the Taliban, and it is absurd to contend that Pakistan had planned creating the latter that early. One can also argue that the circumstances leading to the rise of the Taliban—oppression by the warlords, the near-anarchy conditions and the disruption of trade and commerce in Afghanistan by armed gangs[63]—indicate that the militia of madrasa students initially rose on its own to put an end to the intolerable conditions. Nevertheless, the fact is that the Jalalabad adventure, which had disaster scripted in its genes, had played havoc with the Afghan Mujahideen and cleared the path for the emergence of armed groups that were entirely the ISI's creatures. Was this a mere coincidence?

That it was not is strongly suggested by the manner in which Pakistan prepared for the next offensive in early 1990. The plan, on which the CIA and the ISI worked closely together, involved supporting a new conventional force built around Gulbuddin Hekmatyar's Lashkar-e-Israr (Army of Sacrifice), which, Pakistan, pursuing its own agenda, supplied with artillery and transport. Islamabad wanted this force to counter Ahmed Shah Massoud's army in the north.[64] Meanwhile, during the winter of 1989–90, the CIA helped to coordinate broad attacks against Afghanistan's cities and main roads. It also reached out to Massoud and more than doubled his monthly stipend of $200,000 to $500,000!

The mujahideen, however, seemed lacking in coordination and distracted by internal feuding. Massoud never attacked Najibullah's supply lines which the CIA had wanted him to. The offensive was never launched. After this, the United States' interest in Afghanistan waned. Far-reaching changes were occurring in Europe where the Soviet Union disintegrated and many constituent units of it became independent. Former Warsaw Pact countries were no longer satellites. At home, President Bill Clinton had his own troubles in his second term from 1996 to 2000 over the Monica Lewinsky episode.

Besides, the US Congress had adopted the Pressler Amendment in 1985 as a new section 620E(e) in the Foreign Assistance Act (FAA). It prohibited most economic and military assistance to Pakistan unless the President certified on an annual basis that it did not possess a nuclear explosive device and that the proposed US assistance programme would reduce significantly the risk of Pakistan possessing one. No American President issued such a certification between October 1989 when President Bush senior determined that Pakistan had developed such a weapon and 1995, when the Brown Amendment, piloted by Republican Senator Hank Brown, was adopted. It granted Pakistan a one-time waiver from the Pressler Amendment that barred economic and military aid for Islamabad for violating US nuclear non-proliferation laws. This allowed the United States to release arms worth $368 million to Pakistan that had been blocked earlier. But before the tap could flow again, Pakistan's nuclear tests of May 1998, which followed India's earlier that month, led to another stanching of aid.

Civil war ravaged Afghanistan. Osama bin Laden came from Sudan and set up his headquarters there in May 1996. The Taliban, who had emerged in 1994, captured Kabul in September 1996 with massive help from Pakistan. Meanwhile, the United States became a target of terror attacks at home.

It was, of course, no stranger to these. On 30 July 1916, a massive explosion in an arsenal in what was then called Black Tom Island and was located on the New Jersey side of the New York Harbor shook New York. As Christopher Dickey points out in *Securing the City: Inside America's Best Counterterror Force—The NYPD*, the island, now known as Liberty State Park, was then used as a storage yard for munitions being shipped to Britain during World War I.[65] The explosion was attributed to sabotage by German agents. Again, at noon on 16 September 1920, a horse-drawn carriage blew up in front of J. P. Morgan's headquarters at 23 Wall Street, New York City, leaving behind 40 persons dead and devastation all round.[66] In the 1940s and 1950s, John Metesky—known as the 'mad bomber'—a disabled and disgruntled employee of a public utility company, repeatedly planted explosives at the Grand Central Terminal, Penn Station Terminal, Radio City Music Hall, New

York Public Library, New York Port Authority and, of course, the subway.[67]

Terrorism in its current lethal, collective and organized sense, however, began making an appearance from the late 1980s. One might cite several examples to indicate their nature. A truck bomb attack by adherents of a sectarian group on the Alfred P. Murrah Federal Building in Oklahoma City left 168 persons dead on 19 April 1995.[68] Yu Kikumura, a 35-year-old Japanese affiliated to the Japanese Red Army, was arrested in New Jersey as he was approaching New York with explosives and bomb-making components. Sent by the Japanese Red Army at the behest of Muammar Gaddafi, then President of Libya who was incensed over an American air strike against his country, which he thought was aimed at killing him, Kikumura's target was the United States Navy's recruiting office in Manhattan, which was to be attacked on 14 April 1988. Sentenced in November 1988 to 30 years' imprisonment, he was back in Japan after 22 years minus 'good time'.[69]

In November 1990, Sayyid el-Nosair, an Egyptian by birth who had become an American citizen, shot dead Rabbi Meir Kahane at Marriott Hotel on Lexington Avenue, Manhattan. Kahane, who founded the Jewish Defence League in Brooklyn, New York, in 1970, was known for his violent, extremist views and had served jail terms for arms smuggling. El-Nosair, who had escaped from the hotel, was wounded in an exchange of fire with a postal service policeman on the streets, and was arrested.[70] In 1994, a US federal court sentenced him to imprisonment on gun possession and other charges. While serving his life sentence, he was convicted, along with the blind Egyptian-origin cleric, Omar Abdel-Rahman, in what has come to be known as the New York City Landmark Bomb plot and sentenced to life imprisonment plus 15 years in 1996. Omar Abdel-Rahman was sentenced to life imprisonment. Both of them were denied the facility of parole. The plot, which came to light as investigations by the Federal Bureau of Investigation (FBI) into the World Trade Center bombing on 26 February 1993 proceeded, involved a plot to blow up the United Nations, the Lincoln and Holland tunnels, the George Washington Bridge and 26 Federal Plaza housing the FBI's office in New York,[71] and to assassinate Senator Alfonse M. D'Amato and State Assembly-man Dov Hikind, among other targets.[72]

Several incidents, all with connections with the Af-Pak region, occurred in quick succession, after a lull of about two years following Kahane's killing. On 25 January 1993, Mir Amal Kasi (also spelt Kansi) fired an AK-47 assault rifle at occupants of cars about to turn into the CIA's headquarters in Langley, Virginia. He killed two CIA personnel on the spot, injured three, fled the scene and departed to Pakistan, from where he was arrested on 15 June 1997, brought to the United States,[73] tried and executed. On 26 February 1993, Ramzi Yousef and his associates set off a car bomb in an underground garage at the World Trade Center, New York. killings six persons. He was arrested in Pakistan in February 1995 and brought back to the United States where he is serving a life term without parole.[74]

Americans abroad also became targets. On 25 June 1996, a tanker truck loaded with at least 5,000 pounds of plastic explosives was driven into the parking lot in front of Khobar Towers, a residential complex in Dhahran, Saudi Arabia. A massive explosion destroyed the front part of Building 131, an eight-story structure, moments later, killing 19 Americans and wounding 372.[75] The other attacks which followed bore al Qaeda's unmistakeable signature. The two earlier ones targeted American embassies in Nairobi, capital of Kenya, and Dar-es-Salaam, capital of Tanzania, on 7 August 1998. Steve Coll gives a graphic account of both attacks and the American retaliation.

The one at Nairobi occurred shortly before 10.30 a.m. when a truck laden with explosives blew up at the exit gate of the parking lot behind the embassy, shearing off the embassy's rear facade, killing 231 persons including 12 Americans and 32 Kenyans working at the embassy. About 4,000 persons were wounded. The one at Dar-es-Salaam occurred about nine minutes later when another truck, packed with explosives, blew up. Eleven Africans were killed and 85 wounded. The casualties were fewer in Dar-es-Salaam perhaps because a completely filled water tank that stood between the truck and the building took the brunt of the blast.[76] Who did it? The CIA Director, George Tenet, formally conveyed to President Bill Clinton on 14 August that in his organization's judge·nent bin Laden and his leading Egyptian aides were responsible.[77]

The United States already had Osama bin Laden on its radar for quite some time. By early 1996, the CIA had come to regard him as 'one of the most significant financial sponsors of Islamic extremist activities in the world'.[78] Both under American pressure and keen to improve its ties with the United States, Sudan asked bin Laden, living there since 1991, to leave. In May 1996, bin Laden shifted to Afghanistan and began sending incendiary messages and planning terrorist strikes against Saudi Arabia and the United States. In one of them, called the *Ladenese Epistle*, he called out to 'Muslim brothers' throughout the world, saying that their brothers in Saudi Arabia and Palestine were calling for their help and asking them to participate in their jihad against the enemies of God, the Israelis and Americans. They were asking them (Muslim brothers) to defy them (Israelis and Americans) in whatever they possibly could, 'so as to expel them in defeat and humiliation from the holy places of Islam'.[79]

SANS STRATEGY

Yet, the United States had still to stitch together a coherent plan to deal with him by the time the Nairobi and Dar-es-Salaam attacks occurred. Understandably, its retaliation achieved little. Acting on a CIA report that senior leaders of Islamist terrorist and militant groups would meet that day at al Qaeda's Zawhar Kili camp about seven miles south of the city of Khost on Afghanistan's eastern border with Pakistan, and that Osama bin Laden himself might be present, it ordered a missile strike. At about 10 p.m. local time, 75 Tomahawk cruise missiles hit the camp killing at least 21 Pakistani volunteers for Jihad and wounding dozens more. Simultaneously, 13 Tomahawk cruise missiles slammed into a chemical factory called Al Shifa in Khartoum, Sudan. There were several reasons for it. CIA reports had indicated that bin Laden had ownership links with the factory. Also, an Egyptian agent working with the CIA had returned with soil samples from the factory that showed the presence of substances associated with the manufacture of chemical weapons.[80] There was anger in Sudan and demonstrations in Pakistan against the attack and allegations in the United States that President Bill Clinton had ordered the entire exercise to divert attention from his problems at home, particularly the uproar over his liaison with Monica Lewinsky, a White House intern. Meanwhile, bin Laden remained untouched. According to the CIA, he had been present at the Zawhar Kili camp but had left several hours before the attack.

The attacks persisted. Perhaps the most striking among these outside America was the one on the United States' Navy destroyer, USS *Cole*, on 12 October 2000, as it refuelled outside the Yemeni port of Aden. A boat, filled with explosives and three suicide bombers on board, came close to it and blew up, creating a 40 feet by 20 feet hole in the ship's hull, killing 17 American sailors and wounding over 30. The CIA's Counterterrorism Center found links between the bombers and an al Qaeda operative but could not establish bin Laden's direct hand in it.[81] There was no American retaliation. Bill Clinton was in the last leg of his presidency and opinion among his civilian and military advisors was sharply divided. His own assessment of the relative importance of things was faulty. He repeatedly signalled to Pakistan's highest leadership that securing Osama bin Laden was a lesser priority than nuclear proliferation.[82] As later events were to further indicate, faulty decision-making caused by divided counsel has contributed significantly to the United States' poor progress in the war against al Qaeda and the Taliban.

The circumstances leading to President Clinton's one-day visit to Pakistan following his trips to India and Bangladesh, in March 2000, clearly underlined the perennial flaws of Washington DC's policy toward Islamabad. The American secret service was dead against it for security reasons, including the danger of a stinger missile attack on the presidential aircraft by al Qaeda or the Taliban. Pakistan, however, lobbied hard and made gestures on terrorism—volunteering to help in handing over two Arab militants, who were secretly under arrest, to the Americans and Musharraf announcing that he was 'actively considering' a trip to Kandahar to persuade Mullah Omar to deliver bin

Laden to the US authorities. Steve Coll, who provides many interesting details of the visit, observes that Pakistan's was 'in many ways a cynical charm offensive' and did not indicate a change in its jihad strategy. He adds that the Pakistani army had learnt long ago that 'it could earn credit with the Americans', especially the CIA and the FBI, by cracking down on a relatively small number of al Qaeda personnel who were not important to Pakistan's policies in Kashmir or Afghanistan.[83]

And it worked again. Clinton agreed to the visit. His agenda was to coax Pakistan away from its military nuclear policy and promote American engagement and ensure regional stability.[84] As Coll informs, partly because of so many issues on the plate, Clinton's team did not want to 'push the Pakistani army too hard on terrorism'.[85] Musharraf, reading the American agenda correctly, quietly allowed Kashmiri terrorist groups with close ties with the ISI and al Qaeda to step up recruitment across Pakistan.[86] The talks during Clinton's visit, undertaken under unprecedented security cover, reflected the same order of priorities. In their one-to-one conversation, Clinton pressed Musharraf hard to use Pakistan's influence with Mullah Omar to get him to hand over bin Laden to the United States. Musharraf, according to Coll, promised to do as much as he could but told Thomas Pickering, Under Secretary of State, the next day that Pakistan had little leverage in any event.[87]

Not surprisingly, the Taliban continued to hold sway over most of Afghanistan, bin Laden remained alive and well and at work, and the various Pakistani jihadi groups flourished. The attacks on 11 September next year were waiting to happen. When they did, the United States reacted with fury, just as it had done after Pearl Harbor. Pakistan once again found itself in a corner, and once again it slipped out of it and took the United States for a long and bumpy ride that continues.

The ISI Chief, Lieutenant General Mehmood Ahmed, was in Washington DC when 9/11 happened. On 12 September, the United States Deputy Secretary of State, Richard Armitage, summoned him as well as the Pakistani ambassador to the United States, Maleeha Lodhi, and told them that, on the following day, he would hand over a list of what the United States wanted from Pakistan. Mehmood committed unequivocally that Pakistan would stand by the United States.[88]

If there was blunt talk in Washington, there was fear in Pakistan of being at the receiving end of American wrath. At a meeting with his generals and a few important members of his cabinet on 12 September, President Pervez Musharraf said that the United States would react like a wounded bear and attack Afghanistan. Pointing out that Bush had already said that America would punish not just the perpetrators of the attack but also any state harbouring the terrorists, he said that Pakistan could not oppose American demands and could no longer support the Taliban; he, according to Ahmed Rashid, however, added that Pakistan would not participate in any American attack on Afghanistan either.[89]

On 13 September 2001, Richard Armitage presented Lieutenant General Mehmood Ahmed with a list of seven demands—blanket permission for overflights over Pakistani territory; access to naval bases, airports and borders for operations against al Qaeda; immediate intelligence sharing and cooperation; stopping all al Qaeda operatives at the Pakistan–Afghanistan border and intercepting all arms shipments through Pakistan while ending all logistical support to bin Laden; cutting all fuel shipments to the Taliban; publicly condemning the terrorist acts and, finally, ending support to the Taliban and severing diplomatic ties with them.[90]

The demands, Armitage said, were non-negotiable. Lieutenant General Ahmed replied that Pakistan would do whatever the Americans asked it to do. In another development, Secretary of State Colin Powell rang up Musharraf, telling him that although the United States did not have a war plan yet, he expected an early reply to the American demands. According to Ahmed Rashid, a cabinet meeting in Washington DC on the same day decided that Pakistan would be at the risk of an attack if it did not help the United States.[91]

Arm-twisting did it. On 14 September, Musharraf told his nine corps commanders and a dozen staff officers at a meeting that Pakistan had no alternative to accepting the demands; otherwise the United States would declare it a terrorist state. Several generals protested, three of them particularly strongly. Musharraf silenced them by arguing that if Pakistan accepted the American demands only partially, India, which had been trying to persuade the Americans during the past five years to declare Pakistan a terrorist state, would step into the vacuum, offering bases and support to Washington. He said that Pakistan would then face a hostile India allied with the US military, while hostile US forces in Afghanistan could target Pakistan's nuclear weapons under the guise of preventing them from falling into the hands of Islamist extremists.[92]

Neither Musharraf nor his colleagues, however, had any intention of keeping any of the commitments they might make to the Americans. Ahmed Rashid quotes Abdul Sattar, who attended the meeting as Foreign Minister, as saying, 'We agreed that we would unequivocally accept all US demands, but then later we would express our private reservations to the US and we would not necessarily agree with all the details.' Rashid added that the policy that Pakistan would adopt toward the United States was summed up as, 'First say yes and later say but.' Musharraf followed this policy consistently for the next few years.[93] The ISI, according to Rashid, hoped that by initially complying with US demands, it could create sufficient room to manoeuvre and evade meeting them. It had no intention of dumping Kashmiri militants and their struggle against India.[94]

The implementation of the 'yes but' strategy began almost immediately. Late on 14 September night, Musharraf summoned the US ambassador to Pakistan, Wendy Chamberlin, and told her that he accepted the American demands in toto. Next, he telephoned United States Secretary of State, Colin Powell, and warned him that the domestic fallout of his decision would be unpredictable, and he expected the United States to be patient and understanding.[95] Here Musharraf was applying what has been Pakistan's standard pressure tactics vis-à-vis the United States—emphasizing the dire consequences, including its own collapse and takeover of the region by fundamentalist Islamists, that may ensue if its demands were not met.

Musharraf submitted a huge wish list, including the removal of all US sanctions against Pakistan imposed after the nuclear weapons tests of May 1998 and his own coup on 12 October 1999 which ousted Prime Minister Nawaz Sharif's government. It also included the writing off of Pakistan's gargantuan foreign debt in full, the resumption of military aid and quick disbursal of loans from the US and the World Bank.

The Bush administration and Congress moved swiftly to lift the sanctions. Pakistan was declared a frontline state in the global war against terror. Aid poured in. According to a US Congressional Research Service report, overt economic and military aid to Pakistan came to over $6.5 billion during financial years 2002–05, over $1.8 billion in 2006, and over $1.7 and $2.00 billion in 2007 and 2008 respectively.[96] Pakistan's outstanding debts to the United States and other Western nations were rescheduled or restructured. The Bush administration no doubt rejected Pakistan's request for delivery of 28 F-16s paid for in the 1980s but never delivered because of Pakistan's nuclear weapons programme. Nor was it willing to support Pakistan's request to suspend quota and tariff restrictions on its textile and apparel exports to the United States. Nevertheless, what Pakistan got was a bonanza.

The gains for Pakistan were very considerable. Besides, it had a critical advantage. The Americans distrusted the ISI which was riddled with fundamentalist Islamists who supported the Taliban and were soft toward al Qaeda, and the CIA was apprehensive of entrusting such an unreliable agency with so much of the intelligence-gathering burden. But it had to lump it. Pakistan not only had the longest border with Afghanistan but it was also the only country that could provide intelligence about the Taliban's military preparedness and targets for US bombing.[97]

Islamabad's Goals

In strategic terms, what Pakistan wanted out of its 'cooperation' with the United States in the latter's war against the Taliban and al Qaeda became increasingly clear as events unfolded. Its basic goal was to keep intact as much of the large infrastructure of terror it had assiduously built up to annex Kashmir, balkanize India and set up a puppet government in Kabul through sustained unconventional and, if necessary, conventional warfare backed by nuclear blackmail. In Afghanistan, its first preference was putting Gulbuddin Hekmatyar, a cruel and bitterly anti-American fundamentalist warlord, who had been its protégé since the 1970s, in power. The second preference was to install Taliban groups that would do its bidding. This was an additional reason for the Pakistani establishment's war against Tehrik-e-Taliban Pakistan (TTP), which had courted its wrath by challenging its military's authority.

A subsidiary goal was extracting from the United States as much military and financial assistance as it could to be able to achieve both objectives. The key lay in reducing Washington DC into a position of utter dependence from where it could not turn down at least the more important of Islamabad's demands. The strategy to realize both goals clearly rested on the assumption that the Americans were not fully committed to victory in Afghanistan and would quit as the war prolonged, consuming huge chunks of money and raising casualty figures. This would require prolonging the war to project it as unwinnable by the United States and its North Atlantic Treaty Organization (NATO) allies. This in turn would be done by acting against the Taliban—and that too against those segments of the latter not amenable to Islamabad's hegemony—only when pressure, primarily from America, became intense. The tardy and intermittent action was to be explained in terms of the lack of sophisticated weapons necessary for decisive operations and the need to station a vast chunk of its army on its border with India. This in turn would require keeping tensions with India alive by not punishing those responsible for perpetrating the terror strike in Mumbai beginning on 26 November 2008, continuing terrorist strikes against India and keeping tensions alive along the border by stepping up infiltration of Pakistan-trained terrorists across the line of control in Jammu & Kashmir.

Delayed but successful action against Taliban groups hostile to the Pakistani establishment would show that Pakistan could help if it wanted. This would be accompanied by the message that it could overcome intense domestic opposition to its siding with the United States, and do more, if it could show its people that helping the United States was beneficial for them. For this, more arms and financial aid to it, and the marginalization of India's role in Afghanistan, were essential.

The second process, which was to be stepped up as the war prolonged and Washington DC got desperate to get out, was to convince it as well as other NATO powers that there was no alternative to a negotiated settlement with the 'good' or 'moderate' Taliban and that it could be the honest broker—of course, for a consideration. One way to prolong the war was to enhance the Taliban and al Qaeda's ability to resist and preserve as much of the forces of both as possible. This would also enhance the possibility of achieving Pakistan's post–Afghan war objectives already outlined. Continued supply of arms and fighters was an important way of enhancing their fighting ability, and the minimization of casualties and capture by enemy forces was central to the preservation of their fighting strength. Efforts in both directions began early.

According to a report in the *New York Times* of 8 December 2001, Pakistani border guards at a checkpoint in Khyber Pass waved on convoys heading for Afghanistan on 8 and 12 October—which was a month after the Pakistan government had agreed to end its support to the Taliban. The report stated that trucks in the convoys carried, under tarpaulin covers, rifles, ammunition and rocket-propelled grenade launchers for Taliban fighters. The sender was ISI, which had for long 'provided safe passage to armadas of truckers and smugglers who supplied a mountain of weapons to the Taliban war machine. But the policy was supposed to have changed in September after a Washington ultimatum to Pakistan'. That obviously did not happen and the report pointed out that 'Pakistani intelligence officers and military advisers continued helping the Taliban at least into October, providing tactical advice and helping to strengthen fortifications around Kandahar, the southern stronghold of the Taliban, diplomats and intelligence officials said'.[98]

On 8 November, a month after the first convey crossed into Afghanistan on 8 October, Zahid Hussain, a respected Pakistani journalist, spent a day in Afghanistan's war zone disguised as a doctor in a team sent by a humanitarian organization. He writes in his book, *Front-line Pakistan: The Path to Catastrophe and the Killing of Benazir Bhutto*:

> Whilst the Pakistani government was pledging its support for the US war on the Taliban, I witnessed thousands of Pakistanis pouring into the south-eastern city of Jalalabad in response to Osama bin Laden's call to arms. In their flowing *shalwar* and *kameez*, they stood out instantly.[99]

Pakistan's attempt to preserve the strength of the Taliban and al Qaeda was in evidence a few days after Hussain's visit. The occasion was the airlift from the city of Kunduz in northern Afghanistan, which the United States permitted following a phone call from President Musharraf to President Bush. The incident not only illustrates Pakistan's efforts to preserve its military and strategic assets intact but also provides an example of how it often managed to extract a mile from an American promise of an inch.

The airlift, which lasted for a week from 15 November 2001, 'was meant for the safe evacuation of ISI and Frontier Corps personnel and other Pakistanis stationed there'. Ahmed Rashid, who reveals this, also adds that hundreds of ISI officers, Taliban commanders and soldiers of the IMU (Islamic Movement of Uzbekistan) and al Qaeda boarded the planes. 'What was sold as a minor extraction turned into a major air bridge.'[100] Rashid further adds that foreign terrorists who escaped from Kunduz were believed to have been more numerous than those who escaped later from Tora Bora. In both cases foreign terrorists were allowed to stay in South and North Waziristan, the wildest of Pakistan's tribal areas.[101]

Curiously, the Pentagon denied any knowledge of the airlift, with Defence Secretary Donald H. Rumsfeld saying shortly afterwards, 'I have received no information that would verify or validate statements about aircraft moving in and out. I doubt them.'[102] The airlift, however, was seen to have taken place. A report in the *New York Times* of 23 November 2001 quoted Northern Alliance soldiers saying on the same day that Pakistani planes had once again flown into the city to evacuate Pakistanis fighting alongside Afghan Taliban forces trapped there.[103] It further quoted alliance officials as stating that according to a Taliban leader at least three Pakistani Air Force planes had arrived and departed 'in recent days' on similar missions. The report stated, 'Two more planes landed Thursday night [November 22], according to the latest report. One Northern Alliance official said that a group of people had been observed today waiting for another plane to arrive at the Kunduz airport.'[104]

There were other reports about the airlift. A despatch published in the *Independent*, London, on 26 November, stated that 'fighters around Kunduz had reported spotting Pakistani Air Force planes arriving and departing Kunduz over the past few nights, allegedly transporting Pakistani fighters from the encircled Taliban enclave to safety'.[105] According to it,

> At least three Pakistani aircraft were seen landing in Kunduz in the middle of last week, and two more were sighted subsequently.
>
> The Pentagon, which is monitoring the situation round Kunduz in detail, has been evasive on the subject and has said it has no information about the landings. Pakistani officials have also declined to comment.[106]

The report pointed out that Pakistan had made no secret of its deep concern about the fate of Pakistani nationals fighting in the town and 'potentially facing mass execution', and that General Musharraf 'had pressed the American-led coalition to ensure their safety after the surrender of Kunduz'. According to it, Washington DC had said that it wanted all foreign fighters trapped in Kunduz to be captured but was 'deeply indebted to the Islamabad government for supporting its war against the Taliban' and might 'well have decided for diplomatic reasons not to notice the airlift'.[107]

CAPITULATE AND CONCEAL

On the part of the United States, this was the first major act, post 9/11, of hiding the truth about its actions in Afghanistan from its public and media. It was also the first act of capitulation to Pakistan's pressure post 9/11. In retrospect, the latter was tantamount to taking the first step toward not winning the war in Afghanistan. Retreating from Afghanistan, the majority of foreigners settled down in North and South Waziristan and Bajaur regions in Federally Administered Tribal Areas (FATA), where networks run by Afghan war veterans like Jalaluddin Haqqani and Gulbuddin Hekmatyar, leader of Hizb-e-Islami, sheltered bin Laden's surviving fighters.

Al Qaeda's top brass linked up with the local Taliban, capitalizing on the wave of sympathy for the Afghan Taliban and their leader, Mullah Omar, which the coalition's onslaught had created. The presence of senior al Qaeda leaders, particularly Osama bin Laden and Ayman al-Zawahiri, inspired Waziristan's ultra-conservative and religious tribesmen to join the militants' ranks. The money the Arabs showered on the residents of FATA, whom they trusted, as well as their appeal to concepts of Islamic ideology and Islamic fraternity, moved the emotional tribesmen and hindered governmental action against them. Others also helped. Imtiaz Gul, well-known commentator on al Qaeda, Taliban and Pakistan's tribal areas, writes,

> Sympathetic officials and operatives within the intelligence agencies—the ISI, the Military Intelligence (MI) and the civilian Intelligence Bureau (IB)—as well as those within the armed forces would look the other way when confronted with the challenge of arresting Al Qaeda and Taliban, or stopping their movement to and from Afghanistan.[108]

Protected by the ISI, which maintained a high-profile presence in FATA, the Taliban and al Qaeda began running their own fiefdom in South Waziristan, 'killing tribal elders considered to be spying on them for the Afghans and the Americans and forcing others to flee with their families'.[109] ISI did much more. A secret report compiled by US, NATO and Afghan intelligence in June 2007, and quoted by Ahmed Rashid, said that ISI operatives reportedly paid a significant number of the Taliban to fight and a large number of those fighting were doing so under pressure from the ISI. It categorically stated that the insurgency could not survive 'without its sanctuary in Pakistan' which provided 'freedom of movement, safe havens, logistic and training facilities, a base for recruitment, communication for command and control, and a secure environment for collaboration with foreign extremist groups'. Besides, Pakistan provided a 'seemingly endless supply of potential new recruits for the insurgency'.[110]

The support continues. According to a report in the *New York Times* of 1 April 2009, Michele A. Flournoy, Under Secretary of Defence for Policy, acknowledged before the US Senate Armed Services Committee the administration's concern about a wing of the ISI, which, American intelligence officers said, was providing money and military assistance to the Taliban in Afghanistan. Under sharp questioning by Senator John McCain, she said that she thought the ISI—or at least parts of the latter—were 'certainly a problem to be dealt with'.[111]

Enhancing the military capability of the Taliban and al Qaeda and protecting their cadres and military infrastructure was one way of prolonging the war and undermining the Americans' will to continue fighting. The other was raising objections and withholding cooperation. Pakistan's response to Operation Khanjar (curved sword) in Helmand Province, launched on 1 July 2009, provides an example. Conducted by 4,000-strong US Marine Expeditionary Brigade, joined by 650 Afghan troops, the operation's objective was to push out Taliban forces who had established a dominant presence in the province. Although American and allied forces had earlier swept through, killing and capturing many Taliban fighters, the absence of sufficient ground troops had prevented them from holding on to the large areas which they had cleared of the Taliban.[112]

A report in the *New York Times* of 1 July quoted Brigadier General Larry Nicholson as saying in a statement released after the operation began:

> What makes Operation Khanjar different from those that have occurred before is the massive size of the force introduced, the speed at which it will insert, and the fact that where we go we will stay, and where we stay, we will hold, build and work toward transition of all security responsibilities to Afghan forces.[113]

Further, the *New York Times* dispatch cites a report by The Associated Press, which quotes a spokesman for the Marines, Captain Bill Pelletier, as saying that the Marines will be pushing into areas where NATO and Afghan troops had not previously established a permanent presence. As part of the counter-insurgency strategy, the troops will meet with local leaders, help determine their needs and take a variety of actions to make towns and villages more secure.[114]

This was certainly bad news for the Taliban, whose control of poppy harvests and opium smuggling in Helmand provided major financing for the Afghan insurgency. Obviously, Pakistan too did not relish the development as the success of the marines would mean the Taliban losing a strategically very important province as well as a critical source of money.

Shortly after the operations began, Pakistani officials told the Obama administration that it would force militants across the border into Pakistan and that this could further inflame the latter's troubled province of Balochistan. A report in the *New York Times* of 21 July 2009, which stated this, added that Pakistani intelligence officials claimed that they did not have enough troops to deploy in Balochistan without 'denuding its border with its archenemy, India', and that 'dialogue with the Taliban, not more fighting', was in Pakistan's national interest'.[115]

The report further added that Pakistan's critical assessment was provided as President Obama's then special envoy for the region, Richard C. Holbrooke, arrived in that country on the night of 21 July. Earlier, on Friday, 17 July, senior officials of the ISI briefed, on the condition of anonymity, the staff of the *New York Times* about Pakistan's perspective. It was argued during the briefing that the surge in Afghanistan would further reinforce the perception that foreigners were occupying the country and lead to more civilian casualties, thus further alienating the population and triggering more local resistance to foreign troops.

A HUGE RED HERRING

That the Pakistanis were drawing a huge red herring became clear from the *New York Times* report itself when it cited an email message from a spokesman for the American and NATO forces in Afghanistan, Rear Admiral Gregory J. Smith, on 20 July. The message said that there had been no significant movement of insurgents out of Afghanistan, and no indication of foreign fighters moving into Afghanistan through Balochistan or Iran, another concern of the Pakistanis. The report stated that Obama administration officials praised Pakistani operations in the Swat Valley and parts of tribal areas against the Pakistani Taliban who threatened the government in Islamabad, but were frustrated by lack of action against the Taliban and other militants fighting Americans in Afghanistan or terrorizing India.

Further, while the Americans held that the Afghan Taliban leader, Mullah Mohammad Omar, and his inner circle of commanders, known as the Quetta Shura, were operating out of Quetta, the capital of Balochistan, and were sheltered by the Pakistani authorities, the latter claimed that Mullah Omar was in Afghanistan. There were also differences over the location of the Afghan Taliban leader, Sirajuddin Haqqani, who, the Americans said, operated from North Waziristan under Pakistani protection and equipped and trained Taliban fighters for Afghanistan. Pakistani officials' statement that Haqqani spent most of his time in Afghanistan implied that the American complaints about him being provided sanctuary were baseless.

Pakistan's refusal to act militarily against the Haqqanis, known to have close ties with it, indicated its desire to preserve Taliban groups loyal to it. So did Islamabad's postponement of action against the Quetta Shura to as late as February 2010 when several of its leading members were arrested. As has been seen earlier, far from indicating Pakistan's bona fides, these arrests have raised serious questions, as has the Pakistani government and army's action against the TTP, frequently referred to as Pakistani Taliban. Entitled Rah-e-Raast (the Right Path or the Straight Path), it started in Lower Dir district of Pakistan's NWFP on Sunday, 26 April 2009. On 28 April, it was carried to the neighbouring Buner district of the same province. Then the fighting spread to Swat, Upper Dir, Shangla and several others of the 24 districts comprising the NWFP and large tracts of the country's FATA which includes seven agencies—Khyber, Kurram, Bajaur, Mohamand, Orakzai and North and South Waziristan.

Until 17 October 2009, however, the fighting in FATA was primarily in the nature of aerial attacks and artillery fire on the strongholds of the Taliban, and occasional ambushes and skirmishes involving the latter and Pakistani troops. All this time, the Pakistani army was said to have been preparing for what, the prediction went, would be a very rough and bloody campaign. *Dawn* reported on 18 October 2009 that there were an estimated 10,000 to 12,000 TTP fighters in South Waziristan and up to 25,000 across Pakistan's semi-autonomous tribal belt, which had a history of fierce independence. The reports cited Pakistan's military as saying that Central Asian militants, mainly Uzbeks, as well as Arabs, North Africans and even some Europeans were also in the area.[116] Against them the Pakistani army fielded two divisions consisting of 27,000 soldiers.[117]

There could be no doubt that it would be a difficult campaign. The Taliban had the advantage of a terrain custom-made for guerrilla warfare, familiarity with every bit of it, and long experience of fighting Soviet and American and NATO forces. The Pakistani army, however, had the advantage of air support, far superior fire power and advanced weaponry and equipment for counterterrorism and counter-insurgency operations. It was, therefore, by no means an impossible battle to win, especially since victory depends a great deal on strategy, tactics, morale and the will to win. The question is: Did Pakistan have the will? For an answer, one might look at what its leaders have been saying and the performance of its troops on the ground in its offensive in NWFP.

In an address to the nation on 7 May 2009, on the eve of the Pakistan Army's major offensive in Swat, Prime Minister Syed Yousuf Raza Gilani said, 'We will not bow down before terrorists and extremists and [will] force them to lay down arms.' He added that the time had come when the nation should unite against elements which wanted to take Pakistan hostage at gunpoint and were hell-bent to put the country's future at stake. Asserting that nobody could 'be allowed to challenge the writ of the government', he said that the army had been called out to eliminate terrorists and protect the life and property of people in Swat.[118]

President Zardari clarified during an interview with Margaret Warner of PBS channel on 8 May that the word 'eliminate' used by Gilani meant killing. He had first told Warner that eliminating meant 'clearing out the area of miscreants and bringing life to normalcy'. Warner had pressed on, asking, 'But I mean what happens to them? Are you talking about killing them all or driving them somewhere else? If so, where?' Zardari had replied, 'No, we are talking about—this is an offensive, this is war. They—if they can, they will kill our soldiers and we do the same.' Warner had persisted, 'I am still trying to figure out what eliminate means.' Zardari had replied, 'Well I know what you're trying to figure out. Eliminate means exactly what it means.' Warner interjected, 'Killing them all.' He stated bluntly, 'That's what it means.'[119]

The progress of the offensive so far should provide some idea as to whether Pakistan can eliminate the Taliban and, more important, whether it wants to do it. Success is an indication of the seriousness to achieve the goals of a military campaign.

OFFICIAL CLAIMS, NON-OFFICIAL DOUBTS

One needs to begin with official claims while measuring success. The government declared on 9 July 2009 that military operations in the Swat–Malakand area had been successful, with Prime Minister Syed Yousuf Raza Gilani telling journalists at a press conference, 'We have achieved our target.'[120] He further said, 'The displaced [by fighting] men, women and children will begin returning to their homes with dignity from July 13.' Public utilities like electricity and gas supply, he added, had been restored and banks had reopened.[121]

Not everyone present, however, shared the Prime Minister's assessment. The United Nations' Under-Secretary General for Humanitarian Affairs, John Holmes, had reservations. He told journalists on 10 July that the security situation was 'not going to be 100 per cent' in areas that had seen the most fighting. 'We hope,' he said, 'that the returns are voluntary and the conditions right.'[122] Holmes made it clear that the UN was in constant touch with the government 'to make sure that from our point of view we are satisfied that the conditions are right. Our main concern is to make sure that people are not forced to return before they're ready.'[123] If the situation was not satisfactory, one would witness the worst possible scenario of people having to leave their homes again. Meanwhile, massive assistance would be required over the coming months to assist people pick up their lives again.

The process of sending people back to their homes from the camps began on Monday, 13 July. According to an Agence France-Presse (AFP) report, just over 200 persons were seen leaving the Jalozai camp, where 4,000 families had sought refuge, and a nearby camp in Charsadda. According to a report in the *New York Times*, refugees were eager to return but many had expressed fears about their safety.[124] A *Dawn* report quoted Shamsher Ali, a 55-year-old shopkeeper, as saying that he was worried as previous military operations had failed to crush the Taliban. 'The army promised us twice before that they cleared the area, but then Taliban came again and again to Swat. Perhaps this time the Taliban will come again to Swat,' he said. A government spokesman denied that the process of return was slow, saying it was expected to gain momentum in the coming days.[125]

The *Dawn* report also expressed scepticism about the Pakistani government's claim that more than 1,700 militants had been killed in the offensive. It said that official death tolls were impossible to confirm independently and many suspected that the Taliban simply melted away into the mountains as they had done during past operations. Nevertheless, Interior Minister Rehman Malik said on 14 July that militants had been defeated and security forces were in control of the region. Several militant commanders had been killed in Swat and TTP chief Maulana Fazlullah had been injured. Malik, who was talking to reporters after launching Islamabad Traffic Police's FM channel, had said, while speaking during the ceremony, that the enemies had been flushed out of Swat but a few militant pockets existed in other areas of NWFP.[126]

Dawn, however, reported on Thursday, 16 July, that the security forces had claimed on Wednesday that they had killed 13 militants in clashes in Swat. The report further added that deadly skirmishes triggered fresh concerns about worsening security and that Wednesday was the second consecutive day on which the military reported killings in Swat after announcing nine deaths on Tuesday. It quoted the head of police in Swat, Sajid Mohmand, as stating that the situation had 'not improved to the extent of preventing violent incidents in the valley in the near future.'[127]

Not surprisingly, Gilani's and Rehman Malik's statements were viewed with scepticism given the way official claims had been consistently belied. It will be interesting to recall some instances. Rehman Malik told reporters in Islamabad on 27 June 2009 that military operations against the Taliban would be completed soon. The Taliban would be totally eliminated and would not be able to re-emerge.[128] A meeting in Islamabad on 1 July among President Asif Ali Zardari, Prime Minister Syed Yousuf Raza Gilani and the Chief of Army Staff, General Ashfaq Pervez Kayani, had expressed satisfaction over the progress made by the security forces in Swat where operations had entered the final phase.[129] Again on 1 July, Pakistan's then Foreign Minister, Shah Mahmood Qureshi, said during an interview with the *Guardian* in London that Pakistan had 'turned the tide' in its battle with Islamist militants and al Qaeda was 'on the run' after a series of government offensives.[130]

The question is: How much of all this reflected the reality? Foreign Minister Qureshi's statement that Pakistan had al Qaeda 'on the run' was somewhat mystifying given the fact that the country's government was supposed to have been fighting the Taliban, particularly the segment of it then led by Baitullah Mehsud. Until Qureshi had mentioned al Qaeda, the latter had featured virtually nowhere in Pakistan's media or official statements about the conflict in the country's north-western parts.

CONSTANT HIATUS

Besides, there has been—as reported in Pakistani and international media—a constant hiatus between claims and reality ever since the beginning of Islamabad's offensive in NWFP and FATA. On 11 July, *Dawn News* quoted the Inter Services Public Relations (ISPR), the public relations wing of Pakistan's military, as stating on 10 July—the day after Gilani's statement about the success of the Swat operations—that 26 militants were injured during an operation in the Malam Jabba and Waliabad areas of Swat during the last 24 hours. It further stated that the military had claimed to have intensified its operations in Churkhai, Talang and Sadda Khan areas. Three soldiers had been injured during these operations.[131] The report certainly did not point to a situation in which people who had fled Swat could return to their homes confident that they would be able to stay on.

Other instances are as telling. On 28 April, Major General Athar Abbas, ISPR's Director General, had claimed that the operations in Lower Dir, led by an Inspector-General of Frontier Corps, and backed by army soldiers and Pakistan Air Force (PAF) jets, had been completed. General Abbas, who was addressing a press conference, had added that 70 militants had been killed and others flushed out of the area. Some pockets of resistance, which remained, would be cleared soon, he added.[132] Another report in *Dawn* on 30 April, however, stated that the ISPR's announcement notwithstanding, the situation in the district remained tense and militants were attacked with artillery in Maidan.[133] According to a *Dawn* report on 10 May, 13 militants, including a key commander, were killed and 5 others wounded when security forces pounded militant hideouts in Maidan, Lower Dir.

Success continued to elude the security forces. *Dawn* reported on 20 May that the army had claimed at the time of launching its offensive in Buner (28 April) that there were about 400 to 450 militants in the district and that the operations would be over in a week. But the militants, who put up strong resistance, entrenched themselves in the district's Sultanwas and Pir Baba areas. According to the report, Major General Athar Abbas said on 19 May, 'Security forces have succeeded in clearing about half of Sultanwas and the rest is most likely to be cleared by Wednesday [May 20].'[134]

Dawn, however, reported as late as 15 July 2009 that the security forces had launched a fresh offensive in the headquarters of the militants in Buner district's scenic Gokand valley on the previous day and that helicopter gunships had shelled militants' hideouts in the mountainous areas of Khoz Gokand, Bar Gokand, Batonai and Qadroo Sar to eliminate them. It also quoted local people as saying that the militants were still present in the area, mostly in the mountains between Shangla and Swat.[135]

It was the same story with Swat. The Pakistani army announced the launch of 'full-scale' operations in Swat Valley on 8 May. According to Major General Abbas, some 12,000 to 14,000 troops, backed by attack helicopters and artillery, had been deployed against 4,000 militants. Claiming that the 'militants are on the run', he added that 143 of them had been killed during the past 24 hours and 16 more in Buner and Lower Dir districts.[136] Involving severe fighting and heavy casualties, the offensive had reportedly cleared the Swat Valley, Buner and Lower Dir and other tribal areas of Taliban fighters and had come to be regarded as an indication of Islamabad's determination to wipe out fundamentalist Islamist terrorism from its soil.

Again, a *Dawn* report on 2 July quoted security forces as claiming that all key militant hideouts in Swat district had been secured and local police had resumed patrolling the major cities and towns in Swat valley. It also quoted the ISPR as saying that Shah Dheri had been cleared of militants and that security forces had linked up with other forces in the Langar area. Peace, however, had not returned even by Sunday, 12 July, when a daily military statement rounding up developments over the past 24 hours said that a militant was killed and another arrested during a search operation in Swat valley where troops destroyed five caves in which militants were hiding. According to it, at least 15 other militants had been arrested in different parts of Swat and seven soldiers were wounded.[137] Operations continued 13 days later. *Dawn* reported on 25 July that the security forces killed 14, and apprehended 29, suspected militants and recovered huge quantities of ammunition during search operations in different parts of Swat valley.[138]

Repeated instances of official claims being belied by developments occasioned serious doubts about the success of the offensive. Stating that it was too early to proclaim victory in Swat despite significant military successes, Zahid Hussain wrote in *Dawn* on 27 July 2009:

> Army officials concede that the insurgents have not been completely rooted out and there are still some strong pockets of resistance. 'Taliban are still present in some mountainous areas,' said Brigadier Tahir Hameed. The troops have been battling the Taliban in Shahdehri, Kuza Bandi and Matta, not far from Mingora.[139]

Pointing out that the 'biggest failure of the army operation' had been the escape of the top militant leadership, which raised fears of the militants 'regrouping once the operation is over,' Hussain wrote:

> A major challenge for the government is to boost the morale of police and civilian officials, who had been the main targets of militant attacks, and to restore the confidence of the people in the civilian institutions. The militants have been pushed out of a large part of the valley, but they have not yet been fully defeated. The second stage of the battle, to maintain the gains of the operation is going to be much tougher.[140]

An AFP report, published in *Dawn* a day earlier (Sunday, 26 July), had stated:

> Pakistan says it has eliminated the Taliban in a military offensive launched last April in northwestern districts Buner, Dir and Swat, which rendered nearly two million people displaced.
> But deadly skirmishes continue, raising fears that the Taliban escaped into the mountains and might return, as after previous offensives.[141]

A despatch in the *New York Times* of 27 July 2009 said that reports emerging from Swat showed that Taliban still had the strength to terrorize important areas, and that the army continued to fight them in their strongholds, particularly in Matta and Kabal regions, not far from Mingora where refugees had reclaimed their houses.[142] The report adds:

> In those regions, the Taliban have razed houses, killed a civilian working for the police in Matta and kidnapped another, worrying counterinsurgency experts, who fear that the refugees may have been encouraged by the Pakistani authorities to go back too soon.[143]

NOT AN EASY ANSWER

There was, clearly, a huge hiatus between the Pakistani leaders' claims and military progress on the ground. This in turn raises serious questions about the leaders' credibility as well as the Pakistani army's ability—and also its will—to defeat the TTP. If Pakistan's military could not eliminate the Taliban from Lower and Upper Dir, Buner and Swat roughly three months after launching a much-advertised, massive offensive, can it be expected to eliminate the Taliban—and also al Qaeda which will doubtless come to their support—in the forbidding heights of South and North Waziristan where they have their fortified strongholds and where the terrain is ideal for ambushes and guerrilla warfare?

Many are understandably sceptical. A report in the *New York Times* of 27 June 2009 states:

> The tentative results in Swat also do not bode well for the military's new push in the far more treacherous terrain of South Waziristan, another insurgent stronghold, where officials have vowed to take on the leader of the Pakistani Taliban, Baitullah Mehsud, who remains Pakistan's most wanted man.[144]

Matters are compounded by the absence of independent verification which has been repeatedly mentioned. A report in the *New York Times* of 8 May stated that there was no way of verifying the claims by the Pakistani military's chief spokesman, Major General Athar Abbas, as reporters and most outsiders had been blocked from areas where operations were being conducted. It further quoted a woman in a refugee camp in Mardan as stating, 'The army and the Taliban are not killing each other—they are friends. They are only killing civilians. When civilians are killed, the Government claims they have killed a bunch of terrorists.'[145]

A report in the *New York Times* of 19 May, about urban guerrilla warfare confronting Pakistani army as it closed in on Mingora, quoted a statement by the military as claiming that it had started clearing houses in Kanju, a village in the outskirts of Mingora. Stating that residents who had left Kanju described a mounting civilian death toll, the report added, 'The Pakistani Army has closed Swat to outsiders and essentially ordered residents to leave. The authorities have also mostly barred journalists from entering the area, making it difficult to verify what is happening.'[146]

Referring to the killing of Qari Zainuddin, a militant leader who had decided to take on Baitullah Mehsud in South Waziristan, in Dera Ismail Khan on 23 June, an editorial in the *Dawn* of 24 June 2009 had said, 'The truth is though little is known about what exactly is going on in South Waziristan Agency, who is fighting whom and why, and what is likely to happen in the days and weeks ahead.' It added, 'Reports suggest several militants from Baitullah's camp have been killed so far, but this has not been verified independently. Meanwhile, drones continue to strike targets in South Waziristan Agency, but again it has not been possible to independently verify who had been killed.'[147]

The denial of access to journalists has understandably raised suspicions. The Pakistani army's political role, and its attempts to legitimize the same by projecting itself as a heroic defender of the country's integrity and independence against what it describes as India's attempts to undermine both, is well known. It had, therefore, every reason to make sure that the acts of heroism of its personnel in the campaign against the Taliban received adequate exposure in the section of media, both print and electronic, which commanded credibility at the national and international levels. It should have had no fear of hostile or prejudiced coverage as this section of the media had been sharply critical of the Taliban and al Qaeda for their barbaric ways and regressive social and gender policies. Keeping it out of the scenes of action understandably raises the question whether the military was not being as successful as it had been claiming or whether what had been advertised as 'severe' fighting was not so or even deliberate make-believe or a bit of both.

Scepticism is warranted given the fact that it was the Pakistani army that had been shying away from combat until the launch of the offensive on 26 April 2009. After describing the Taliban's barbaric reign of terror and oppression in Swat, prior to the offensive, the *New York Times* had reported on 24 January 2009 that interviews 'with a half-dozen senior Pakistani government, military and political officials' involved in the fight against the Taliban revealed that from 2,000 to 4,000 of the latter's fighters roamed the district. By contrast, the Pakistani military had four brigades with 12,000 to 15,000 men.[148]

The report, however, added:

> But the soldiers largely stay inside their camps, unwilling to patrol or exert any large presence that might provoke—or discourage—the militants, Swat residents and political leaders say. The military also has not raided a small village that locals say is widely known as the Taliban's headquarters in Swat.
>
> Nor have troops destroyed mobile radio transmitters mounted on motorcycles or pickup trucks that Shah Doran[149] and the leader of the Taliban in Swat, Maulana Fazlullah, have expertly used to terrify residents.[150]

Another report in the *New York Times* of 27 July 2009 stated that a landlord from Swat Valley, Sher Mohammad, was still bitter that the army refused to help last year when he, his brother and nephew fought off the Taliban for 13 hours, even though the soldiers were stationed less than a mile away. Mohammad was hit in the groin by a bullet and lost two fingers.[151]

Nor did the army—as the *New York Times* reported on 24 January 2009—seem prepared for or capable of taking on the Taliban. The report stated:

> When the army does act, its near-total lack of preparedness to fight a counterinsurgency reveals itself. Its usual tactic is to lob artillery shells into a general area, and the results have seemed to hurt civilians more than the militants, residents say.[152]

The same tactical approach was in evidence during the offensive launched on 26 April 2009. According to a report in the *Dawn* of 19 June 2009,

> Troops, backed by combat helicopters, jets and armoured personnel carriers, launched a fresh offensive in the areas of Mehsuds in South Waziristan on Friday and bombed suspected hideouts of militants....
>
> (According to AP news agency, jetfighters flattened at least three suspected Taliban training facilities in South Waziristan, killing or wounding several insurgents, two senior intelligence officials said....
>
> The Taliban also opened fire on troops elsewhere in the mountainous area, starting an exchange of fire that was still going on hours later, said an intelligence official, without giving any further details....)[153]

The AFP report cited earlier, published in *Dawn* on 26 July 2009, stated:

> In mid-June, the military said it had received orders and was preparing to launch an offensive against Pakistani Taliban chief Baitullah Mehsud and his network in the South Waziristan tribal district bordering Afghanistan.
>
> Troops have sealed off much of the eastern border between South Waziristan and areas under government control, and carried out air raids in what the military calls softening up for a full-scale ground operation.[154]

They had still not launched their offensive by the end of August. According to a report datelined 31 August 2009 in *Dawn*,

> With Baitullah Mehsud dead, troops may be bracing for a new round of offensive against the Tehrik-i-Taliban Pakistan in the days and weeks ahead to prepare the ground for a decisive assault on South Waziristan, knowledgeable sources say.[155]

The report added:

> The military and paramilitary operations against the remaining pockets of militants will resume after a wait-and-see strategy in the aftermath of the death of the TTP chief in a drone attack in the first week of this month, resulting in a power struggle that many in the military and security establishment believe also led to the death of Baitullah's key lieutenant Hakeemullah.[156]

Taliban officials rang up journalists in north-west Pakistan on Saturday to say that Hakimullah Mehsud, a young militant who commanded fighters in the Orakzai, Khyber and Kurram tribal regions, had been chosen as the new chief by a leadership council, or *shura*. Saturday was 22 August; Baitullah was killed on 5 August. The Pakistani army should have struck immediately after Baitullah's killing to take advantage of the demoralization and confusion—compounded by factional warfare—in the ranks of the TTP. Its failure to do so as well as to adopt an appropriate strategic and tactical approach certainly did not reflect a burning desire to win which, in turn, raises the question whether it indicates an unwillingness on the part of the civilian government and the military's top brass to eliminate the Taliban altogether.

A Strange Kind of Fighting

The relevance of asking this is underlined by the fact that questions arise not only about the success but also of the intensity of the fighting the Pakistani troops had been engaged in. Was the latter as severe as had been claimed by Islamabad? The *Dawn* report, datelined 19 June 2009, cited earlier, stated with reference to the fighting in South Waziristan, 'According to sources, heavy clashes took place between security forces and militants loyal to Baitullah Mehsud. No casualty was reported.'[157]

If the idea of heavy clashes without casualties appears intriguing, so do some other aspects of the operations. Referring to Pakistani military's claim 'for the past month and a half' of its success in retaking Swat Valley from the Taliban, a report (cited earlier) in the *New York Times* of 27 June 2009 stated:

> Yet from a helicopter flying low over the valley last week, the low-rise buildings of Mingora, the largest city in Swat, now deserted and under a 24-hour curfew, appeared unscathed. In the surrounding countryside, farmers had harvested wheat and red onions on their unscarred land.
>
> All that is testament to the fact that the Taliban mostly melted away without a major fight, possibly to return when the military withdraws or to fight elsewhere, military analysts say.[158]

Mentioning the heavy fighting that lay ahead of the Pakistani troops as they entered Mingora, another report (also cited earlier) in the *New York Times* on 19 May 2009 had stated that, according to Pakistani 'analysts and politicians', the fight for the town would present 'a decisive test of the military's ability to defeat the Taliban in Swat, a once popular scenic resort 100 miles from the capital, Islamabad'. The report had added:

> Unaccustomed to urban guerrilla warfare, the military has so far concentrated on battling the militants in the rural and mountainous areas of Swat. Inside Mingora, the militants command the rooftops and the main buildings, according to residents and government officials.
>
> In a statement issued Tuesday, the army said it had started clearing houses in Kanju, a village on the outskirts of Mingora, and residents who had left Kanju described a mounting civilian death toll.

'They will leave Mingora until last,' said Aftab Ahmed Sherpao, a former interior minister, whose political base is adjacent to the Swat area. 'You have to clear each and every house, and the Taliban are going to give their own pitched battle.'[159]

What happened to the 'decisive test' and the Taliban's 'pitched battle'? How could the Taliban have just melted away when Pakistani troops were in the very outskirts of Mingora? Did the troops look the other way while they fled? If not, then it reflects very poorly on their quality as military men and puts a huge question mark against their ability to defeat the Taliban. If they did connive in the 'melting away', then at whose instance? All this raises further doubts not only about Pakistan's claims of success, casualties inflicted and the actual severity of the fighting but also whether the melting away had not been according to an arrangement agreed upon before the operations began.

One has doubtless seen television news clips of Pakistani army directing artillery fire and rockets. But at whom? A report in the New York Times of 28 April 2009 stated, 'After a week of strong criticism here and abroad over its inaction, the Pakistani military deployed fighter jets and helicopter gunships to flush out hundreds of Taliban militants who overran the strategic district of Buner last week.'[160] The Taliban, however, had started retreating from Buner on 24 April under orders from its leader in Swat, Maulana Fazlullah.[161] The report, which stated this, quoted Taliban spokesman, Muslim Khan, as stating, 'Our leader has ordered that Taliban should immediately be called back from Buner.' He added that there were only around 100 fighters in Buner.

According to television channels, the order followed a meeting between Taliban leaders Qari Muhammad Khan and Muslim Khan and the Commissioner of the Malakand division, Syed Muhammad Javed, in the presence of Maulvi Sufi Mohammad, the founder of Tehrik-e-Nifaz-e-Shariat-e-Mohammadi (Movement for the Establishment of Islamic Law) who acted as an intermediary.[162] Further, television channels showed dozens of militants, masked and heavily armed, driving away in pickup trucks and minibuses. Muslim Khan said on 25 April that all militants who had come from Swat had withdrawn and that only local Taliban fighters from Buner remained in the area.[163]

Yet heavy fighting was reported on 6 May from Buner district where troops are said to have blasted Taliban fortifications in Pir Baba and Sultanwas areas, killing 27 militants.[164]

If Muslim Khan's claim on 24 April that only 100 Taliban fighters remained in Buner was correct, and the same holds for his statement on the following day that only local Taliban fighters remained in the district, then it is surprising that heavy fighting was still going on in the district on 6 May. A *Dawn* report no doubt stated that the security forces launched their operation in Buner after intelligence agencies intercepted a telephone conversation between Maulana Fazlullah and his 'commanders' which revealed their plan to take over the area after faking a withdrawal. But then one can hardly accept Pakistani intelligence agencies'—or for that matter any intelligence agency's—claims without corroborating evidence.[165]

Some may also cite the killing of TTP chief Baitullah Mehsud to trash the suspicion that serious clashes had not occurred and much of the offensive by Pakistani troops had been in the nature of shadow boxing. The killing, however, was the result not of a Pakistani military operation but a missile attack from an American drone. Pakistan has been severely critical of drone attacks and demanding an end to these. What is at issue is not the accuracy and/or justification of drone strikes but the authenticity of Pakistan's claims that there had been severe fighting and that it was both capable of, and determined to, stamp out Islamist terrorism.

Besides, during the campaign, an element of doubt attached to Pakistan's claims of important militant leaders being killed or seriously injured. *Dawn* had reported on 25 June 2009 that Qari Hussain, a lieutenant of Baitullah who was popularly known as Ustad-i-Fidayeen, or teacher of suicide bombers, and who had been tipped as Baitullah's successor, had been killed on 23 June by a missile strike on people present at the burial of an Afghan militant leader, Khoze Ali. According to the report, Mehsud, who was also present, had escaped by the skin of his teeth.[166] On 23 June itself, TTP spokesman Mufti Waliur Rehman dismissed reports of Qari Hussain's death and said that only one local commander, Bilal, had been killed in the missile strike.[167]

According to another report in *Dawn* on 1 July 2009, Interior Minister Rehman Malik had said during an interview with the BBC that Maulana Fazlullah, the TTP's chief in Swat, had been badly wounded in the ongoing military operations.[168] The chief of ISPR, Major General Athar Abbas, reiterated the claim on 9 July.[169] On 11 July, Maulvi Omar, whom *Dawn* described as 'self-styled spokesman' for TTP and who was later arrested, dubbed the claim as 'totally baseless'. He said that he had talked to Fazlullah on telephone that very day and that the top leadership of the Taliban in Malakand had gone underground according to a plan.[170] Muslim Khan, Fazlullah's spokesman, asserted on 23 July, that Swat's Taliban chief 'is alive, healthy and has never been wounded'.[171]

Meanwhile, there were ample indications that the Pakistani army's campaign in areas like Swat valley had little impact. A report in the *Los Angeles Times* of 7 October 2009 makes this amply clear. It reads:

> The tragedy of more than 2 million people being displaced in less than two months may have vanished from the headlines, but the civilian drama continues. If there is less attention to their needs, it's partly because it is still hard for anyone other than the armed forces or a native Swati to reach most of the district north of Mingora. The army can take foreign journalists on periodic tours of the 'cleared' areas in the south but rarely in the north, where the situation remains uncertain. One thing is obvious: Beyond Mingora, the Swat Valley is still an insecure place.[172]

The report adds:

> The situation in other parts of the North-West Frontier Province remains unstable. Reporting about a militant attack in a market, last month in Kohat, a local Pakistani news paper wrote that for several hours after the blast, an enraged crowd did not allow the bomb disposal squad to enter the market. Huge must be the people's grief and the animosity towards those responsible for the mayhem, for them to shoo away Samaritans coming to the rescue of their loved ones.[173]

NOTES

1. The term 'Memogate' has come to apply to a scandal over a message allegedly delivered by a Pakistani-American businessman, Mansoor Ijaz, to the then US National Security Adviser, General James L. Jones, for being forwarded to Admiral Mike Mullen, then the Chairman of the United States Joint Chiefs of Staff. The memorandum reportedly sought American military and political aid to prevent Pakistan's military from wresting direct control over the government from the country's civilian rulers in the wake of the killing of Osama bin Laden on 2 May 2011 and provided a detailed list of steps that were needed to be taken. According to Ijaz, he sent the memorandum at the instance of Pakistan's then ambassador to the United States, Husain Haqqani, who had contacted him via BlackBerry on 9 May 2011. Ijaz further claimed that he had pointed out that his American interlocutors asked for a written communication, and had sent a draft memorandum to Haqqani the following day asking him to proofread and approve it and also whether the move had the Pakistani President's approval. Haqqani proof read and approved it and confirmed that he had the 'boss's' approval.

   Ijaz wrote a piece in the *Financial Times* on 10 October 2011 mentioning the memorandum which he said had been drafted by a Pakistani official in Washington at the instance of President Zardari. A storm exploded in Pakistani media. Mullen first denied any knowledge of the memorandum and then said he knew of it but 'thought nothing of it'. The Pakistani cricketer-turned-politician, Imran Khan, first mentioned Haqqani as the author at a rally in Lahore on 30 October 2011. Later, Ijaz confirmed that he had sent the memorandum at Haqqani's instance. The latter was recalled to Pakistan where he resigned on 17 November 2011 after a meeting with President Asif Zardari. The Pakistani President and the Prime Minister, Yousuf Raza Gilani, had, earlier in the day, an official meeting with Pakistan's Chief of Army Staff, General Ashfaq Pervez Kayani, and the then head of the Inter-Services Intelligence (ISI) Directorate, Lieutenant General Ahmad Shuja Pasha.
2. Husain Haqqani, *Pakistan between Mosque and Military* (Washington DC: Carnegie Endowment for International Peace, 2005), p. 32.
3. Then Lord Mountbatten's chief of staff in India.
4. Shuja Nawaz, *Crossed Swords: Pakistan, Its Army, and the Wars Within* (Karachi: Oxford University Press, 2008), p. 93.
5. Ibid., p. 94.
6. Ayesha Jalal, *The State of Martial Rule* (Cambridge: Cambridge University Press, 1990), p. 112.
7. Haqqani, *Pakistan between Mosque and Military,* pp. 32–33.
8. Nawaz, *Crossed Swords: Pakistan, Its Army, and the Wars Within*, p. 98.
9. Ibid., p. 106.
10. Ibid., p. 108.
11. Ibid., p. 114.
12. Ibid., p. 116.

13. Ibid., p. 118.
14. Ibid., p. 122.
15. Ibid., p. 107.
16. Ahmed Rashid, *Descent into Chaos: How the War against Islamic Extremism Is Being Lost in Pakistan, Afghanistan and Central Asia* (London: Allen Lane, 2008), p. 36.
17. Nawaz, *Crossed Swords: Pakistan, Its Army, and the Wars Within*, p. 136.
18. Ibid., p. 135.
19. Ibid., p. 188.
20. Ibid.
21. Haqqani, *Pakistan between Mosque and Military*, p. 35.
22. Shirin Tahir-Kheli, *The United States and Pakistan: Evolution of Influence* (New York: Praeger, 1982), p. 4.
23. Haqqani, *Pakistan between Mosque and Military*, pp. 35–36.
24. Mohammad Yousaf and Mark Adkin, *The Bear Trap: Afghanistan's Untold Story* (Lahore: Jang Publishers, 1992), p. 25.
25. Ibid.
26. Ibid., p. 26.
27. Nawaz, *Crossed Swords: Pakistan, Its Army, and the Wars Within*, pp. 369–70.
28. Haqqani, *Pakistan between Mosque and Military*, p. 187.
29. Steve Coll, *Ghost Wars: The Secret History of the CIA, Afghanistan and Bin Laden, from the Soviet Invasion to September 11, 2001* (United States: Penguin Books, 2004), p. 93.
30. Haqqani, *Pakistan between Mosque and Military*, p. 188.
31. Coll, *Ghost Wars*, pp. 81–82.
32. Haqqani, *Pakistan between Mosque and Military*, p. 188.
33. V. R. Raghavan, 'Strategic Depth in Afghanistan', *Hindu*, 7 November 2001.
34. Aslam Siddiqi, *Pakistan Seeks Security* (Karachi: Longmans Green, 1960), p. 53.
35. Ibid., p. 52.
36. Raghavan, 'Strategic Depth in Afghanistan', 7 November.
37. Ibid.
38. Yossef Bodansky, *Bin Laden: The Man Who Declared War on America* (Rocklin, California: Forum: An Imprint of Prima Publishing, 1999), p. 18.
39. Javed Hassan, *India: A Study in Profile* (Rawalpindi: Services Book Club, 1990), p. 111.
40. Ibid., p. 139.
41. Haqqani, *Pakistan between Mosque and Military*, p. 269.
42. Ibid., p. 365.
43. Ibid., p. 266.
44. Ibid., p. 267.
45. Ibid.
46. Bodansky, *Bin Laden*, p. 18.
47. Apratim Mukharji, 'Terrorism Claimed More Lives Than Wars', *Hindustan Times*, Delhi, 8 December 1999.
48. Coll, *Ghost Wars*, p. 29.

49. Ibid.

50. Ibid., p. 31.

51. Ibid., p. 34.

52. Ibid., p. 91.

53. Ibid.

54. Ibid., pp. 67–68.

55. Ibid.

56. Ibid., p. 68.

57. Ibid., p. 99.

58. Ibid., p. 100.

59. Ibid., p. 62.

60. Haqqani, *Pakistan between Mosque and Military*, p. 188.

61. Coll, *Ghost Wars*, pp. 190–91.

62. Bodansky, *Bin Laden*, p. 25.

63. For a detailed study see Rashid, *Taliban*, pp. 22–27.

64. Coll, *Ghost Wars*, pp. 210–11.

65. Christopher Dickey, *Securing the City: Inside America's Best Counterterror Force* (New York: Simon & Schuster, 2009), pp. 43–44.

66. Ibid., p. 47.

67. Ibid., p. 48.

68. Federal Bureau of Investigation, *Terrorism in the United States 1999* (Washington DC: Counterterrorism and Threat Assessment Unit, Counterterrorism Division, 1999), p. 10, http://www.fbi.gov/publications/terror/terror99.pdf.

69. Dickey, *Securing the City*, pp. 54, 251.

70. Ibid., p. 57.

71. Ronald Sullivan, 'Minor Figure in Bomb Plot Sentenced to Time Served', *New York Times,* online edition, 21 July 1994, http://www.nytimes.com/1994/07/21/nyregion/minor-figure-in-bomb-plot-sentenced-to-time-served.html.

72. Ralph Blumenthal, 'Tapes in Bombing Plot Show Informer and F.B.I. at Odds', *New York Times*, online edition, 27 October 1993, http://www.nytimes.com/1993/10/27/nyregion/tapes-in-bombing-plot-show-informer-and-fbi-at-odds.html?pagewanted=all&src=pm.

73. Coll, *Ghost Wars*, pp. 5–6.

74. Ibid., pp. 5–6, 272–74.

75. Federal Bureau of Investigation, Press release, Washington DC, 21 June 2001, http://www.fbi.gov/pressrel/pressrel01/khobar.htm.

76. Coll, *Ghost Wars,* pp. 403–12. See these pages for a graphic account of the attacks and American retaliation.

77. Ibid., p. 407.

78. Ibid., p. 320.

79. Osama bin Laden, *Messages to the World: Statements of Osama bin Laden*, ed. and introduction by Bruce Lawrence, trans. James Howarth (London and New York: Verso, 2005), p. 30.

80. Coll, *Ghost Wars*, pp. 411–12.

81. Ibid., pp. 537–38.

82. Ibid., p. 442.

83. Ibid., p. 511.

84. Ibid.

85. Ibid.

86. Ibid.

87. Ibid., p. 512.

88. Rashid, *Descent into Chaos*, p. 27.

89. Ibid., pp. 27–28.

90. Ibid., p. 28.

91. Ibid.

92. Ibid., pp. 28–29.

93. Ibid., p. 28.

94. Ibid., pp. 32–33.

95. Ibid., p. 30.

96. K. Alan Kronsdradt, *Pakistan-U.S. Relations: A Summary*, Table I, Congressional Research Service, Washington DC, 21 October 2011, http://www.fas.org/sgp/crs/row/R41832.pdf.

97. Rashid, *Descent into Chaos*, p. 32.

98. Douglas Frantz, 'A Nation Challenged: Supplying the Taliban; Pakistan Ended Aid to Taliban only Hesitantly', *New York Times*, online edition, 8 December2001, http://www.nytimes.com/2001/12/08/world/nation-challenged-supplying-taliban-pakistan-ended-aid-taliban-only-hesitantly.html?pagewanted=3.

99. Zahid Hussain, *Frontline Pakistan:The Path to Catastrophe and the Killing of Benazir Bhutto* (New Delhi: Penguin, 2008), p. viii.

100. Rashid, *Descent into Chaos,* p. 92.

101. Ibid., p. 93.

102. Michael Moran, 'The "Airlift of Evil": Why Did We Let Pakistan Pull "Volunteers" out of Kunduz', MSNBC, 29 November 2001, http://www.msnbc.msn.com/id/3340165/ns/world_news-brave_new_world/t/airlift-evil/.

103. Dexter Filkins and Carlotta Gall, 'Alliance Reports Planes Flew Into Kunduz to Rescue Fighters', online edition, 23 November 2001, http://www.nytimes.com/2001/11/23/international/23CND-AFGH.html?pagewanted=1.

104. Ibid.

105. Marcus Tanner, 'Pakistan Air Force Seen Evacuating Foreign Fighters from Kunduz', London, *Independent*, 26 November 2001, http://www.independent.co.uk/news/world/asia/pakistan-air-force-seen-evacuating-foreign-fighters-from-kunduz-618144.html.

106. Ibid.

107. Ibid.

108. Imtiaz Gul, *The Al Qaeda Connection: The Taliban and Terror in Pakistan's Tribal Areas* (Penguin: 2010), p. 29.

109. Rashid, *Descent into Chaos*, p. 269.

110. Ibid., p. 368.

111. Elisabeth Bumiller, 'Petraeus Warns about Militants' Threat to Pakistan', *New York Times*, 1 April 2009, http://www.nytimes.com/2009/04/02/washington/02military.html.

112. Thom Shankar and Richard A. Oppel, 'In Tactical Shift, Troops Will Stay and Hold Ground in Afghanistan', *New York Times*, online edition, 2 July 2009, http://www.nytimes.com/2009/07/03/world/asia/03afghan.html.

113. Richard A. Oppel Jr., 'U.S. Marines Try to Retake Afghan Valley from Taliban', *New York Times*, online edition, 1 July 2009, www.nytimes.com/2009/07/02/world/asia/02afghan.html.

114. Ibid.

115. Eric Schmitt and Jane Perlez, 'Pakistan Objects to U.S. Plan for Afghan War, *New York Times*, online edition, 21 July 2009, http://www.nytimes.com/2009/07/22/world/asia/22pstan.html?_r=1&th&emc=th.

116. *DawnNews*/AFP, 'Security Forces Battle Militants in South Waziristan', *Dawn*, online edition, 18 October 2009, http://www.dawn.com/wps/wcm/connect/dawn-content-library/dawn/news/pakistan/04-troops-pound-south-waziristan-militant-positions-qs-06.

117. Sayed Bokhari, 'The Battle for Wazirisran', *Dawn*. online edition, 18 October 2009, http://www.dawn.com/wps/wcm/connect/dawn-content-library/dawn/news/pakistan/04-the-battle-for-waziristan-qs-01.

118. Iftikhar A. Khan, 'Army Told to Crush Swat Militants. Militants Mistook Govt's Sincerity for Weakness. Women Subjected to Discrimination. PML-N, ANP, JUP Back Operation. Rs 1 Bn Allocated for Displaced People', *Dawn*, online edition, 8 May 2009, http://www.dawn.com/wps/wcm/connect/dawn-content-library/dawn/the-newspaper/front-page/army-told-to-crush-swat-militants-militants-mistook-govts-sincerity-for-weakness-women-subjected-to-discrimination-pmln%2C-anp%2C-jup-back-operation-rs1bn-859.

119. Margaret Warner, 'Zardari Assesses War on Taliban, Appeals for Aid', interview, Public Broadcasting Service Channel, Newshour, aired on 8 May 2009, http://www.pbs.org/newshour/bb/asia/jan-june09/zardari_05-08.html.

120. Nirupama Subramanian, 'Success in Swat: Pakistan: Di splaced People Can Return to Their Homes, It Says', *Hindu*, New Delhi, 11 July 2009.

121. Ibid.

122. Ibid.

123. Ibid.

124. Salman Masood and Sabrina Tavernise, 'Refugees from Region in Pakistan Trickling Home', *New York Times*, online edition, 13 July 2009, http://www.nytimes.com/2009/07/14/world/asia/14pstan.html?_r=1&th&emc=th.

125. 'Displaced Families Being Transported Back to Swat', *Dawn*, online edition, 13 July 2009, http://www.dawn.com/wps/wcm/connect/dawn-content-library/dawn/news/pakistan/04-displaced-families-being-transported-back-to-swat-qs-08m.

126. Munawer Azeem, 'Taliban Defeated in Swat, Claims Interior Minister', *Dawn*, online edition, 14 July 2009, http://www.dawn.com/wps/wcm/connect/dawn content-library/dawn/news/pakistan/12-taliban+defeated+in+swat+claims+interior+minister-bi-05.

127. 'Thirteen Militants Die in Fresh Swat Clashes', Report, *Dawn*, online edition, 16 July 2009, http://www.dawn.com/wps/wcm/connect/dawn-content-library/dawn/the-newspaper/front-page/13-militants-die-in-fresh-swat-clashes-679.

128. Syed Irfan Raza, 'Military Operation to Be Completed Soon: Malik', *Dav n*, online edition, 27 June, http://www.dawn.com/wps/wcm/connect/dawn-content-library/dawn/news/pakistan/metropolitan/06-military-operation-to-be completed-soon-rehman-malik-rs-10.

129. Iftikhar A. Khan 'Terror to Be Fought with Full Force', *Dawn*, online edition, 2 July 2009, http://www.dawnnews.net/wps/wcm/connect/dawn-content-library/dawn/news/pakistan/12-terror+to+be+fought+with+full+force-bi-04.

130. Dawn Special Correspondent, 'Pakistan Winning Fight against Extremists: Qureshi', *Dawn*, online edition, 2 July 2009, http://www.dawnnews.net/wps/wcm/connect/dawn-content-library/dawn/news/world/09-pakistan-winning-fight-against-extremists-qureshi-szh-09.

131. *DawnNews*, 'Malakand Operation Continues, 26 Injured: ISPR', *Dawn*, online edition, 11 July 2009, http://www.dawn.com/wps/wcm/connect/dawn-content-library/dawn/news/pakistan/provinces/04-malakand-operation-continues-26-injured-ispr-qs-13.

132. Iftikhar A. Khan, 'Action Triggered by Taliban Plan to Take Over Buner', *Dawn*, online edition, 29 April 2009, http://www.dawn.com/wps/wcm/connect/dawn-content-library/dawn/the-newspaper/front-page/action-triggered-by-taliban-plan-to-take-over-buner-949.

133. Abdur Rahman Abid and Haleem Asad, 'Forces Regain Control of Dagger', *Dawn*, online edition, 30 April, http://www.dawn.com/wps/wcm/connect/dawn-content-library/dawn/the-newspaper/front-page/forces-regain-control-of-daggar-049.

134. Ifthikar A. Khan, 'Troops Claim Clearing Most of Sultanwas', *Dawn*, online edition, 20 May 2009, http://www.dawn.com/wps/wcm/connect/dawn-content-library/dawn/the-newspaper/front-page/troops-claim-clearing-most-of-sultanwas-059.

135. Abdur Rahman Abid, 'Fresh Offensive Launched in Buner', *Dawn*, online edition, 15 July 2009, http://www.dawn.com/wps/wcm/connect/dawn-content-library/dawn/news/pakistan/11-fresh-offensive-launched-in-buner-il-13.

136. Nirupama Subramanian, 'Pakistan Army Strikes in Swat: Up to 14,000 Troops Are Aided by Attack Helicopters and Artillery, *Hindu*, New Delhi, 9 May 2009

137. 'Three Soldiers, 14 Taliban Killed in Multiple Clashes', *Dawn*, online edition, 12 July 2009, http://www.dawn.com/wps/wcm/connect/dawn-content-library/dawn/news/pakistan/09-three-soldiers-14-taliban-killed-in-multiple-clashes-szh-01.

138. 'Security Forces Kill 14 Militants, Arrest 29 in Swat Operation', *Dawn*, online edition, 25 July 2009, http://www.dawn.com/wps/wcm/connect/dawn-content-library/dawn/news/pakistan/provinces/06-eleven-militants-killed-in-swat-operation-rs-08.

139. Zahid Hussain, 'Swat—It's Too Early to Proclaim Victory', *Dawn*, online edition, 27 July 2009, http://www.dawn.com/wps/wcm/connect/dawn-content-library/dawn/news/pakistan/13+swat+too+early+to+declare+victory-za-13.

140. Ibid.

141. AFP, 'Pakistan Stretched Thin for Mehsud Battle', *Dawn*, online edition, 26 July 2009, http://www.dawn.com/wps/wcm/connect/dawn-content-library/dawn/news/pakistan/04-pakistan-stretched-thin-mehsud-battle-qs-01.

142. Jane Perlez and Pir Zubair Shah, 'Landowners Still in Exile from Unstable Pakistan Area', *New York Times*, online edition, 27 July 2009, www.nytimes.com/2009/07/28/world/asia/28swal.html.

143. Ibid.

144. Jane Perlez and Pir Zubair Shah, 'Taliban Losses Are No Sure Gain for Pakistanis', *New York Times*, online edition, 27 June 2009, http://www.nytimes.com/2009/06/28/world/asia/28swat.html?_r=1&th&emc=th.

145. Dexter Filkins, 'Pakistan Pounds Taliban, Swelling the Tide of Refugees', *New York Times*, online edition, 8 May 2009, http://www.nytimes.com/2009/05/09/world/asia/09pstan.html.

146. Jane Perlez and Pir Zubair Shah, 'Urban Battle Looms Ahead for Pakistan in Swat', *New York Times*, online edition, 19 May 2009, http://www.nytimes.com/2009/05/20/world/asia/20swat.html.

147. Editorial, 'Waziristan Uncertainty', *Dawn*, online edition, 24 June 2009, http://www.dawn.com/wps/wcm/connect/dawn-content-library/dawn/the-newspaper/editorial/waziristan-uncertainty-469.

148. Richard A. Oppel Jr. and Pir Zubair Shah, 'In Pakistan, Radio Amplifies Terror of Taliban', *New York Times*, online edition, 24 January 2009, http://www.nytimes.com/2009/07/26/world/asia/26marines.html?pagewanted=2&_r=1&th&emc=th.

149. Shah Doran, a Taliban commander and deputy to the Taliban supremo, Moulvi Fazlullah, had become notorious for his venomous speeches over the militants' FM radio in Swat. According to one report, Pakistan's security forces had killed him in June 2009; according to another he had prostrate and kidney cancer and died in December that year.

150. Ibid.

151. Perlez and Shah, 'Landowners Still in Exile from Unstable Pakistan Area'.

152. Oppel Jr. and Shah, 'In Pakistan, Radio Amplifies the Terror of Taliban.'

153. Our Correspondent, 'Troops Pound Hideouts of Baitullah's Men', *Dawn*, 19 June, http://archives.dawn.com/archives/34004.

154. AFP, 'Pakistan Stretched Thin for Mehsud Battle'.

155. Ismail Khan, 'Troops Brace for Decisive Offensive', *Dawn*, online edition, 31 August 2009, http://www.dawn.com/wps/wcm/connect/dawn-content-library/dawn/news/pakistan/09-troops-brace-for-decisive-offensive-szh-13.

156. Ibid.

157. Our Correspondent, 'Troops Pound Hideouts of Baitullah's Men'.

158. Perlez and Shah, 'Taliban Losses Are No Sure Gain for Pakistanis'.

159. Perlez and Shah, 'Urban Battle Looms Ahead for Pakistan in Swat'.

160. Carlotta Gall and Elisabeth Bumiller, 'Pakistani Military Moves to Flush Out Taliban', *New York Times*, online edition, 28 April 2009, http://www.nytimes.com/2009/04/29/world/asia/29pstan.html.

161. Agencies, 'Taliban Retreat from Buner, Back in Swat: Cleric Sufi Muhammad Brokers Deal with Govt.', *Times of India*, New Delhi, 25 April 2009.

162. Ibid.

163. PTI, 'Taliban Pullout from Buner Complete: 'Militants from Swat Have Withdrawn, but Local Taliban Fighters Still Present', *Times of India*, 26 April 2009.

164. PTI, 'Pak Steps up Offensive to Reclaim Swat: 62 Militants Killed; 50,000 Flee Valley; Exodus Figure to Touch 5 Lakh', *Tribune*, New Delhi, 7 May 2009.

165. Agencies, 'Taliban Retreat from Buner, Back in Swat: Cleric Sufi Muhammad brokers deal with Govt.'.

166. Alamgir Bhittani and Pazir Gul, 'Missile Kills Key Trainer of Taliban Suicide Bombers', *Dawn*, online edition, 25 June 2009, http://www.dawn.com/wps/wcm/connect/dawn-content-library/dawn/the-newspaper/front-page/baitullahs-narrow-escape-in-drone-attack-missile-kills-key-trainer-of-taliban-suicide-bombers-569.

167. Alamgir Bhittani, 'Qari Hussain Is Alive, Claim Taliban', *Dawn*, online edition, 26 June, http://www.dawn.com/wps/wcm/connect/dawn-content-library/dawn/the-newspaper/national/qari-hussain-is-alive%2C-claim-taliban-669.

168. 'I confirm Fazlullah Is Seriously Injured: Rehman Malik', *Dawn*, 2 July 2009, online edition, http://www.dawnnews.net/wps/wcm/connect/dawn-content-library/dawn/news/world/07-fazlullah-seriously-injured-rehman-malik-ha-06.

169. 'Swat Taliban Chief Fazlullah Injured, Says ISPR', *Dawn*, online edition, 2009, http://www.dawn.com/wps/wcm/connect/dawn-content-library/dawn/news/pakistan/provinces/12-fazlullah+is+alive+claim+taliban-bi-08.

170. Anwarullah Khan, 'Taliban Reject Claim about Fazlullah', *Dawn*, online edition, 12 July 2009.

171. 'Maulana Fazlullah Is Alive, Claim Taliban', *Dawn*, online edition, 24 July 2009, http://www.dawn.com/wps/wcm/connect/dawn-contentd-library/dawn/news/pakistan/provinces/12-fazlullah+is+alive+claim+taliban-bi-08.

172. Anna Husasrska, 'No Peace in the Valley: The People of Pakistan's Swat Valley Remain Tragically Trapped between the Army and the Taliban', Los Angeles, 7 October 2009.

173. Ibid.

CHAPTER 6

THE SHADOW OF JIHADIS

Pakistan's dismal record in fighting terrorism has been attributed to its military's lack of preparedness. Oriented mainly toward waging conventional wars with India, it lacked the training and weaponry needed for complex counter-insurgency operations. This can only be a partial explanation. For decades, the Pakistani army has been engaged in savage counter-insurgency operations in Balochistan as well as Gilgit-Baltistan. One must, therefore, look for other explanations. As seen, one is the attempt to keep the Afghan Taliban, the Haqqani network and organizations like Lashkar-e-Toiba (LeT) intact to achieve its objective of having a pliant Afghan government which would allow Pakistan to use its territory to gain strategic depth against India. The growth of intense anti-American feelings in the Pakistani army and polity and the inclination to view the war on terror as the United States' war is also said to have impeded cooperation, as has the growing presence of Islamist, pro-jihadi hardliners in the military.

The first explanation, as has been seen, flies too blatantly in the face of facts to require a detailed rebuttal. The validity of the second should be clear to all who have followed the developments in Afghanistan and Pakistan and witnessed Pakistan's efforts to keep its strategic assets in Afghanistan—and against India—intact. This chapter will examine the last two explanations and also whether the Americans and their North Atlantic Treaty Organization (NATO) allies can win the Afghan war even if Pakistan persists in its present course.

We will confine ourselves primarily to the Pakistani army. The dominant arm of the military, it plays the most critical role in counter-insurgency operations, has been the principal mover in all coups and has run the military dictatorships that Pakistan has suffered. As we have seen, anti-American sentiments have been growing in the Pakistani military almost ever since military and economic assistance began arriving from the United States. The latter's enforcement of the Pressler Amendment, which stanched aid, as well as refusal to help Pakistan install Hekmatyar in Afghanistan after the Soviet withdrawal from the country, incensed Pakistanis further. In his essay 'In the Doghouse', in *On the Abyss: Pakistan after the Coup*, Tariq Ali quoted a retired Pakistani General telling him, 'Pakistan was the condom the Americans needed to enter Afghanistan,' and adding, 'We've served our purpose and they think we can just be flushed down the toilet.'[1]

As to the growing presence in the Pakistani army of fundamentalist Islamists, sympathetic to al Qaeda and the Taliban, which is also said to explain Pakistan's dismal record in fighting terrorism, Tariq Ali writes that it is no secret that 'the fundamentalists have penetrated the [Pakistani] army on every level. What distinguishes them from the old-style religious groups is that they want to seize state power and for that they need the army.'[2] He further states, 'Their [fundamentalists'] preferred model is that of the Taliban. If such a faction were ever to take over the Pakistani Army—and the possibility is not as remote as it seemed a few years ago—the possession of nuclear weapons [by Pakistan] would acquire a frightening new significance.'[3]

The ranks of the jihadis in the Pakistani army include not only foot soldiers and non-commissioned officers but a growing number of middle-level officers and quite a few officers of the rank of major generals and above. The arrest of Brigadier Ali Khan on 6 May 2011 on the charge of being linked to the Hizbut Tahrir (HuT), a banned Islamist militant group believed to be linked with al Qaeda, once again underlined the issue. A Lieutenant Colonel who worked under Khan was also detained. Earlier, on 4 May 2009, Pakistani military intelligence apprehended the then commanding officer of the Shamsi air force base in Balochistan province, alleging links with HuT. Arrested along with him were a retired fighter pilot–turned-lawyer, Squadron Leader Nadeem Ahmad Shah, and Awais Ali Khan, a US-educated mechanical engineer who held a green card. The fate of the accused, who were court-martialled, is unknown.[4]

The ideological conflict bedevilling the Pakistani army and affecting discipline was further reflected in the refusal of several units to be posted in South Waziristan and dozens of troops refusing to fight the tribes. The development shocked the military high command, which had to recall most of the troops from the front line.[5] If this indicated how Islamist penetration was hobbling Pakistani military's ability to fight terrorism, so did the attack on PNS Mehran. The attack could not have been staged without help from within the naval establishment. Significantly on 30 May, hardly a week after the naval base attack, Pakistani military authorities arrested a former navy commando, Kamran Ahmed, and his younger brother, Zaman Ahmed, for aiding the attackers. Kamran, who joined the navy in 1993 and was trained as a Special Services Group commando, was detained on charges of providing the attackers with maps of the base.[6]

Kamran was a member of the Mehsud tribe which has produced many Taliban leaders, like Tehrik-e-Taliban Pakistan's (TTP's) founder-commander, Baitullah Mehsud, Qari Hussain Mehsud and the incumbent TTP chief, Hakimullah Mehsud. The banned organization has claimed responsibility for the naval base attack as an act of vengeance for the killing of bin Laden. The military court, which had discharged Kamran from service in 2003 for assaulting a senior officer, had also declared him unfit for the job because of his extremist views.[7]

The question is whether these incidents were independent episodes triggered by the charged atmosphere created in the Pakistani military by its participation in America's war on terror or manifestations of a growing movement aimed at taking the armed forces over. For an answer, one must have a close look at the process of Islamization of the armed forces as well as in Pakistan's government and civil society since 1947, when Pakistan emerged as a separate, sovereign entity, and the ground it has gained so far. An understanding of the roots and history of Islamization in Pakistan is necessary for an idea of its destination.

JINNAH'S LANDMARK ADDRESS

That one is even considering the process is in a sense ironic. Muhammad Ali Jinnah, Pakistan's creator, was a secular, westernized Muslim who wanted Pakistan to be a moderate, modern, democratic State. He stated in his much-cited address in Pakistan's Constituent Assembly on 11 August 1947:

> You are free to go to your temples; you are free to go to your mosques or any other places of worship in this state of Pakistan. You may belong to any religion or caste or creed that has nothing to do with the business of the state.

He then cited the example of Britain where Protestants and Roman Catholics once persecuted one another but were now—though existing as separate communities—'equal members of the nation' and added:

> Now I think we should keep that in front of us as our ideal and you will find in course of time that Hindus would cease to be Hindus and Muslims would cease to be Muslims, not in the religious sense, because that is the personal faith of each individual, but in the political sense as citizens of the State.[8]

The cause of secularism suffered a severe blow with Jinnah's death on 11 September 1948. The fundamentalist ideologue, Abu Ala Maududi, who established Jama'at-e-Islami in undivided India in 1941, had shifted to Pakistan, the creation of which he had opposed earlier, after its emergence. He had become the head of the Jama'at in that country and mounted a vicious attack against Jinnah while the latter was alive. He now launched a furious campaign for a fundamentalist constitution for Pakistan. As early as 12 March 1949, the Pakistani constituent assembly succumbed to pressure from him and other leaders of his hue when it adopted an Objectives Resolution stating that it was obligatory for the State in Pakistan to enable Muslims to order their lives in accordance with the teachings and requirements of Islam as set out in the Holy Quran and the Sunnah, in effect declaring Pakistan to be an Islamic State.[9]

Maududi and his Jama'at shot into the limelight in Pakistan during the riots against Ahmadiyas in 1953 in which hundreds of members of the community were killed before the military ended the violence.[10] Arrested for his role in the riots and sentenced to death, he was released following domestic and international pressure.[11] He then resumed his campaign for an Islamist constitution for Pakistan. There were few takers for his ideas and Jama'at remained a fringe force, capable of violence but with little public support.

The corrupt and unstable civilian governments—seven prime ministers between 1950 and 1958[12]—had little stomach for fighting fundamentalists. Pakistan's first constitution, finally adopted in 1956, described the country as an 'Islamic Republic', the first Islamic country in the world to mention its religious character in its official name.[13] The constitution prescribed that no law could be passed against the teachings of the Quran and Sunnah and the existing laws would be made Islamic in character. It provided that the President should set up an organization for promoting Islamic Research and Training while the Directive Principles incorporated the injunction of the Objectives Resolution mentioned above. The president had to be a Muslim.

The constitution, which came into force on 23 March 1956, became a victim of infant mortality. It was summarily set aside by the country's President, Major General (Retired) Iskander Mirza, after the Chief of Army Staff, General Mohammad Ayub Khan, staged a coup on 7 October 1958. In another coup on 27 October, Ayub sent Mirza packing into comfortable exile in London and became the sole dictator. Ayub and the military brass were 'still steeped in Sandhurst culture' and 'made clear their dislike for Maududi and his socio-political agenda'.[14] M. J. Akbar points out in his incisive book, *Tinderbox: The Past and Future of Pakistan*, that 'Ayub Khan dismissed the Mullah as an enemy of modern education, and for him the success of Pakistan lay in its ability to modernize'. He cited a famous speech to a gathering of Deoband *ulema* (Islamic scholars and religious leaders), who had migrated to Pakistan, in which Ayub Khan said that Islam had started as a dynamic and progressive movement, but now suffered from dogmatism:

> Those who looked forward to progress and advancement came to be viewed as disbelievers and those who looked backward were considered devout Muslims. It is a great injustice to both life and religion to impose on twentieth century man the condition that he must go back several centuries in order to prove his bona fides as a true Muslim.[15]

Ayub Khan wanted to reduce the Islamic content in his 1962 constitution, and even to remove the word 'Islamic' before 'Republic' in Pakistan's name, making it just 'Republic of Pakistan'. He dropped the direct reference to the Quran and Sunnah in the Repugnancy Clause and made it read to the effect that no law should be repugnant to Islam. His modernizing intention became further evident when the Muslim Family Law Ordinance of 15 July1964 created a referral body for arbitrary divorce through instant talaq. Anyone remarrying within a year without permission from the Arbitration Council faced a year's imprisonment plus a fine of Rs 5,000.[16]

Maududi declared war on Ayub Khan's constitution as soon as it was made public. The Jama'at-e-Islami also agitated against the government's establishment of the Advisory Council of Islamic Ideology and the Pakistan Arts Councils, the promulgation of the family law ordinance, and permission for running Girl Guides troops, cinema halls and importing books critical of Islam. Ayub Khan began feeling the heat when Maududi joined the National Democratic Front, formed by Huseyn Shaheed Suhrawardy in 1962, thus merging the pro-democracy and the Islamist movements. The word 'Islamic' was restored to Pakistan's name in 1963, once again making it the 'Islamic Republic of Pakistan'.[17]

It was, however, not just the pressure of opposition that made the military regime retreat. It was not itself averse to playing the Islamic card. Ayub Khan mobilized a section of the ulema against Fatima Jinnah, sister of Muhammad Ali Jinnah, who contested him in the presidential elections of 1965. His Interior Ministry had a fatwa issued to the effect that Islam did not allow women to be the head of a State.[18] The regime also used Islamic symbolism and calls to jihad during the war with India later that year. On the day—5 September—of India's advance in the Lahore sector following Pakistan's offensive in the Chhamb-Jaurian sector, he said in his address to the nation, 'The 100 million people of Pakistan, whose hearts beat with the sound of "Lai illaha illallah, Muhammad Ur Rasool Ullah [There is no God but One God and Muhammad is His Messenger]" will not rest till India's guns are silent.'[19] Pakistan's state-controlled media whipped up a jihadi frenzy, extolling the virtues of Pakistan's 'Soldiers of Islam'.[20]

General Yahya Khan, then Pakistan's Chief of Army Staff, to whom President Ayub Khan handed over power after being forced to step down following widespread opposition to his rule in 1968, returned to Islam. Commenting on the development, M. J. Akbar observes that to protect the army's shattered credibility, the 'armed forces would henceforth also be guardians of Pakistan's "ideological frontiers". As defender of both faith and geography, the Army could claim to be the spine of the nation'.[21] Yahya Khan's strategy, as Zahid Hussain states, 'was to create an alliance between the military and the Islamists in order to check the rising power of the forces in favour of secular de-mocracy and maintain the preeminence of the military in Pakistani politics'.[22]

This political strategy of Pakistani military became the principal cause of the accelerating Islamization of Pakistan's army. Contrary to what one would have expected, the process was not reversed by Zulfikar Ali Bhutto, considered a secularist, socialist and a democrat who assumed power after Yahya Khan had to resign as president fol-lowing Pakistan's debacle in the 1971 war with India. The constitu-tion he promulgated on 3 April 1973 made Pakistan a parliamentary democracy where effectively all power vested in the prime minister and not the president. It included in the preamble the text of the 'Ob-jectives Resolution' of 1949, declared Islam as Pakistan's state religion and reserved the offices of the prime minister and the president for

Muslims. The constitution made the state duty-bound to enable Muslims lead an Islamic life, promote the study of the Quran and Sunnah and teach Islamiyat in schools. A Council of Islamic ideology was created to ensure that every law was in harmony with the tenets of the faith.[23] Clearly, there is truth in Akbar's scathing comment:

> Self-professed liberals like Bhutto have been as instrumental in the Islamization of Pakistan as ideologues. The momentum lay in the idea of Pakistan. Bhutto's motivation might have been expedience rather than conviction, but he too encouraged the growth of a strain in Pakistan's metabolism that had preceded him, and would acquire viral strength after his departure.[24]

The validity of Akbar's observation becomes clear on recalling that it was Bhutto's government that buckled under the pressure of religious parties and enacted a constitutional amendment that effectively declared Ahmadiyas as non-Muslims in 1974.[25] Significantly, in February that year Bhutto staged a grand Islamic summit in Lahore under the patronage of the Saudi King, Feisel bin Abdel Aziz. With the exception of the Shah of Iran, almost all Muslim leaders were present including, remarkably, Sheikh Mujibur Rahman of Bangladesh who was in a Pakistani prison for most of 1971. Another noteworthy presence was that of Colonel Muammar Qaddafi of Libya who called Pakistan the 'fortress of Islam' in Asia and placed Libya's resources at 'Bhutto's command'.[26]

It was a heady period for Bhutto. But *sic transit gloria mundi*.[27] On 1 March 1976, he superseded six generals and appointed Lieutenant General Muhammad Zia-ul Haq, with the most undistinguished record among all the claimants, as Chief of Army Staff.[28] Zia, who had ingratiated himself into Bhutto's favour by his obsequious behaviour, and was thought incapable of causing trouble as he was a *Mohajir* (Muslims who came over to Pakistan after India's partition), overthrew the Pakistan People's Party (PPP) leader in a coup on 5 July 1977 and had him executed on 21 April 1979 on a charge of murder following a dubious judgement.

ZIA'S AGENDA

Zia had his own agenda. An indication of its nature had become available even in Bhutto's lifetime when he had changed the army's motto from Jinnah's 'Unity, Faith and Discipline' to 'Faith, Obedience of God, and Struggle in the path of Allah' (*Iman, Takwa, Jihad fi Sabeelillah*) soon after taking over as army chief.[29] Bhutto, however, did not object and the move went largely unnoticed. Once in the saddle as dictator, Zia went full throttle to implement his idea of what Pakistan and its military should be. The results were far-reaching. As Wilson John states, 'nicknamed *maulvi* (preacher) among his peers', he 'systematically and radically changed what was, till then, essentially a professional army in the tradition of British days'.[30]

Commenting on the same process, Zahid Hussain writes in *Frontline Pakistan: The Path to Catastrophe and the Killing of Benazir Bhutto*, 'Islam was incorporated into the Army's organizational fabric. For the first time Islamic teachings were introduced into the Pakistan Military Academy.' Hussain further writes that 'Islamic training and philosophy were made a part of the curriculum at the Command and Staff College. A Directorate of Religious Instruction was instituted to educate the officer corps on Islam'. Islamic education became a subject of promotion examinations. Officers were required to read *The Quranic Concept of War*, a book written by a serving officer, Brigadier S. K. Malik, who later became a major general, and taught to be not just professional soldiers, but also soldiers of Islam.[31] In his foreword to the book, Zia wrote, 'The professional soldier in a Muslim army, pursuing the goals of a Muslim state, CANNOT become "professional" if in all his activities he does not take the "colour of Allah."'[32]

Zia also upgraded the status of maulvis attached to each army unit, who were until then barely tolerated by the military elite. He integrated them into the ethos of army life and made it compulsory for them to go into battle with the troops.[33] An officer had to be a devout Muslim to be promoted.

> Scores of highly professional and secular officers were sidelined for not meeting the criteria of being a 'good Muslim.' ...

many conservative officers reached the senior command level. Radical Islamist ideology permeated the army with the free flow of religious political literature in the armed forces training institutions. Friday prayers at regimental mosques, a matter of individual choice in the past, became obligatory.[34]

If all these measures made for the Islamization of the Pakistani army, so did the change in the social composition of the officers' corps which was, until the 1970s, dominated by upper class elements and rural aristocracy. Post-1970s, new officers came mostly from the 'lower and middle social strata' which were conservative and easily influenced by Islamic fundamentalism.[35] Zahid Hussain further says that unlike their predecessors they came not from elite English-language schools but modest state-run educational institutions. Less westernized, they knew virtually nothing of the spirit of liberalism common in the 'old' army.[36] The narrow nationalist orientation and education as well as the professional training and culture of these new officers made them most vulnerable to the appeal of the Jama'at-e-Islami which was allowed to freely conduct its propaganda and distribute Islamic literature in the armed forces.[37] Stating that these young officers constituted the main base of President Zia's regime, Zahid Hussain says, citing a retired Pakistani general, that 25 to 30 per cent of the officers had fundamentalist Islamist leanings.[38]

Also interesting is a geographical phenomenon. Wilson John points out that the Pakistani 'Army's traditional recruiting ground for men and officers' has shifted 'from north and central Punjab (Rawalpindi, Abbotabad and Jhelum) to the south (Multan, Jhang, Bhawalpur, etc.) which happens to be the core zone of *jihadi* recruitment since the Afghan days'. Stating that it can be safely assumed that a large number of these recruits have had 'direct or indirect experience of participating in either the Afghan or Kashmir *jihad*', he adds, if such a possibility were 'to be seen in parallel to the streak of radicalism among the officer cadre mentioned earlier, the vulnerability of Pakistan to extremist ideologies and movements like Al Qaida can be more clearly understood'.[39]

The attempt to Islamize Pakistan's society and governance was made simultaneously, and as assiduously, as the one to transform the military. A decision to enforce Islamic laws on theft, drinking, adultery and 'protection of freedom of belief' from February 1979 was announced on 2 December 1978. The government, it was further stated, would constitute provincial *shariat* benches at the High Court level and an appellate shariat court at the level of the Supreme Court. These courts were empowered to decide, even if no suit had been filed before them, whether any law was wholly or partly un-Islamic and the government would have to amend the law according to the court's directive.[40] Zia started a debate on how to rid the banking system of usury, which was forbidden in Islam.[41]

A major step toward Islamization was taken in 1980 when the government announced that it would set up a central *zakat* administration to collect and distribute zakat, the amount representing 2.5 per cent of the value of their assets and savings that Muslims have to give to charity every year. Shias, who claimed that their faith did not allow compulsion in the collection of zakat, were exempted from the scope of the order. Nevertheless, the thousands of local committees through which zakat was distributed were happy with Zia as were the recipients.[42] This doubtless conduced to building up a large, patronage-based support network.

Zia's drive was jurisprudentially, socially and culturally regressive. Women suffered particularly. His legal amendments significantly devalued their evidence. Women signing financial contracts had to have their signatures witnessed by another woman or man. An order that women should cover their heads in public was issued and enforced in public schools and colleges, as well as on state television. Women's participation in sports and the performing arts was severely restricted.[43] Minorities were subjected to gross discrimination. For example, a Muslim murdering a Hindu could not be punished without confirming evidence by four Muslims.[44]

The results were far-reaching. Succinctly summing these up, Haqqani writes that Zia undoubtedly 'went farthest in defining Pakistan as an Islamic state'. He 'nurtured the jihadi ideology that now threatens do destabilize much of the Islamic world; but in doing so he saw himself as carrying forward the nation-and-state-building process that started soon after the demise of Pakistan's founder, Muhammad Ali Jinnah'.[45]

The jihadi ideology threatens much of not just the Islamic but the whole world. While nations like India and Afghanistan, which are adjacent to Pakistan, have had to bear the brunt of the vicious terrorism it has spawned, other parts of the world have not been left unscarred. Recall 9/11, the attack on London's subway system in July 2005 and many other horrifying terrorist acts that have occured. It is, therefore, important to note Zia's efforts to Islamize Pakistan's society and governance as it has reinforced the process of the Islamization of the military in terms of both providing official sanction for the process and influencing the ethos of the people from whose ranks recruitment is made to the forces.

THE STRENGTH OF JIHADIS

Estimates of the strength of Islamists in Pakistan's army are essentially intelligent guesses. Shuja Nawaz, a distinguished military historian and a brother of General Asif Nawaz, who was a Chief of Army Staff of Pakistan, writes that of the 804 officers commissioned into the Pakistani army in 1978 and 1979, 29 were recommended for promotion to the rank of major general in 2006. A select few of them have taken over, or would take over, as lieutenant generals by now. Known as 'Zia bhartis', or 'Zia recruits', they were certainly a more conservative lot given more to rituals than their predecessors.[46] Nawaz further points out that Zia recruits would run the Pakistani army once the senior lieutenant generals, commissioned during the 1960s and 1970s, retired. Many of them have been exposed to Zia's propagation of Islamist ideology in staff colleges and academies. Affected by American and Western European embargo on aid to Pakistan, they never had any opportunity for advanced overseas training during their formative years. Nor had they any exposure to the outside world till late in their careers, by which time their world views had been formed and, in many cases, become entrenched.[47]

The jihad in Afghanistan against Soviet occupation further contributed to the Pakistani army's Islamization. It, Wilson John points out,

> ... saw the army openly use Islamic concepts and symbols to raise a force of *Mujahideen* mercenaries with funds and weapons generously supplied by the US and its Western allies to fight Soviet troops ... Middle-rank officers (Pervez Musharraf was one of them) took charge of the covert operations in Afghanistan; new recruits in large numbers joined the Army as well as the ISI. A number of men were recruited from *madrassa* for the ISI. Saudi Arabia stepped in with enormous funding for the operations and, packaged in this generosity was the Wahhabi ideology, an extremely radical school of thought. The *jihad* saw the birth of terrorist groups in Pakistan, with links to global terrorist networks, and the emergence of a more radical set of officers and men in the Army and the ISI.[48]

Besides, as Zahid Hussain points out, the situation in Afghanistan inspired a whole generation of Pakistani Islamic radicals who 'considered it their duty to fight the oppression of Muslims anywhere in the world'. This gave 'a new dimension to the idea of jihad' which the Pakistani state had used until then to mobilize support against India.[49] The atrocities on Muslims in Bosnia reinforced the globalization of the concept of jihad which, as people like Abdullah Azzam, Osama bin Laden and Ayman al-Zawahiri came to proclaim, had to be waged against the United States and the West as well.

Zia died in a mysterious air crash on 17 August 1988. Neither General Mirza Aslam Beg, who succeeded him as Pakistan's Chief of Army Staff, nor any of the others who held that office—Generals Asif Nawaz, Abdul Waheed, Jehangir Karamat and Pervez Musharraf—was a fundamentalist like General Zia. They presented themselves as pro-American Pakistani generals of the Cold War era like Ayub Khan and Yahya Khan. They were, however, not averse to presiding over 'jihadi policies aimed against India but occasionally spilling beyond South Asia'.[50] This detracted from the single-minded effort that might have halted the progress of Pakistani army's Islamization, which continued apace.

General Asif Nawaz was perhaps one of the two exceptions. While fully subscribing to the view that the army had to play a dominant role in Pakistan's life, he was alarmed by the increasing influence the Islamists wielded and sought to restore to the army some semblance of professionalism which 'politics and ideology had eroded'.[51] His death in January 1993, following a heart attack, sparked a huge controversy with his widow, Nuzhat Nawaz, alleging that he had been poisoned to death and the prime minister of Pakistan might have been among the plotters,[52] and demanding a judicial inquiry into the circumstances of his death. Though a judicial inquiry found no evidence of a conspiracy or of poisoning, the suspicion that he was killed remains.

General Abdul Waheed, who became Pakistan's Chief of Army Staff after General Asif Nawaz's passing, was a straightforward professional army man who was not politically or ideologically motivated. He made it clear that he would not countenance officers 'interfering in politics or becoming involved with contentious matters outside their profession'.[53] The caretaker government, headed by a former World Bank executive, Moeen Qureshi, that came into power following Nawaz Sharif's sacking, made, with General Waheed's active cooperation, an effort to clean up the Inter-Services Intelligence (ISI). Scores of officers, who had become closely linked with extremist Afghan Mujahideen groups during the anti-Soviet jihad, were systematically removed. About 1,100 operatives were either retired or sent back to their army units.[54] Lieutenant General Javed Nasir, a dyed-in-the-wool Islamist fundamentalist, whom Nawaz Sharif made the head of the ISI, and who aggressively stepped up aid to Kashmiri terrorists and is said to have enlisted the services of Mumbai's underworld don, Dawood Ibrahim, for staging devastating serial bomb explosions in the city on 12 March 1993, was sacked as ISI's chief and prematurely retired from the army in May 1993, following the dismissal of Sharif's government.

The purge had perhaps restored some discipline in the ISI but did not change its basic orientation. It had become very deeply involved in helping the secessionist struggle in Kashmir. The military too was unwilling to withdraw support from the militants and many in its establishment believed that 'Kashmiri freedom fighters' were ensuring Pakistan's safety by engaging about half-a-million Indian troops in Kashmir.[55] Islamization of Pakistan's military continued apace, in spite of disturbing indications of trouble brewing.

One of these indications was an attempted coup by a group of Islamist army officers who wanted to capture power with the help of extremist militant groups and clerics. Their plan to storm a corps commanders' meeting, chaired by the Chief of Army Staff, kill all present and then 'eradicate the cabinet', was foiled with the arrest of Major General Zaheerul Islam Abbasi and 35 other officers on 26 September 1995.[56] Abbasi was at the centre of the attempt along with Brigadier Mustansir Billa, perhaps a more extreme radical Islamist than him. They were sentenced to 7 and 14 years of rigorous imprisonment respectively.

Many have argued that the 'coup' charge was trumped up. One of them, Yossef Bodansky, said, 'In reality the coup was a setup, a purge of current or former ISI elements who had actively sponsored terrorism against the United States.'[57] According to Bodansky, Pakistan had concluded in September that the interrogation of Ramzi Yousuf, the main perpetrator of the World Trade Center bombing of 26 February 1993 in the United States, and Fuad Talat Qassim, the leader of the Egyptian terrorist organization, Gama'a Islamiyya, in Cairo, must have given Washington DC an idea 'of how extensively these individuals, particularly the senior ISI officers, were involved in Islamic terrorism'.[58] These officers had to be sacrificed to maintain the credibility of Prime Minister Benazir Bhutto who denied Pakistan's involvement in promoting terrorism.

Bodansky, a former director of the United States' Congressional Task Force on Terrorism and Unconventional Warfare, ought to know. But even if the coup episode was trumped up, the Pakistani army's fear of exposure indicated the presence of Islamists in its ranks. And it would be laughable to believe that the arrests had ended the Islamist presence in Pakistan's army.

Cousins in Culture

Wilson John writes that over the years, the army and the ISI became culturally sympathetic to the extremists if not entirely radicalized. There were numerous instances of regular officers and men from the army being involved in terrorist activities 'either directly or indirectly as facilitators and trainers for groups like LeT and JeM'.[59] He cites the example of Tanzeem-ul Ikhwan, a radical group of retired army officers and men which held that Pakistan could be converted into an Islamic state if 1 per cent of its population could be made to support its cause. Ikhwan has often trained or sent its cadres for training with LeT. All its leaders being retired senior army officers, it drew hundreds of serving officers and soldiers to the group's ideological training sessions.[60] Its cadres included, besides Major General Zaheerul Islam Abbasi and Brigadier Mustansir Billa, Colonels Mohammad Azad Minhas and Inayatullah Khan. All four were among those jailed in connection with the 1995 coup attempt.[61]

Lieutenant Generals Gul Hasan and Javed Nasir, both of whom headed the ISI, maintain close links with Islamist organizations, which continue to have a strong presence in Pakistan's armed forces. Pervez Musharraf shifted out three of his senior-most lieutenant generals, who had helped him to carry out the coup of October 1999 and were known for their hard-line Islamist views, several hours before American airstrikes began in Afghanistan on 7 October 2001. They were the ISI chief, Mehmood Ahmed, the corps commander, Lahore, Muhammad Aziz Khan, a former ISI officer who had run the Taliban in the 1990s and the Deputy Chief of Army Staff, Muzaffar Usmani, who 'resigned after being replaced'.[62] Aziz Khan became Chairman, Joint Chiefs of Staff Committee.

Lieutenant General Ehsan ul-Haq, who was made the new ISI chief, removed dozens of mid-level ISI officers who had been involved with the pro-Taliban policy. But an organization, that had trained and motivated hundreds of its officers to support Islamists in Afghanistan and Kashmir for two decades, could not be expected to change its views overnight.[63] Extremists continued to be present in the army and the ISI. According to a report in the *Telegraph* of the United Kingdom, on 1 September 2003, the Pakistani military spokesman, Major General Shaukat Saulat, admitted that three or four mid-level officers, including a lieutenant colonel, were being investigated for violation of discipline and suspected links to Islamic extremist groups. None of the officers was named.[64] The report further stated that American, British and Afghan officials believed that the ISI, the army's main tool in backing fundamentalist movements, was still full of Islamic extremist officers. They had ceased providing support to the Taliban after the September 11 terrorist attacks on America, but had resumed doing it.

The presence of extremists in the ranks of Pakistan's military—including navy and air force—was sharply underlined by the two attempts on Musharraf's life on 14 and 25 December respectively in 2003. On the first occasion, a massive bomb exploded under a bridge in Rawalpindi a mere 30 seconds after Musharraf's convey had driven over it. A jamming device, provided by the Federal Bureau of Investigation (FBI) and attached to Musharraf's car, had saved him by momentarily blocking all telephone signals and delaying the blast.[65] The attack on 25 December, very close to the scene of the 14 December attack, involved two suicide bombers in two explosives-laden vans trying to dash against the car in which the Pakistani president was travelling.[66] It was, according to official admission, the fourth attempt on the general-turned-president's life since 13 September 2001 when he decided to support American action in Afghanistan.[67]

The attacks, staged very close to the army headquarters and Musharraf's residence, could not have been mounted without help from people within the armed forces and the security agencies. This becomes further clear on recalling that Musharraf's movements were kept strictly secret and very few people knew about it. In fact, the military was already under the scanner. A naval soldier and a paramilitary ranger were among those arrested in connection with an earlier attempt on Musharraf's life in April 2002. They were accused of providing the terrorists with information about Musharraf's route.[68]

More than 150 police and military personnel were arrested and interrogated after the December 2003 attacks. Finally, a secret court martial tried six non-commissioned officers of the air force, and several military personnel and civilians. Twelve were found guilty and sentenced to death in 2006.[69] The December 2003 attacks led to a major reshuffle of the Pakistani army's higher command which put Major General Nadeem Taj, a close confidante of Musharraf, at the head of military intelligence, which now looked after his security. A further attempt to strengthen his grip over the army led to Lieutenant General Ahsan Saleem Ayat's appointment as vice-chief of the army and Lieutenant General Shuja Pasha becoming the head of the ISI. Seven major generals were made lieutenant generals superseding 37 of their colleagues.[70] The move rewarded senior officers who had borne the burden of the war on terrorism alongside him and ensured an obedient top brass as the new lieutenant generals, juniors who owed everything to Musharraf, were in no position to criticize his policies.[71]

Musharraf, as Syed Saleem Shahzad says, was

> unable to completely eradicate the radical tendency, which had become deep-rooted in Pakistan's security services from 1979 to 2001. Al Qaeda aimed, through organizations like Jundullah, to divert the allegiance of this impressive pool of Islamists into its own fold, along with others.[72]

Saying that Pakistan's Army was not 'itself immune from the influence of radicalism', Syed Saleem Shahzad adds:

> Several army officers had pledged their allegiance (*bait*) to different jihadi spiritual leaders, including Maulana Akram Awal of Chakwal. These groups were known in Pakistan army as *pir bhai* groups (*pir bhai* are those who [had] pledged their allegiance to a person, in a way that means the whole circle of disciples acted as brothers to each other).[73]

The arrests mentioned above underscored the validity of Shahzad's statement.

The question is whether the deep-rooted radical tendency in Pakistan's security services, particularly the army, is irreversible and will lead to a jihadi takeover of the Pakistani military. One cannot rule out the possibility given the spread of jihadi ideology and sympathy for the Taliban, al Qaeda and organizations like the LeT and HuT in the armed forces. Growing anger against the United States also helps the intensely anti-American jihadi elements, inside and outside the military. The Pakistani army, however, is still a disciplined force. By all indications, its top brass would not want to have an irreparable breach with the United States. It is true that officers with liberal backgrounds and warm links with the West are getting increasingly fewer. But even the conservative ones may not want a sharp deterioration of ties with the United States because that may mean a drastic curtailment, if not complete stoppage, of military aid, which has been considerable.

THE CASCADE OF AID

Chapter 5 has detailed the huge amount of aid the United States has given Pakistan, including the economic and military package announced after Islamabad's becoming an ally in America's post-9/11 war against al Qaeda and Taliban, since the 1950s. According to a report by the United States' Congressional Research Service dated 7 June 2011, the United States has pledged more than $30 billion in direct aid, about half for military assistance, to Pakistan since 1948. Two-thirds of this total was appropriated from financial year 2002 to financial year 2010.[74] In September 2009, the United States Congress passed the Enhanced Partnership with Pakistan Act, also called the Kerry-Lugar-Berman Act after its main sponsors.[75] It authorizes the American President to provide $1.5 billion in annual bilateral economic aid to Pakistan from financial year 2010 to financial year 2014. It also provides as a sense of Congress that the same level of economic aid should continue in financial year 2015 to financial year 2019 'subject to an improving political and economic environment in Pakistan'.[76]

Also in 2009, the United States Congress established the Pakistan Counterinsurgency Fund (PCF) within the Defence Department appropriations and the Pakistan Counterinsurgency Capability Fund

(PCCF) within the State-Foreign Operations Appropriations—to build Pakistan's counter-insurgency capabilities. Within the financial year 2010 supplemental appropriations, Congress provided $349 million in military and economic assistance to Pakistan. Taking into account military reimbursements under the 'coalition support fund', America provided a total of $4.5 billion for Pakistan for financial year 2010 alone, making it the second-highest recipient after Afghanistan. Besides these ongoing programmes, the United States pledged, in mid-2010, an additional $592 million in emergency and recovery aid, plus more than $95 million of in-kind aid after extensive flooding resulted in a severe humanitarian crisis that affected an estimated 20 million Pakistanis. In October 2010, Secretary of State Hillary Clinton announced the United States Administration's intention to increase American Foreign Military Financing for Pakistan to $2 billion over a five-year period, a $100 million annual increase from the then current level.[77]

There has been considerable grumbling in the Pakistani establishment over the conditions for actual disbursement. For example, the Act provides that the availability of the economic aid of $1.5 billion annually will depend on the US administration submitting to appropriate Congressional committees a *Pakistan Assistance Strategy Report*, which it did on 14 December 2009.[78] The other condition remains, which is that the aid will be limited to $750 million in a year unless the President's Special Representative to Afghanistan and Pakistan or, in his or her absence, the Secretary of State certifies that Pakistan was making reasonable progress toward achieving the United States' objectives[79] or the Secretary of State waives the certification in the United States' national interest.[80]

The most stringent conditions, however, apply to security-related assistance for financial years 2011–14, and arms transfers for financial years 2012–14. The law precludes such assistance and transfers until the Secretary of State certified annually for Congress that the Government of Pakistan continued to cooperate with the United States in efforts to dismantle supplier networks relating to the acquisition of nuclear weapons–related materials, such as providing relevant information from or direct access to Pakistani nationals associated with such networks; that it had demonstrated during the preceding fiscal year a sustained commitment to, and was making significant efforts towards, combating terrorist groups; that it was ending support, including by any elements within the Pakistan military or its intelligence agency, to extremist and terrorist groups, particularly to any group that has conducted attacks against United States or coalition forces in Afghanistan, or against the territory or people of neighbouring countries.[81]

The Secretary of State had also to certify that Pakistan's government was preventing al Qaeda, the Taliban and associated terrorist groups, such as LeT and JeM, from operating in Pakistan's territory, carrying out activities that included cross-border attacks into neighbouring countries, in closing terrorist camps in the Federally Administered Tribal Areas (FATA), and dismantling terrorist bases of operations in other parts of the country, including Quetta and Muridke. The Secretary of State had also to certify that the Pakistani government had been taking action when provided with intelligence about high-level terrorist targets; strengthening counterterrorism and anti-money laundering laws; and that Pakistan's security forces were not materially and substantially subverting the country's political or judicial processes.[82]

It is important to note the conditions for two reasons. First, these reflect Washington DC's growing realization that Pakistan was using its participation in America's war on terror to further its own interests in Afghanistan at the cost of the United States and arm itself against India. A number of instances indicating this have been cited in earlier chapters. According to a report in the *New York Times* of 24 December 2007, the Bush administration and American military officials believed that much of the $5 billion provided to Pakistan under a programme called 'Coalition Support Fund', which reimburses Pakistan for its military operations against terrorism, were diverted to finance the acquisition of weapons systems designed to counter India.[83] The funds did not reach the men fighting al Qaeda and the Taliban on the ground.

The very fact that Pakistan accepted these tough conditions, albeit kicking and protesting, showed that it was loathe to lose American aid. Instead, its objective during the present Afghan war, as during the entire span of its relationship with the United States, was to eat its cake and also have it. There have been other indications. According to a report in the *New York Times* of 9 July 2011, the Obama administration was suspending, and in some cases cancelling, the release of military aid and equipment to the tune of about $800 million in a move to chasten Pakistan for expelling American military trainers and to press its army to fight militants more effectively. The report further stated that many of the recent aid curtailments were clearly intended to force the Pakistani military to choose between backing the country that financed much of its operations and equipment, and continuing to support in secret Taliban and other militants fighting American soldiers in Afghanistan.[84]

Pakistan's first response was defiance. Stating that the Pakistani army had not officially heard from the United States in the matter, Major General Athar Abbas, the Pakistani army's spokesman, said on 11 July, 'The Army in the past, as well as at present, had conducted successful military operations using its own resources without any external support whatsoever.'[85] On the following day, the country's Defence Minister, Ahmed Mukhtar, threatened to pull Pakistani forces out of the sensitive border region with Afghanistan if the United States followed through on some $800 million in cuts to an annual $2 billion in military assistance.[86] On 13 July, the very next day, however, Lieutenant General Shuja Pasha, then head of the ISI, was on a visit to Washington DC! Prime Minister Yusuf Raza Gilani expressed his concern about how the cuts would affect Pakistan's fight against extremism and said, 'It is our own war, but we are fighting this war for the entire world.'[87]

OF SPATS, TANTRUMS AND NEAR BREAK-UPS

In spite of the spats, tantrums and near break-ups like the one after the American air strikes of 26 November 2011, United States–Pakistan relations have not sundered and have continued on their roller-coaster ride. The *New York Times* provided an example of this when it revealed on 9 March 2012 that the ISI and the Central Intelligence Agency

(CIA) had quietly worked to 'rebuild their ties in the past month'.[88] The reason is simple. Pakistan's present leadership, both civilian and military, fully realize that they are in no position to dispense with American civilian and military aid. Equally, they do not want to destroy the Haqqani network and the Afghan Taliban which they consider to be their strategic assets, or desist from activities that undermine the American position and the Karzai government in Afghanistan, and install a pliant government there. They are, besides, inheritors of a skill that their predecessors had turned into an art—taking Americans for a ride. They will, therefore, huff and puff on the brink but take care not to leap over.

Things will, of course, change if Islamists either take over or dominate the army as to them jihad takes precedence over everything else. As of now, they will be able to do so only if a Taliban–al Qaeda takeover of Afghanistan boosts their morale and prestige immensely and demoralizes and weakens the moderate forces in Pakistan's military and civilian spheres. This in turn is unlikely to happen before the bulk of American forces leave Afghanistan after 2014. Thereafter, it would depend on how much resistance the Karzai regime or its successor can offer and how much support the United States and other countries like India and Russia extend to it. Surprising almost everybody, the Najibullah[89] government did not collapse immediately after the Soviet withdrawal from Afghanistan completed on 15 February 1989. Propped up by substantial economic and military aid from the Soviet Union, he continued in power until the dissolution of the Soviet Union on 26 December 1991 deprived him of foreign aid, and internal differences in his government undermined him, leading to his ouster on 14 April 1992.

Given the escalating demand in the United States to end its involvement with Afghanistan, a renewed deterioration in the still tense ties between the United States and the Karzai government may lead to the stoppage or serious curtailment of American economic and military aid to Kabul not long after 2014. In that case the Afghan government of the day may not even last as long as the Najibullah government did in Afghanistan, and the consequent Taliban–al Qaeda takeover may then lead to an Islamist takeover of Pakistan's army and government.

A Taliban–al Qaeda takeover of Afghanistan would render irrelevant the question of Pakistan's role in the United States' war against terror. What matters is Islamabad's role till then. Given the internal pressures in Pakistan, its own interests in Afghanistan, and its belief that the United States cannot win in Afghanistan, it is unlikely to extend to Washington DC anything more than the highly selective and inadequate support it is now providing. The question is: Can the United States arm-twist it into playing an effective role? It can no doubt extract a promise—as it did after 9/11—that Pakistan would extend wholehearted cooperation by issuing a stern ultimatum. It would, however, be highly unrealistic to expect that Islamabad would not again go back on its promise as it did earlier. Hence the question: Can the United States, which is in the process of withdrawing its troops from Afghanistan, win the war in the country? The answer will depend on the soundness of the new strategy it has adopted and the determination with which it is implemented. Before considering both, however, one must look at a problem which has bedevilled the American war effort in Afghanistan from the very beginning—that of routing supplies.

For about seven months, supply routes to American troops in Afghanistan stood blocked ever since the American air strikes in Pakistan's border areas killed 24 of the latter's soldiers on 26 November 2011. Supplies to NATO/International Security Assistance Force (ISAF) troops in Afghanistan have so far depended mainly on convoys using two routes through Pakistan—one across the Khyber Pass in the Khyber Pakhtunkhwa province to the border town of Torkham and from there to Kabul, and the other running through Balochistan province to the border town of Chaman and thence to Kandahar.[90]

Safety, however, has been a major concern. According to Amir Mir, Taliban militants had targeted a total of 109 NATO convoys, killing 52 persons, mostly truck drivers, since January 2011. The targeted convoys included fuel tankers, each carrying 45,000 litres, and containers with unspecified quantities of logistic material for the 120,000-strong NATO/ISAF forces. Armoured transport vehicles were also set aflame or looted.[91] Pakistan's government has not exactly been helpful. Mir mentions an incident on 30 September 2009, which killed two Pakistani troops. NATO apologized for the incident saying that the helicopter gunships mistook warning shots by Pakistani forces for a militant attack. Nevertheless, Pakistan kept the supply routes suspended for 10 days.[92]

Given all this, it is hardly surprising that a report by the Foreign Relations Committee of the United States Senate, released on 19 December 2011, by Senator John Kerry, its chairman, stated that the United States had 'steadily increased traffic on the Northern Distribution Network (NDN)' since 2009. The report further stated that the NDN comprised

> three principal land routes: one stretching from the Georgian Black Sea port of Poti, through Baku, Azerbaijan, across the Caspian Sea, and into Central Asia; one from the Latvian port of Riga through Russia, Kazakhstan, and Uzbekistan; and a final route that originates in Latvia and travels through Russia, Kazakhstan, Kyrgyzstan, and passes into Afghanistan via Tajikistan. An estimated 70 percent of cargo transiting the NDN enters at Uzbekistan's Hairaton Gate.[93]

There has been a marked change in the pattern of routing supplies. The report of the Senate Foreign Relations Committee states, 'According to U.S. Transportation Command, close to 75 percent of ground sustainment cargo is now shipped via the NDN. An estimated 40 percent of all cargo transits the NDN, 31 percent is shipped by air, and the remaining 29 percent goes through Pakistan.'[94] This is in sharp contrast to the situation in 2009 when about 90 per cent of the United States' non-lethal cargo to Afghanistan was routed through Karachi.

NOT WITHOUT PROBLEMS

The despatch of supplies through the NDN has, however, not been without its problems. As the Senate Committee on Foreign Relations has pointed out, only one-way transit of goods to Afghanistan is now permitted, though discussions have been underway to make it two ways. Besides, the present permission covers the transit of only non-lethal supplies such as cement, lumber, blast barriers, septic tanks and matting. Sensitive and high-technology equipment are being air-lifted. Moreover, the NDN is not cheap. 'It costs roughly an additional $10,000 per twenty-foot container to ship via the NDN instead of Pakistan. But airlifting supplies is estimated to cost $40,000 more per twenty-foot container, according to US Transportation Command.'[95]

Besides the NDN, the Manas Transit Centre in Kyrgyzstan is a critical air mobility hub. About 13 million pounds of cargo transit through it every month. The entry and exit point for virtually all coalition forces, it enables critical missions including aerial refuelling and medical evacuation and consumes one million gallons of fuel every two days.[96] There are, however, problems here as well. In 2006, Kyrgyzstan demanded a substantial increase in lease payments. The settlement reached included an announcement that the United States would provide $150 million in total 'assistance and compensation.'[97] The United States concluded a five-year agreement with Kyrgyzstan in 2009 increasing the rent from $17.4 million to $60 million per year. But uncertainties remain. Many in Kyrgyzstan are deeply suspicious about United States' presence at Manas and the centre has often been a subject of domestic controversy.[98]

There is also the Russian factor. An issue is NATO's Active Layered Theatre Ballistic Missile Defence (ALTBMD) programme. The NATO acquired the first phase of an initial capability to protect its forces against missile threats in early 2010. The November 2010 NATO summit in Lisbon decided to expand the command, control and communication capabilities of the programme to protect its forces, to include NATO's European populations and territory. It welcomed the United States' European Phased Adaptive Approach (EPAA) and contributions from other nations as valuable additions to the alliance's missile defence architecture.[99] Russia has serious reservations about the shield which it considers to be a threat. In November 2011 its President, Dmitry Medvedev, threatened to withdraw from the New Strategic Arms Reduction Treaty—known as New START—on nuclear weapons reductions if NATO proceeded with the missile-defence system.

He also said that Russia would prepare to deploy new ballistic missiles on its European border.[100]

In what appeared to be yet another escalatory step, Russia's ambassador to NATO, Dmitry Rogozin, stated that if the alliance did not respond seriously to its concerns, 'we have to address matters in relations in other areas'. Russian news services, which reported his remark, also quoted him as saying that Russia's cooperation on Afghanistan may be an area for review.[101] Be that as it may, the matter remains a potential source of trouble because NATO has signalled its intention to go ahead with the shield. Addressing a news conference at the end of a meeting of NATO foreign ministers on 7 December 2011, NATO Secretary General Anders Fogh Rasmussen said that Russia's threat to install countermeasures against a planned missile-defence system in Europe were reminiscent of 'the confrontation of a bygone era' and reflected a 'fundamental misunderstanding' of the West's intentions.[102] Rasmussen further said, 'We need missile defence for our own security. We believe our defences would be more effective if we cooperate ... this is why we invited our Russian partners' to participate in the system.

Rasmussen said that Russia's comments about the supply network were 'an empty threat ... because it is clearly in Russia's self-interest to contribute to success in Afghanistan'. Russia, he said, 'knows from bitter experience that instability in Afghanistan has negative repercussions in Russia as well'.[103] Besides, according to the Obama administration and its European allies, the system is directed against possible long-range and medium-range missiles from the Middle East. Russia, they have insisted, needs protection from the same threat. They, however, dubbed as unnecessary Russia's demand for a binding guarantee that the system would never be used to undermine or counter its defences, and the negotiations stalled over this.[104]

ACCOMMODATING RUSSIANS

To be fair to Russia, it has been more than accommodating in permitting overflights and railway transportation to Afghanistan across its territory. According to a media note issued by the Office of the Spokesman, United States Department of State, on 20 April 2011, the day recorded a significant milestone in cooperation with Moscow with the 1,000th supply mission transiting Russian airspace.[105] These overflights, the note said, resulted from a bilateral agreement in support of operations in Afghanistan announced during the July 2009 United States–Russia Summit. The agreement, in turn, 'has been a major success of the "reset" in U.S.-Russian relations and has resulted in the transfer of over 150,000 personnel in support of international efforts in Afghanistan to date. The flights will continue in the weeks and months ahead'.[106]

Under a separate NATO–Russia transit arrangement, complementary to the Russo-American one, supplies have been shipped by rail through Russia and Central Asia to support ISAF forces in Afghanistan. By 20 April 2011, these shipments totalled more than 25,000 containers.[107] Taken together, these transit arrangements with Russia have allowed the United States to diversify crucial transportation routes into Afghanistan, significantly improving its ability to support its troops. That Russia has done so despite the key role the United States played in the 1980s to ensure its defeat in Afghanistan is a tribute to the wisdom of its leaders. Their conduct stands in sharp contrast to that of the Reagan administration which blindly backed rabidly anti-American fundamentalist Islamist groups, with little thought of the consequences to follow, to avenge the United States' defeat in Vietnam.

The United States will show a similar lack of wisdom if it now takes Russia's support for granted and pays scant regard to Moscow's concerns particularly since the latter's support is indispensible to the success of any effort to stabilize Afghanistan and Central Asia. Indeed, Vladimir V. Putin was the first world leader to call President George W. Bush after 9/11 offering assistance and Moscow readily agreed to permit American bases in the former Soviet republics of Central Asia to support the war effort in Afghanistan. And even before 9/11, during the Clinton administration, Putin had proposed Russo-American cooperation against the Taliban, a proposal Washington DC had turned down for political reasons.[108]

Those opposing close Russo-American cooperation may argue that the interests of the two countries conflict in Central Asia and that Washington DC cannot endorse Moscow's record in human rights and manner of holding elections. But the United States' interests in Afghanistan also conflict with Pakistan's. While the United States wants a stable, democratic and peaceful Afghanistan making economic progress and respecting human rights and gender equality, Pakistan wants a pliant government in Kabul which will provide it with 'strategic depth' against India and disallow any Indian presence in Afghanistan. Its instruments for securing both objectives are the Afghan Taliban and the Haqqani network, who reject democracy and uphold theocracy and have little respect for human rights and gender equality. They are pathologically anti-American, deeply linked to al Qaeda and share with the latter the goal of global supremacy of their version of obscurantist Islam through worldwide jihad.

One can doubtless argue that Pakistan's cooperation is perhaps more important than Russia's in ensuring an Afghan settlement. Such cooperation, however, has not been coming and, by the look of things, is unlikely to come. On the other hand, Russia's support will have to be a key element in defeating the Taliban and al Qaeda and ensuring a peaceful, stable, democratic order, respecting human rights and gender justice, in Afghanistan and Central Asia.

NOTES

1. Ali Tariq, Contribution entitled 'In the Doghouse', *On the Abyss: Pakistan after the Coup* (India: HarperCollins Publishers, 2000), p. 7.
2. Ibid., p. 26.
3. Ibid., p. 30.
4. Amir Mir, 'Islamists Break Pakistani Military Ranks', *Asia Times Online*, 24 June 2011, http://www.atimes.com/atimes/South_Asia/MF24Df04.html.
5. Ibid.
6. Ibid.
7. Ibid.
8. Quoted in Husain Haqqani, *Pakistan between Mosque and Military* (Washington DC: Carnegie Endowment for International Peace, 2005), pp. 12–13.
9. Ibid., pp. 16–17.

10. Haqqani, *Pakistan between Mosque and Military*, p. 21.

11. Zahid Husain, *The Scorpion's Tail: The Relentless Rise of Islamic Militants in Pakistan—And How It Threatens the World* (New York: Free Press, 2010), p. 46.

12. Ibid., p. 47.

13. Haqqani, *Pakistan between Mosque and Military*, p. 25.

14. M. J. Akbar, *Tinderbox: The Past and Future of Pakistan* (New Delhi, India: HarperCollins Publishers, 2011), p. 242.

15. Ibid., p. 243.

16. Ibid.

17. Ibid., p. 245.

18. Haqqani, *Pakistan between Mosque and Military*, p. 44.

19. Ibid., p. 48.

20. Ibid.

21. Akbar, *Tinderbox*, p. 248.

22. Husain, *The Scorpion's Tail*, p. 49.

23. Akbar, *Tinderbox*, p. 252.

24. Ibid.

25. Haqqani, *Pakistan between Mosque and Military*, p. 107.

26. Akbar, *Tinderbox,* p. 254.

27. A Latin phrase that means 'Thus passes the glory of the world', which in turn, has been interpreted to mean that earthly glory is fleeting or vanishes quickly.

28. Akbar, *Tinderbox*, pp. 255–56.

29. Shuja Nawaz, *Crossed Sword: Pakistan, Its Army and the Wars Within* (Karachi: Oxford University Press, 2008), p. 384.

30. Wilson John, 'Radical Islam's Long War in Pakistan: An Assessment', in *Radical Islam: Perspectives from India and Russia*, eds Vikram Sood and Sergey Kurginyan (Delhi: Observer Research Foundation in association with Macmillan, 2011), p. 396.

31. Zahid Hussain, *Frontline Pakistan: The Path to Catastrophe and the Killing of Benazir Bhutto* (London: Penguin Books, 2008), p. 19.

32. S. K. Malik, *The Qur'anic Concept of War* (New Delhi: Adam Publishers and Distributors, 2008).

33. Brian Cloughley, *A History of Pakistan Army: Wars and Insurrections*, second edition (New Delhi: Lancer Publishers & Distributors, 1999), p. 278.

34. Hussain, *Frontline Pakistan*, p. 19.

35. Ibid., p. 20.

36. Ibid.

37. Ibid.

38. Ibid., p. 21.

39. John, 'Radical Islam's Long War in Pakistan: An Assessment', p. 403.

40. Haqqani, *Pakistan between Mosque and Military*, p. 134.

41. Akbar, *Tinderbox*, p. 258.

42. Haqqani, *Pakistan between Mosque and Military*, pp. 140–41.

43. Ibid., pp. 144–45.

44. Akbar, *Tinderbox*, p. 258.
45. Haqqani, *Pakistan between Mosque and Military*, p. 131.
46. Shuja Nawaz, *Pakistan: Its Army and the Wars Within* (Karachi: Oxford University Press, 2008), p. 572.
47. Ibid.
48. John, 'Radical Islam's Long War in Pakistan: An Assessment', p. 398.
49. Hussain, *Frontline Pakistan*, p. 21.
50. Haqqani, *Pakistan between Mosque and Military*, p. 281.
51. Ibid., p. 225.
52. Ibid., p. 228.
53. Cloughley, *A History of Pakistan Army*, p. 354.
54. Hussain, *Frontline Pakistan*, p. 27.
55. Ibid.
56. Cloughley, *A History of Pakistan Army*, p. 355.
57. Yossef Bodansky, *Bin Laden: The Man Who Declared War on America* (Rocklin, California, United States: Forum, an imprint of Prima Publishing, 1999), p. 146.
58. Ibid.
59. John, 'Radical Islam's Long War in Pakistan: An Assessment', p. 398.
60. Ibid.
61. Ibid., p. 399.
62. Ahmed Rashid, *Descent into Chaos: How the War Against Islamic Extremism Is Being Lost in Pakistan, Afghanistan and Central Asia* (London: Allen Lane, 2008), p. 79.
63. Ibid.
64. Ahmed Rashid, 'Pakistani Army Officers Arrested in Terror Swoop', *Telegraph*, United Kingdom, 1 September 2003, online edition, http://www.telegraph.co.uk/news/worldnews/asia/pakistan/1440284/Pakistan-army-officers-arrested-in-terror-swoop.htm.
65. Rashid, *Descent into Chaos*, p. 230.
66. For details, see Hussain, *Frontline Pakistan*, p. 1.
67. Ibid., p. 2.
68. Rashid, *Descent into Chaos*, p. 154.
69. Ibid., p. 231.
70. Ibid., p. 239.
71. Ibid.
72. Syed Saleem Shahzad, *Inside Al-Qaeda and the Taliban: Beyond 9/11* (London and South Yarra: Pluto Press and Palgrave Macmillan, 2011), pp. 8–9.
73. Ibid., p. 8.
74. Susan B. Epstein and K. Alan Kronstadt, *Pakistan: Foreign U.S. Assistance, Congressional Research Service*, Washington DC, 7 June 2011, http://fpc.state.gov/documents/organization/166839.pdf.
75. Senators John Kerry and Richard Lugar and Representative Howard Berman.
76. Susan B. Epstein and K. Alan Kronstadt, *Pakistan: Foreign U.S. Assistance, Congressional Research Service*, Washington DC, 7 June 2011.
77. Ibid.

78. Ibid.
79. To improve the Government of Pakistan's capacity to address the country's most critical infrastructure needs; help the Pakistani government address basic needs and provide improved economic opportunities in areas most vulnerable to extremism; and strengthen Pakistan's capacity to pursue economic and political reforms that reinforce stability.
80. Ibid.
81. Ibid.
82. Ibid.
83. David Rhode, Carlotta Gall, Eric Schmitt and David E. Sanger, 'U.S. Officials See Waste in Billions Sent to Pakistan', *New York Times*, 24 December 2007, online edition, http://www.nytimes.com/2007/12/24/world/asia/24military.html?pagewanted=all.
84. Eric Schmitt and Jane Perlez, 'U.S. Is Deferring Millions in Pakistani Military Aid', *New York Times*, 9 July 2011, online edition, http://www.nytimes.com/2011/07/10/world/asia/10intel.html?pagewanted=all.
85. Issam Ahmed, 'Pakistan Says It Doesn't Need US Military Aid', *Christian Science Monitor*, 11 July 2011, online edition, http://www.csmonitor.com/World/Asia-South-Central/2011/0711/Pakistan-says-it-doesn-t-need-US-military-aid.
86. Howard LaFranchi, 'Why Pakistan Wants to Keep that $ 800 Million in Aid after All,' *Christian Science Monitor*, 13 July 2011, online edition, http://www.csmonitor.com/USA/Foreign-Policy/2011/0713/Why-Pakistan-wants-to-keep-that-800-million-in-aid-after-all.
87. Ibid.
88. Declain Walsh and Salman Masood, 'Pakistan Picks New Director for Spy Agency', *New York Times*, 2012, online edition, http://www.nytimes.com/2012/03/10/world/asia/powerful-pakistan-intelligence-agency-the-isi-gets-new-leader.html?nl=todaysheadlines&emc=edit_th_20120310.
89. Full name Mohammad Najibullah Ahmedzai.
90. Amir Mir, 'US May Abandon Pakistan Supply Routes'.
91. Ibid.
92. Ibid.
93. Committee on Foreign Relations, The United States Senate, 'Central Asia and the Transition in Afghanistan: A Majority Staff Report', p. 6. Printed for the use of the Committee on Foreign Relations, U.S. Government Printing Office, Washington, 2011, www.foreign.senate.gov/.../central-asia-and-the-transition-in-afghanistan. Also available at www.fdsys.gpo.gov.
94. Ibid., p. 5.
95. Ibid., p. 6.
96. Ibid.
97. Ibid.
98. Ibid.
99. NATO Homepage, *Missile Defence*, http://www.nato.int/cps/en/natolive/topics_49635.htm (accessed on 30 December 2011).

100. Karen DeYoung, 'NATO Chief Rebuffs Russian Threats to Counter Missile Shield', *Washington Post*, 8 December 2011, online edition, http://www.washingtonpost.com/world/nato-chief-rebuffs-russian-threats-to-counter-missile-shield/2011/12/07/gIQAtyRxcO_story.html.

101. Alan Cullison, 'Russia Considers Blocking NATO Supply Routs', *Wall Street Journal*, 28 November 2011, online edition, http://online.wsj.com/article/SB1000142405 2970204753404577066421106592452.html.

102. DeYoung, 'NATO Chief Rebuffs Russian Threat to Counter Missile Shield'.

103. Ibid.

104. Ibid.

105. U.S. Department of State, '1000th ISAF Supply Mission Transits Russian Airspace', Office of the Spokesman, 20 April 2011, http://www.state.gov/r/pa/prs/ps/2011/04/161318.htm.

106. Ibid.

107. Ibid. April 20 is the date of the issue of the media note.

108. Dov S. Zakheim and Paul J. Saunders, 'Can Russia Help Us Withdraw From Afghanistan?' *New York Times*, 1 December 2011, online edition, http://www.nytimes.com/2011/12/02/opinion/can-russia-help-us-withdraw-from-afghanistan.html.

CHAPTER 7

AS THE DICE ROLLS

T he summit meeting of the North Atlantic Treaty Organization (NATO) in Chicago on 20 and 21 May 2012 produced
no breathtaking surprises. A statement issued at the end of it
referred to the 'irreversible' transition strategy that began in July 2011
and said that it was on track and would be completed by 2014.[1] Noting that '75% of Afghanistan's population will soon be living in areas
where the ANSF have taken the lead for security', it stated:

> By mid-2013, all parts of Afghanistan will have begun transition
> and the Afghan forces will be in the lead for security nation-
> wide. This will mark an important milestone in the Lisbon road-
> map.[2] ISAF is gradually and responsibly drawing down its forces
> to complete its mission by 31 December 2014.[3]

Noting the improvements in the lives of the people of Afghanistan
during the past 10 years, the statement declared the resolve of the
nations contributing to the International Security Assistance Force
(ISAF[4]) 'to work together to preserve the substantial progress ...
made during the past decade'. It then added,

> The nations contributing to ISAF will therefore continue to sup-
> port Afghanistan on its path towards self-reliance in security,
> improved governance, and economic and social development.
> This will prevent Afghanistan from ever again becoming a safe
> haven for terrorists that threaten Afghanistan, the region, and the
> world. A secure and stable Afghanistan will make an important
> contribution to its region, in which security, stability and devel-
> opment are interlinked.[5]

According to the statement, the NATO allies and ISAF partners reiterated their strong commitment to continue beyond the end of the transition period the process of training, equipping, financing and capability development of the Afghan National Security Forces (ANSF), decided upon at the International Conference on Afghanistan in Bonn on 5 December 2011. Saying that they will also play their part in financially sustaining the ANSF, the statement called upon the International Community to commit to this long-term programme.

Several things strike one as one hacks one's way through the statement's pompous jargon. First, some NATO forces—read overwhelmingly American troops—will stay on in Afghanistan after 31 December 2014. It does not say how many nor does it spell out their role. It only says, 'NATO will have made the shift from a combat mission to a new training, advising and assistance mission, which will be of a different nature to the current ISAF mission.' It is equally vague about funding the ANSF. All it says is that the preliminary model for the ANSF's numerical strength puts it at 228,500 with a budget of $4.1 billion, and that it will be 'reviewed regularly against the developing security environment'. There is no mention of how much each individual NATO member or country contributing to the ISAF will give. On its part, the Afghan government will have to progressively increase its contribution from $500 million in 2015 to the total cost of supporting its security forces by 2024.[6]

A person trying to find out how events will unfold in Afghanistan after 2014 will not find the NATO statement overly helpful. It contains a number of expressions of intent without indicating how these will be implemented. Nor does a look at the strategic partnership agreement between Afghanistan and the United States, signed by Presidents Obama and Karzai, on 1 May 2012, make one any the wiser. The *New York Times*, reporting on the initialling of the draft agreement on 22 April 2012 by the US ambassador in Afghanistan, Ryan C. Crocker, and Afghanistan's National Security Adviser, Rangin Dadfar Spanta, noted that its text had not been made public.[7] The report, however, gave a few broad indications beginning with the observation that the agreement was in many respects 'more symbolic than substantive'.

It did not mention aid in terms of dollars and programmes that Americans would support. Besides, financing had to be authorized and appropriated by the US Congress year to year. Nor did it lay down specifically what American military and security presence will be after 2014. Nevertheless, it observed:

> Even so, the United States expects to make substantial contributions toward the cost of Afghanistan's security forces beyond 2014. A total figure for the United States of $2.7 billion a year has been discussed, and it could easily be more; there would most likely be aid for civilian programs as well.

That would be a steep reduction from the amount the United States now spends here, which has been $110 billion to $120 billion a year since the 'surge' in American troop levels began in 2010, according to the Congressional Research Service.[8]

The *New York Times* report of 1 May 2012, however, cited Western diplomats in Kabul as saying the agreement was an important and positive marker because it would help persuade other Western countries to continue to support Afghanistan and would signal to all sides, including the Taliban, that they would not have a free hand to manipulate the country after 2014.[9]

Such 'positive markers' have their value but will not be enough in themselves to defeat al Qaeda and the Taliban. Much will depend on a host of factors including the number of NATO troops present, the nature of their activities, the adequacy of Western—which would be overwhelmingly American—economic and military aid reaching the Kabul government and the ability of the ANSF to hold its own against the Taliban and al Qaeda.

ELUSIVE INFORMATION

Any effort to visualize the shape of things to come post-2014 will require a minimum level of information about the factors cited above. Since neither the statement emanating from NATO's Chicago summit nor the Afghanistan–United States Strategic Partnership Agreement provides any significant information, one needs to look at other sources. According to a report in the *Guardian* of Britain, while there has been no announcement about the number of NATO troops that will stay in Afghanistan after 2014, US commanders in Kabul have put it around 15,000–20,000.[10]

The *New York Times* reported on 4 February 2012 that the United States' plan to wind down its combat role in Afghanistan by the summer of 2013 would rely heavily on Special Operations forces personnel who would train a variety of Afghan security forces, while elite commando teams of the Special Operations forces would continue with their raids to hunt down, capture or kill insurgent commanders, and keep terrorist/insurgent cells under pressure to prevent them from launching attacks.[11] Some conventional units will remain, but mainly in a supporting role, handling logistics, transportation, medical care and security. In terms of organizational structure, the plan calls for the creation of a two-star command position in charge of the entire Special Operations effort in Afghanistan. This would be the first step to be followed by the next, which would be handing over to a Special Operations officer the three-star corps headquarters that now commands the quotidian operations of the war and is headed by an army officer from the conventional forces.[12]

Whether this would be enough will depend to a great extent on the ANSF's ability to prevent the Taliban and al Qaeda from taking over Afghanistan. We have examined the matter in chapter 1 and concluded that it was unlikely to be able to do that on its own for some time. There is as yet no credible indication that the handicaps these have been suffering from are going to be removed. Consider, for example, the numerical strength of the ANSF which consists of the Afghan National Army (ANA), the Afghan National Police, the Afghan Border Police, the Afghan National Civil Order Police and other smaller authorized militia across the country. Its primary component is the ANA, of which the ANA Air Corps (formerly Afghan Air Force) is a part.[13]

According to a report in the *New York Times*, ANSF numbered 305,000 in December 2011, and were expected to expand to 352,000 by the end of 2012.[14] As of March 2011, there were 160,000 troops on its rolls, 4,000 ahead of the March goal. There was a proposal to increase its strength to between 195,000 and 208,000 by October 2012. As early as 1 February 2012, the US Defence Secretary, Panetta, however, had indicated the possibility of downsizing of the ANSF's proposed strength because of the expenses required in supporting such a large body. He had said that the United States and other NATO countries supported those forces at a cost of around $6 billion a year, but financial crises in Europe were causing countries to balk at the bill.[15]

The downsizing seems to have been decided upon. As seen earlier, the NATO's post–Chicago summit declaration says that the preliminary model for the ANSF's numerical strength puts it at 228,500 with a budget of $4.1 billion, and that it will be 'reviewed regularly against the developing security environment'. As has been shown in chapter 1, even a strength of 352,000 would be far below the required strength of anything between 568,000 and 710,000 that, according to the United States' counter-insurgency doctrine, would be required for a country with Afghanistan's population.

The trouble is that one does not yet know from where the $4.1 billion will come every year. As seen earlier in this chapter, the *New York Times* report of 22 April 2012, on the draft strategic agreement between Afghanistan and the United States, stated that a 'total figure for the United States of $2.7 billion a year has been discussed' and added that 'it could easily be more; there would most likely be aid for civilian programs as well'. An Associated Press report on the Chicago summit, published in the Long Island newspaper, *Newsday*, stated that about $1.3 billion was expected to come from NATO members other than the United States and quoted a 'senior Western official' as saying on the condition of anonymity that about '$ 1 billion of that has already been pledged'.[16]

According to the report, the United States 'and some nations outside the military coalition' were expected to contribute $2.3 billion. While it stated nothing about the amounts to be contributed by the other nations, the total of $2.3 billion suggests a much reduced contribution by the United States compared to the $2.7 billion which the

New York Times report cited above indicated as a possible American contribution. Nevertheless, the sum of $2.3 billion plus $1.3 billion from non-US NATO members add up to $3.6 billion. One gets the figure of $4.1 billion if one adds to this the $500 million the Afghan government is expected to contribute to the ANSF's maintenance from 2015 onward.

The question is whether the contributions will be as expected. According to a report in the *Guardian* of 20 May 2012, Britain was promising a contribution of $110 million a year, Germany and Australia of $200 and $100 million respectively (making for a total of $410 million), and the United States was to 'to take up the bulk of the costs, anything from between 50% and 75%'.[17] The maths still do not work out; a total of $410 million is way short of the expected $1.3 billion. Besides, the question of the adequacy of the ANSF's projected reduced strength of 228,500 remains.

Scalpel, Not the Hammer

One, however, needs to recognize that the United States has worked out a new counter-insurgency/unconventional warfare strategy that marks a radical departure from the conventional one of deploying a large number of troops to deny territory to the insurgents and attacking the latter's stronghold by land, air and (though not in the present case) sea. The emphasis is now more on expansion and intensification of intelligence-gathering, intelligence-driven raids that seek to cripple the insurgents' military capability, undermine their morale and destabilize their organization by physically eliminating their top leadership through drone and commando attacks. It also involves increasing reliance on a network of private contractors to gather intelligence and train local operatives to go after terrorists. A report on the new strategy in the *New York Times* quotes one of its architects and President Obama's top terrorism adviser, John O. Brennan, as saying in a speech in May 2010 that instead of the 'hammer' America will rely on the 'scalpel' while pledging a 'multigenerational' campaign against al Qaeda and its extremist affiliates.[18]

The new strategy involves activities of the Central Intelligence Agency (CIA) coming to include operations like drone strikes that are normally undertaken by military and the American military conducting clandestine operations that belong to the territory of intelligence/covert operations agencies. President Obama's appointment of his CIA chief, Leon Panetta, as defence secretary and General David Petraeus, head of the ISAF and US forces in Afghanistan, as the head of CIA in July and September 2011, respectively, perhaps reflected his expectation that the change will enable the army and the spy agency to discharge their new roles better.

Meanwhile, in keeping with its new strategic approach, the US Army has been reshaping its training programme and deployment of troops, involving the placement of some conventional troops under Special Operations forces commanders and others assigned to parts of the world, like Africa, viewed as emerging security risks. According to a report in the *New York Times*, the changes visualized reflected efforts by the US Army's top officer, General Raymond T. Odierno, to institutionalize many of the successful tactics adopted ad hoc in Afghanistan and Iraq.[19]

Units, which will remain in the conventional army, will be told in advance about the regions abroad where they may be deployed, which will enable the officers and men to develop regional expertise. The military's global combat operations commanders could guide the units whether they should focus on developing high-end combat skills, disaster relief or training missions. The *New York Times* report cited Pentagon and US Army officials as saying that the first unit to undergo this regional orientation would be a full brigade that would train for missions in support of the military's Africa command.[20] It further pointed out that the training would focus on what the military described as 'hybrid' scenarios, in which 'a single battle space may require the entire continuum of military activity from support to civil authorities to training local security forces to counterinsurgency to counterterrorism raids to heavy combat'.[21]

The United States' new counter-insurgency/counterterrorism strategy is part of a reorientation of its wider military vision that involves a downsizing of its army, an avoidance of fighting expensive, high-casualty ground wars, as in Iraq and Afghanistan, and the transference of its principal strategic concern to Asia where China's growing presence, North Korea's unpredictability and developments in Iran have been causing the United States concern. Encapsulating the essence of the new approach at Pentagon's briefing room on 5 January 2012, President Obama said:

> We will be strengthening our presence in the Asia Pacific, and budget reductions will not come at the expense of that critical region. We're going to continue investing in our critical partnerships and alliances, including NATO, which has demonstrated time and again—most recently in Libya—that it's a force multiplier. We will stay vigilant, especially in the Middle East.
>
> As we look beyond the wars in Iraq and Afghanistan—and the end of long-term nation-building with large military footprints—we'll be able to ensure our security with smaller conventional ground forces. We'll continue to get rid of outdated Cold War-era systems so that we can invest in the capabilities that we need for the future, including intelligence, surveillance and reconnaissance, counterterrorism, countering weapons of mass destruction and the ability to operate in environments where adversaries try to deny us access.[22]

Marking a departure from Pentagon's old strategic emphasis on being able to fight and win two wars simultaneously, the new doctrine emphasized the US military's ability to fight one war and also deny 'the objectives of—or imposing unacceptable costs on—an opportunistic aggressor in a second region'.[23]

Two Questions

Two questions strike one at the very outset. First, will the shift to Asia and Asia-Pacific as the main focus of the United States' strategic military concern not detract from the war against al Qaeda and the Taliban? Can the United States regard that war as won or almost won? Second, can the new strategy against the Taliban and al Qaeda, with its emphasis on intelligence-driven covert operations by special forces and drone attacks and air strikes, deliver victory?

Taking up the second question first, one notes some significant successes, the most striking of them being the commando raid that killed Osama bin Laden early in the morning of 2 May (Pakistan time) 2011. President Obama clearly had these in mind when, announcing a schedule for the withdrawal of American troops from Afghanistan, he declared in an address from the White House on 22 June 2011 that the United States had largely achieved its goals in the country which no longer represented a terrorist threat to it. An intense campaign of drone strikes and other covert operations in Pakistan had crippled al Qaeda's original network in the region and its leaders were either dead or pinned down in the rugged border between Pakistan and Afghanistan. Twenty of the thirty top al Qaeda leaders, identified by American intelligence, had been killed during the previous year and a half, administration officials said.[24]

The drones have continued taking a severe toll of al Qaeda and Taliban leaders, and not only in Pakistan. On 30 September 2011, an attack killed Anwar al-Awlaki, a cleric with a dual American-Yemeni citizenship, who had shifted to Yemen in 2006 and whose fiery English sermons inspired terrorism.[25] Also killed with him was Samir Khan, an American citizen of Pakistani origin, who was the editor of *Inspire*, the sophisticated English-language Internet magazine of Al Qaeda in the Arabian Peninsula (AQAP).[26] Al-Awlaki had reportedly motivated, among others, a 39-year-old US Army psychiatrist, Nidal Malik Hasan, who was facing deployment in a war zone in Iraq or Afghanistan. On 5 November 2009, Hasan fired from two hand guns, killing 13 and wounding 30 in a shooting spree at Fort Hood, Texas. Situated near Killeen, 100 miles south of Dallas, Fort Hood is the largest active duty military post in the United States. Spread over 340 square miles housing training and support facilities and homes, it is a virtual city for more than 50,000 military personnel and some 150,000 family members and civilian support personnel. It has been a major centre for troops being deployed to or returning from service in Iraq and Afghanistan.[27]

Hasan attended the controversial Dar al-Hijrah Mosque in Falls Church, Virginia, in 2001, at the same time as two 9/11 terrorists, when al-Awlaki was a preacher there. An article in the *Sunday Telegraph* cited a fellow Muslim officer at Fort Hood as saying that his eyes lit up while mentioning his deep respect for al-Awlaki's teachings.[28] Major Hasan had himself told investigators that he had corresponded with al-Awlaki before going on the shooting rampage.[29]

Al-Awlaki was also very much behind the attempt by Umar Farouk Abdulmutallab, a 23-year-old Nigerian citizen, to set off an explosion on board Northwest Airlines Flight 253, bearing Delta Air Lines' name, flying from Amsterdam to Detroit on Christmas day in 2009. The bid failed. The bomb, which he had sewn into his underpants, failed to explode properly. Abdulmutallab, who was overwhelmed by his fellow passengers, is the son of a Nigerian banker and had been trained in the use of explosives by AQAP in Yemen. According to a report in the *Washington Post* of 11 February 2012, as far back as 2009, investigators had linked Abdulmutallab with al-Awlaki. The report cites a United States Justice Department memo, released ahead of al-Awlaki's sentencing in February 2012,[30] as describing how the Yemeni American tested the Nigerian's commitment to jihad, arranged for him to meet a bomb maker, and told him to get on a US airliner and detonate his explosives over the United States.[31] Besides, a report in the *New York Times* of 31 December 2009 cites American military and law enforcement agencies as saying that both Umar Farouk Abdulmutallab and Major Nidal Malik Hasan had exchanged email with the Islamic cleric Anwar al-Awlaki.[32]

Al-Awlaki was a leading member of the AQAP based in Yemen that had claimed responsibility for the crash of a United Parcel Service (UPS) jet in Dubai on 3 September 2010 that killed two pilots. While some question the claim's validity, there is no doubt that, in October that year, it had sought to despatch through a UPS cargo plane and two commercial flights packages containing ink toner cartridges filled with pentaerythritol tetranitrate (PETN) chemical explosives inside Hewlett-Packard printers. Loaded at Sana'a, and meant for out-of-date addresses of two Jewish synagogues in Chicago, these were detected on 29 October in Dubai and East Midlands airport near Nottingham in Britain, after Saudi intelligence officials had provided their American counterparts with the precise tracking number of the packages. If the manufacture of the bombs showed the remarkable sophistication achieved by AQAP, so did the editorial and production quality of its magazine, *Inspire*. Though the terror attack, code-named Operation Haemorrhage, was foiled, *Inspire*, in its issue posted on the AQAP's website on 17 November 2010, claimed success in terms of the fear and disruption it caused. It claimed that the operation, which cost only $4,200 to launch, reflected a new strategy of low-cost attacks designed to cause widespread economic damage.[33]

That Anwar al-Awlaki and the Saudi bomb maker Ibrahim Hassan al-Asiri were involved in what has come to be regarded as the parcel bomb case was strongly indicated when Yemen launched a manhunt for both of them for involvement in the attempt. Not only that, Yemen put al-Awlaki on trial in absentia on 2 November 2010, accusing him and two other men of plotting to kill foreigners and being members of the AQAP.[34]

Many believe that both AQAP and Al Qaeda in the Islamic Maghreb (AQIM) suffered major blows in 2011. Even before al-Awlaki's and Samir Khan's death on 30 September, Fazul Abdullah Mohammed, al Qaeda's leader in East Africa and the mastermind of the bombing of American embassies in Dar es Salaam and Nairobi on 7 August 1998, had been killed in a shoot-out in Somalia in June 2011. President Obama remarked at General Martin E. Dempsey's swearing-in ceremony as the chairman of the US Joint Chiefs of Staff on 30 September 2011 that al-Awlaki's death was 'a major blow to Al Qaeda's most active operational affiliate'. He added that the cleric, whom he described as 'the leader of external operations for Al Qaeda in the Arabian Peninsula', had taken 'the lead role in planning and directing the efforts to murder Americans'.[35] The *New York Times* report, which mentioned Obama's remark, quoted a senior American military official, who monitored Yemen closely, as saying that al-Awlaki's death would send an important message to the surviving leaders and foot soldiers in the AQAP. Saying that this was 'critically important', the senior official added, 'It sets a sense of doom for the rest of them. Getting Awlaki, given his tight operational security, increases the sense of fear. It is hard for them to attack when they are trying to protect their own back side.'[36]

The question is whether these and other killings of al Qaeda's leaders have significantly destabilized the parent organization as well as AQAP and AQIM. Significantly, similarly optimistic pronouncements by American officials followed a CIA-mounted drone attack that eliminated a critically important American target, al Qaeda's deputy leader, Abu Yahya al-Libi, at Hassu Khel village in North Waziristan on Monday, 4 June 2012. A *New York Times* report quoted the White House spokesman, Jay Carney, as saying that, as a result of al-Libi's death, there was 'no clear successor to take over the breadth of his responsibility, and put additional pressure' on al Qaeda, 'bringing it closer to its ultimate demise than ever'.[37]

It will be entirely understandable if such a statement arouses a feeling of déjà vu. It reminded one of President Obama's claim on 22 June 2011 that the United States had largely achieved its goals in Afghanistan, which no longer posed a terrorist threat to it. He also said that an intense campaign of drone strikes, and other covert operations in Pakistan, had crippled the organization's original network in the region.[38] It also reminded one of Leon Panetta's statement during his flight to Kabul—where he arrived on 6 July 2011—that the United States was 'within reach of strategically defeating al Qaeda' and that America's focus had narrowed to capturing or killing 10 to 20 crucial leaders of the terrorist group in Pakistan, Somalia and Yemen.[39]

The very fact that Jay Carney's observation on 5 June 2012 projected an assessment of al Qaeda's dire straits similar to Obama's and Panetta's in June and July 2011 suggested that the situation had not changed much since then and that the Spectacular Episodes Syndrome (SES) was alive and well. It is not surprising that some independent experts were more cautious. The *New York Times* report that quoted Carney also quoted Bill Roggio of the website the *Long War Journal* as saying, 'Killing the top leadership harms Al Qaeda, but it won't defeat them.' Roggio added, 'There are people who will step up to fill the void. Al Qaeda has a far deeper bench than the [Obama] administration gives it credit for.' Roggio made a basic point when he said that while drone strikes offered an attractive short-term tactic, they did not present a complete strategy, and added, 'Until we tackle Al Qaeda's ideology, state support and ability to exploit ungoverned space in countries like Pakistan, Somalia and Yemen, you're not going to defeat the organization.'[40]

By No Means Out

There is sense in what Roggio said. Besides, activities on the ground indicate that the al Qaeda–Haqqani network alliance has by no means been put out of action in the Af-Pak area. Indeed, on 6 June, just two days after al-Libi's death, two explosions—at least one set off by a suicide bomber on a motorcycle—killed 23 civilians near Kandahar Airfield, one of the largest coalition bases in Afghanistan, according to the Kandahar police chief and witnesses. The attack's target, according to officials, was a small market and a hotel where Afghan security escorts for NATO supply trucks stopped between escort runs to rest and have tea.[41] There were other attacks and casualties. In northern Afghanistan, a suicide bomber detonated himself in the middle of a bazaar in Maimana, the capital of Faryab province, usually a relatively calm area, killing at least one civilian and wounding 10. In Paktika province, a civilian who was travelling with family members was killed along with a child, and four other children were wounded, when a roadside bomb exploded in Yahya Khel district.[42]

At 6.15 in the morning of Wednesday, 2 May 2012, hours after President Obama left Kabul after signing the strategic partnership agreement with President Karzai, a team of suicide attackers struck a private residential compound used by hundreds of foreigners in the east of the city. Wearing suicide vests the attackers drove a car packed with explosives to the main gate of the complex called Green Village and detonated it, blowing the gate open, allowing at least two of them to slip inside. They occupied a parking garage, set off other explosions and engaged in a firefight with private guards and Afghan security forces who prevented them from entering the main residential complex. The entire incident lasted for more than four hours and it left at least eight dead—seven Afghans and a guard—and 17 wounded.[43]

Earlier, exactly at 1:45 p.m. on Sunday, 15 April, Taliban suicide bombers and gunmen launched a series of coordinated attacks—at least three in Kabul, two in Nangarhar province and one each in Paktia and Logar provinces—that bore the clear imprimatur of an evolved Haqqani network. As a *New York Times* report pointed out, each attack followed an identical pattern—'light gunfire, followed by explosions and then protracted firefights with Afghan security forces, with the militants in several cases fighting from empty buildings or construction sites near their main targets'.[44] The attacks, according to senior Afghan officials, ended on Monday morning with 39 of the attackers killed, 16 of them in Kabul. Accounts of the number of security force members killed differed: the Interior Ministry put it at 8, the president's office at 11, with 42 wounded.[45]

Western military and intelligence officers admitted on Monday to being surprised by the scale and sophistication of the synchronized attacks and saw it as a disturbing step in the Haqqani network's evolution form a criminal mob to a leading militant force.[46] According to a *New York Times* report, the attacks indicated

> more than just the ability to paralyze the mostly tightly secured districts of Kabul for hours. They were proof that the Taliban offshoot could create the vast network of logistical support and planning needed to mount terrorist attacks without anything leaking to the intelligence groups so tightly focused on it.[47]

Second, as President Karzai put it, the assaults—involving dozens of attackers who crossed hundreds of miles to strike at seven different secured targets, all around 1:45 p.m. on Sunday—represented an 'intelligence failure' on the part of both the Afghan government and NATO.[48]

The attacks raised two critical questions. One was whether the militants were now able to mount such audacious assaults repeatedly as opposed to once every several months. The second was whether the Afghan government could blunt such attacks post-2014, after the lapse of the deadline for the withdrawal of Western troops when they would have limited access to NATO intelligence assistance.[49] As to the first, time alone will tell. Military capability vis-à-vis enemies is not something unchanging. An army can lose its superiority if its enemy increases its arsenal and the quality of its troops through training and vice versa. In the present instance, much would depend on whether American and NATO forces are able to significantly degrade the capability of the Haqqani network and its al Qaeda allies through drone strikes and covert operations to prevent them from taking over Afghanistan after 2014.

ANSF DOES WELL

An important aspect of the attacks on 15 April 2012 was the performance of the ANSF personnel who managed the response almost entirely on their own, with embedded Western training teams and helicopters providing limited support. They did very well not only in eliminating the attackers but keeping civilian casualties down to an incredibly low figure of six![50] In a statement on 16 April, President Karzai praised the performance and the caution of the Afghan security forces, which he said had prevented further civilian deaths and led to a 'relatively quick control of the situation'.[51] The United States' ambassador to Kabul, Ryan C. Crocker, had words of high praise for the Afghan forces who, he said, had 'acquitted themselves very, very well, very professionally'.[52] Equally forthcoming was the NATO commander in Afghanistan, General John R. Allen. While saying that nobody was underestimating the seriousness of the attacks, he added, 'Each attack was meant to send a message: that legitimate governance and Afghan sovereignty are in peril. The A.N.S.F. response itself is proof enough of that folly.'[53]

While the bravery of Afghans had never been in question, their inadequate numerical strength, training and equipment, and uneven performance had been causing concern. Things continue to be bad. According to an Associated Press report, a contingent of 20 ANA soldiers posted at Chinari outpost in Logar province knew of a meeting called by the Taliban at a village less than a kilometre from where they were but they could not act because they had no way of pinpointing where the insurgents were gathering and lacked the firepower to launch an attack. Besides, the report, published in the *Hindu* of 11 June 2012, pointed out that the 20 had only one helmet to share among themselves! The report quoted a Director of Public Relations of the US Army, Lieutenant Colonel Timothy M. Stauffer, as saying late in May that there was 'definitely a logistical problem within the ANA' and that there was 'an awful lot of equipment purchased and sitting in warehouses'. The logistics had to be fixed and the ANA trained to request for and use these.[54]

Besides, the question remains whether the professionalism shown by the troops who dealt with the 15 April attacks is shared by a significant section of the ANSF. Much would depend on that, as much would depend on the adequacy of the financial and military aid to ensure the continuing ability of the Afghan government and its military to defend their country. The matter is critically important. A look at some of the attacks that preceded those on 15 April will amply bear out the conclusion that the Taliban and al Qaeda are by no means finished. On 10 April, suicide bombers had struck Herat and Helmand, killing 16 people. Twelve people died in Herat. Casualties might have been higher if the two attackers, who came under police fire, had not detonated the sports utility vehicle in which they travelled, as they approached the government centre at Guzara district.[55] In Helmand province, where at least four police officers were killed in the Musa Qala district, the target might well have been the provincial police chief who had fought staunchly against the Taliban.[56]

Herat, where the target seems to have been the provincial governor who was scheduled to travel on the road to the airport, is Afghanistan's second most populous city and a place that has seen relatively little violence in recent years. In Helmand, the bomb attack was an ominous sign in that it occurred despite strenuous and prolonged effort by American and Afghan forces to clear the province of Taliban and al Qaeda forces who had dominated the province for several years. It stoked fears about what might happen after thousands of American marines move out over the next eight months.[57]

Earlier, a series of Taliban attacks during the first week of April left 9 Afghan police officers dead and 14 missing. The deadliest of these, on a police post in Helmand province, killed four officers and two civilians on Monday, 2 April. In another attack, insurgents killed three police officers at a checkpoint in Badakhshan province. A total of 14 police officers went missing following the two raids. Two other Afghan police officers were killed in Kandahar province when their truck hit a buried bomb on Tuesday, 3 April, the provincial police said.[58]

All this, of course, does not indicate that the Taliban and al Qaeda are inexorably set to conquer Afghanistan not very long after the bulk of the American and NATO forces leave the country in 2014. But it does indicate that the danger is quite real. Significantly, referring to the Taliban and the Haqqani network in the context of the attacks the latter launched in Afghanistan on 15 April, Ryan C. Crocker had told the CNN as the firefights raged, 'There's a very dangerous enemy out there with capabilities and with safe havens in Pakistan,' and added:

> To get out before the Afghans have a full grip on security, which is a couple of years out, would be to invite the Taliban, Haqqani, and Al Qaeda back in and set the stage for another 9/11. And that, I think, is an unacceptable risk for any American.[59]

And it is not just Pakistan. As Bill Roggio wrote in the *Long War Journal* on 9 June 2011, 'Yemen has become one of al Qaeda's most secure bases and a hub for its activities on the Arabian peninsula and on the Horn of Africa.' He further pointed out that AQAP maintained safe havens in various parts of the country and operated terror camps in Aden, Marib and Abyan, and in the Alehimp and Sanhan regions in Sana'a. Besides serving as a hub for attacks against the West, the AQAP base in Yemen served as a 'command and control centre, a logistics hub, a transit point from Asia and the [Arabian] Peninsula and a source of weapons and munitions for the al Qaeda-backed Shabaab in Somalia'.[60]

JIHADIS IN YEMEN

This, of course, took several decades to come about. Thousands of Yemenis fought in the jihad against the Soviet Union in Afghanistan in the 1980s and were warmly welcomed on their return. A significant number among them were linked to al Qaeda. They formed Islamic Jihad in Yemen, the Army of Aden Abyan and Al Qaeda in Yemen (AQY).[61] The attack on the United States Navy destroyer, USS *Cole*, on 12 October 2000, while it was refuelling outside the Yemeni port of Aden provided an early indication of AQY's strength and capability. A boat filled with explosives and three suicide bombers on board came close to the ship and blew up, creating a 40 feet by 20 feet hole in the hull, killing 17 Americans. This triggered strong action against the Islamists in which the Yemeni government under President Ali Abdullah Saleh fully participated. The marked decline in Islamist militant activity that followed, however, did not last long. Things changed with the escape of 23 al Qaeda suspects from prison in Sana'a, Yemen's capital, on 3 February 2006. Only a few were captured or killed.

The AQY's first major post-jailbreak strikes were near simultaneous suicide attacks against oil facilities in Yemen in September 2006. It claimed responsibility for these in its first Internet announcement in November that year and vowed further attacks. Ayman al-Zawahiri, then al Qaeda's second in command, congratulated it in a statement in December and encouraged further attacks.[62]

There was a sharp increase in its activities in 2008 which saw an attack on Belgian tourists in January, four oil pipeline bombings, attacks on oil facilities and the bombing of a Japanese oil tanker in April 2008.[63] In March, mortar shells directed at the US embassy detonated in a nearby girls' school, killing a security guard and injuring more than a dozen students.[64] On 3 May, a group calling itself 'Al Qaeda Organisation in the Arabian Peninsula—Yemen Soldiers Brigades' claimed responsibility for a mortar attack on the Italian embassy in Sana'a. The two shells fired, however, landed in the parking lot of a nearby customs building.[65] Perhaps the most major of the other attacks was the one on the US embassy in Sana'a on 17 September.

According to a report in the *Washington Post*, the attackers used vehicle bombs, rocket-propelled grenades and automatic weapons. They left 10 guards and civilians dead outside the main gate but failed to breach the walled compound.[66] The total number of those killed was 20 including 10 Yemeni guards and 4 civilians along with the 6 attackers.[67]

Islamist militancy in Yemen received a new boost in January 2009 with the formation of AQAP[68] through a merger of al Qaeda's Yemeni and Saudi Arabian wings. The development was facilitated by a successful crackdown by the Saudi government in 2008, following which, the country's al Qaeda leaders urged their followers to flee to Yemen.[69] Nasser al-Wuhayshi, one of those who broke out of a Sana'a jail in February 2006, and subsequently emerged as a prominent leader, is believed to have been the driving force behind the merger.[70] Qassim al-Raimi, another escapee became part of al Qaeda's core leadership in Yemen and a military commander of the group. The nucleus of the group's leadership expanded when two Guantanamo Bay inmates, Said Ali al-Shihri, a Saudi Arabian national, and Ibrahim Suleiman al-Rubaysh, joined them after their release.[71]

A renewed burst of activity followed. In March 2009, AQAP suicide bombers killed four South Korean tourists and their local Yemeni guide near the city of Shibam. A week later, they attacked a convoy of South Korean officials who had travelled to Yemen to investigate the murders.[72] On 27 August 2009, AQAP operative Abdallah Hassan al-Asiri, pretending to surrender to Saudi authorities, detonated a bomb hidden in his undergarments while in the presence of Prince Muhammad bin Nayef. Al-Asiri spent weeks negotiating his false surrender and was invited, as other penitent ex-militants, to meet the prince during a Ramadan fast-breaking event. He bypassed some airport inspections because he was flown from southern Saudi Arabia on the prince's own jet and was not required to change clothes nor be thoroughly searched before he met the prince.[73] In late December 2009, al Qaeda militants made a rare public appearance in southern Yemen, telling an anti-government rally that the group's war was with the United States, and not with the Yemeni army. Also in late 2009, Yemeni government officials said that al Qaeda was responsible for a daring armoured car robbery in Aden, which netted $500,000. No arrests have been made.[74]

On Christmas Day in 2009, AQAP's hand was seen in Umar Farouk Abdulmutallab's attempt to blow up Northwest Airlines Flight 253 from Amsterdam to Detroit. Reacting, the United States designated it as a Foreign Terrorist Organization on 19 January 2010, and two of its leaders, Nasser al-Wuhayshi and Said Ali al-Shihri, as terrorists.[75] That did not seem to have much impact on the organization. The year 2010 saw AQAP launch its sophisticated English-language magazine *Inspire*, edited by Samir Khan, who, as has been seen, was killed along with Anwar al-Awlaki. It also saw the organization launch a series of attacks which included an attempted suicide bombing of the car carrying the British ambassador to Yemen, Timothy Torlot, in April. Torlot survived the attack unhurt.[76] On 6 October, Fionna Gibb, Britain's deputy ambassador to Yemen, survived a rocket-propelled grenade attack on the car in which she was travelling to the British embassy in Sana'a along with four of her colleagues. One of the latter was injured while she escaped unhurt.[77] Three weeks after the incident were loaded the parcel bombs containing ink toner cartridges filled with PETN chemical explosives inside Hewlett-Packard printers that were discovered before they reached their destinations in the United States.

CRISIS, INSTABILITY AND AQAP

The fear that AQAP will expand its tentacles in Yemen rose as the political crisis that led to the ouster of President Ali Abdullah Saleh's 30-year rule started gathering momentum from the beginning of 2011. An early cause of concern was the delivery of a speech on 1 March by the radical Islamist cleric, Abdul Majid al-Zindani, once a mentor of Osama bin Laden, who addressed several thousands of anti-government protestors from an open-air stage in Sana'a, guarded by 10 men carrying AK-47 rifles.[78] According to a report in the *New York Times*, his declaration that an Islamic state was coming drew cries of 'God is great' from some in the crowd.[79]

In March itself, al Qaeda–linked militants, fighting under the banner of Ansar al-Sharia, took over the town of Jaar in Abyan province.[80] The nearby coastal city of Zinjibar fell on Sunday 29 May,[81] and the Islamists quickly expanded their control over the rest of the province of Abyan, facing little resistance from the Yemeni military. As the movement against Saleh grew in strength and increasingly serious clashes followed, Yemeni troops who had been battling al Qaeda–linked Islamists in the troubled south of the country were pulled back to the capital, Sana'a.[82]

The United States paid little attention to Yemen until the attack on USS *Cole* in October 2000 and 9/11. The CIA inaugurated its drone programme in Yemen on 3 November 2002 with a Hellfire missile strike that killed an al Qaeda top operative, Qaed Salim Sinan al-Harethi, and five others in Marib province, about 100 miles east of the capital city of Sana'a. Thereafter, there were no reported US air strikes or drone attacks in Yemen until December 2009, when a sustained campaign of attacks began.[83] The strategy now being implemented followed President Obama's order for a policy review after Abdulmutallab's bid to blow up Northwest Airlines' Detroit-bound flight. The outcome was a threefold approach: concentrating on combating AQAP in the short run, increasing development assistance to Yemen in the long term and organizing international support for stabilization efforts.[84]

The United States has mainly depended on drone strikes and missile and bomb attacks by aircraft to combat AQAP and its allies. In a piece entitled 'Obama Ramps Up Covert War in Yemen', updated on CNN's website on 12 June 2012, Peter Bergen and Jennifer Rowland state that drones have killed at least 16 leading al Qaeda militants during Obama's presidency. Those killed include Anwar al-Awlaki and Fahd al-Quso (who was suspected of involvement in the 2000 bombing of the USS *Cole*). Bergen and Rowland have also cited New American Foundation's data putting the number of people killed in drone and air strikes at 531 and 779 respectively in Yemen as of 6 June 2012. Of them, 509 to 713 were identified in media reports as militants. Of these deaths, 99 per cent occurred during Obama's presidency.[85]

Pentagon's Joint Special Operations Command (JSOC) spearheads the United States' covert war in Yemen in close coordination with the CIA. From a command post in Sana'a, American military and intelligence operatives track intelligence about militants and plan future strikes. The *New York Times* report which said this added that the CIA believed that al Qaeda's affiliate in Yemen posed 'the greatest immediate threat to the United States, more so than even Qaeda's senior leadership believed to be hiding in Pakistan'.[86]

To facilitate drone strikes in Yemen, the CIA was reportedly building a secret airbase in a West Asian/African country. It was to have been completed by the end of last year.[87] Besides, the White House approved a new policy on drone attacks on 25 April 2012. It permitted what are called 'signature strikes' that target groups of men believed to be militants associated with terrorist organizations, but whose identities are not always known. Earlier, the administration only allowed the JSOC and the CIA to launch drone attacks in Yemen against top-level militants whose names appeared on secret JSOC and CIA target lists and whose locations could be confirmed.[88] Meanwhile, efforts to enhance the capacity of Yemen's military continue.

One part of the programme is training. The *New York Times* reported in September 2010 that as many as 75 American Special Forces personnel were then training Yemeni troops.[89] Even in the midst of Yemen's domestic upheaval, US counterterrorism cooperation with specially trained Yemeni troops, who worked with the US JSOC and the CIA, continued, and targeted AQAP leaders such as Anwar al-Awlaki.[90] American, as well as British trainers, however, stopped much of their activity in May 2011 amidst the government's crackdown on protestors demanding President Saleh's ouster.[91] American and Yemeni officials, however, agreed to resume training programmes to help the new Yemeni President, Abed Rabbo Mansour Hadi, who replaced Ali Abdullah Saleh, in February 2012 and who pledged to continue counterterrorism cooperation with the United States against AQAP.[92] The agreement came in the wake of a series of attacks—besides one on a US convoy in Aden—by Islamist militants that killed nearly 200 Yemeni soldiers and sparked a crisis for President Hadi.[93]

The resumption of military and economic aid is also on its way. According to a *New York Times* report, American military aid to Yemen soared to $155 million in fiscal year 2010 from less than $5 million in fiscal year 2006.[94] The same report also mentioned that the US Central Command had proposed supplying Yemen with $1.2 billion in military equipment and training programme financing over the next six years. The aid would provide for the supply of automatic weapons, coastal patrol boats, transport planes and helicopters, as well as tools and spare parts. Training could expand to allow American logistical advisers to accompany Yemeni troops in some non-combat roles.[95] The proposal, however, had, according to the report, run into opposition on the ground that the presence of 500 to 600 hard-core members of al Qaeda's local affiliate did not justify building a 21st-century military in the poorest country of the Arab world that had no hostile neighbour.[96]

The Obama administration had set aside about $50 million in military assistance for Yemen in 2011. A part of it was suspended when the country's military forces split during the agitation against the rule of President Ali Abdullah Saleh, and troops began shooting at one another.[97] US economic assistance for fiscal year 2012 is $50 million, equal to the military assistance, with a similar amount projected for 2013. The *Washington Post* report which stated this quoted a senior US official as saying that the United States was prepared to increase the assistance if the new government moved quickly to restructure its military force, stem official corruption and implement electoral reforms.

Meanwhile, the situation has started changing on the ground. The Yemeni army's US-backed offensive, launched on 12 May 2012 to regain territory lost to AQAP and al Qaeda–linked Ansar al-Sharia, led to the recapture of the cities of Zinjibar and Jaar on 12 June[98] and Shuqra on 15 June.[99] On 16 June, followers of Ansar al-Sharia were reported to be leaving their bastion of Azzan in the south-eastern Yemeni province of Shabwa in what some described as redeployment.[100] According to the Al Jazeera blog which said this, many al Qaeda fighters had escaped to Azzan after pulling out of Jaar, Zinjibar and Shuqra.

While the gains of the latest offensive have been significant and their symbolic impact must have been considerable, it would be too early to write the AQAP and Ansar al-Sharia off. They may well have made a tactical retreat from the four cities to preserve their strength to fight another day. The Taliban have repeatedly done that in Afghanistan and they are still in business. Besides, al Qaeda affiliates still control large areas in southern parts of Yemen. Even if they are driven out of these, they may escape into Somalia, where the al Shabaab is still very strong, or other adjoining countries and stage a comeback—as the Taliban and al Qaeda did in Afghanistan after the United States' involvement in the Iraq war—if the Yemeni government's pressure slackens.

The suicide bomb explosion during a military parade rehearsal in Sana'a on 20 May 2012, which left over 90 Yemeni soldiers dead, indicated the kind of attack that Islamist extremists can mount, and which their counterparts in Afghanistan have been launching with deadly effect. The ability to mount such attacks, however, does not necessarily indicate a capacity to launch a large-scale offensive and take over a country. In Yemen, the danger lies in circumstances that make the population vulnerable to the appeal of extremist organizations like the AQAP.

According to a report by the majority staff of the US Senate Foreign Relations Committee, Yemen's oil reserves, which accounts for 75 per cent of its income, will be exhausted by 2017, and the country has no apparent way of transiting to a post-oil economy.[101] Worse, rapidly depleting water supply—a result of a much faster consumption than replenishment—has created acute shortages throughout the country and Sana'a may become the world's first capital city to run out of water. A large amount of Yemen's water is used for irrigating qat—a semi-narcotic plant. Habitually chewed by about 75 per cent of Yemen's men, it is blamed for decreasing productivity and depleting resources and contributing to the country's abysmal poverty with half its population earning less than $2 a day. As if all this was not enough, Yemen faces one of the world's highest population growth rates, 3.4

per cent a year, which strains the government's ability to provide serv-ices and contributes to an illiteracy rate of more than 50 per cent.[102]

Such conditions constitute a fertile breeding ground of extremist militancy. Given the geo-strategic location of Yemen, the world may have to pay a heavy price if it becomes complacent about combating AQAP and Ansar al-Sharia. The point needs to be emphasized because Yemen is next door to Somalia, which lies in the Horn of Africa, across the narrow Gulf of Aden and which has been plagued by Islamist mili-tants, clan warlords, factional armies and innumerable men who live by the gun.

SOMALIA'S CURSE

Somalia's current curse is an organization called al Shabaab, which is also known as Harakat al-Shabaab al-Mujahidin, al Shabaab, the Youth, Mujahidin al-Shabaab Movement and Mujahideen Youth Movement.[103] Originally the militant wing of the Islamic Courts Union, which cap-tured power in the country on 5 June 2006, it remained a fringe force until Ethiopia, with the backing of the United States, invaded Somalia in December 2006 and installed the Transitional Federal Government. The development, however, stoked extremist sentiments and al Shabaab emerged as a full-fledged insurrectionary force.[104] Declared a terrorist organization by the United States in 2008, its leaders have claimed affiliation with al Qaeda since 2007.[105]

Al Shabaab imposes strict sharia law in the southern territories it controls. It has claimed responsibility for several suicide attacks, including one in February 2009, which killed 11 Burundian soldiers in the deadliest strike against African Union peacekeepers since their de-ployment in the country. And following the lethal US attack on Saleh Ali Nabhan, a top al Qaeda leader, on 14 September 2009, al Shabaab launched a suicide attack that killed 17 peacekeepers and a number of civilians.[106]

While estimates of al Shabaab's size vary, a general agreement among analysts tends to veer round to several thousand fighters, many of them from the Hawiye clan. It has been able to expand in Somalia with relatively small numbers because of the country's lack of a central government since 1991, and the willingness of many clan warlords, who filled the power vacuum, to cooperate with it, at least in the south. Al Shabaab, however, has been forcibly recruiting, so it is unclear how many members of the group truly believe in its ideology. According to experts, however, the number of hard-core ideological believers could range between 300 and 800 individuals.[107]

Since 2007, al Shabaab has been battling troops of the countries participating in the African Union Mission in Somalia (AMISOM), set up by the African Union with the approval of the United Nations. It is mandated by the UN Security Council Resolution 1744 (2007) to support dialogue and reconciliation in Somalia, provide appropriate protection to the Transitional Federal Institutions to help them carry out their functions of government and ensure security for key infrastructure. It is also mandated to assist with implementation of the National Security and Stabilization Plan, in particular the effective re-establishment and training of all-inclusive Somali security forces; and to contribute to the creation of the necessary security conditions for the provision of humanitarian assistance.[108] Its duties have come to include supporting the Transitional Federal Government's forces against al Shabaab militants.

Troops from Uganda, Kenya, Burundi, Ethiopia and Djibouti constitute the main bulk of AMISOM forces. Though al Shabaab still controls most of the country's area, it is at last beginning to lose ground and support fast enough to prompt speculation about its impending rout. While some may consider the speculation premature, the fact is that al Shabaab, which appeared to be riding high some time ago, has taken several hard body blows in the last few months. The latest, at the time of writing, was on 31 May when it admitted to have withdrawn from the town of Afmadow in southern Yemen, 115 kilometres from Kismayo, where it has its headquarters. The victors were soldiers of the Kenyan Defence Forces, who had entered the fray in October 2011, and Somali troops.[109] Afmadow was one of their key targets from the very beginning not only because of its proximity to Kismayo but for the network of roads that radiate all over the country from the town.[110] Earlier, in August 2011, AMISOM troops had pushed al Shabaab militants out of Mogadishu after a long and bloody struggle.

A few days prior to the capture of Afmadow, on 26 May 2012, al Shabaab had to abandon the important city of Afgoye, about 30 kilometres to the West of Mogadishu. Afgoye, which was captured by Somali and African Union troops, was an important stronghold of al Shabaab and gave them easy access to Mogadishu, the country's capital, where they had carried out several suicide attacks.[111] These successes had led to a mood of confidence among the African Union forces. Thus, after the capture of Afmadow, a spokesman of the Kenyan army, Colonel Cyrus Oguna, told the BBC that he hoped the African Union forces would be able to take Kismayo before 20 August—the deadline for the completion of the transition process leading to a new constitution and parliament, and the election of a president.[112]

The question is: Do these successes warrant talk of al Shabaab being on the run? The search for an answer has to begin with a look at the causes of the reverses it has suffered. There are two distinct sets of reasons. The first is a wave of defections from its fighting force, with the defectors helping the African Union and their Somali interim government allies to arrest yet more fighters. Simultaneously, there has been an erosion of its support base.[113]

There have been several reasons for both developments. Many had initially joined al Shabaab because the latter had appealed to their patriotism by projecting the Ethiopian and African Union troops as invaders, and to their religious sentiments by saying that these troops, mostly Christians, threatened Islam. Their conduct, however, soon disillusioned people. A BBC report quoted one of the defectors, who went by the name of Gashan (Shield) as saying that he noticed al Shabaab demanding tax by force, confiscating animals from nomads and carrying out harsh punishments and realized that 'they were not about religion', and adding, 'They were about killing people.'[114]

Extreme, wanton cruelty has been the hallmark of al Shabaab's conduct. An example was the public execution of two girls, aged 18 and 14 years, by a firing squad at the centre of Beledweyne town near the Ethiopian border, on 27 October 2010.[115] The gory event was preceded by pickup trucks with loudspeakers driving into the town, ordering residents to watch the execution but not to take pictures or bring their cell phones. While an al Shabaab official told local journalists that the two girls were found guilty of spying for the Ethiopian government, townspeople argued that they were innocent. According to them, the girls, who had been travelling away from their families, were caught in a crossfire just outside the town. They fled to the bush where they were finally caught. Some of the women who watched the execution fainted. Meanwhile, the al Shabaab official, Sheik Yusuf Ali Ugas, said that the two teenagers were not the only ones in his organization's custody, adding, 'There are many people now in Shabab prisons in Beledweyne.'[116]

ANGER IN MOGADISHU

One of the most striking demonstrations of the growing popular anger against al Shabaab occurred in Mogadishu on 29 March 2010, when hundreds of men, women and children marched through the city's streets shouting slogans against the organization which had been using amputation as punishment and digging up and desecrating the graves of renowned Sufi clerics.[117] Besides its savagery, intolerance and violent enforcement of its version of sharia law and Islamic conduct, al Shabaab's banning of several relief organizations——and even the United Nations High Commissioner for Refugees, United Nations Children's Fund and World Health Organization——during the widespread famine in southern Somalia in 2011, also cost it a lot of support. In a statement, it accused the organizations of exaggerating the scale of problems for political reasons and raising money, and alleged that the agencies were working with church groups to convert vulnerable Muslim children and opposing its attempts to impose sharia law.[118] But it does seem to have had many takers among the famine victims.

The second development responsible for al Shabaab's reverses is the increase in the numerical strength of the African Union troops in early 2012 from 12,000 to nearly 18,000 through the incorporation of Kenyan soldiers, who entered Somalia in October 2011, in pursuit of al Shabaab militants. They have been accusing the latter of involvement in kidnappings on Kenyan soil and of destabilizing the border region.[119] Not only that, the troops are now better equipped and armed. The American government is helping by contributing more than $400 million[120] to equip and maintain the African Union troops whose number may increase even further. African Union troops also receive operational support and tactical and strategic advice from the United States.

Oman-based planes of the American navy have been flying reconnaissance missions over Somalia, and an international fleet has been monitoring sea traffic. US military has stationed an aircraft carrier and three other warships off the coast to patrol the waters, and in 2007 it began carrying out 'targeted killings', through air strikes, of senior al Qaeda leaders within the country. On 1 May 2008, American war planes reportedly killed Aden Hashi Ayro, the former leader of al Shabaab.[121] On 14 September 2009, American commandos killed one of the most wanted Islamic militants in Africa, Saleh Ali Saleh Nabhan, in a daylight helicopter-borne raid near the town of Baraawe in southern Somalia. Western intelligence agencies have described him as the ringleader of the al Qaeda cell in Kenya responsible for the bombing of an Israeli hotel on the Kenyan coast in 2002. Nabhan may have also played a role in the attacks on two American embassies in East Africa in 1998.[122]

In April 2010, President Barack Obama issued an executive order to block the finances of al Shabaab's leaders and those contributing to the conflict in Somalia. Following the bomb attacks on Sunday, 11 July 2010, on crowds watching the football World Cup final in Kampala, Uganda, which left at least 70 persons dead,[123] the Obama administration also indicated that it would boost its efforts against al Shabaab, which claimed responsibility for these, most probably in the form of increased aid to AMISOM as well as the Transitional Federal Government.[124] On 8 June 2012, the US State Department placed, for the first time, seven top al Shabaab leaders on its wanted list offering a total of $33 million for clues to help in the hunt for them.[125] It placed a $7 million bounty on al Shabaab founder Ahmed Abdi aw-Mohamed, and $5 million each on Ibrahim Haji Jama, Fuad Mohamed Khalaf, Bashir Mohamed Mahamoud and Mukhtar Robow. It had placed a further $3 million each on Zakariya Ismail Ahmed Hersi and Abdullahi Yare.[126]

An ABC report cited Somali government and observers as saying that the bounty might be just what was needed to crush the al Shabaab, which was already reeling from military assaults and air strikes. It quoted from a statement by the government as saying that the 'announcement from the U.S. government ... will certainly help the Somali government's efforts to end al Qaeda's reign of terror in Somalia,' and adding, 'This is an important juncture in Somali history, where the possibility of full recovery from years of chaos is within reach.'[127]

Such, and perhaps even more, optimistic statements had been made before. Fazul Abdullah Mohammed, al Qaeda's leader in East Africa and the mastermind of the bomb attacks on the American embassies in Nairobi and Dar es Salaam on 7 August 1998, was killed by Somali soldiers in a shoot-out at a checkpoint in Mogadishu on 7 June 2011. Following the incident, officials of the country's Transitional Federal Government had expressed the hope that the killing could be a turning point against al Shabaab.[128] Serious doubts about this actually happening, however, arose on 10 June when Somalia's Interior Minister, Abdi Shakur Sheikh Hassan, was killed at his residence by a suicide bomber said to be his niece. Al Shabaab claimed responsibility for the act.[129]

As seen, al Shabaab has suffered several blows since then. Yet, it is too early to write it off. Military operations like those by AMISOM troops, and foreign assistance like the kind provided by the Americans—and to some extent by the French—provide temporary respite and not more. A permanent solution would require initiating a political process that would address the circumstances that have led to the emergence of al Shabaab and account for such appeal as it still exercises. Unfortunately, the prospects of such a political process emerging seem as bleak as ever. The Transitional Federal Government, the country's internationally recognized authority that the African Union protects, is a collection of corrupt politicians and warlords who control almost no territory and are exceedingly unpopular.[130]

On the military front too, concerns remain despite the ground gained by African Union troops. For one thing, they need to be better armed and equipped. American officials, who consider the AMISOM to be under-financed, insist that the African troops need better flak jackets, more armoured trucks and helicopters.[131] In the absence of the latter, the injured often die before being evacuated to hospitals.

Unfortunately, the African Union troops are unlikely to get better equipment given the budget cuts at the Pentagon and the US State Department.[132] The wider question is whether America, facing continuing economic problems, and increasingly inward-looking thanks to war weariness, will maintain even its present level of aid to and involvement in West Asia and North Africa. If it does not, one can hardly rule out both regions falling to al Qaeda and its affiliates.

TROUBLED NORTH AFRICA

Islamist militancy has been growing in almost the whole of North Africa for over two decades. As the book is being written, two major terrorist organizations are active in the region besides al Shabaab. They are AQIM based in Algeria and Jama'atu Ahlis Sunnah Lidda'awati Wal-Jihad, commonly referred to as Boko Haram (literally meaning Western education is sinful). There are other smaller ones.

Emily Hunt rightly states that North Africans tend to be more

> religiously moderate than their counterparts in the Gulf. The vast majority of citizens in the region do not adhere to Salafist Islam; indeed, many deliberately hold themselves apart from what they consider to be radical tendencies in the 'East,' including Saudi Arabia.[133]

She, however, further points out that

> the region has not been entirely insulated from trends elsewhere in the Middle East. Islamic revivalism has been on the upswing since the 1970s, and in the past two decades political Islam has become a popular vehicle of opposition to increasingly undemocratic regimes.[134]

External sponsorship of mosques, religious schools and scholarships for locals to study religion in countries such as Saudi Arabia and Iran has also helped conservative strands of Islam gain a foothold.[135]

The 1979–89 jihad against Soviet occupation of Afghanistan was a further radicalizing factor. Arab North African countries constituted a major recruiting ground for the mujahideen. Hundreds of 'Afghan Arabs', as participants in the jihad were known throughout the Middle East, began returning to their countries of origin by the end of the 1980s. Their arrival infused emerging local Islamist groups, such as the Algerian Armed Islamic Group (GIA) and the Nigerian Taliban, with an 'uncompromising radical outlook, coupled with a set of external connections and expertise'.[136] As political conditions conducive to the rise of Islamist militancy in north-western Africa continued unchanged, radical networks metastasized and embedded themselves deeper in society. Simultaneously, the original leadership of al Qaeda has pursued a strategy of harnessing local groups with local grievances to the wider global jihad against the West which proved highly successful.[137]

While the countries affected early also included Tunisia, Morocco, Mauritania and Libya, the conflict was particularly savage in Algeria where violence flared up after the country's secular military cancelled the second round of the elections in 1992, which the Islamic Salvation Front, a coalition of militant and moderate Muslims, appeared set to win. The insurrection claimed 150,000 lives before it gradually subsided following tough counterterrorism measures by the government as well as the latter's offer of an amnesty to the Islamists in 1999.[138] The most dreaded militant organization, the GIA, however, rejected the promised amnesty and continued a violent campaign to establish an Islamic state. The movement had split by then, with a body called the Salafist Group for Preaching and Combat (GSPC) having broken away from the GIA in 1998, believing that the latter's savage tactics were damaging the Islamist cause.[139]

The GSPC declared its allegiance to al Qaeda as early as 2003, but Ayman al-Zawahiri, then the latter's second in command, officially approved its merger in a videotape released on 11 September 2006.[140] In January 2007 GSPC announced that it had changed its name to al Qaeda in the Lands of Islamic Maghreb to reflect its new allegiance.[141] Led by Abdelmalek Droukdal, aka Abu Musab Abdul Wadoud, the AQIM has been declared a Foreign Terrorist Organization by the United States.

Since the announcement of its changed moniker, AQIM has claimed responsibility for attacks under its new name.[142] In April 2007 at least 30 people were killed in bomb attacks on official buildings in Algiers. More attacks followed: on buses carrying foreign oil workers; on American diplomats; on soldiers; and in September 2007, a suicide bomb attack in Batna, aimed at a motorcade of President Abdelaziz Bouteflika. The President was not injured, but 20 people were killed. Two days later, a car bomb killed more than 30 people at a coastguard barracks in the town of Dellys. In December, twin car bombs killed at least 37 people in Algiers, including 17 UN staff.[143]

In 2008, a suicide car bombing at a police college in Issers, east of Algiers, killed 48 people on 19 August. A day later, two more car bombings occurred in quick succession in Bouira, south-east of Algiers. The second explosion killed 12 Algerian employees of a Canadian engineering firm. In February 2009, suspected al Qaeda militants killed nine security guards who were working for the state-owned gas and electricity distributor Sonelgaz at a camp near Jijel, east of Algiers.[144]

In 2010, however, AQIM failed to conduct the high-casualty attacks in Algeria that it had in previous years, and multinational counterterrorism efforts—including a joint French-Mauritanian raid in July on an AQIM camp—led to the deaths of some of the organization's members and possibly disrupted some of its activity. But then it killed two French hostages in 2011 during an attempted rescue operation.

At the time of writing, it continues to hold four French hostages as well as an Italian tourist.[145]

There has been a surge in large attacks in northern Algeria since early 2011. To cite the more important ones, attackers identified as activists of AQIM killed at least 13 Algerian soldiers at a Kabylia outpost in April, and at least 29 in a suicide bombing attack on a police headquarters in the Kabyle city of Tizi Ouzou in August. In the same month they also carried out a double suicide attack at an elite military academy in the usually secure western town of Cherchell, killing at least 18, and fired a rocket launcher at a regional airport in the Kabyle city of Jijel in September.[146]

Clearly, AQIM is far from finished. Rather, it may grow stronger by taking advantage of, among other things, the civil war in Libya that led to Qaddafi's ouster and its unsettled aftermath. In November 2011, AQIM's commander Mokhtar Belmokhtar confirmed that the group had used the ensuing chaos to acquire weapons.[147] Nor does it seem to be starved of funds. Besides smuggling, kidnapping for ransom is its most important source of money. According to an article in *Der Spiegel Online* of 4 January 2012, it had allegedly netted itself some $65 million in ransom money since 2005 and was holding 13 hostages from six countries.[148] The Sahara desert, which covers almost the whole of North Africa, offers Islamist terrorist groups active in countries like Algeria, Chad, Egypt, Libya, Mali, Mauritania, Morocco, Niger, Sudan and Tunisia a tremendous advantage. Its vast open spaces facilitate smuggling and diverse other forms of criminal activity, which even the best-trained police forces find hard to control, and which are a source of funds for terrorist groups which operate with relative impunity and can hold their hostages without being easily detected. In fact, AQIM is known to have held several hostages along Algeria's Saharan border with Mali and Niger.

MALI'S TRAVAILS

In fact, Mali is facing a serious Islamist threat. The French President, François Hollande, said in June 2012 that it could become a home for terrorist groups which could threaten the region. He was reacting to the expression of concern by the President of Niger, Mahamadou Issoufou, over the report that Malian rebels were being trained by jihadis in Pakistan and Afghanistan.[149] Niger's President said that he intended to ask the United Nations to allow the despatch of troops to Mali and West African countries and would ask the Security Council to supervise the operation with logistical support from France and the United States. President Hollande said that he would support the move but Niger and its neighbours must take the lead.[150]

A military takeover in Mali on 22 March 2012, following widespread rioting and looting by soldiers the day before, seems to have given a new thrust to the Islamist threat facing the country whose government had earlier acknowledged that several AQIM fighters had found sanctuary in its desert reaches.[151] It also highlighted the destabilizing impact that the movement bringing down Libya's Qaddafi regime has had on the region. The Libyan leader's downfall has sent a flood of weapons into Mali, bolstering a longstanding rebel movement in the desert area and inflicting several defeats on the Malian forces. The junior officers and enlisted men who led the coup said on state television that they were fed up with the way the government dealt with the rebellion and complained of lack of weapons and effective leadership.[152]

In the turmoil that gripped Mali following the coup, the north was captured by a loose coalition of Tuareg separatists and Islamist fundamentalists including the AQIM and another group calling itself Ansar Dine (Army of the Faith). Much of the weapons and many of the Islamist fighters came from Libya.[153] Even the Nigerian Islamist group, Boko Haram, has reportedly established a presence in northern Mali where Islamists are seeking to set up a theocratic state, based on sharia law. They have raised their black flags, shut down nightclubs and forced women to wear veils.[154] And, in a move reminiscent of Taliban's destruction of Buddha statues in Afghanistan in March 2001, militants of Ansar Dine defied international requests and destroyed mausoleums of Sufi saints in Timbuktu in northern Mali, on Sunday, 1 July 2012.[155]

At a meeting in Ivory Coast in June 2012, Western African military chiefs claimed to have secured commitments from Nigeria, Senegal and Niger to provide the bulk of the 3,270-strong force that would intervene in Mali. The going will be tough and would possibly involve bitter hand-to-hand fighting in Timbuktu and other northern cities. The West African troops are inadequately armed and do not even have proper vehicles for northern Mali's rugged desert terrain. They will clearly need a lot of help from the United States and the West.

The matter is important. The whole of northern Africa is in danger. Morocco has known Islamist violence beginning with the attack on Atlas-Asni Hotel in Marrakech on 24 August 1994 when terrorists, French-Algerian citizens, entered it and fired with automatic weapons, killing two and injuring several persons.[156] On 16 May 2003, five coordinated attacks targeting foreign and Jewish interests, launched in Casablanca, Morocco's 'economic capital', killed 45 and injured around 100.[157] After a gap of over eight years, during which repeated attempts at terrorist strikes were foiled by Morocco's security agencies which also neutralized several terrorist groups, attacks resumed in April 2010 when a terrorist, reportedly expelled from Spain in 2004 after the bombing attack in Madrid, stabbed two police officers guarding the royal palace at Tétouan. On 15 April 2011, a terrorist stabbed two men, including a French tourist, at a restaurant in Tangiers.[158]

A far bigger strike, however, occurred on 28 April when terrorists staged an explosion at the Argana cafe in Marrakech, which killed 17 persons[159] and wounded over 80. Briefing the government in Rabat, Morocco's Interior Minister, Taieb Cherkaoui, said on the following day that the bomb attack appeared to have the hallmark of the AQIM. 'The manner reminds us of the style used generally by Al Qaeda,' he said, adding, 'And this leads us to think that there is a possibility of more dangers to come.'[160] AQIM doubtless said in a statement issued on 7 May and carried by Nouakchott Information Agency in Mauritania, 'We deny involvement in the bombing and assure that we have nothing to do with it, neither up close nor from afar.'[161] Significantly, however, the statement came after thousands of people, including trade union members, had marched through the cities of Morocco on 1 May demanding both a more rapid transition to democracy and decrying terrorism.[162] Understandably, it did not carry much conviction.

A report in the *Guardian* of Britain of 26 June 2012 quoted General Carter Ham, head of the US Army's Africa Command, as saying that there were signs that the AQIM, Boko Haram and al Shabaab were sharing money and explosive materials and training fighters together. The General, who was addressing an African Centre for Strategic Studies seminar in Washington, specifically stated, 'Most notably I would say that the linkages between AQIM and Boko Haram are probably the most worrisome in terms of the indications we have that they are likely sharing funds, training and explosive materials that can be quite dangerous.'

Events in Nigeria indicate how lethal the results of such cooperation can be. Boko Haram, formed in Maiduguri, a city in the northeastern part of the country in the mid-1990s, demands the imposition of sharia law in Nigeria and stands for the al Qaeda brand of reductionist Islam. It was using poisoned darts and machetes to kill and maim police officers until a few years ago.[163] Indeed, it appeared to have been crippled by a harsh government crackdown on the violent agitation it had launched in 2009. It, however, has reorganized itself since then, affiliated itself with a global terrorist network that includes al Shabaab, militant groups in Pakistan and AQIM and has carried out a series of devastating attacks. In 2011 alone, the group killed up to 600 people.[164]

SPAWNING OF DISCONTENT

Poverty and lack of development in the Muslim-majority northern part of the country coupled with administrative corruption and inefficiency have spawned the discontent that has contributed to Boko Haram's emergence. The latter has also been helped by the discontent created by the harsh measures used to crush the 2009 agitation. By no means, however, could it have unleashed the kind of violence it has without help from AQIM and al Shabaab, violence that threatens to plunge Nigeria in a civil war between Muslims and Christians as the latter turned toward retaliation. Rioting killed 1,000 persons in 2001 and subsequent violence in 2004 and 2008 killed another 1,000. Smaller but equally vicious attacks killed dozens in 2009.[165] The BBC reported on 2 July 2012 that the spate of Boko Haram bomb attacks was intended to fuel religious violence, possibly in an effort to make Nigeria ungovernable.[166] The motive may also be to gain further strength from bitter communal polarization.

Given the manner in which events are unfolding in Africa, the outcome in Nigeria will influence, and will be influenced by, events in the rest of the continent. A country to watch is Kenya. As one would recall, American embassies in its capital, Nairobi, as well as Dar es Salaam, the capital of neighbouring Tanzania, were targets of devastating terror attacks by al Qaeda on 7 August 1998.[167] Another major attack occurred on 28 November when three suicide bombers drove themselves up to the doors of an Israeli-owned hotel in the coastal city of Mombasa and detonated their explosives. All of them and twelve others—three Israelis and nine Kenyans—were killed. Dozens were wounded. Minutes before the explosion, terrorists had fired a shoulder-launched missile, which, fortunately, had missed its target.[168] On 2 December, al Qaeda claimed responsibility for the attacks in a message posted on an Islamist website, azfalrasas.com (literally meaning 'melody of gunfire').[169]

After years of relative quiet, the kidnapping of Westerners from parts of Kenya close to Somalia led the entry of hundreds of Kenyan troops, backed by helicopters and tanks, into Somalia on 15 October 2011, in a campaign against al Shabaab. While the Kenyan government blamed al Shabaab for the kidnappings, some analysts attributed these to Somali bandits and pirates.[170] Al Shabaab threatened to hit back as fighting progressed. A spokesman of the organization, Sheik Ali Mohamud Rage, warned on 16 October, 'The Kenyan government does not know war!' He then added, 'We know what war is. War is destruction, displacement, and your tall buildings will be immediately brought to the ground.' Al Shabaab, he further said, would attack Kenya if it did not withdraw its troops immediately and that Kenyan planes had bombed al Shabaab positions killing civilians.[171]

There have been several deadly attacks in Kenya since then but, according to a *New York Times* report, most terrorism analysts believed that the perpetrators were most likely not al Shabaab operatives from Somalia but the organization's sympathisers within the country.[172] Several attacks occurred on 24 November 2011. In one, a large military truck carrying troops struck a landmine near Mandera, a remote outpost straddling the Kenya–Somalia border. One soldier was killed and five severely injured. In another, a grenade attack on a hotel and a shopping centre in the northern town of Garissa killed at least three and wounded six.[173]

Among the other incidents that followed, a grenade attack outside a nightclub in Mombasa killed a woman and wounded several people on 15 May 2012.[174] The terrorists struck again on 23 June, a day after the US embassy in Kenya had warned of an 'imminent' attack in Mombasa and asked all its government workers to leave or not to travel to the city, as the case might be.[175] A grenade attack on a bar in the city killed one and injured several others.[176] The biggest attack after the start of the Kenyan offensive against al Shabaab, however, occurred on 1 July 2012 when armed men killed a total of at least 15 people in two separate strikes on two churches in Garissa.[177]

Al Shabaab's growing reach and organizational capability in Africa had been in evidence almost two years before the 1 July attacks when two deadly bomb explosions in Uganda's capital, Kampala, had killed at least 70 persons on 11 July 2010. The targets were an Ethiopian garden restaurant and a rugby field in two disparate parts of the city where people had gathered to watch the football World Cup final in Johannesburg. There was no mistaking the fact that the staging of synchronized bomb attacks in two different parts of Uganda, located hundreds of miles apart, required sophistication. Such outrages, however, did not go down well with the people. If the angry demonstration against al Shabaab in Mogadishu on 29 March 2010 reflected alienation in Somalia, the hostile response in Kenya to the bomb attacks on 1 July 2012 indicated that the majority of Muslims elsewhere in the continent had little use for its ways.

Adan Wachu, head of the Supreme Council of Kenyan Muslims, who also chairs the Inter-Religious Council of Kenya, told BBC on 3 July that there were 'people out there' who were 'determined to make Kenya another Nigeria'. A sectarian division of the country would not be allowed and whoever was attempting it would fail. He went on to add that a meeting of the Inter-Religious Council on 3 July unanimously agreed that the church attacks were acts of 'terrorists and terrorism' and that 'Muslims felt that because those Christians are a minority in their domain they must be protected at all cost'. Muslim youth would 'provide a vigilante service to the churches not only in Garissa but in any other places that the Christians may deem fit'.[178]

In Bamako, the capital of Mali, some 2,000 people held a sit-in on 4 July 2012 in pouring rain demanding weapons to liberate the north of the country where the Ansar Dine had imposed a harsh, Taliban-style Islamist rule and had been demolishing ancient monuments. Complaining that the 'north of our country has been abandoned by our leaders who have other concerns', they demanded weapons to liberate the region. Oumar Maiga, a leader of a collective of the citizens of the north, said, 'If the army doesn't want to go to war, then give us the means to liberate the north.'[179]

Things are at a turning point. The Islamists are unpopular but are fanatical and ruthless killers. The armies and police forces fighting them are ill-equipped and often inadequately trained while the governments are corrupt and inefficient. The regimes fighting organizations like the AQIM and al Shabaab will have further problems if what is perceived as a Taliban/al Qaeda victory in Afghanistan boosts Islamist morale and undermines theirs besides unleashing a wave of radical Islamism by glamorizing it as the wave of the future and its protagonists as heroes who vanquished the mighty United States of America.

The consequences of an Islamist takeover of North Africa and the Arabian peninsula have been discussed in some detail and require no further elaboration. Besides, the frightening consequences of the Sahara becoming a terrorist sanctuary have already been mentioned. What does bear some elaboration, however, is the kind of threat terrorism now poses to the world. The first thing to note is that organizations like the AQAP, AQIM and al Shabaab have the potential to perpetrate terror attacks in Europe and the United States. Second, the dimensions of the threat have to be assessed in terms of an increase in the incidence and danger of actual terror strikes and the enhancement of the damage done by these.

THE GROWING REACH OF AL QAEDA AFFILIATES

Europe has seen a series of terror strikes since 9/11. On 15 and 20 November 2003, bomb explosions directly linked to al Qaeda killed 57 persons and wounded 700 in Istanbul, Turkey.[180] The casualties were much higher—191 killed and over 1,800 injured—in near-simultaneous bomb explosions in commuter trains in Madrid, Spain, on 11 March 2004.[181] On 7 July 2005, 56 persons, including four suicide bombers, were killed when the latter struck in three London underground system trains and a double-decker bus in central London.[182] In March 2012, a gunman shot dead three soldiers—one on the 11th, two on the 15th—and three Jewish children and a rabbi on the 19th before being shot by police personnel on the 23rd.

Besides the ones executed, a number of terrorist strikes, some of which could have wrought death and havoc on a large scale, have been foiled. The more diabolical among them included one to attack unspecified targets in the United Kingdom potentially including nightclubs and shopping centres using fertilizer-based bombs.[183] A joint operation effort by the police and MI5 code-named 'Operation Crevice' led to the arrest of a number of people between 29 March and 1 April 2004.[184]

In August 2006, the British police foiled a terrorist plot to explode at least 10 trans-Atlantic aeroplanes carrying passengers to North America.[185] It thwarted two more strikes on 29 and 30 June respectively. In the former, it discovered and disabled bombs in two cars in London; in the second, two men drove a dark green Cherokee jeep into the main door of the Glasgow Airport and set fire to it as they could not break through. One of them died of burn injuries; the other was tried and sentenced to 32 years of imprisonment.

The threats continued. In late September, Western intelligence agencies claimed that an al Qaeda plot to carry out coordinated terrorist attacks in the United Kingdom, France and Germany, akin to the ones that began in Mumbai, India, on 26 November 2008 and lasted for about 60 hours, had been uncovered. According to a BBC report, both France and Germany were on a heightened state of alert.[186] The report quoted British officials as saying that the plot had not been halted but an attack was not expected immediately.

Understandably, the 2012 London Olympics sharply heightened fears of a terrorist strike while it was being held. There were a number of arrests and the most elaborate security arrangements made. All this once again raised the question of how safe Britain and the rest of Europe were from terror attacks. Al Qaeda, its affiliates and those inspired by its affiliates have doubtless both in their sights and have been responsible for the attacks that have succeeded or been thwarted. As James Brandon points out, it was becoming clear with the emergence of more evidence from police and judicial investigations that 'many of the United Kingdom's largest terrorist plots developed as a direct result of the plotters' close involvement with senior members of al-Qa'ida in Pakistan'.[187]

'Lone wolves' and 'self-radicalised' young people who have emerged as jihadi terrorists have predominated the British terror scene since the busting of the big and better-organized plots after 2006. They have displayed a low level of expertise and 'poor tradecraft'. But, as Michael Clarke, Director General of the Royal United Services Institute (RUSI),[188] has pointed out, the large number of such individuals may be 'lucky in a few attempts'. The danger is all the greater because they are 'harder to track and their behaviour much harder to predict'.

As for Europe, Jason Burke, who has written extensively on al Qaeda, has pointed out that the organization did not play any role in funding the attacks or training people for the Madrid bomb attacks. He, however, adds:

> The Madrid bombings were the work of a disparate group of individuals drawn together by two motivated, angry, twisted

individuals who were heavily influenced by something that might be called 'al-Qaida-ism' but whose links to any global terrorist group were very scant indeed. And that is the nature of modern Islamist militancy. And that is not good news.[189]

It is certainly not good news. British officials have warned in recent years that a wide network of Islamist militants' cells has been established throughout the country. Some of them, they say, were actively planning terrorist attacks, often benefiting from the cultural, political and religious alienation that has become common among Britain's million-and-a-half strong Muslims.[190] The AQIM has been steadily expanding its network in Europe. In June 2008, Spanish authorities unearthed a terrorist cell in their country, arrested 8 men and detained 10, accusing them of providing logistical and financial support to it. In December 2007, French police uncovered a similar cell in the outskirts of Paris. Terrorists with suspected AQIM links have been arrested in the United Kingdom, Germany, Italy, Portugal and the Netherlands. Some analysts point to the thwarted attacks and arrests of AQIM-linked terrorists as evidence that the group is capable of attacks in Western Europe.[191]

North Africa and the Arabian peninsula are increasingly the areas to watch. Michael Clarke has written that Britons were thought to constitute 25 per cent of the 200 or so foreign fighters fielded by al Shabaab in Somalia and in a deepening war on neighbouring Kenya and its tourism. He has further stated that the survivors among young British men, and some women, who went to fight in Somalia, Yemen and border areas of Pakistan tended to return in months or perhaps a year. It was only a matter of time before their commitment to the cause and their newly acquired expertise were likely to be seen on British streets.[192]

The danger from them will be all the greater because their return

> will coincide with the steady release from prison of those convicted of terrorist offences in Britain over the last decade. For good legal reasons their sentences have not, on average, been very

long. Less than 20 per cent of convicted terrorists are serving life or indeterminate sentences and another 20 per cent have been given more than ten years. The largest single proportion—32 per cent—have been serving sentences of between eight months and four years for their offences.[193]

The United States too faces a similar threat. On 5 June 2010, two men, 20-year-old Mohamed Mahmood Alessa and 24-year-old Carlos Eduardo Almonte, both from New Jersey, who were flying to Somalia with the stated intention of joining al Shabaab, were arrested from Kennedy International Airport, New York.[194] American citizens began turning up in Somalia in late 2006 ready to fight; the number sharply increased in 2007, when as many as 20 young men from the Minneapolis area travelled to join al Shabaab.[195] According to a report in the *New York Times* of 30 October 2011, the FBI estimated that Abdisalan Hussein Ali, a Somali-American who had blown himself up in an attack on African Union troops in Mogadishu, was one of the 30 Americans who had joined al Shabaab.[196] American counterterrorism officials estimate that 8 to 12 US citizens have been killed in fighting in Somalia since 2006.[197]

The chances are strong that some American jihadis would plot terrorist attacks on returning to the United States. According to the criminal complaint against Alessa and Almonte, they talked about their obligation to wage violent jihad, and at times expressed a willingness to commit acts of violence in the United States.[198] On the other hand, Abdisalan Hussein Ali reportedly told a friend in Minneapolis two years ago that he would never attack the United States. 'Why would I do that?' the friend recalled Mr Ali saying. 'My mom could be walking down the street.'[199]

Not on Returning Jihadis Alone

Not surprisingly, al Qaeda does not depend on returning jihadis alone. In *Obama's Wars*, Bob Woodward mentions a briefing by Mike McConnell, director of national intelligence during the Bush administration, to Obama who was then president-elect. McConnell said that al Qaeda was recruiting people from 35 countries who did not require visas to enter the United States, paying them well and bringing them into ungoverned regions by the dozens. It was training them in all aspects of warfare—explosives and chemicals—and trying to have them acquire biological weapons.[200]

The reference to biological weapons once again underlined the chilling mass lethality that contemporary terrorism has acquired. The United States had already been hit by biological terrorism. On 18 September 2001, exactly a week after 9/11, letters postmarked Trenton, New Jersey, were mailed to the NBC news anchor, Tom Brokaw, and the editor of the *New York Post*.[201] These were laced with the bacterium *Bacillus anthracis*, which causes an infectious disease, anthrax, whose victims display symptoms similar to those of common flu, causes pulmonary, intestinal and skin lesions, and can be fatal. A CBS employee and the seven-month-old baby of an ABC producer also tested positive for cutaneous anthrax, suggesting that additional letters may have been sent to the New York offices of CBS and ABC. No letters, however, were recovered from these locations.[202]

In October 2001, letters addressed to US senators, Tom Daschle and Patrick Leahy, were found to contain anthrax powder. While Senator Daschle's letter was opened by a staff member, spilling out a small cloud of anthrax, the letter addressed to Senator Patrick Leahy, Chairman, Senate Judicial Committee, was recovered from a quarantined postal facility on 16 November 2001. The US capital police in Washington DC and the FBI were notified and the area was vacated and secured immediately.[203]

Five of the 18 confirmed cases of anthrax infection led to death. There were four suspected cases. By way of precaution, an additional 20,000 people were given antibiotics and 21 buildings, including offices of the US House of Representatives and the US Senate and postal facilities, were temporarily shut down due to contamination.[204]

The two letters mailed to the senators contained a more refined form of anthrax powder. They had the same fictitious return address: 4th Grade, Greendale School, Franklin Park, NJ 08852. Who sent them? The messages they contained were perhaps meant to provide a clue as well as a warning. The two letters addressed to the media stated:

9-11-01
THIS IS NEXT
TAKE PENACILIN NOW
DEATH TO AMERICA
DEATH TO ISRAEL
ALLAH IS GREAT[205]

The two letters sent to the senators stated, 'YOU CAN NOT STOP US. WE HAVE THIS ANTHRAX. YOU DIE NOW. ARE YOU AFRAID? DEATH TO AMERICA. DEATH TO ISRAEL. ALLAH IS GREAT.[206]

Christopher Dickey, who refers to the anthrax attacks in his *Securing the City: Inside America's Best Counterterror Force—The NYPD*, states that investigators subsequently traced the bacterium's DNA to a strain that originated at the US army's biological weapons research facility at Fort Detrick, Maryland. An American was also named as 'a person of interest' to the investigation. The trail, however, went cold.[207]

The absence of a successful biological weapons strike in the United States since then should not spawn complacence. Meanwhile, two other threats to the United States, Europe and the rest of the world are growing—cyber and nuclear terror. As early as the summer of 2008, the Chinese had hacked into the campaign computers of Barack Obama and the Republican candidate for the American presidency, John McCain.[208] In *Obama's Wars*, Bob Woodward gives a graphic and detailed account of the briefing Mike McConnell gave Obama on 6 November 2008. One of the things he told the latter, who had been elected President two days earlier, was that the 9/11 terrorists would have wrought far greater havoc on the American and global economies than they did had they attacked the Bank of New York and the Citibank instead of the twin towers of the World Trade Center. Considering that each handled $3 trillion in financial transfers every day and the annual US GDP was $14 trillion, there would have been financial chaos if the banks' data had been destroyed.[209]

McConnell, Woodward wrote, told Obama that there was no real protection and the system was totally open to attacks. Power grids, telecommunications lines, air traffic control—all computer-dependent enterprises—were vulnerable to cyber attacks.[210] The United States had a taste of what a cyber attack could do when Google came under one in December 2009. It was some time before it could be traced to China. Washington DC and corporate America were stunned that such a technologically smart company in the Silicon Valley was so completely penetrated. The identity of the Chinese attackers and their links with their governments, if any, remained a mystery.[211]

David E. Sanger, who refers to the incident in his absorbing work *Confront and Conceal: Obama's Secret Wars and Surprising Use of American Power*, mentions three simulated terror attacks that left those who witnessed these shell-shocked. The one in January 2010, staged for the benefit of the Pentagon's top leadership, concerned possible response to a sophisticated cyber attack targeting America's power grids, communications systems and financial networks. 'The results', in Sanger's words, 'were dispiriting'. No one could detect the origins of the attack, which made a deterring follow-on attack nearly impossible.[212]

In September 2011, the US Department of Homeland Security staged for reporters a cyber attack on a simulated chemicals factory by a mock competitor company. The defenders trying to protect the target were quickly overwhelmed.[213] In March 2012, a special demonstration in Washington DC's Capitol Hill showed a group of US Senators invited by the White House the possible consequences of an effort by a dedicated hacker or an enemy state trying to turn off New York City's lights. It was not long before the entire city was plunged into darkness.[214]

The United States has taken precautions. On 21 May 2010 it completed setting up a U.S. Cyber Command (USCYBERCOM) under the U.S. Strategic Command (USSTRATCOM). According to USCYBERCOM Fact Sheet dated 25 May 2010, it plans, coordinates, integrates, synchronizes, and conducts activities to: direct the operations and defense of specified Department of Defense information networks and; prepare to, and when directed, conduct full-spectrum military cyberspace operations in order to enable actions in all domains, ensure US/ Allied freedom of action in cyberspace and deny the same to our adversaries.[215]

Run by the US National Security Agency and the Pentagon from the latter's headquarters at Fort George G. Meade in Maryland, and headed at the time of writing by General Keith B. Alexander, it, in short, is the overarching institution operating the United States' offensive and defensive cyber capability. The importance the United States attaches to cyber defence is further clear from the fact that the Pentagon spends $3.4 billion annually on cyber defence and offence. The Cyber Command at Fort Meade has a budget of $182 million.[216] There can be no underestimating America's cyber warfare capacity. Despite the embarrassment caused by the escape of the worm, named 'Stuxnet'—designed in the United States and Israel—into the Internet, the attack on Iran's nuclear establishment it spearheaded hurt the Iranians and caused delays, as had the earlier attacks.[217]

Nevertheless, there can be no underestimation of the danger cyber terrorism poses to the United States, or for that matter any other country. It can cause a mind-boggling range of damages from crippling a country's infrastructure to paralysing its command and control structure during a war. It can strike through seemingly innocent emails without being noticed until the havoc unfolds. A cyber attack's origin can be next to impossible to detect as it can be routed through computers based in several countries and does not cause a bang like a nuclear explosion. Finally, old concepts of defence like a 'firewall' do not serve. Sanger quotes William Lynn III, a former US Deputy Secretary of Defence who oversaw the simulated attack on a mock chemicals company in 2010, as saying that the collapse of the defence reminded him of the Maginot Line the French had built before World War II and boasted of its impregnability.[218] Lynn III, he added, further stated, 'A fortress mentality will not work in cyber. We cannot retreat behind a Maginot Line of firewalls. We must also keep maneuvering.'[219]

One can argue that the Taliban, al Qaeda and their affiliates lack the computer skills to launch crippling attacks on the United States. This may be true of the Taliban but one cannot be sure that it is the same with al Qaeda and affiliates. The AQAP showed remarkable so-phistication in manufacturing parcel bombs and sending them off to Chicago by air in October 2010.[220] They have proved themselves to be computer savvy by putting out the English-language online jihadi magazine *Inspire*. Nor can one ignore the mushrooming jihadi websites that provide detailed instructions on manufacturing bombs.

Samir Khan, the main architect of *Inspire*, was killed with Anwar al-Awlaki in a drone strike in 2011. Also, it is one thing to be compu-ter savvy and quite another to be able to hack into US cyber systems. Nevertheless, given the growing number of young men and women with backgrounds in science and technology who are being attracted to Islamist militancy, one cannot rule out al Qaeda or its affiliates achieving the capability to attack and cripple US and European com-puter systems. After all, only a very few people had imagined some-thing like 9/11 happening before the outrage occurred.

NUCLEAR ARMAGEDDON

The third thing that has given a new, frightening dimension to the Islamist threat is the danger of nuclear terrorism. David Sanger gives a graphic account of the panic and confusion that had followed early in the summer of 2009 after intelligence briefers had told President Obama that Tehrik-e-Taliban Pakistan (TTP) might have got hold of a nuclear bomb or nuclear materials.[221] The information, obtained through transcripts of intercepted conversations, was vague. But one could hardly have ignored it, particularly since it raised two critical questions. Was the bomb or the materials stolen? If so, were they from the Pakistani military's stocks? How could the United States search for such missing items given Islamabad's paranoia about American designs on its nuclear arsenal and establishments?

Islamabad dismissed the report. But the issue of the safety of Pakistan's nuclear arsenal, which it once again underlined, came up repeatedly as the Obama presidency rolled on. The murder of Salman Taseer, Governor of Pakistan's Punjab province, in Islamabad on 4 January 2011 by one of his own bodyguards, a member of Pakistan's elite force, again raised it. As Sanger has put it, 'If Taseer's bodyguards weren't adequately vetted, how was one to rest assured that the thousands who protected Pakistan's nuclear weapons were better screened?'[222]

The issue was again underlined by the attack on PNS Mehran, Pakistan Navy's important airbase near Karachi, which began at 10:30 p.m., Pakistan time, on Sunday 22 May 2011, and Pakistan's efforts to prevent the full facts—particularly al Qaeda's reported role—from coming to light. If the attackers, heavily armed and familiar with the layout of the base, could enter it, hold security forces at bay for about 16 hours and wreak havoc in a highly protected area, what guarantee was there that they would not be able to enter a nuclear arsenal or facility and remove a bomb or material for making it?

There is the danger of another kind of entry, though not forced. In an article in the *New York Times Magazine* of 8 January 2009, David Sanger mentioned an alarming stream of intelligence that began circulating in early 2008 in the top tier of President George W. Bush's national security leadership in Washington DC. In Sanger's words,

> The highly restricted reports described how foreign-trained Pakistani scientists, including some suspected of harboring sympathy for radical Islamic causes, were returning to Pakistan to seek jobs within the country's nuclear infrastructure— presumably trying to burrow in among the 2,000 or so people who have what Kidwai calls 'critical knowledge' of the Pakistani nuclear infrastructure.[223]

Sanger wrote that a very senior official in the Bush administration had told him that he had two worries. One was that some group might try to provoke an India–Pakistan confrontation hoping that Pakistani military would then move tactical nuclear weapons closer to the front lines, where they would be vulnerable to seizure. The second, in the official's words, was 'steadfast efforts of different extremist groups to infiltrate the labs and put sleepers and so on in there'.[224]

Such sleepers can play havoc. To cause massive damage and even to merely spread panic and confusion, one need not steal an entire nuclear bomb but just the materials for making it. The latter can be used in manufacturing a 'dirty bomb' that does not cause a nuclear explosion but spreads radioactive material over a large parts of a city by triggering a conventional explosive device. In fact, one need not steal anything. As Sanger puts it, 'Terrorists with a credible story of infiltrating the Pakistani nuclear storage areas could easily convince the world they have a crude nuclear capability.'[225] This could lead to a whole range of consequences from inhibiting action against them to panic and paralysis of entire cities and regions. Sanger quotes an Indian official telling him that India would have thought twice about counter-attacking if the Lashkar-e-Toiba (LeT) had announced at the time of the terror attack on Mumbai on 26 November 2008 that it had a nuclear weapon.[226] Indian nuclear forces would have been put on alert and there would have been the threat of a nuclear strike and counter-strike[227] and a replay of the confrontation during the Kargil War.

Pakistan's nuclear storage areas, therefore, should not only be very safe but seen to be so. According to a report in the *New York Times* of 31 January 2011, the United States had spent over $100 million helping Pakistan build fences, install sensor systems and train personnel to handle the weapons. But senior officials remained deeply concerned over the fact that weapons-usable fuel, which is kept in laboratories and storage centres, was more vulnerable and could be diverted by insiders in Pakistan's vast nuclear complex.[228] And, as Sanger points out in his article in the *New York Time Magazine*, it is 'next to impossible to stop engineers from walking out [through] the door with the knowledge how to produce fuel, which Khan provided to Iran, and bomb designs'.[229]

According to Sanger, the problem was made worse in Pakistan by the fact that the universities—from where the nuclear programme drew its young talent—were now more radicalized than at any time in memory, and the nuclear programme itself had greatly expanded.

According to him, Kidwai[230] estimated that there were roughly 70,000 people who worked in the nuclear complex in Pakistan, including 7,000 to 8,000 scientists and the 2,000 or so with 'critical knowledge'. If even 1 per cent of those employees were willing to spread Pakistan's nuclear knowledge to outsiders with a cause, Kidwai—and the United States—had a problem.[231]

Sanger wrote in the *New York Times Magazine* that four years later no one in Washington DC had a clear sense whether the covert programme to help Pakistan to help secure its weapons and laboratories was actually working. Kidwai took the money, sent progress reports but rebuffed all American efforts to find out how the money was being spent.[232]

According to a report by the US Congressional Research Service in February 2010, Pakistan had 'in recent years taken a number of steps to increase international confidence in the security of its nuclear arsenal'. In addition to dramatically overhauling its nuclear command and control structures since 11 September 2001, Islamabad had implemented new personnel security programmes.[233] In his report in the *New York Times Magazine*, David Sanger said that when he met Lieutenant General Khalid Kidwai, head of the Strategic Plans Division, charged with safeguarding the country's nuclear weapons, 'Kidwai spent considerable time describing the extensive "personal-reliability program" that he has created to screen existing employees and applicants to the program'. Sanger added that Kidwai's intelligence agency monitored nuclear employees' private bank accounts, foreign trips and meetings with anyone who might be considered an extremist. He, however, pointed out that Americans still had their doubts and quoted Robert Gates, then US Defence Secretary, as telling him, that 'there is no human vetting system that is entirely reliable', pointing out that lie detector tests and other screening techniques that CIA employees regularly underwent had, at times, failed to identify spies.[234]

The other problem is that Pakistanis are rapidly increasing their nuclear weapons stockpile and expanding their laboratories. According to a report in the *Washington Post* of 31 January 2011, Pakistan had over 100 nuclear weapons, representing a doubling of its stockpile over the past several years.[235] The report stated that, four years ago, the Pakistani arsenal was estimated at 30 to 60 weapons. Meanwhile, production of nuclear materials is the bigger worry. A report in the *New York Times* of the same date cited experts saying, on the basis of estimates by the International Panel on Fissile Materials,[236] that Pakistan had now produced enough material for 40 to 100 additional weapons, including a new class of plutonium bombs. If correct, those estimates would put Pakistan on a par with long-established nuclear powers.[237]

The greater the production of nuclear materials and the larger the arsenal, the greater the danger of theft. This is because it is harder to screen and keep under adequate surveillance the larger number of people employed. The danger, particularly of surveillance lapses, increases when storage and processing sites are scattered all over, which is the case in Pakistan. As the United States prepared to attack the Taliban in Afghanistan post-9/11, Musharraf reportedly ordered a redeployment of Pakistan's nuclear arsenal to 'at least six secret new locations'. This action came at a time of uncertainty about the future of the region, including the direction of United States–Pakistan relations. Pakistan's president was uncertain whether the United States would target Pakistan's nuclear assets if Islamabad did not assist it against the Taliban.[238]

In the autumn of 2007 and early 2008, some observers had expressed concern about the security of Pakistan's nuclear arsenal if the country continued to be politically unstable. During the period, American military officials too expressed the fear of radical groups taking over the country and its nuclear weapons, a fear that was shared by the then Director General of the International Atomic Energy Agency, Mohamed El Baradei. Experts were also worried that even if nuclear weapons were then under firm control, insiders could sell off technology during an intensifying crisis.[239]

Every few months, David Sanger states, Americans reportedly conduct a simulated exercise of how Washington DC might respond if a terrorist group infiltrates the Pakistani nuclear programme or manages to take over one or two of its weapons. The results are kept highly secret for fear of tipping off the Pakistanis about what the United States knows and does not know about the location of the country's weapons.[240] The exercises invariably end without anybody getting a clear idea of what happened and if anything was missing. The reason was simple. US knowledge of Pakistan's arsenal remained limited. By way of example, Sanger quoted Admiral Mike Mullen[241] saying as much and Leon Panetta, then Director of the CIA, as acknowledging in a speech on 18 May 2010 that the United States did not possess the intelligence to locate all of Pakistan's nuclear weapons–related sites.

It is not a very reassuring scenario. Islamist terrorism globally threatens, besides the great religion of Islam itself, modernity and all it stands for. Not recognizing this would be as dangerous as trying to use it to promote national ends or settle national scores. The recognition of this alone, however, will not help. The world needs a coordinated approach by all the big powers.

That, however, will take time to happen, if it happens at all. Meanwhile, the United States will have to deal with the situation in Afghanistan as it unfolds. To start with, it has to be firm with Pakistan. In the immediate aftermath of 9/11 its virtual ultimatum forced Pakistan to support its war against the Taliban in Afghanistan, however duplicitously. Firmness again paid in the stand-off following the death of 24 Pakistani army personnel in an attack by US aircraft on 26 November 2011. Pakistan clutched at a non-apology by Secretary of State Clinton to allow the resumption of US supplies to NATO forces in Afghanistan through its territory.

As has been said, Pakistan cannot afford to annoy the United States beyond a point. This has been once again underlined by Islamabad's response to the designation of the Haqqani network as a Foreign Terrorist Organization (FTO) by the United States. The decision, signed by Secretary of State Hillary Clinton, followed two years of debate within the Obama administration 'about the merits of formally ostracizing a powerful element of the Afghan insurgency that American officials say has uncomfortably close ties to Pakistan'.[242] There was apprehension that the move might jeopardise US ties with Pakistan, or at least the war against the Taliban and al Qaeda.

In the event, Pakistan's response has been remarkably muted. 'This is an internal matter for the United States. It's not our business,' Sherry Rehman, its ambassador to the United States, said in a statement. 'We are not in the business of coddling terrorists and those who challenge the writ of our state.' According to a *New York Times* report published on 7 September 2012, which quoted Ambassador Rehman's observation, 'The restraint was consistent with indications from Pakistani officials in recent weeks that they would publicly accept the designation, even if they privately opposed.'[243]

Designating the Haqqani network as an FTO, however, will not be enough to change the course of events in Afghanistan and Pakistan's role vis-à-vis the network and that country. C. Christine Fair, an assistant professor at the Center for Peace and Security Studies, within Georgetown University's Edmund A. Walsh School of Foreign Service, suggests in an article in *Foreign Policy*, that the declaration should pave 'the way for public discussions about declaring Pakistan to be a state that supports terrorism. After all, surely Pakistan's support for terrorism exceeds that of Cuba and Iran, two of the four countries so designated?'[244] She adds:

> Of course, one of the principal reasons *not* to declare Pakistan a state sponsor of terrorism is that it is virtually impossible to get off that list. It also punishes the elected civilian government, which has no control over Pakistan's jihad policies even if it objects to them. The United States needs to find a way to be selective in its punitive actions—there should be a clear path forward with identified and verifiable steps that Pakistan can take to rehabilitate itself over time. Efforts to designate Pakistan as a state that sponsors terrorism must lay out key milestones that would enable it to remove this pariah status should it choose to, and offer inducements for doing so.[245]

Stating that the United States should 'consider creative ways to pursue specific individuals for whom there is credible evidence of material support to designated groups,' Fair goes on to say:

> This could include U.S. Department of Treasury moves against personal financial resources, coordinated visa restrictions among

the United States and European partners, and coordinated actions through Interpol that could lead to the arrest and prosecution of the individuals in question. All that might make the Pakistani ISI finally sit up and take notice.[246]

The main thing is that the United States must clearly indicate that it means business. The Pakistani army and the ISI will get the message.

NOTES

1. Press Release (2012) 065, 'Chicago Summit Declaration on Afghanistan', issued by the Heads of State and Government of Afghanistan and Nations contributing to the NATO-led International Security Assistance Force (ISAF), 21 May 2012, online edition, http://www.chicagonato.org/reports-and-declarations-pages-243.php.
2. The Lisbon conference of NATO heads of state, held on 19 and 20 November 2010, set the end of 2014 as the deadline for ending combat role by the alliance's troops in Afghanistan and the withdrawal of most of them from the country.
3. Ibid.
4. ISAF was created following a decision at the first Bonn Conference on Afghanistan in December 2001. It came under NATO's leadership on 11 August 2011. ISAF's mandate was initially limited to providing security in and around Kabul. In October 2003, the United Nations extended ISAF's mandate to cover the whole of Afghanistan (UNSCR 1510), paving the way for an expansion of its mission across the country. While 50 countries have contributed troops, the contribution of the United States has been overwhelmingly the largest.
5. Press Release (2012) 065, 'Chicago Summit Declaration on Afghanistan.'
6. Ibid.
7. Alissa J. Rubin, 'With Pact, U.S. Agrees to Help Afghans for Years to Come', *New York Times*, online edition, 22 April 2012, http://www.nytimes.com/2012/04/23/world/asia/us-and-afghanistan-reach-partnership-agreement.html?pagewanted=2&_r=1&nl=todaysheadlines&emc=edit_th_20120423.
8. Ibid.
9. Ibid.
10. Ewen MacAskill, 'Obama and Karzai Outline Post-2014 Afghanistan Vision at NATO Summit', *Guardian*, online edition, 20 May 2012. http://www.guardian.co.uk/world/2012/may/20/obama-karzai-afghanistan-nato.
11. Thom Shanker and Eric Schmitt, 'U. S. Plans Shift to Elite Units as It Winds Down in Afghanistan', *New York Times*, online edition, 4 February 2012, http://www.nytimes.com/2012/02/05/world/asia/us-plans-a-shift-to-elite-forces-in-afghanistan.html?pagewanted=all.
12. Ibid.

13. Dhruv C. Katoch, 'The Afghan National Army' in *Afghanistan: A Role for India*, ed. R. K. Sawhney, Arun Sahgal and Gurmeet Kanwal (New Delhi: Centre for Land Warfare Studies, 2011), p. 21.

14. Thom Shanker, 'U.S. Shift May Push Afghans into Lead Role', *New York Times*, online edition, 13 December 2011, http://www.nytimes.com/2011/12/14/world/asia/us-plans-afghan-shift-to-lessen-nato-combat-role.html?_r=1&nl=todaysheadlines&emc=tha22.

15. Elisabeth Bumiller, 'Panetta Says U.S. to End Afghan Combat Role As Soon As 2013', *New York Times*, online edition, 1 February 2012.

16. The Associated Press, 'NATO Touts Afghan War's End as Fighting Goes On', *Newsday*, online edition, 21 May 2012, http://www.newsday.com/nato-touts-afghan-war-s-end-as-fighting-goes-on-1.3729244.

17. MacAskill, 'Obama and Karzai Outline Post-2014 Afghanistan Vision at NATO Summit'.

18. Scott Shane, Mark Mazzetti and Robert F. Worth, 'Secret Assault on Terrorism Widens on Two Continents', *New York Times*, online edition, 14 August 2010, http://www.nytimes.com/2010/08/15/world/15shadowwar.html?pagewanted=all.

19. Thom Shanker, 'Army Will Reshape Training, With Lessons From Special Forces', *New York Times*, online edition, 2 May 2012, http://www.nytimes.com/2012/05/03/us/politics/odierno-seeks-to-reshape-training-and-deployment-for-soldiers.html?pagewanted=2&nl=todaysheadlines&emc=edit_th_20120503.

20. Ibid.

21. Ibid.

22. Matt Compton, 'President Obama Outlines a New Global Military Strategy', The White House Blog, 5 January 2012, http://www.whitehouse.gov/blog/2012/01/05/president-obama-outlines-new-global-military-strategy.

23. Elisabeth Bumiller and Thom Shanker, 'Obama Puts His Stamp on Strategy for a Leaner Military', *New York Times*, online edition, 5 January 2011, http://www.nytimes.com/2012/01/05/us/in-new-strategy-panetta-plans-even-smaller-army.html.

24. Mark Landler and Helene Cooper, 'Obama Will Speed Pullout from War in Afghanistan', *New York Times*, online edition, 22 June 2011, http://www.nytimes.com/2011/06/23/world/asia/23prexy.html?pagewanted=2&nl=todaysheadlines&emc=tha2.

25. Mark Mazzetti, Eric Schmitt and Robert F. Worth, 'Two-year Manhunt Led to Killing of Awlaki in Yemen', *New York Times*, online edition. 30 September 2011, http://www.nytimes.com/2011/10/01/world/middleeast/anwar-al-awlaki-is-killed-in-yemen.html?pagewanted=all.

26. Ibid.

27. Robert D. McFadden, 'Army Doctor Held in Fort Hood Rampage', *New York Times*, online edition, 5 November 2009, http://www.nytimes.com/2009/11/06/us/06forthood.html?pagewanted=2&th&emc=th.

28. Philip Sherwell and Alex Spillius, 'Fort Hood Shooting: Texas Army Killer Linked to September 11 terrorists', *Guardian*, online edition, 7 November 2009, http://

www.telegraph.co.uk/news/worldnews/northamerica/usa/6521758/Fort-Hood-shooting-Texas-army-killer-linked-to-September-11-terrorists.html.

29. Yassin Musharbash, 'Anwar al-Awlaki: The Death of Jihad's English-language Mouth-piece', Spiegel Online International, 30 September 2011, http://www.spiegel.de/international/world/anwar-al-awlaki-the-death-of-jihad-s-english-language-mouth-piece-a-789427.html.

30. Abdulmutallab was sentenced to imprisonment for life without the facility of parole.

31. Peter Finn, 'Awlaki Directed Christmas "Underwear Bomber" Plot, Justice Depart-ment Memo Says', *Washington Post*, online edition, 2011, http://www.washing-tonpost.com/world/national-security/al-awlaki-directed-christmas-underwear-bomber-plot-justice-department-memo-says/2012/02/10/gIQArDOt4Q_story.html.

32. Eric Schmitt and Eric Upton, 'Focus on Internet Imams as Recruiters for Al Qaeda', *New York Times*, online edition, 31 December 2009, http://www.nytimes.com/2010/01/01/us/01imam.html?th&emc=th.

33. Scott Shane, 'Qaeda Branch Aimed for Broad Damage at Low Cost', *New York Times*, online edition, 20 November 2010, http://www.nytimes.com/2010/11/21/world/middleeast/21parcel.html?nl=todaysheadlines&emc=a22.

34. Report, 'Yemen Hunts Parcel Bomb Pair as Oil Pipeline Attacked', BBC, 2 November 2010, http://www.bbc.co.uk/news/world-middle-east-11675984.

35. Mazzetti, Schmitt, and Worth, 'Two-Year Manhunt Led to Killing of Awlaki in Yemen'.

36. Ibid.

37. Declan Walsh and Eric Schmitt, 'Drone Strike Killed No. 2 in Al Qaeda, U.S. Officials Say', *New York Times*, online edition, 2012, http://www.nytimes.com/2012/06/06/world/asia/qaeda-deputy-killed-in-drone-strike-in-pakistan.html?pagewanted=2&_r=1&nl=todaysheadlines&emc=edit_th_20120606.

38. Landler and Cooper, 'Obama Will Speed Pullout from War in Afghanistan'.

39. Elisabeth Bumiller, 'Panetta Says Defeat of Al Qaeda Is "Within Reach"', *New York Times*, online edition, 9 July 2011, http://www.nytimes.com/2011/07/10/world/asia/10military.html?_r=1&ref=leonepanetta.

40. Walsh and Schmitt, 'Drone Strike Killed No. 2 in Al Qaeda, U.S. Officials Say'.

41. Alissa J. Rubin and Taimoor Shah, 'Afghanistan Faces Deadliest Day for Civilians This Year in Multiple Attacks', *New York Times*, online edition, 6 June 2012, http://www.nytimes.com/2012/06/07/world/asia/suicide-attack-kills-at-least-20-civilians-in-afghanistan.html?_r=1&nl=todaysheadlines&emc=edit_th_20120607.

42. Ibid.

43. Graham Bowley and Sangar Rahimi, 'Hours after Obama's Visit, Suicide Attackers Kill at Least 8 in Afghanistan', *New York Times*, online edition, 2 May 2012, http://www.nytimes.com/2012/05/03/world/asia/kabul-afghanistan-suicide-blasts-after-obama-visit.html?nl=todaysheadlines&emc=edit_th_20120502.

44. Alissa J. Rubin, Graham Bowley and Sangar Rahimi, 'Complex Attack by Taliban Sends Message to the West', *New York Times*, online edition, 15 April 2012, http://

www.nytimes.com/2012/04/16/world/asia/attacks-near-embassies-in-kabul.html?pagewanted=2&_r=1&nl=todaysheadlines&emc=edit_th_20120416.

45. Alissa J. Rubin, 'Afghan Forces Quell Attack; Few Civilians Are Killed', *New York Times*, online edition, 16 April 2012, http://www.nytimes.com/2012/04/17/world/asia/complex-attack-by-taliban-sends-message-to-the-west.html?pagewanted=2&nl=todaysheadlines&emc=edit_th_20120417.

46. Eric Schmitt and Alissa J. Rubin, 'Afghan Assaults Signal Evolution of a Militant Foe', *New York Times*, online edition, 16 April 2012, http://www.nytimes.com/2012/04/17/world/asia/afghan-assaults-signal-evolution-of-haqqani-network.html?pagewanted=2&_r=1&nl=todaysheadlines&emc=edit_th_20120417.

47. Ibid.

48. Ibid.

49. Ibid.

50. The attackers too reportedly tried to avoid civilian casualties.

51. Rubin, 'Afghan Forces Quell Attack; Few Civilians Are Killed'.

52. Rubin, Bowley and Rahimi, 'Complex Attack by Taliban Sends Message to the West'.

53. Ibid.

54. Associated Press, 'Afghan Army Unit Highlights the Challenges: The Distance between Soldiers and Enemy Can Be Perilously Small', *Hindu*, New Delhi, 11 June 2012.

55. Alyssa J. Rubin, 'Attacks Attest to Afghan Insurgents' Spring Offensive', *New York Times*, online edition, 10 April 2012, http://www.nytimes.com/2012/04/11/world/asia/suicide-bomber-kill-civilians-and-officers-in-western-afghanistan.html?nl=todaysheadlines&emc=edit_th_20120411.

56. Ibid.

57. Ibid.

58. Mathew Rosenberg, 'Taliban Attacks Kill 9 Afghan Police Officers', *New York Times*, online edition, 3 April 2012, http://www.nytimes.com/2012/04/04/world/asia/taliban-attacks-kill-9-afghan-police-officers.html?nl=todaysheadlines&emc=edit_th_20120404.

59. Rubin, Bowley and Rahimi, 'Complex Attack by Taliban Sends Message to the West'.

60. Bill Roggio, 'US Kills AQAP Leaders in Airstrikes in Southern Yemen: Report', *Long War Journal*, online edition, 9 June 2011, http://www.longwarjournal.org/archives/2011/06/us_kills_mid-level_a.p.

61. Jonathan Masters, 'Al-Qaeda in the Arabian Peninsula (AQAP)', backgrounder, Council on Foreign Relations, New York, 24 May 2012, http://www.cfr.org/yemen/al-qaeda-arabian-peninsula-aqap/p9369?breadcrumb=%2Fpublication%2Fby_type%2Fbackgrounder.

62. NCTC Counterterrorism Calender, 'Al-Qa'da in the Arabian Peninsula (AQAP)', United States National Counterterrorism Centre, 2012, http://www.nctc.gov/site/groups/aqap.html.

63. Masters, 'Al-Qaeda in the Arabian Peninsula (AQAP)'.

64. CBC News, 'Explosion Reported Near Italian Embassy in Yemen', CBC News, online edition, 30 April 2008, http://www.cbc.ca/news/world/story/2008/04/30/yemen-attack.html?ref=rss.

65. Reuters, 'Qaeda Claims Attack on Italian embassy in Yemen', Reuters website, 3 May 2008, http://www.reuters.com/article/2008/05/03/idUSL03718052.

66. Ellen Knickmeyer, 'Attack Against U. S. Embassy in Yemen Blamed on Al-Qaeda', *Washington Post*, online edition, 2011, http://www.washingtonpost.com/wp-dyn/content/article/2008/09/17/AR2008091700317_2.html.

67. Atul Aneja, 'Al-Qaeda Spreads Its Tentacles in Yemen', *Hindu*, online edition, 18 January 2010, http://www.thehindu.com/opinion/lead/article81682.ece.

68. It was really a rebirth as the *US Country Report on Terrorism 2010* says it had staged attacks in Saudi Arabia under this name between 2004 and 2006, http://www.state.gov/j/ct/rls/crt/2010/170264.htm.

69. Julie Cohn, 'Islamist Radicalism in Yemen', backgrounder, *Council on Foreign Relations*, updated 29 June 2010, http://www.cfr.org/publication/9369/islamist_radicalism_in_yemen.html.

70. Aneja, 'Al-Qaeda Spreads Its Tentacles in Yemen'.

71. Ibid.

72. Majority Staff, Committee on Foreign Relations, United States Senate, 'Al Qaeda in Yemen and Somalia: A Ticking Time Bomb', Committee on Foreign Relations, United States Senate, Washington DC, 2010, p. 12, http://www.foreign.senate.gov/imo/media/doc/Yemen.pdf.

73. Ibid., p. 12.

74. Ibid., p. 11.

75. PTI, 'Al-Qaeda in Arabian Peninsula Declared Terrorist Organisation', *Hindu*, online edition, 20 January 2010, http://www.thehindu.com/news/international/article82847.ece.

76. Richard Spencer, 'British Deputy Ambassador to Yemen Survives Mortar Attack,' *Telegraph*, the United Kingdom, online edition, 6 October 2010, http://www.telegraph.co.uk/news/worldnews/middleeast/yemen/8045407/Britains-deputy-ambassador-to-Yemen-survives-mortar-attack.html.

77. Mathew Weaver and agencies, 'British Deputy Ambassador to Yemen Survives Rocket Attack', *Guardian*, the United Kingdom, online edition, 2010, http://www.guardian.co.uk/world/2010/oct/06/yemen-middleeast.

78. Laura Kasinof and Scott Shane, 'Radical Cleric Demands Ouster of Yemen Leader', *New York Times*, online edition, 1 March 2011, http://www.nytimes.com/2011/03/02/world/middleeast/02yemen.html?_r=1&nl=todaysheadlines&emc=tha2.

79. Ibid.

80. Adam Baron, McClatchy Newspapers, 'Yemen's Defence Minister Visits Zinjibar; Jaar—Freed from al Qaida-linked Militants', *Miami Herald*, online edition. 13 June 2012, http://www.miamiherald.com/2012/06/13/2848255/yemens-defense-minister-visits.html.

81. Nasser Arrabyee and Laura Kasinof, 'Islamists Seize a Yemeni City, Stoking Fears', *New York Times*, online edition, 29 May 2011, http://www.nytimes.com/2011/05/30/

world/middleeast/30yemen.html?pagewanted=2&src=un&feedurl=http://json8.
nytimes.com/pages/world/middleeast/index.jsonp.

82. Mark Mazzetti, 'U.S. Is Intensifying a Secret Campaign of Yemen Airstrikes', *New York Times*, online edition, 8 June 2011, http://www.nytimes.com/2011/06/09/world/middleeast/09intel.html?_r=1&nl=todaysheadlines&emc=tha22.

83. Peter Bergen and Rowland Jennifer, 'Obama Ramps Up Covert War in Yemen', CNN, 2010, http://edition.cnn.com/2012/06/11/opinion/bergen-yemen-drone-war/index.html.

84. Masters, 'Al-Qaeda in the Arabian Peninsula (AQAP)'.

85. Bergen and Rowland, 'Obama Ramps Up Covert War in Yemen'.

86. Mazzetti, 'U.S. Is Intensifying a Secret Campaign of Yemen Airstrikes'.

87. Mark Mazzetti, 'C.I.A. Building Base for Strikes in Yemen', *New York Times*, 14 June 2011, http://www.nytimes.com/2011/06/15/world/middleeast/15yemen.html?nl=todaysheadlines&emc=tha22.

88. Bergen and Rowland, 'Obama Ramps Up Covert War in Yemen'.

89. Eric Schmitt and Scott Shane, 'Aid to Fight Qaeda in Yemen Divides U.S. Officials', *New York Times*, online edition, 15 September 2010, http://www.nytimes.com/2010/09/16/world/middleeast/16yemen.html.

90. Karen De Young, 'U.S. Plans to Step Up Aid to Yemen if Conditions Are Met', *Washington Post*, online edition, 21 February 2012, http://www.washingtonpost.com/world/national-security/us-plans-to-step-up-aid-to-yemen-if-conditions-are-met/2012/02/20/gIQA0r4AQR_story.html.

91. Margaret Coker, Hakim Almasmari and Julian E. Barnes, 'U.S., Yemen Restart Training', *Wall Street Journal*, 7 March 2012, http://online.wsj.com/article/SB10001424052970204276304577265321207513952.html.

92. Ibid.

93. Ibid.

94. Schmitt and Shane, 'Aid to Fight Qaeda in Yemen Divides U.S. Officials'.

95. Ibid.

96. Ibid.

97. De Young, 'U.S. Plans to Step Up Aid to Yemen if Conditions Are Met'.

98. Laura Kasinof, 'Yemen Says Militants Are Driven from 2 Cities', *New York Times*, online edition, 12 June 2012, http://www.nytimes.com/2012/06/13/world/middleeast/yemeni-forces-drive-militants-from-2-cities.html.

99. News agencies, 'Another al-Qaeda Stronghold "Falls" in Yemen', *Al Jazeera*, 15 June 2012, http://www.aljazeera.com/news/middleeast/2012/06/201261511115945 1314.html.

100. Live Blogs, *Al Jazeera*, http://blogs.aljazeera.com/liveblog/tag/snc-4516, accessed on 17 June 2012.

101. Majority Staff, Committee on Foreign Relations, United States Senate, 'Al Qaeda in Yemen and Somalia: A Ticking Time Bomb', 2010, p. 8, http://www.gpoaccess.gov/congress/index.html.

102. Ibid., p. 9.

103. Stephanie Hanson, 'Al-Shabaab,' Backgrounder, Council on Foreign Relations, New York, 10 August 2011, http://www.cfr.org/somalia/al-shabaab/p18650.

104. Julie Cohn, 'Terrorism Havens: Somalia', Backgrounder, Council on Foreign Relations, New York, June 2010, http://www.cfr.org/somalia/terrorism-havens-somalia/p9366.

105. Hanson, 'Al-Shabaab'.

106. Cohn, 'Terrorism Havens: Somalia'.

107. Hanson, 'Al-Shabaab'.

108. Resolution 1744, United Nations Security Council, adapted at 5633rd meeting on 20 February 2007, http://daccess-dds-ny.un.org/doc/UNDOC/GEN/N07/245/31/PDF/N0724531.pdf?OpenElement.

109. BBC News, 'Somalia Forces Capture Key al-Shabaab Town of Afmadow', BBC News, online edition, 31 May 2012, http://www.bbc.co.uk/news/world-africa-18288639.

110. Ibid.

111. BBC News, 'Somalia's al-Shabaab Ambush President Ahmed's Convoy', BBC News, 29 May 2012, http://www.bbc.co.uk/news/world-africa-18255185.

112. David Smith, 'Kenyan and Somali Forces Capture Town from al-Shabaab', *Guardian*, online edition, 1 June 2012, http://www.guardian.co.uk/world/2012/jun/01/kenyan-somali-forces-al-shabaab.

113. Gabriel Gatehouse, 'Defections Put Militant al-Shabab on the Run in Somalia', *BBC*, 9 June 2012, http://www.bbc.co.uk/news/magazine-18364762.

114. Ibid.

115. Mohammed Ibrahim, 'Somali Islamists Kill Two Girls Branded Spies', *New York Times*, online edition, 28 October 2010, http://www.nytimes.com/2010/10/29/world/africa/29somalia.html?nl=&emc=a22.

116. Ibid.

117. Mohammad Ibrahim and Geoffrey Gettleman, 'Somali Protest against Shabab in Mogadishu', *New York Times*, online edition, 29 March 2010, http://www.nytimes.com/2010/03/30/world/africa/30shabab.html.

118. BBC News, 'Somalia's al-Shabab Militants Close UN Aid Offices', BBC, 28 November 2011, http://www.bbc.co.uk/news/world-africa-15916940.

119. BBC News, 'Somalis Flee Afgoye Advance by African Union Troops,' BBC, 23 May 2012, http://www.bbc.co.uk/news/world-africa-1817335.

120. Geffrey Gettleman, 'African Union Force Makes Strides Inside Somalia', *New York Times*, online edition, 24 November 2011, http://www.nytimes.com/2011/11/25/world/africa/africa-forces-surprise-many-with-success-in-subduing-somalia.html?pagewanted=2&nl=todaysheadlines&emc=tha22.

121. Cohn, 'Terrorism Havens: Somalia'.

122. Geffrey Gettleman and Eric Schmitt, 'U.S. Kills Top Qaeda Militant in Southern Somalia', *New York Times*, online edition, 14 September 2009, http://www.nytimes.com/2009/09/15/world/africa/15raid.html?_r=1&th&emc=th.

123. Mark Landler, 'After Attacks in Uganda, Worry Grows Over Group', *New York Times*, online edition, 12 July 2010, http://www.nytimes.com/2010/07/13/world/africa/13policy.html?th&emc=th.

124. Hanson, 'Al-Shabaab'.

125. Report, 'US Offers Bounty for al-Shabab Leaders', Al Jazeera news channel, 8 June 2012, http://abcnews.go.com/Blotter/us-offers-33-million-capture-al-shabaab-leaders/story?id=16528673&page=2#.T-MetJHTSdo.

126. Ibid.

127. Mohamed Ibrahim, 'Somalis Say US Rewards Will Help End "Reign of Terror" By Al Qaeda Offshoot', *ABC News*, 9 June 2012, http://abcnews.go.com/Blotter/us-offers-33-million-capture-al-shabaab-leaders/story?id=16528673&page=2#.T-MetJHTSdo.

128. Jeffrey Gettleman, 'Somalis Kill Mastermind of 2 U.S. Embassy Bombings', *New York Times*, online edition, 11 June 2011, http://www.nytimes.com/2011/06/12/world/africa/12somalia.html?pagewanted=2&nl=todaysheadlines&emc=tha2.

129. Ibid. Also, Abdi Sheikh, 'Somali Interior Minister Dies after Suicide Blast,' Reuters, 10 June 2011, http://af.reuters.com/article/topNews/idAFJOE7590PV20110610?pageNumber=2&virtualBrandChanne.

130. Gettleman, 'African Union Force Makes Strides Inside Somalia'.

131. Ibid.

132. Ibid.

133. Emily Hunt, 'Islamist Terrorism in Northwestern Africa: A "Thorn in the Neck" of United States?', Policy Focus # 65, The Washington Institute for Near East Policy, February 2007, http://www.washingtoninstitute.org/uploads/Documents/pubs/PolictyFocus65.pdf.

134. Ibid.

135. Ibid.

136. Ibid.

137. Ibid.

138. Backgrounder, 'Profile: Al-Qaeda in North Africa', *BBC*, 9 March 2012, http://www.bbc.co.uk/news/world-africa-17308138.

139. Ibid.

140. Andrew Hansen and Lauren Vriens, 'Al-Qaeda in the Islamic Maghreb (AQIM)', Council on Foreign Relations, New York, 21 July 2009, http://www.cfr.org/north-africa/al-qaeda-islamic-maghreb-aqim/p12717.

141. Backgrounder, 'Profile: Al-Qaeda in North Africa'.

142. Hansen and Vriens, 'Al-Qaeda in the Islamic Maghreb (AQIM)'.

143. Backgrounder, 'Profile: Al-Qaeda in North Africa'.

144. Ibid.

145. Profile, 'Al-Qa'ida in the Lands of the Islamic Maghreb (AQIM)', National Counterterrorism Center, Maclean, Virginia, United States. n.d., http://www.nctc.gov/site/groups/aqim.html.

146. Alexis Arieff, 'Algeria: Current Issues', Congressional Research Service, United States Congress, Washington DC, 18 January 2012, http://www.fas.org/sgp/crs/row/RS21532.pdf.

147. Aaron Y. Zelin and Andrew Lebovich, 'Assessing Al-Qa'ida's Presence in the New Libya', Combating Terrorism Center, West Point, 2012, http://www.ctc.usma.edu/posts/assessing-al-qaidas-presence-in-the-new-libya.

148. Horand Knaup, 'Suicide Attacks in Nigeria Islamist Terror Network Gains Strength in Africa', *Der Spiegel Online International*, 4 January 2012, translated from the German by Jan Liebelt, http://www.spiegel.de/international/world/suicide-attacks-in-nigeria-islamist-terror-network-gains-strength-in-africa-a-806749.html.

149. BBC News, 'Mali "Terror Threat" Warning Given to Africa', BBC, 11 June 2012, http://www.bbc.co.uk/news/world-africa-18401223.

150. Ibid.

151. Adam Nossiter, 'Soldiers Overthrow Mali Government in Setback for Democracy in Africa', *New York Times*, online edition, 22 March 2012, http://www.nytimes.com/2012/03/23/world/africa/mali-coup-france-calls-for-elections.html?pagewanted=all.

152. Ibid.

153. Geoffrey York, 'Mali's Neighbours Plan Military Intervention to Re-conquer Parts Of Country Seized by Rebels,' *The Globe and Mail*, Johannesburg, online edition, 17 June 2012, http://m.theglobeandmail.com/news/world/malis-neighbours-plan-military-intervention-to-re-conquer-parts-of-country-seized-by-rebels/article4299616/?service=mobile.

154. Ibid.

155. Reuters, 'Mali Islamists Destroy Timbuktu Holy Sites', *Indian Express*, Delhi, 2 July 2012.

156. Claude Moniquet, 'Marrakech Attack: Is Terrorism Returning in Morocco?', European Strategic Intelligence Center, Brussels, 28 April 2011, http://www.esisc.net/en/p.asp?TYP=TEWN&LV=187&see=y&t=69&PG=TEWN/EN/detail_os&l=3&AI=2321.

157. Ibid.

158. Ibid.

159. Fiona Govan, 'Marrakech Cafe Bomber's Linked to al-Qaeda', *Daily Telegraph*, the United Kingdom, 6 May 2011, http://www.telegraph.co.uk/news/worldnews/africaandindianocean/morocco/8498469/Marrakesh-cafe-bombers-linked-to-al-Qaeda.html.

160. Souad Mekhennet and Steven Erlanger, 'Fatal Bomb in Morocco Shows Signs of Al Qaeda,' *New York Times*, online edition, 29 April 2011, http://www.nytimes.com/2011/04/30/world/africa/30morocco.html.

161. News report, 'Al-Qaeda Denies Role in Morocco Cafe Blast', Al Jazeera channel, 7 May 2011, http://www.aljazeera.com/news/middleeast/2011/05/201157211841813188.html.

162. Souad Mekhennet and Steven Erlanger, 'Protesters in Morocco Seek Quicker Shift to Democracy and Denounce Terror', *New York Times*, 1 May 2011, http://www.nytimes.com/2011/05/02/world/africa/02morocco.html.

163. Knaup, 'Suicide Attacks in Nigeria Islamist Terror Network Gains Strength in Africa'.

164. Ibid.

165. Meg Handley, 'The Violence in Nigeria: What's Behind the Conflict?', *Time*, online edition, 10 March 2010, http://www.time.com/time/world/article/0,8599,1971010,00.html.

166. BBC News, 'Will Nigeria's Boko Haram Add Fuel to Jos Fires?', BBC, 2 July 2012, http://www.bbc.co.uk/news/world-africa-18649354.

167. Steve Coll, *Ghost Wars: The Secret History of the CIA, Afghanistan and Bin Laden from the Soviet Invasion to September 10, 2001* (New York, Penguin: 2004), pp. 403–12. See these pages for a graphic account of the attack and American retaliation.

168. Dexter Filkins and James Bennet, 'Terror in Africa: The Attacks; 12 Die as Israelis Are Attacked in Kenya', *New York Times*, online edition, 29 November 2002, http://www.nytimes.com/2002/11/29/world/terror-in-africa-the-attacks-12-die-as-israelis-are-attacked-in-kenya.html?pagewanted=all&src=pm.

169. Staff and agencies, '"Al-Qaida" Message Claims Responsibility for Kenya Attacks', *Guardian*, the United Kingdom, online edition, 3 December 2002, http://www.guardian.co.uk/world/2002/dec/03/kenya.israel.

170. Jeffrey Gettleman, 'Kenyan Forces Enter Somalia to Battle Militants', *New York Times*, online edition, 16 October 2011, http://www.nytimes.com/2011/10/17/world/africa/kenyan-forces-enter-somalia-to-battle-shabab.html?ref=kenya.

171. Jeffrey Gettleman, 'Somali Militants Threaten Kenya over Cross-Border Troops', *New York Times*, online edition, 17 October 2011, http://www.nytimes.com/2011/10/18/world/africa/somali-militants-vow-to-attack-kenya.html?ref=kenya.

172. Jeffrey Gettleman, 'Fatal Attacks Tied to Raid by Kenya', *New York Times*, online edition, 24 November 2011, http://www.nytimes.com/2011/11/25/world/africa/fatal-attacks-in-kenya-tied-to-incursion-into-somalia.html?ref=kenya.

173. Ibid.

174. Reuters, 'Kenyan Police Arrest Suspect in Mombasa Grenade Attack', Reuters Home Page Africa, 16 May 2012, http://af.reuters.com/article/topNews/idAFJOE84F09M20120516?pageNumber=2&virtualBrandChannel=0.

175. BBC News, 'US Warns of "Imminent" Threat of Attack in Mombasa', BBC, 23 June 2012, http://www.bbc.co.uk/news/world-africa-18563678.

176. AFP, 'Mombasa Bar Hit by Grenade Attack,' *Telegraph*, the United Kingdom, online edition, http://www.telegraph.co.uk/news/worldnews/africaandindianocean/kenya/9353158/Mombasa-bar-hit-by-grenade-attack.html.

177. Jeffrey Gettleman, 'At least 15 Die in Kenya Church Attacks', *New York Times*, online edition, 1 July 2012, http://www.nytimes.com/2012/07/02/world/africa/at-least-15-dead-in-attacks-on-2-churches-in-kenya.html.

178. BBC News, 'Kenyan Muslim Groups "to Protect Churches"', BBC, Africa, 4 July 2012, http://www.bbc.co.uk/news/world-africa-18703171.

179. AFP, 'Malians Seek to Liberate North from Islamists', *Hindu*, New Delhi, 5 July 2012.

180. Paul Carsten, 'Al Qaeda Attacks in Europe since September 11', *Telegraph*, the United Kingdom, 21 March 2012, http://www.telegraph.co.uk/news/worldnews/al-qaeda/9157929/Al-Qaeda-attacks-in-Europe-since-September-11.html.

181. Ibid.

182. Ibid.

183. James Brandon, 'Al-Qaida's Involvement in Britain's "Homegrown" Terrorist Plots', Combating Terrorism Center, United States Military Academy, West Point, 15 March 2009, http://www.ctc.usma.edu/posts/al-qaida%E2%80%99s-involvement-in-britain%E2%80%99s-%E2%80%9Chomegrown%E2%80%9D-terrorist-plots. Also see Peter Bergen and Paul Cruickshank, 'Al Qaeda-on-Thames: UK Plotters Connected', *Washington Post*, 30 April 2007, http://onfaith.washingtonpost.com/postglobal/needtoknow/2007/04/al_qaedaonthames_plotters_well.html.

184. Kim Howells MP, 'Could 7/7 Have Been Prevented? Review of the Intelligence on the London Terrorist Attacks on 7 July 2005', Intelligence and Security Committee, presented to British Parliament on 19 May 2009, http://www.official-documents.gov.uk/document/cm76/7617/7617.pdf.

   According to its website (http://isc.independent.gov.uk), Britain's Intelligence and Security Committee (ISC) was established by the Intelligence Services Act 1994 to examine the policy, administration and expenditure of the Security Service, Secret Intelligence Service (SIS) and the Government Communications Headquarters (GCHQ). The British Prime Minister appoints the ISC Members after considering nominations from Parliament and consulting with the Leader of the Opposition. The Committee reports directly to the Prime Minister, and through him to Parliament, by the publication of the Committee's reports.

185. Carsten, 'Al Qaeda Attacks in Europe since September 11'.

186. BBC News, 'Al-Qaeda Terror Plot Targeting Europe Uncovered,' BBC, 29 September 2010, http://www.bbc.co.uk/news/world-europe-11432849.

187. James Brandon, 'Al-Qaida's Involvement in Britain's "Homegrown" Terrorist Plots', CTC Sentinel, Combating Terrorism Center, United States Military Academy, West Point.

188. RUSI is an independent think tank engaged in cutting edge defence and security research based in London and founded by the Duke of Wellington in 1831.

189. Jason Burke, 'What Role Did al-Qaida Play?', *Guardian*, the United Kingdom, online edition, http://www.guardian.co.uk/commentisfree/2007/oct/31/whatroledidalqaidaplay.

190. John Burns, 'In Scare over Cigarette, Signs of a Britain on Edge', *New York Times*, online edition, 5 July 2012, http://www.nytimes.com/2012/07/06/world/europe/british-police-arrest-6-in-suspected-terror-plot.html.

191. Hansen and Vriens, 'Al-Qaeda in the Islamic Maghreb (AQIM)'.

192. Michael Clarke, 'Global Origins of New Terrorism', UK Terrorism Analysis No 1, February 2012, RUSI Briefings, The Royal United Services Institute, London, http://www.rusi.org/downloads/assets/UKTA1.pdf.

193. Ibid.

194. William Rashbaum, 'Two Arrested at Kennedy Airport on Terror Charges', *New York Times*, online edition, 6 June 2010, http://www.nytimes.com/2010/06/07/nyregion/07terror.html?pagewanted=all.

195. Dana Hughes, Kirit Radia and Jason Ryan, 'American Jihadi Killed in Somalia Shoot-out', *ABCnews*, 10 September 2010, http://abcnews.go.com/Blotter/american-jihadi-killed-somalia-shootout/story?id=11604972#.T_rnN5HTSdo.

196. Josh Kron, 'American Identified as Bomber in Attack on African Union in Somalia', *New York Times*, online edition, 30 October 2011, http://www.nytimes.com/2011/10/31/world/africa/shabab-identify-american-as-bomber-in-somalia-attack.html.

197. Ibid.

198. Rashbaum, 'Two Arrested at Kennedy Airport on Terror Charges'.

199. Kron, 'American Identified as Bomber in Attack on African Union in Somalia'.

200. Bob Woodward, *Obama's Wars* (New York, London, Toronto, Sydney: Simon & Schuhster, 2010), p. 5.

201. Terrorism 2000/2001, *September-November 2001: Bacillus Anthracis Mailings*, Federal Bureau of Investigation, United States Government, http://www.fbi.gov/stats-services/publications/terror/terrorism-2000-2001/.

202. Ibid.

203. Ibid.

204. Ibid.

205. Ibid.

206. Ibid.

207. Christopher Dickey, *Securing the City: Inside America's Best Counterterror Force* (New York, London, Toronto, Sydney: Simon & Schuster, 2009), p. 70.

208. Woodward, *Obama's Wars*, p. 9.

209. Ibid., p. 10.

210. Ibid., p. 11.

211. David E. Sanger, *Confront and Conceal: Obama's Secret Wars and Surprising Use of American Power* (New York: Crown Publishers, 2012), p. 263.

212. Ibid., p. 267.

213. Ibid., p. 208.

214. Ibid., p. 262.

215. U.S. Cyber Command Fact Sheet, US Department of Defence, 25 May 2010, http://www.defense.gov/home/features/2010/0410_cybersec/docs/cyberfactsheet%20updated%20replaces%20may%2021%20fact%20sheet.pdf.

216. Sanger, *Confront and Conceal*, p. 264.

217. For details about the Stuxnet episode, see Sanger, *Confront and Conceal*, pp. 190–207.

218. Hitler's mechanized Panzer divisions and infantry just outflanked it by attacking through Belgium and the Netherlands and overwhelming the French military.

219. Sanger, *Confront and Conceal*, p. 268.

220. As seen, these were detected and disarmed.

221. Sanger, *Confront and Conceal,* pp. 58–62.

222. Ibid., p. 76.

223. David E. Sanger, 'Obama's Worst Pakistan Nightmare', *New York Times Magazine,* online edition, 8 January 2009, http://www.nytimes.com/2009/01/11/magazine/11pakistan-t.html?pagewanted=all. The reference was to Lieutenant General Khalid Kidwai, head of Strategic Plans Division, which is in charge of protecting Pakistan's nuclear weapons.

224. Ibid.

225. Sanger, *Confront and Conceal,* p. 111.

226. Ibid.

227. Ibid.

228. David E. Sanger and Erich Schmitt, 'Pakistani Nuclear Arms Pose Challenge to U.S. Policy', *New York Times,* online edition, 31 January 2011, http://www.nytimes.com/2011/02/01/world/asia/01policy.html?pagewanted=all.

229. Sanger, 'Obama's Worst Pakistan Nightmare'.

230. Lieutenant General Khalid Kidwai, head of Pakistan's Strategic Plans Division charged with keeping Pakistan's nuclear arsenal safe.

231. Ibid.

232. Ibid.

233. Paul K. Kerr and Mary Beth Nikitin, 'Pakistan's Nuclear Weapons: Proliferation and Security Issues', Congressional Research Service, US Congress, 23 February 2010, http://www.fas.org/sgp/crs/nuke/RL34248.pdf.

234. Sanger, 'Obama's Worst Pakistan Nightmare'.

235. Karen de Young, 'New Estimates Put Pakistan's Nuclear Arsenal at More Than 100', *Washington Post,* online edition, 31 January 2011, http://www.washingtonpost.com/wp-dyn/content/article/2011/01/30/AR2011013004136_3.html.

236. According to the website (http://fissilematerials.org/ipfm/) of the International Panel on Fissile Materials (IPFM), the organization was founded in January 2006 and is an independent group of arms-control and non-proliferation experts from both nuclear weapon and non-nuclear weapon states. Its mission is to

> analyze the technical basis for practical and achievable policy initiatives to se-cure, consolidate, and reduce stockpiles of highly enriched uranium and plu-tonium. These fissile materials are the key ingredients in nuclear weapons, and their control is critical to nuclear weapons disarmament, to halting the pro-liferation of nuclear weapons, and to ensuring that terrorists do not acquire nuclear weapons.

237. Sanger and Schmitt, 'Pakistani Nuclear Arms Pose Challenge to U.S. Policy'.

238. Kerr and Nikitin, 'Pakistan's Nuclear Weapons: Proliferation and Security Issues'.

239. Ibid.

240. Sanger, 'Obama's Worst Pakistan Nightmare'.

241. Admiral Glenn 'Mike' Mullen, a retired admiral of the US Navy, served as Chairman of the Joint Chiefs of Staff of the US from 1 October 2007 to 30 September 2011.

242. Declan Walsh and Eric Schmitt, 'U.S. Blacklists Militant Haqqani Network', *New York Times*, online edition, 7 September 2012, http://www.nytimes.com/2012/09/08/world/asia/state-department-blacklists-militant-haqqani-network.html?_r=1&nl=todaysheadlines&emc=edit_th_20120908.

243. Ibid.

244. C . Christine Fair, 'State of Terror: Why Obama Should Blacklist Pakistan—Not Just the Haqqanis', *Foreign Policy*, National Security, 10 September 2012, http://www.foreignpolicy.com/articles/2012/09/10/state_of_terror?page=0,3.

245. Ibid.

246. Ibid.

INDEX

ABOUT THE AUTHOR

Hiranmay Karlekar, a distinguished Indian journalist, is Consultant Editor of the *Pioneer* where he writes under his byline in the editorial page every alternate Saturday and the op-ed page every alternate Thursday. Over the past decade-and-a-half, one of his main concerns has been the war in Afghanistan and its possible consequences for the region and the world. He has written extensively on the subject.

A former Nieman Fellow at Harvard (class of 1967), Mr Karlekar, in his career in journalism spanning nearly five decades, has been Editor of the *Hindustan Times*, Deputy Editor of the *Indian Express* and an Assistant Editor of the *Statesman* in Delhi and Kolkata and the erstwhile *Hindusthan Standard* in Kolkata. Starting his career in journalism as a Staff Reporter in *Ananda Bazar Patrika* in 1963, he has also been an Associate Editor of another Bengali newspaper from the same city, *Aajkaal*.

Apart from his journalistic writings, Mr Karlekar has written three books in English—*Savage Humans and Stray Dogs: A Study in Aggression* (SAGE 2008), *Bangladesh: The Next Afghanistan?* (SAGE 2006) and *In the Mirror of Mandal: Social Justice, Caste, Class and the Individual* (1992). He has edited—and contributed two chapters to—*Independent India: The First Fifty Years* (1998), an anthology of essays published to mark 50 years of India's independence. He is also author of two novels in Bengali, *Bhabishyater Ateet* (1994) and *Meherunnisa* (1995).

A member of the Press Council of India in two stints during 1978–80 and 2004–07, Mr Karlekar has also been a General Secretary of the Editors Guild of India, a member of the board of directors of the Press Trust of India, one of India's two national news agencies, and a nominee of the Editors' Guild to the Government of India's Central Press Accreditation Committee.

A former member of the Animal Welfare Board of India, Mr Karlekar is actively involved in India's animal rights movement. He is also a keen photographer.